COLLECTED STUDIES SERIES

Tradition and Exegesis in
Early Christian Writers

Dr C.P. Bammel

C. P. Bammel

————

Tradition and Exegesis in
Early Christian Writers

————

VARIORUM
1995

This edition copyright © 1995 by C.P. Bammel.

Published by VARIORUM
  Ashgate Publishing Limited BT
  Gower House, Croft Road, 25
  Aldershot, Hampshire GU11 3HR   , H345
  Great Britain   1995

  Ashgate Publishing Company
  Old Post Road,
  Brookfield, Vermont 05036
  USA

ISBN 0-86078-494-0

British Library CIP Data
  Bammel, C.P.
  Tradition and Exegesis in Early Christian Writers
  (Variorum Collected Studies Series; CS 500)
  I. Title II. Series
  230

US Library of Congress CIP Data
  Hammond Bammel, Caroline P.
  Tradition and Exegesis in Early Christian Writers / C.P. Bammel.
  p. cm. — (Variorum Collected Studies Series: CS500)
  Includes bibliographical references and index.
  ISBN 0-86078-494-0
  1. Theology—History—Early Church, ca. 30–600. 2. Bible—
  Criticism, interpretation etc.—History—Early Church, ca. 30–600.
  3. Church history—Primitive and Early Church, ca. 30–600.
  4. Christian literature, Early. I. Title. II. Series: Collected Studies:
  CS500.
  BT25.H345 1995   95–12455
  270.1—dc20   CIP

The paper used in this publication meets the minimum requirements of the
  American National Standard for Information Sciences - Permanence
  of Paper for Printed Library Materials, ANSI Z39.48-1984. ∞ TM

Printed by Galliard (Printers) Ltd
  Great Yarmouth, Norfolk, Great Britain

COLLECTED STUDIES SERIES CS500

CONTENTS

This volume contains xii + 312 pages

PUBLISHER'S NOTE

The articles in this volume, as in all others in the Collected Studies Series, have not been given a new, continuous pagination. In order to avoid confusion, and to facilitate their use where these same studies have been referred to elsewhere, the original pagination has been maintained wherever possible.

Each article has been given a Roman number in order of appearance, as listed in the Contents. This number is repeated on each page and quoted in the index entries.

PREFACE

This collection of essays has two main themes. The first is unity and diversity in the pre-Constantinian church; the variety of traditions which came together to form main-stream Christianity as we know it from its surviving literary products and from Eusebius' account in his Ecclesiastical History. The second is biblical exegesis and its contribution to the history of ideas.

A general overview of the first theme is given in VI, where it is argued that, despite the evidence for religious intolerance within early Christianity, there must also have been tendencies towards tolerance which worked to counter the processes of fragmentation and to bring the divergent trends together again. In VII one of the topics touched on in VI is examined in more detail, the recognition by a number of early Christian writers of variety in the traditions of the church with regard to certain practices (such as the celebration of Easter) and their reactions to this phenomenon. The articles are arranged more or less in chronological order. The first paper suggests a new solution to a contradiction in the Gospel accounts of the earliest resurrection appearance. It touches on the variety of traditions about the resurrection appearances and their association with different streams within early Christianity. Articles II–V illustrate some of these streams by looking at four very different Christian writers. Essay II considers the evidence of Ignatius' letters for early Christianity at Antioch and in Asia Minor. In this paper I suggested that Ignatius may have been familiar with a form of 'Johannine' Christianity associated with a John who had flourished at Ephesus but was not the son of Zebedee.[1] Justin (III) is a complete contrast to Ignatius both as an individual and in respect of the Christian tradition he represents. Contrary to what is usually written about Justin, I consider that there is no adequate evidence to associate him with Ephesus (cf. pp. 55 and 63–4). Heracleon (IV) was an important representative of Valentinianism, the closest

---

[1] I have been glad to find support for my view of this John as a Christian leader who really existed and is referred to by second-century writers in the publications of Martin Hengel; *The Johannine Question* (London 1989), especially pp. 14–15 on Ignatius; *Die johanneische Frage. Ein Lösungsversuch* (Tübingen 1993), especially pp. 68–71. Differently from E. Bammel; *Journal of Theological Studies* n.s. 42 (1991), pp. 666–8, and from G. Zuntz; 'Papiana', *Zeitschrift für die neutestamentliche Wissenschaft* 82 (1991), pp. 242–63, I find myself substantially in agreement with Hengel. I was also glad that this article received positive use in Christine Trevett; *A Study of Ignatius of Antioch in Syria and Asia* (Lewiston 1992) and Charles Munier; *Où en est la question d'Ignace d'Antioche?* in W. Haase and H. Temporini (ed.); *Aufstieg und Niedergang der Römischen Welt II.27.1* (Berlin 1993), pp. 359–484.

of the Gnostic schools to main-stream Christianity.[2] Article V (Hippolytus) illustrates how the writings and even the reputation of a schismatic Christian leader at Rome were salvaged for later generations.[3] The last paper in the general section (VIII) is on a different topic (conversion), but it touches on a subsidiary theme which reappears in a number of the contributions, that of the relations between Christian and philosophical thought (VIII pp. 98–9 and 102–106 on ideas about conversion in general and the influence on Origen of Stoic psychology; cf. also III pp. 51–5 on Justin's attitude to philosophy and his criticisms of Platonism, and XVI p. 8f. on African Manichaeism as a response to philosophical objections to Christianity, and p. 10ff., on Augustine's Christian Platonism).

The majority of the papers in the second section are devoted to Pauline exegesis but these are preceded by four contributions on other parts of the Bible. The chronological range stretches from the second-century Gnostic Heracleon to Augustine. A number of items are on early Christian exegesis in general but pay particular attention to Origen (IX, X, XI, XIV) and two are devoted specifically to Origen (XII and XIII). XV is on Jerome's use of Origen, XVIII on Rufinus, and XVI and XVII on Augustine. Article X also looks at the use of Origen in these later writers. Essay IX can be taken as a general introduction to patristic New Testament exegesis using the exegesis of the Johannine farewell discourse as an example. The exegetical methods of Heracleon and Origen's reaction to them in his commentary on John are examined in IV (cf. also IX pp. 196–7). Article X is concerned with the textual basis of Old Testament exegesis, the work of Origen in the Hexapla, and looks at the attitude to the Hebrew text, the Septuagint and the other Greek versions of Origen himself, his predecessors and later exegetes and translators (Eusebius, Epiphanius, Rufinus, Jerome and Augustine). It emerges that the later reports on Origen's work are often strongly biased. Essay XV takes Jerome's four Pauline commentaries as examples of the application of Greek scholarly techniques in Latin exegesis and examines Jerome's use of his Greek sources. Three contributions look at aspects of the attitude of early Christian writers to their Jewish heritage (X, XI and XIII). In making clear their own relation to Judaism in answer to pagan enquiries and over against the more negative Gnostic position Christian writers had to explain the role of the Old Testament Law and expound a view of salvation history compatible with their belief in divine providence (cf. III pp. 61–3, and IV; also XVI p. 2ff. on the Manichaean rejection of "Jewish superstition" and Augustine's reply). These questions are dealt with more generally in item XI and in an account of Origen's exegesis of the relevant chapters of

---

[2] The influence of Valentinianism on Origen has recently been examined by Holger Strutwolf; *Gnosis als System* (Göttingen 1993).

[3] The problems surrounding Hippolytus have now received very detailed treatment in the forthcoming book of Allen Brent; *Hippolytus and the Roman Community* (Brill, Leiden 1995). Brent makes the interesting and attractive suggestion that the writings listed on the base of the famous statue may be those of a school rather than of a single individual.

Romans in paper XIII.[4] Article XIV uses the exegesis of relevant verses in I Corinthians in order to look at what patristic exegetes have to say about Christian prophecy, a topic which was much discussed in connection with the Montanist movement.

The history of early Christian thought reflects a complex interplay of influences from tradition (Jewish and Christian), philosophy and biblical exegesis. The two most substantial contributions in this collection are concerned with ideas about the fall in Origen, the greatest thinker of the pre-Constantinian Greek church, and Augustine, the greatest and most influential of the Latin fathers. Article XII attempts to convey something of the richness and sophistication of Origen's exegesis in relation to the figure of Adam.[5] Essay XVII looks at Augustine's Pauline exegesis up to the beginning of the Pelagian controversy, comparing it with that of Origen, and concluding that, whereas partly because of indirect influence and partly because of the Platonist background the structure of Augustine's early thought is similar to Origen's (pp. 347–8), his direct encounter with Origen's Pauline exegesis in the form of Rufinus' translation of the Commentary on Romans came at a time when his own ideas had moved on. This encounter, it is argued, provided powerful stimulation both positive and negative in Augustine's earliest anti-Pelagian writings. The related article XVIII attempts to make clear the setting in which Rufinus composed his Latin translation of Origen on Romans amidst the ferment of ideas caused by the condemnation of Origenism and the debates that were to result shortly afterwards in the Pelagian controversy.[6] Whereas the Pelagians agreed with Origen's anti-determinist emphasis on free will but took a more optimistic view of the human condition, Augustine followed Origen in his view of the human condition in this life as a fallen one, but because, like the Pelagians, he now explicitly rejected the Origenist (and Platonist) theory of the fall of the pre-existent soul, he was forced to place the whole burden of responsibility for this condition on Adam alone, a view difficult to reconcile with the assertion of divine justice. Article XVI looks at the influence of Paul in the early Augustine, considering first the evidence for African Manichaeism from Augustine's own anti-

---

[4] This theme in Origen's Commentary on Romans is given much prominence by Theresia Heither; *Translatio Religionis. Die Paulusdeutung des Origenes* (Cologne 1990). My own paper was complemented by that of Hermann Josef Vogt; 'Die Juden beim späten Origenes', given at the same conference and published in the same volume, Herbert Frohnhofen (ed.), *Christlicher Antijudaismus und jüdischer Antipaganismus* (Hamburg 1990), pp. 152–169.

[5] The Platonist background to Origen's understanding of Gen 1:27, 2:7 and 3:21 is expounded by Hermann S. Schibli; 'Origen, Didymus, and the Vehicle of the Soul', in Robert J. Daly (ed.), *Origeniana Quinta* (Leuven 1992), pp. 381–91.

[6] The wider context is now illuminatingly described by Elizabeth A. Clark; *The Origenist Controversy* (Princeton 1992). I agree with her reading of Rufinus the Syrian's *De Fide* (cf.XVII pp. 356–8, XVIII pp. 139–40) and am not persuaded to reject this view by W. Dunphy; 'Marius Mercator on Rufinus the Syrian', *Augustinianum* 32 (1992), pp. 279–88.

Manichaean writings and secondly Augustine's earliest treatises from the period after his conversion and contrasting the Christian Platonism of the latter with the Manichaean outlook which it replaced.

A number of these papers were written as contributions for the annual conferences organised at the Institutum Patristicum "Augustinianum" in Rome. The themes of the conferences were conversion (VIII); Christianity and Judaism (X); dreams, visions and prophecy (XIV); tradition (VII); and Latin Christianity and Greek culture (XV). I am grateful to Professor Vittorino Grossi and Professor Angelo Di Berardino and their colleagues for their hospitality on these occasions. Other items were written for conferences held in Leuven (I); Pretoria (IX); Wiesbaden (XIII); Oxford (XVII); and Portogruaro (XVIII). Thanks are due to their organisers. Two of the papers are extended book reviews, both of them concerned with writings whose authenticity (indeed writers whose existence) has been questioned (II and V). Article VI is the only contribution which has not previously been published. Essay IV appeared in an abbreviated form in the Theologische Realenzyklopädie. Three of the papers (XI, XII and XVI) were written for volumes dedicated to revered older scholars, all three of them inspiring teachers, and to all three of whom, in their various ways, I owe an inestimable debt not only academically but also personally.

Acknowledgements

Grateful thanks are due to the following for permission to reprint: Professor Vittorino Grossi, editor of Augustinianum (VII, VIII, X, XIV, XV, XVII); Cambridge University Press (XII); Oxford University Press (II); Sheffield Academic Press (XI); Professor T.J. Deidun, editor of the Heythrop Journal (V); Professor H.C. van Zyl, editor of Neotestamentica (IX); Kohlhammer Verlag, Stuttgart (III); E. J. Brill, Leiden (XVI); Professor F. Neirynck, editor of the Bibliotheca Ephemeridum Theologicarum Lovaniensium (I); the Arti Grafiche Friulane (XVIII). The index to this volume was kindly prepared by Nathalie Henry.

CAROLINE BAMMEL

Girton College, Cambridge
February 1995

I

THE FIRST RESURRECTION APPEARANCE TO PETER

JOHN 21 AND THE SYNOPTICS

I address you as an outsider, as one who might politely be described as a specialist in a related field of studies, and I will attempt to present you with a very simple idea about the first resurrection appearance to Peter. It may be that this will appear as a somewhat naive attempt to harmonise the account of John 21 with the reference in Luke 24,34. The main part of this paper will be spent in introductory observations in order to make clear the presuppositions from which I reached the conclusion that I will put before you at the end.

The reader who attempts to harmonise the New Testament accounts of resurrection appearances to the disciples is presented with puzzling contradictions[1]. The penultimate verse of Mark's Gospel at 16,7 gives the impression that a resurrection appearance in Galilee to Peter and the disciples should follow. Matthew provides one, to the eleven, at a prearranged site on a mountain in Galilee. The author of Luke and Acts on the other hand knows nothing of this and seems instead to wish to emphasise that the disciples remained in Jerusalem until Pentecost[2]. The Gospel of John agrees with Luke in narrating an appearance late on Easter Sunday to the disciples in Jerusalem, but in chapter 21 preserves the tradition of an appearance to Peter and six others at the sea of Galilee[3]. The earliest account of all, that which Paul reports in

1. An account of the literature on this subject would fill many volumes. Only a very small selection of references can be given here. I have attempted to include some of the earlier as well as of the more recent contributions. Hans GRASS, *Ostergeschehen und Osterberichte*, Göttingen, 1956; ²1962, gives a conveniently systematic discussion of a variety of earlier views and arguments. Also very useful are the summaries and bibliographies in the commentaries on John and Luke in the Anchor Bible series: Raymond E. BROWN, *The Gospel according to John (xiii-xxi)*, Garden City, NY, 1971, pp. 966ff., and J.A. FITZMYER, *The Gospel according to Luke (x-xxiv)*, Garden City, NY, 1985, pp. 1533ff.

2. Cf. esp. Acts 1,4. Acts 13,31 also implies that the appearances took place in Jerusalem rather than Galilee.

3. The question whether the resurrection appearances took place at Jerusalem or in Galilee or in both locations, and, if the latter, in what order, has often been discussed. Cf. for example, Kirsopp LAKE, *The Historical Evidence for the Resurrection of Jesus Christ*, London, 1907, pp. 206ff., Ernst LOHMEYER, *Galiläa und Jerusalem*, Göttingen, 1936, the summaries of arguments in GRASS, *op. cit.*, pp. 113-127; also Bernd STEINSEIFER, *Der Ort der Erscheinungen des Auferstandenen*, in *ZNW* 62 (1971) 232-265, together with the reply by Thorwald LORENZEN, *Ist der Auferstandene in Galiläa erschienen?*, in *ZNW* 64 (1973) 209-221. For an attempt to harmonise the disagreement cf.   Rud. HOFMANN, *Galiläa auf dem Ölberg*, Leipzig, 1896.

Reprinted from A. Denaux (ed.), *John and the Synoptics* (BETL 101) Leuven, University Press–Peeters, 1994, pp. 620–631.

I

1 Cor 15,3-8, lists appearances to Cephas, the twelve, to more than five hundred brothers at once, to James, to all the apostles, and finally to himself. Of these, that to James is not narrated in the canonical Gospels, only in the Gospel of the Hebrews[4], that to Peter is mentioned but not narrated in Luke 24,34[5], and those to more than five hundred brothers and to all the apostles have no obvious equivalents, though it has been suggested that the former should be identified with the events at Pentecost[6]. The question arises: why, if these traditions were handed down to Paul at an early date, are all the appearances in question not narrated fully and clearly in the gospels, why also do Luke and John ignore the appearance narrated by Matthew and vice versa?

Consideration of the report in I Cor draws our attention to certain important features of the resurrection traditions — firstly that at the time that Paul was writing he still felt it appropriate to include at least one appearance that took the form of a vision, namely his own; secondly that there were more appearances than are narrated even in the fullest of our Gospels, something that is also made clear by the mention of unnarrated appearances in Acts 1,3; and thirdly that already at the time that the traditions reported by Paul were formed a resurrection appearance was being used as an authorisation of apostleship — hence Paul's emphasis here and at 1 Cor 9,1[7] on the appearance to himself. It may be for this reason that Paul omits to mention any appearances to the women, and it is in this context that it is important that he lists the appearance to Peter first. That Jesus appeared to Peter first corresponds to Peter's position as leading apostle[8].

It has been suggested that 1 Cor 15,5-8 combines two lists, the one

4. As reported by Jerome; cf. E. HENNECKE and W. SCHNEEMELCHER, *Neutestamentliche Apokryphen* Vol. 1, [5]Tübingen, 1987, p. 147; ET, London, 1963, p. 165. On the appearance to James cf. Martin HENGEL, *Jakobus der Herrenbruder - der erste "Papst"?*, in Erich GRÄSSER and Otto MERK (eds.), *Glaube und Eschatologie. Festschrift für Werner Georg Kümmel zum 80. Geburtstag*, Tübingen, 1985, pp. 82-3 and p. 100; also p. 86 on the appearances to James and Peter in the *Epistula Jacobi apocrypha*.

5. It is probably presupposed in the prediction of Luke 22,31-32.

6. E.g. by E. von DOBSCHÜTZ, *Ostern und Pfingsten*, Leipzig, 103, pp. 34 ff., and A. VON HARNACK, *Die Verklärungsgeschichte Jesu, der Bericht des Paulus und die beiden Christusvisionen des Petrus* (first published in *Sitzungsberichte der preussischen Akademie der Wissenschaften*, 1922) in *Kleine Schriften zur Alten Kirche* 2, Leipzig, 1980, p. 603.

7. Cf. also Acts 1,22.

8. The traditions about the resurrection appearances will have been influenced both by rivalry within Christianity and by arguments with outsiders. The appearance to over five hundred brethren at once will obviously have been particularly useful in the latter context. On the evidence of apologetic tendencies in the narratives about the empty tomb cf. Hans VON CAMPENHAUSEN, *Der Ablauf der Osterereignisse und das leere Grab*, in *Tradition und Leben. Kräfte der Kirchengeschichte*, Tübingen, 1960, pp. 66 ff., ET *The Events of Easter and the Empty Tomb*, in *Tradition and Life in the Church*, Philadelphia, 1968, pp. 54 ff.

I

headed by Peter, the other by James[9]. If this is so, it may be that the resurrection account of Luke 24 reflects the first list but combines it with the story of the Emmaus disciples. The complete silence of the Gospels about the appearance to James could perhaps result from a rejection of exaggerated leadership claims by James and his followers. It seems particularly strange that the appearance to Peter is nowhere narrated, but various reasons have been suggested for this, for example that it was only a vision or that an appearance before one witness alone was felt to have inadequate attestation[10]. Such suggestions find support in the fact that the Jewish critic of Christianity cited by Celsus in Origen, *Contra Celsum* II.55, mocks the Christians for believing in the resurrection on the evidence of a hysterical female and perhaps some other individual who had had a dream or a hallucination or who wished to impress the others by a fantastic invention[11].

I will return now to John 21. It would appear to be one of the aims of the writer of John 21 to set the beloved disciple in relation to Peter. The beloved disciple is the first to recognise the Lord in John 21,7, just as in John 20,3-8 he had been the first of the two to reach the empty tomb and the first to believe. It has often been suggested that John 21 uses an existing tradition about a resurrection appearance to Peter and his companions which was also narrated in the Gospel of Peter. In the last verse of the surviving fragment of that Gospel before it breaks off, Peter states that on the last day of unleavened bread, he and his brother Andrew took their nets and went to the sea and that Levi the son of Alphaeus was with them[12]. It is a natural assumption that an appearance similar to that of the Johannine narrative followed[13]. In the

9. Ernst BAMMEL, *Herkunft und Funktion der Traditionselemente in 1.Kor.15,1-11*, in *TZ* 11 (1955) 401-419, esp. 406-408. Cf. also A. VON HARNACK, *art. cit.*, p. 605; Hans-Werner BARTSCH, *Das Auferstehungszeugnis, sein historisches und sein theologisches Problem*, Hamburg, 1965, pp. 7-8; Reginald H. FULLER, *The Formation of the Resurrection Narratives*, London, ²1980, pp. 27f.; and Gerd LÜDEMANN, *Paulus, der Heidenapostel II. Antipaulinismus im frühen Christentum*, Göttingen, 1983, pp. 76ff. The view of H. VON CAMPENHAUSEN, *art. cit.*, p. 53; ET, p. 45, that the list gives a single chronological sequence is opposed by Raymond E. BROWN, *op. cit.*, p. 970.

10. Cf. for example K.G. GOETZ, *Petrus als Gründer und Oberhaupt der Kirche und Schauer von Gesichten nach den altchristlichen Berichten und Legenden*, Leipzig, 1927, p. 74; Oscar CULLMANN, *Petrus*, Zürich, ²1960, p. 69; ET *Peter*, London, 1953, p. 62.

11. As was pointed out by A. VON HARNACK, *Petrus im Urteil der Kirchenfeinde des Altertums*, in *Festgabe Karl Müller zum 70. Geburtstage*, Tübingen, 1922, p. 2, this is likely to refer to Peter. It shows that Celsus' Jew (who was not simply a fiction; cf. Ernst BAMMEL, *Der Jude des Celsus*, in *Judaica: Kleine Schriften I*, Tübingen, 1986, pp. 265-283) was in touch with an early stage of the tradition.

12. *Evangelium Petri XIV 59-60*, ed. Erich KLOSTERMANN, *Apokrypha I*, Berlin, 1933, p. 8. HENNECKE and SCHNEEMELCHER, *op. cit.*, vol. 1, p. 188, ET, p. 187. Cf. R.E. BROWN, *The Gospel of Peter and Canonical Gospel Priority*, in *NTS* 33 (1987) 333-340, and KOESTER, *Ancient Christian Gospels*, London, 1990, pp. 239-40.

13. In the *Didascalia* however Jesus appears to the apostles in the house of Levi and R.H. CONNOLLY (ed., *Didascalia Apostolorum*, Oxford, 1929, p. 183, n. 4) surmises that it was this appearance that was narrated in the Gospel of Peter.

I

context of this Gospel it would be the first one. More boldly, certain scholars have taken the view that the same appearance was once narrated in a lost conclusion to Mark's gospel[14]. Such a theory however would exacerbate the difficulties of the harmonisation attempt with which I started out. An appearance to Peter and companions in Galilee could not be the same as the appearance to Peter of Luke 24,34, which took place in Jerusalem already on Easter Sunday.

The main reason why I would reject a theory of a lost ending of Mark containing a narrative of an appearance or appearances in Galilee parallel either to John 21 or indeed to Matthew 28,16-20 is that I incline rather to follow the view that Mark 16,8 is the original ending[15]. The absence of any contact between the resurrection accounts of Matthew and Luke would seem to me to indicate not only that they had no written Marcan account before them but also that they had no fixed common tradition to draw on, and thus that the oral tradition about Jesus' life which has been recorded in written form in the Synoptic Gospels did not include a narrative about the resurrection appearances. If this is correct, the early Christian preaching prior to Mark will indeed have contained proclamations about Jesus' resurrection and exaltation and brief mentions of appearances such as we find in Paul and in Peter's speeches in Acts, but not full accounts containing details of timing and location[16]. Such longer accounts may have been developed separately in different groups within the Christian movement.

Rather than speculating about a lost ending to Mark I would prefer to take account of the view which has often been put forward, that the

14. Paul ROHRBACH, *Der Schluss des Markusevangeliums*, Berlin, 1894, and *Die Berichte über die Auferstehung Jesu Christi*, Berlin, 1894, followed by many later scholars. This hypothesis strongly encouraged the idea that the account of the Gospel of Peter is substantially correct and that the disciples fled to Galilee and witnessed the first resurrection appearances there.

15. This is well argued by R.H. LIGHTFOOT, *The Gospel Message of St. Mark*, Oxford, 1950, pp. 80-97. Cf. also FULLER, *op. cit.*, pp. 65-8, and p. viii, where he states: "There seems to be general agreement that Mark did end his Gospel at 16:8, and that consequently there is no 'lost ending'".

16. Cf. E. BAMMEL, *art. cit.*, p. 419, n. 83; C.H. DODD, *The Appearances of the Risen Christ: An Essay in Form-Criticism of the Gospels*, in D.E. NINEHAM (ed.), *Studies in the Gospels: Essays in Memory of R.H. Lightfoot*, Oxford, 1955, p. 29. On the form of the earliest traditions about Jesus' resurrection and exaltation cf. Jacob KREMER, *Die Oster-evangelien - Geschichten um Geschichte*, Stuttgart, 1977, pp. 9-13; Otto MICHEL, *The Conclusion of Matthew's Gospel*, in Graham STANTON (ed.), *The Interpretation of Matthew*, London, 1983, p. 37 (first published as *Der Abschluss des Matthäusevangeliums* in *EvT* 10 [1950-51] 16-26); and J.A. FITZMYER, *op. cit.*, pp. 1533-4, also pp. 1588-9 and MICHEL, *loc. cit.*, on the uncertainty in the tradition about the timing of the ascension (on this cf. also VON DOBSCHÜTZ, *op. cit.*, p. 32). For an interesting attempt to identify different stages in the development of the tradition and their relationship to the development of ideas concerning the parousia cf. Hans-Werner BARTSCH, *op. cit.* (above, note 9).

awareness of the post-resurrection events has coloured the pre-resurrection traditions to the extent that it is possible to see certain of the earlier narratives about occurrences in Jesus' lifetime as doublets of resurrection experiences. There are at least two ways in which we may detect this tendency. One is in the secondary transposition of a post-resurrection event back into Jesus' lifetime[17]. This view is often taken with regard to the account of the miraculous draught of fishes in Luke 5[18] and of the commissioning of Peter in Matthew 16[19]. Another possibility is that in certain cases both pre- and post-resurrection traditions may be genuine[20]. Thus it has been suggested that there was a resurrection appearance to Peter which was parallel to the narrative of the transfiguration and which is reflected in 2 Peter 1,16-18. Harnack thought of both the transfiguration and this resurrection appearance as being visions experienced by Peter[21]. Moreover it is possible to see a reflection of the sequence of experiences of the disciples between the last supper and the first resurrection appearance in the succession of events narrated in Mark 6,30-51 together with the parallel passages in the other Gospels; namely the miraculous eucharistic meal, the separation of the disciples from Jesus, his departure alone to a mountain, their toil and testing in the boat in the darkness of the night, Jesus' mysterious apparition on the water and his reassurance of them[22]. In Matthew 14 this apparition is combined with Peter's attempt to come to Jesus on the water, an episode which has often been viewed as derived from a

17. Such transpositions have often been proposed and accepted and often also rejected; cf. O. CULLMANN, op. cit., pp. 68-69; ET, p. 61. FULLER, op. cit., pp. 160-167, considers and rejects six examples of "alleged transpositions of appearance stories into the earthly ministry". A negative view is also taken by K.H. RENGSTORF, Die Auferstehung Jesu, Witten/Ruhr, ⁵1967, pp. 146ff.

18. Cf. the works cited below note 40. W. DIETRICH, Das Petrusbild der lukanischen Schriften, Stuttgart, 1972, pp. 23-81, argues against this view.

19. Cf. CULLMANN, op. cit., p. 209; ET, p. 180. E. STAUFFER, Zur Vor- und Frühgeschichte des Primatus Petri, in ZKG 62 (1943/4) 25-26, argues that reports on the first appearance to and commissioning of Peter were retrojected into Jesus' lifetime as a means of strengthening Peter's claims against those of Paul, which were based only on a vision.

20. A third possibility is that in the case of certain episodes, to quote the words of FULLER, op. cit., p. 167, "the Easter faith has contributed to the shaping of the narrative in its context of the earthly ministry".

21. HARNACK, art. cit., pp. 612-616. Others have preferred to see the account of the transfiguration as derived from a resurrection appearance; cf. GOETZ, op. cit., pp. 76ff., and, more recently, James M. ROBINSON, Jesus: From Easter to Valentinus, in JBL 101 (1982) 9. For a quite different reconstruction of a report of the first appearance to Peter cf. Hans-Werner BARTSCH, op. cit., p. 12.

22. C.H. DODD, art. cit., pp. 22-26, shows that the pericopé about Jesus walking on the water in Jn 6,16-21, Mk 6,45-51 shows many of the features of post-resurrection narratives especially in its Johannine form, whereas Lk 5,1-11 (the miraculous draught of fishes), Mark 9,2-8 and parallels (the transfiguration), and Mk 4,35-41 and parallels (the stilling of the storm) do not.

I

resurrection story, and which is reminiscent of Peter's jumping into the sea to join Jesus in John 21[23].

At this point I would like to introduce the theory which I wish to propose to you. If we start with the assumption that the first resurrection appearance was to Peter, as implied in I Cor 15, and with the problem of the contradiction in our sources over whether this appearance took place in Galilee or Jerusalem, we may solve the dilemma by means of a very simple hypothesis, namely that Peter, while at Jerusalem, experienced a vision in which he was encountered by the risen Jesus at the Sea of Galilee. Thus he was in Jerusalem in the flesh but in Galilee in the spirit; perhaps he regarded himself as having been bodily transposed there.

Obvious as this hypothesis may seem, I have not been able to find it expounded in the copious literature on the subject — where the evidence for a first appearance at the Sea of Galilee is accepted, it is regarded as necessitating Peter's physical presence in Galilee[24]; where the idea of a vision is favoured, scholars have thought in terms of a commissioning of Peter or of a vision whose contents were similar to the account of the transfiguration[25]. There seems no reason however why Peter should not have experienced more than one vision or indeed a series of visions and this indeed may seem probable in view of the multiplicity of surviving traditions[26]. Disputes about the validity of what were only visions could have resulted in a certain reticence in speaking about them[27], and in the meantime accounts of more concrete manifestations were proliferating. When the tradition about the appearance at the Sea of Galilee did resurface it was assimilated to the narrative form of other accounts and thus caused a divergence of views over where the first appearances occurred, in Galilee or Jerusalem. It may be that the claims of Jerusalem were being appropriated by the followers of James as head of the Jerusalem church and that rivalry between adherents of Peter and James reinforced the divergence[28].

23. Cf. Dodd, *art. cit.*, p. 23 note; H. Sasse, *Die erste Erscheinung des Auferstandenen*, in *Theologische Blätter* 1 (1922) 59-61; Emanuel Hirsch, *Osterglaube: Die Auferstehungsgeschichten und der christliche Glaube*, Tübingen, 1988 (first published 1940), pp. 51-52.

24. Thus for example Arnold Meyer, *Die Auferstehung Christi*, Tübingen, 1905, pp. 168 and 302; Sasse, *art. cit.*, col. 61; Stauffer, *art. cit.*, pp. 13ff. Emmanuel Hirsch, *op. cit.*, pp. 49-54, while thinking in terms of a vision to Peter reflected in Luke 5, John 21 and Matthew 14,28-31, rejects the idea that this vision could have taken place at Jerusalem.

25. Thus Goetz, *op. cit.*, pp. 76ff.

26. On the traces of such traditions in canonical and non-canonical literature cf. Goetz, *op. cit.*, pp. 89ff.; Stauffer, *art. cit.*, pp. 26ff.

27. Cf. Goetz, *op. cit.*, p. 73, Cullmann, *op. cit.*, p. 70, ET, p. 62, and Lüdemann, *op. cit.* (above, n. 9), pp. 248-251, on the evidence of the Pseudo-Clementines for distrust of visions. Robinson, *art.cit.* (above, n. 21), pp. 7-17, gives a forceful account of the increasing divergence between concrete (orthodox) and spiritualising (gnostic) understandings of the resurrection appearances.

28. On James and his followers cf. M. Hengel, *op. cit.*, esp. pp. 71-72, on the negative

If one accepts the view which I have just outlined there is no reason why the accounts of Luke and John about the appearance to the twelve should not be correct in their location and perhaps even in their timing[29]. Of the possible settings for the appearance to the twelve reported by Paul that of a room in Jerusalem where they had assembled soon after the crucifixion (Luke 24,34; John 20,19) seems to me to have more inherent plausibility than the hypothesis of many modern scholars that the disciples fled individually to Galilee[30] and had to be sought out and collected together again by Peter after he had received his vision. The account of Matthew on the other hand is likely to be derived from the prophecies in Mark 14,27 and 16,7[31]. The location on a mountain may perhaps have been chosen as being theologically appropriate or perhaps Matthew utilises an earlier tradition of an appearance on a mountain[32]. In the earlier tradition the location of this mountain may not have been specified[33]. If the Jerusalem location is correct, the question must be asked why Matthew ignores or suppresses it, whereas Luke preserves it. Perhaps the reason is that the tradition represented by Matthew rejected the claims of a branch of Christianity appealing to

view of Jesus' brothers in the Gospels, pp. 98ff. on the relation of James and Peter and the supplanting of Peter by James, and p. 89 on the Petrine tradition behind Mark as perhaps associated with a preference for Galilee over against Jerusalem in that gospel. On James and Peter cf. also Ernst BAMMEL, *Jesu Nachfolger: Nachfolgeüberlieferungen in der Zeit des frühen Christentums*, Heidelberg, 1988, pp. 31-60, esp. p. 57 on the more modest claims for Peter as representative rather than successor and on the evidence in Mark of "ein versteckter Kampf um die Frage, wer an die Stelle Jesu gehört".

29. The Lukan account has often been rejected as tendentious, but the fact that it is possible to imagine reasons why Luke might have transferred a Galilee narrative to Jerusalem or have compressed the time sequence is not in itself proof that he actually did so. H. CONZELMANN, *Auferstehung Christi*, in *RGG*[3] I, Tübingen, 1957, pp. 698-700, argues in favour of a location in Jerusalem. W. MARXSEN, *Der Evangelist Markus*, Göttingen, 1956, p. 52, argues that the later assumption of appearances in Galilee are derived from the prophecies of Mk 16,7 and 14,28.

30. Such a flight of the disciples is thought to be proved by Mk 14,27 (Mt 26,31; quoting Zech 13,7) and Jn 16,32 (cf. LORENZEN, *art. cit.*, pp. 209-211) but these prophecies are sufficiently fulfilled in the flight and scattering of the disciples at the time of Jesus' arrest and crucifixion. On this cf. already P. GARDNER-SMITH, *The Narratives of the Resurrection*, London, 1926, p. 144.

31. Cf. STEINSEIFER, *art. cit.*, pp. 246-251 with references to earlier discussions.

32. Cf. VON CAMPENHAUSEN, *art. cit.*, p. 58, n. 36; ET, p. 48, n. 25; GRASS, *op. cit.*, p. 28; FULLER, *op. cit.*, p. 81 (referring to the possibility that the mountain has something to do with the mountain of the transfiguration).

33. The mountain of 2 Peter 1,18 (often regarded as a reference to a resurrection appearance) is simply described as "the holy mountain". The *Apocalypse of Peter* (E. HENNECKE and W. SCHNEEMELCHER Vol. II [Tübingen, 1964], pp. 472 and 483, ET [London, 1964], pp. 668 and 682-3) describes a revelation discourse set on the Mount of Olives whose conclusion incorporates features of the transfiguration but may be intended as a post-Easter triumphal ascension to heaven; cf. also *Pistis Sophia 2* (HENNECKE and SCHNEEMELCHER, *op. cit.*, Vol. I, p. 292, ET, p. 253).

I

THE FIRST RESURRECTION APPEARANCE

the authority of James as first leader of the Jerusalem church, whereas Luke, while representing the heritage of the Pauline mission to the Gentiles, is ready to acknowledge Jerusalem as the centre from which the spread of the Christian Gospel started (cf. Lk 24,47; Acts 1,8) and to give some recognition to the role of Jesus' family in the Jerusalem church[34].

The prophecies in Mark of an appearance in Galilee perhaps originally referred to the *parousia*[35], but it may well be that the evangelist included them under the impression that the first resurrection appearance had actually taken place there[36]. None the less Mark still preserves a certain ambiguity. Whereas in Matthew Jesus himself gives specific instructions for a joint exodus of the eleven to Galilee and this is stated to have been obeyed (27,10; cf. 27,16), in Mark the young man's message that Jesus will be seen there is not even delivered[37]. The modern reader is left asking the question "What happened next?"[38]

---

34. Luke gives some recognition but not full recognition to the role of Jesus' family (cf. on this E. BAMMEL, *op. cit.*, p. 47). He ignores the resurrection appearance to James, but he does allow that others were present at the appearance to the eleven. In addition the inclusion of the story of the Emmaus disciples may represent a recognition of claims of the Jerusalem church. The Cleopas of Luke 24, 18 is probably the brother of Joseph and father of Simeon, James' successor as head of the Jerusalem church (cf. EUSEBIUS, *Ecclesiastical History*, III.11), and it is possible that his companion was Simeon; cf. Theodor ZAHN, *Brüder und Vettern Jesu* (Forschungen zur Geschichte des neutestamentlichen Kanons und der altkirchlichen Literatur, VI.ii), Leipzig, 1900, pp. 350ff. Walter GRUNDMANN, *Das Evangelium nach Lukas*, Berlin, 1964, pp. 442-444 (referring to A. SCHLATTER, *Das Evangelium des Lukas*, 1931, p. 454) characterises the story of the Emmaus disciples as "die Ostergeschichte der Familie Jesu, die zum Urbestand der Jerusalemer Gemeinde gehört und u.U. mit den Zwölfen in Konkurrenz um den Vorrang stand". Contrasting with both Matthew and Luke, the Pseudo-Clementines give evidence for a variety of Jewish Christianity which subordinated Peter to James and was strongly hostile to Paul; cf. HENGEL, *op. cit.*, pp. 76-7, 81-2 and 87; E. BAMMEL, *op. cit.*, pp. 48-50; LÜDEMANN, *op. cit.* (above, n. 9), pp. 228-257.

35. Cf. FULLER, *op. cit.*, pp. 57-64; LORENZEN, *art. cit.*, p. 212, n. 15; W. MARXSEN, *op. cit.*, pp. 53ff. and pp. 73ff., (and, more briefly, *Die Auferstehung Jesu von Nazareth*, Gütersloh, 1968, p. 167; ET *The Resurrection of Jesus of Nazareth*, London, 1970, p. 164), following LOHMEYER, *op. cit.*, pp. 10ff. This interpretation is accepted by Otto MICHEL, *art. cit.* (above, note 16), p. 31. On Mk 16,1-8 cf. also KREMER, *op. cit.*, pp. 41-9. On the reinterpretation of sayings about the parousia to refer to the resurrection cf. Joachim JEREMIAS, *Die Drei-Tage-Worte der Evangelien*, in Gert JEREMIAS, Heinz-Wolfgang KUHN and Hartmut STEGEMANN (eds.), *Tradition und Glaube*. FS Karl Georg Kuhn, Göttingen, 1971, pp. 221-229.

36. Thus LORENZEN, *art. cit.*, p. 213. On Mk 16,1-8 cf. also KREMER, *op. cit.*, pp. 41-9.

37. It has often been pointed out that Mk 14,27 and 16,7 form an interruption in the contexts in which they appear, which could easily be read without these verses (cf. STEINSEIFER, *art. cit.*, pp. 251-6). Thus it may be that Mark has inserted them into the tradition he had received. The view however which is adopted by STEINSEIFER, *art. cit.*, p. 255, from Ludger SCHENKE, *Auferstehungsverkündigung und leeres Grab*, Stuttgart, 1968, pp. 43-53, that Mark inserted these verses together with 16,8b in order to show that the disciples stayed in Jerusalem is rightly rejected by LORENZEN, *art. cit.*, p. 212, n. 14.

38. Mark's intended audience may have known what followed; cf. LIGHTFOOT, *op. cit.*, p. 95.

The only answer he receives is when he turns back again to the preceding narrative and realises that it is not the report of an impartial outside observer, nor of the followers of a failed mission but rather that it reflects the experience of one who had himself encountered Jesus as his risen Lord[39].

APPENDIX: THE FORM OF THE TRADITION BEHIND JOHN 21

The resurrection narrative in John 21 consists of a number of episodes: the appearance at the Sea of Galilee, the meal on the shore, the commissioning of Peter by Jesus and the dialogue of Peter and Jesus about the beloved disciple. It is unlikely that this complex narrative reached the redactor of the chapter (whether or not he is the same as the author of the Gospel) in this form. It is questionable whether the individual episodes originally belonged together. The redactor himself may well be responsible for the role of the beloved disciple in Jn 21,7 and 20ff. In addition the initial fishing episode shows certain inconsistencies which indicate that it is the result of a combination of separate traditions[40]. One of these traditions was clearly the story of the miraculous draught of fishes which appears also in Luke 5. If we subtract that story, leaving aside the question of whether it too was originally a resurrection narrative[41], we are left with a scene

---

39. I would accept the traditional view of the dependence of Mark on Peter; cf. Martin HENGEL, *Studies in the Gospel of Mark*, London, 1985, pp. 47-53; *Jakobus der Herrenbruder*, p. 101.

40. Cf. J. WELLHAUSEN, *Das Evangelium Johannis*, Berlin, 1908, pp. 96f. Wellhausen himself regarded the second tradition as merely a variant of Mark 6. SASSE, *art. cit.* (above, n. 23), separates the story of the miraculous draught of fishes from the tradition of a resurrection appearance reflected also in Mk 6, Jn 6 and Mt 14. Rudolf PESCH, *Der reiche Fischfang*, Düsseldorf, 1969, summarises some earlier interpretations (pp. 42ff.) and concludes that a tradition about the miraculous draught of fishes has been combined with a tradition of a resurrection appearance which included a meal. He does not examine the parallel to Mk 6, Jn 6 and Mt 14. STEINSEIFER, *art. cit.*, pp. 258ff., follows Pesch's analysis but subtracts the appearance at the Sea of Galilee from it. LORENZEN, *art. cit.*, pp. 214ff., against both Pesch and Steinseifer, regards the miraculous draught of fishes as having originally been a resurrection story. Agreeing with Steinseifer, he thinks it was combined with an originally separate meal story. G.R. OSBORNE, *John 21: Test Case for History and Redaction in the Resurrection Narratives*, in R.T. FRANCE and D. WENHAM (eds.), *Gospel Perspectives: Studies of History and Tradition in the Four Gospels II*, Sheffield, 1981, pp. 293-328, esp. p. 298, rejects the theory that two traditions have been combined, following Raymond E. BROWN, *John 21 and the First Appearance to Peter*, in E. DHANIS (ed.), *Resurrexit*, Rome, 1974. Although I take the view that two traditions have been combined to form the narrative of Jn 21,1-14, I do not think that it is possible to separate this passage out verse by verse into two separate sources.

41. F. SPITTA, *Das Johannes-Evangelium als Quelle der Geschichte Jesu*, Göttingen, 1910, pp. 3-4, suggested it came from an earlier source narrating miracles performed by Jesus. On the possibility of derivation from the so-called "signs-source" cf. also PESCH, *op. cit.*, p. 130, n. 56 and p. 149 with n. 9. The form of this theory put forward by M.-É. Boismard is examined and rejected by F. NEIRYNCK, *Jean et les Synoptiques*,

I

reminiscent of the *pericopé* about the walking on the water in Mk 6,45-51, Jn 6,16-21, and especially Mt 14,22-33, in which the disciples are in a boat at night, Jesus appears to them across the water and Peter jumps from the boat in an attempt to join him. I have above proposed the view that this scene may reflect the first resurrection appearance of Jesus to Peter in the form of a vision. My aim is not to deny that an episode of the kind described in Mk 6 and Jn 6 took place during Jesus' lifetime, but to suggest that Peter's post-resurrection vision mirrored this episode in certain respects and that in subsequent reflection the traditions of the two events became confused[42]. Peter's attempt to cross the water to Jesus will belong to the post-resurrection vision. It could be that this vision continued with a meal or a commissioning of Peter or perhaps the three episodes represent separate resurrection appearances which were later combined. The hypothesis that I would like to propose now concerns not the original vision but the form of one of the traditions used by the Johannine redactor.

It has often been seen that the meal on the shore in Jn 21,12-13 shows eucharistic features which are taken up in representations of a eucharistic meal of loaves and fishes in early Christian art[43]. Less obvious to the modern reader is the fact that Peter's action in Jn 21,7 and Mt 14,29-31 is reminiscent of baptism. These overtones are concealed in the Johannine narrative by the intrusion of elements from the fishing miracle but also by the unfamiliarity to modern readers of the concept of self-baptism. Self-baptism is however normal in Jewish proselyte baptism and is likely to have been the earliest practice in Christianity. Originally the minister or officiant present at the baptism will have acted as a witness and the person undergoing baptism will himself have uttered an invocation as he left the water[44]. Viewed in this light Jesus acts as the witness of Peter's self-baptism but he is also

Leuven, 1979, pp. 121ff. It is also a matter for dispute whether the Johannine redactor used some such earlier tradition or Luke 5 direct, or indeed both; on this cf. F. NEIRYNCK, *op. cit.*, pp. 139ff. and the contributions of F. Neirynck and R.T. Fortna to this conference, together with the books and articles referred to there. I am not here concerned with these questions but rather with the hypothesis that the story of the miraculous draught of fishes has been combined in Jn 21 with the tradition of a resurrection appearance at the Sea of Galilee. It will be apparent, however, that I do not regard the Gospel of John as having been composed (or intended to be read) simply as a literary exercise based on the Synoptics without other traditions to draw on.

42. Cf. GARDNER-SMITH, *op. cit.*, pp. 146f.

43. Cf. R. E. BROWN, *op. cit.*, pp. 1098-1100; J. STEVENSON, *The Catacombs*, London, 1978, p. 90; F. VAN DER MEER and Christine MOHRMANN, *Atlas of the Early Christian World*, London, 1958, pp. 42-43.

44. Cf. the clear account of the earliest Christian development by Burton Scott EASTON, *Self-Baptism*, in *AJT* 24 (1920) 513-518. For the invocation cf. Acts 22,16 and 1 Pet 3,21. On self-baptism cf. also Gregory DIX, *Confirmation, or Laying on of Hands?* = *"Theology" Occasional Papers 5*, Guildford, pp. 12-13, and Thecla's self-baptism in the Acts of Paul and Thecla 34 (HENNECKE-SCHNEEMELCHER, Vol. II, p. 249, ET p. 362).

invoked by Peter and helps him out of the water according to the version of Mt 14,29-32. This episode too is depicted in Christian art and often the accounts of Matthew 14 and John 21 (which I am here supposing to reflect a joint underlying tradition) are confused or combined[45]. The earliest surviving depiction, that in the Christian baptistery at Dura Europus, is of Peter walking on the water[46] and is associated with baptism by its context[47].

The question whether the apostles received a Christian baptism became a matter for discussion in later generations. Tertullian cites persons, with whom he disagrees, who regarded Peter's walking on the water as a baptism[48], and Clement of Alexandria states that Christ baptised Peter only, Peter baptised Andrew, Andrew James and John, and they the rest[49].

Whereas Tertullian and his opponents think in terms of a baptism during Jesus' lifetime, the setting of a resurrection appearance fits better to the earliest imagery of baptism as being buried with Christ in his death and sharing in the new life of his resurrection (Rom 6,3ff., Col 2,12)[50]. In Mt 14,30 the water is a hostile medium in which one risks drowning, and the same is true in the case of the crossing of the Red Sea[51] and the floods through which Noah travelled in the ark, cited as types of baptism in 1 Cor 10,1-2 (cf. also Hebr 11,29) and 1 Peter 3,20-22.

It was the practice of the early church to emphasise the association of baptism with Christ's death and resurrection by carrying out baptisms at the end of the Easter vigil at cockcrow on the morning of Easter

---

45. Cf. R. LAUER - W. KEMP, art. *Rettung Petri aus dem Meer*, in Engelbert KIRSCHBAUM (ed.), *Lexikon der christlichen Ikonographie*, vol. 3, Rome, 1971, col. 546f., and W. MEDDING, art. *Erscheinung des Auferstandenen (7) am See Genesareth*, in *op. cit.*, vol. 1, Rome, 1968, col. 672-3; Gertrud SCHILLER, *Ikonographie der christlichen Kunst*, vol. 1, Gütersloh, 1966, pp. 176-7 and vol. 3, Gütersloh, 1971, pp. 114-5.

46. Cf. Carl H. KRAELING, *The Christian Building*, New Haven, 1967, pp. 61-5 (description) and pp. 209-210 (comparison with later depictions).

47. Cf. also R. LAUER - W. KEMP, art. cit., "Auslegung dieser Szene im Sinne der Taufsymbolik wird nahegelegt durch Tertullian und durch Parallelbeispiele".

48. TERTULLIAN, *De Baptismo*, 12 (ed. F. OEHLER, *Tertulliani quae supersunt omnia*, vol. 1, Leipzig, 1853, p. 631).

49. CLEMENT states this in a fragment of his lost *Hypotyposeis* (ed. Otto STÄHLIN, vol. 3, Leipzig, 1909, p. 196).

50. Cf. E. DINKLER, art. *Taufe II. Im Urchristentum*, in *RGG* [3]VI, Tübingen, 1962, col. 627-637. The association with Christ's death is already present in the sayings of Mk 10,38f., Lk 12,50 and Mt 20,22f.

51. J. JEREMIAS, *Der Ursprung der Johannestaufe*, in *ZNW* 28 (1929) 312-320, in an examination of the development of Jewish proselyte baptism as a rite of initiation, argues that the idea of a baptism of the followers of Moses in the cloud and in the sea (1 Cor 10,1-2) is a rabbinic "theologoumenon" which aims to provide a biblical basis for proselyte baptism.

I

Sunday[52]. If we regard the tradition of Peter's self-baptism as the first Easter appearance, then it anticipates this timing. Likewise the association of baptism with a Eucharistic meal anticipates the later Christian practice of following the baptism with the Eucharist of the newly baptised[53] (probably corresponding to the sacrifice offered by the newly baptised Jewish proselyte)[54]. For this reason the possibility should be considered that the tradition used in John 21 did combine Peter's crossing the water with the episode of the meal on the shore.

The hypothesis suggested here implies that the tradition used in John 21 had been viewed in terms of baptism at some earlier stage in its transmission, but that this was no longer recognised by the Johannine redactor[55]. At a later stage, the symbolism of the miraculous draught of fishes had been felt to be more important and this story had been incorporated and had been allowed to obscure the baptismal overtones of the earlier version[56].

The evidence from the liturgical practice of the early church for a special association of baptism with the ending of the Easter vigil belongs to the late second or early third century, but the connexion of Christian baptism with Christ's death and resurrection goes back to the very beginning of the Christian movement. The memory that in Peter's own experience there was a special personal link between Christ's resurrection and the new birth of baptism may be preserved in the baptismal imagery of the epistle I Peter and especially its opening proclamation: "Blessed be the God and Father of our Lord Jesus Christ, who according to his abundant mercy has begotten us again to a living hope by the resurrection of Jesus Christ from the dead".

52. Easter is stated to be a particularly appropriate time for baptism by TERTULLIAN, *De Baptismo* 19. HIPPOLYTUS, *Apostolic Tradition* 20-21, specifies cockcrow on Sunday preceded by a fast and vigil, probably referring to the Easter vigil. Cf. Karl BAUS, *Von der Urgemeinde zur frühchristlichen Grosskirche*, Freiburg, 1963, pp. 312-3, ET *From the Apostolic Community to Constantine*, Freiburg, 1965, pp. 272-273. There was some variation in the exact timing of the ending of the Easter fast; the problem is discussed by DIONYSIUS OF ALEXANDRIA in his *Epistle 14* (ed. C.L. FELTOE, *The Letters and Other Remains of Dionysius of Alexandria*, Cambridge, 1904, pp. 91ff.).

53. The Eucharist of the newly baptised is described by JUSTIN, *First Apology* 65 and by HIPPOLYTUS, *Apostolic Tradition* 23. Baptism and Eucharist are associated in early Christian art; cf. J. STEVENSON, *op. cit.*, pp. 89-90. The descriptions of baptism in Acts do not reflect this practice, but this need not mean that it originated later than the composition of Acts; there is likely to have been variation in the matter within early Christianity.

54. Cf. JEREMIAS, *art. cit.*, p. 313; DIX, *art. cit.*, p. 13.

55. It would be natural to suppose that it was not a "Johannine" tradition but rather a "Petrine" tradition (probably reflected also in the lost ending to the Gospel of Peter), which was taken over and utilised by the Johannine redactor for his own purposes.

56. On the ecclesiastical symbolism of the use of the fishing story in Jn 21 cf. the contribution of B. Standaert to this conference.

II

IGNATIAN PROBLEMS

THE authenticity of Ignatius' letters has been a favourite field of disputation for centuries. Until the mid seventeenth century the letters were only known in an interpolated form. Critical suspicions were spurred on by dislike of Ignatius' advocacy of a hierarchical church order and, a full array of weapons having once been amassed, it is natural that they should again and again be brought out and redeployed. In more recent times the extreme scepticism fashionable in New Testament Studies has extended itself also to Ignatius. The two authors whose books are examined in this article both reject the authenticity of the letters in their generally accepted form but apart from this their approaches are very different.[1]

Professor Rius-Camps begins his study with a discussion of the rather complicated problems of the manuscript transmission, which form the necessary basis for further study. The Long Recension of Ignatius' epistles, which held the field until the mid seventeenth century, is known both in Greek and in Latin translation and consists of the seven epistles now usually accepted as genuine but in an interpolated form and interspersed with six spurious epistles. In 1644 Ussher published his discovery of a Latin translation of the Middle Recension in which the seven genuine letters are free from the interpolations of the Long Recension. Publication of the uninterpolated Greek text of the Middle Recension followed soon after from manuscripts in Florence and Paris (1646 and 1689).

A fresh bout of controversy was inaugurated in 1845 by the publication by Cureton of an abbreviated Syriac version of the epistles, containing what is known as the Short Recension, consisting of three epistles only, those to Polycarp, to the Ephesians, and to the Romans, in a briefer form than that in which they appear in the Middle Recension. Cureton claimed that this form alone of the Ignatian epistles was genuine whereas his opponents maintained that his Syriac version was an epitome.

The position which is nowadays generally but not universally accepted was established above all by the detailed studies and editions of

---

[1] J. Rius-Camps, *The Four Authentic Letters of Ignatius, the Martyr* (Pontificium Institutum Orientalium Studiorum, Rome, 1979), pp. 1–414. Robert Joly, *Le Dossier d'Ignace d'Antioche* (Éditions de l'Université de Brussels, 1979), pp. 1–144.

Journal of Theological Studies, N.S., Vol. XXXIII, Pt. 1, April 1982.

Lightfoot and Zahn.[1] The Syriac Short Recension is an epitome of a Syriac translation of the Greek Middle Recension; this Syriac translation survives in the form of extracts and was also the basis for subsequent Armenian and Arabic versions. The seven uninterpolated letters of the Middle Recension are vindicated above all by the fact that they coincide with the collection of Ignatius' letters known to Eusebius. In his *Ecclesiastical History* (iii. 22) Eusebius lists the seven letters individually with the names of their recipients and place of composition and quotes from the letters to the Romans and to the Smyrnaeans. Thus any theory that these letters are forged has to date the forgery before Eusebius.

The interpolations which occur in the seven genuine letters in the manuscripts of the Long Recension together with the six additional spurious letters, which appear in manuscripts both of the Long and the Middle Recensions, are usually ascribed to a single forger working in the latter part of the fourth century in Syria. He shows close acquaint-ance with the Apostolic Constitutions and has been identified by some scholars with the author of that work.

It may be worth noting that the extent of interpolation varies in the different letters, the *Epistle to the Romans* and the *Epistle to Polycarp* being less heavily interpolated than the others. Both are set apart somewhat from the other letters by their subject matter, since the *Epistle to the Romans* is concerned with Ignatius' approaching martyr-dom and the *Epistle to Polycarp* is addressed to a single individual rather than a church. Zahn argued that the *Epistle to the Romans* was unknown to the interpolator of the other epistles and was interpolated separately and added to the Long Recension collection later. Professor Rius-Camps (*Four Authentic Letters*, p. 23 n. 35) refers to Lightfoot's refutation of this theory (*Apost. Fathers*, ii. 1, pp. 263 ff.), but himself introduces a new variation of it.

The seven letters vouched for by Eusebius consist of four written from Smyrna and three written from Troas. Those from Smyrna are addressed to three nearby churches which had sent delegations to greet Ignatius at Smyrna (Ephesus, Magnesia, and Tralles), and to the church at Rome. From Troas Ignatius writes to two churches he had passed through, Philadelphia and Smyrna, and also to Polycarp, the bishop of Smyrna.

Closely connected with the occasion of Ignatius' letters, although separately transmitted, is Polycarp's letter to the Philippians, in which

---

[1] J. B. Lightfoot, *The Apostolic Fathers*, ii. 1 and 2. 1–2 (London, 1885, and 2nd edn., 1889); T. Zahn, *Ignatius von Antiochien* (Gotha, 1873) and *Patrum Apostolicorum Opera*, ii (Leipzig, 1876).

Polycarp mentions Ignatius' recent journey and states that he has sent to the Philippians 'the letters of Ignatius which he sent to us and as many others as we had by us'. It would be natural to assume that the seven letters of Ignatius known to us go back to this collection made by Polycarp, particularly since two of the letters are addressed to Polycarp and his church. It has sometimes been stated and is maintained by Rius-Camps that Polycarp could only have collected the letters sent to nearby churches and would therefore have been unable to obtain a copy of the letter to the Romans; but this is a fallacy, since it ignores the possibility of copies of the letters being kept at the place from which they were written (the same fallacy sometimes occurs in discussions of the collection of St. Paul's epistles). Our collection of Ignatian letters contains four letters written from Smyrna, two written to Smyrna, and one written to a nearby church (Philadelphia).

Since Rius-Camps takes up the hypothesis that the order of the letters in the manuscripts gives support to the theory of a separate early transmission of the letter to the Romans, it may be worth looking briefly at this question. Our earliest evidence comes from Eusebius, who had all seven letters before him and lists them chronologically, the four written from Smyrna and then the three from Troas. This arrangement does not recur in the manuscripts, and it is not clear whether it represents the form in which Eusebius possessed the collection or merely the form in which he chose to cite the letters. In the manuscripts of the Long Recension the seven genuine letters have been interspersed with the spurious ones. *Romans* follows *Ephesians* at the end. The transmission of the Middle Recension is represented by two main branches, the Greek manuscripts together with the Latin translation, which was made in the thirteenth century from a superior but closely related Greek copy; and the partly lost Syriac translation, which is thought to have been made in the fourth century and was the basis for the Armenian translation. The fragments of the Coptic translation (of which more have been found since the time of Lightfoot) give evidence of the same arrangement as the Armenian translation (except that the Coptic fragments begin with the spurious letter to Hero). This arrangement starts with the two letters written to Smyrna, *Smyrnaeans* and *Polycarp*, and then with three letters written from Smyrna, *Ephesians*, *Magnesians*, and *Trallians*, and continues with *Philadephians* and lastly *Romans*. After this follow the spurious letters. The form of the collection represented by the Greek manuscripts and the Latin translation differs in two respects: *Philadelphians* precedes *Trallians*, and the Antiochene *Acts of Martyrdom*, which incorporate the *Epistle to the Romans*, have been added at the end after the spurious letters, with the result that *Romans*

IGNATIAN PROBLEMS

is omitted from its earlier position. It should also be mentioned that our main witnesses for the Greek text are incomplete—the Florence manuscript breaks off in the course of the spurious letter to the Tarsians, so that for the Greek text of the *Epistle to the Romans* it is necessary to turn to other Greek manuscripts which give the *Acts of Martyrdom* separately. The result of this is that the Greek text of *Romans* has indeed been transmitted to us separately, but this is merely the consequence of an accident. Moreover the removal of *Romans* from its position with the other six genuine letters and its insertion in the Antiochene *Acts of Martyrdom* cannot have taken place before these *Acts* came into existence. Lightfoot assigns them to Antioch in the fifth or more probably the late sixth century, associating their composition with a report in Evagrius' church history that Ignatius' bones at Antioch were translated from the cemetery outside the Daphnitic Gate to the Tychaeum under Theodosius II (i.e. in the first half of the fifth century) and that in the late sixth century the patriarch Gregory expanded the celebration of the festival of Ignatius to greater magnificence (op. cit., vol. ii, p. 387). It would seem then that the order of the letters given in the Armenian translation is likely to be the most primitive one. The position of *Romans* at the end, rather than with the other letters written from Smyrna, could be explained either on the basis of its different subject-matter, or, if one is determined to assert its separate transmission, by the hypothesis that it had indeed circulated separately earlier.

Anyone who rejects the authenticity of some or all of the Ignatian letters has to take account of certain basic facts concerning their attestation. As we have seen, the seven letters of the Middle Recension were known to Eusebius in the early fourth century, and subsequently also to the forger who supplemented them to create the Long Recension as well as the translators who produced the Syriac and Coptic versions. Prior to Eusebius we have evidence from Origen that a collection of the letters was known. Origen quotes from *Ephesians*, as from 'one of the letters of a certain martyr, I mean Ignatius, the second bishop of Antioch after the blessed Peter, the one who fought with beasts in the persecution in Rome'.[1] He also quotes twice from *Romans*, once without any ascription, once as from 'one of the saints, Ignatius by name'.[2]

[1] *Homily on Luke*, vi, ed. M. Rauer, *G.C.S. Origenes* ix (Berlin, 1959), pp. 34–5. This remark is preserved in a Greek catena extract as well as in Jerome's Latin translation.

[2] *On Prayer*, 20, ed. P. Koetschau, *G.C.S. Origenes* ii (Leipzig, 1899), p. 344 (an allusion only to *Romans* iii. 3), and, surviving in Rufinus' translation, *Comm. on Song of Songs*, Prologue, ed. W. A. Baehrens, *G.C.S. Origenes* viii (Leipzig, 1925), p. 71.

Irenaeus also quotes from *Romans*, introducing the quotation with the words, 'as one of our people said when condemned to the beasts on account of his witness of God'.[1] The letter of Polycarp to the Philippians refers three times to Ignatius, once indirectly and twice by name, and states that Polycarp has made a collection of Ignatius' letters which he is forwarding to the Philippians.

Both Rius-Camps and Joly dismiss the evidence of Polycarp by supposing that his letter is interpolated, and both posit forgeries which were already established by the time of Eusebius. Apart from this their theories differ.

According to Professor Joly the letters of Ignatius were composed by a forger writing at Smyrna soon after the death of Polycarp and the composition of the account of Polycarp's martyrdom. He assigns both writings to the seventh decade of the second century. Ignatius bishop of Antioch did not exist—the forger took the name of a Philippian martyr mentioned in chapter 9 of Polycarp's letter to the Philippians as the starting-point for his forgery. The forged collection of letters was already available to Irenaeus and Origen, who, however, show their embarrassment concerning the authorship by the evasive way in which they refer to them. The identification of Ignatius as bishop of Antioch in one of Origen's references may be either an interpolation in Origen's text, or derived from Julius Africanus, whose evidence is untrust-worthy (pp. 99–100).

The hypothesis of Rius-Camps is much more complicated. He attempts to distinguish within the seven Ignatian letters between a genuine core and the activities of a third-century forger who inter-polated this core. The bishop Ignatius of Antioch really existed, but he only wrote four letters, not seven. The letters to the Philadelphians, to the Smyrnaeans, and to Polycarp bishop of Smyrna are the creations of the forger—but the forger did not simply compose these letters himself, he divided up what Rius-Camps assumes to have been the original letters to the Ephesians and Magnesians and used material from them in composing the extra letters. In addition he interpolated what remained of the original letters to the Ephesians and Magnesians and the letter to the Trallians, which Rius-Camps states was not divided up. The letter to the Romans was transmitted separately from the other Ignatian letters and was not available to the forger, and hence remained uninterpolated. The genuine Ignatius, author of four letters only, travelled to Rome by a different route and at an earlier date than that assigned to him by Eusebius, namely by ship to Ephesus, where

---

[1] *Adversus Haereses*, v. xxviii. 3. References are to the edition of W. H. Harvey (Cambridge, 1857). The numbering of chapters varies in different editions.

he received delegations from Magnesia and Tralles, and from there on by land to Smyrna, where he wrote all four genuine letters. The contacts between Ignatius and Polycarp are a fabrication of the forger. The genuine Ignatius passed through Smyrna before Polycarp became bishop there, and not only that but before the activities of John in this area referred to by Irenaeus, who states that John stayed at Ephesus until the times of Trajan. Thus Rius-Camps tentatively dates his four Ignatian letters between the years 80 and 100. The forger, who divided up and interpolated these letters and who constructed the new more complicated itinerary via Philadelphia, Smyrna, and Troas, introducing the contacts with Polycarp and interpolating Polycarp's letter to the Philippians to authenticate his forgery, lived in Asia Minor in the middle of the third century and drew heavily on the *Didascalia* (p. 242). He shows concern about divisions in the church at Philadelphia and was probably himself the bishop of Philadelphia (p. 341). Irenaeus had no knowledge of Ignatius and knew the saying he quotes from Romans only from hearsay (p. 86).

Rius-Camps' volume represents the English translation of an elaborated version of two long articles which had previously appeared in Spanish together with a new third section. It is a monumental piece of work. He himself describes it as systematic and exhaustive and it incorporates an impressive amount of erudition and ingenuity. An attempt has been made to assist the reader by means of a detailed list of contents, frequent sub-headings and numbering of arguments, summaries of conclusions, and even an appendix printing the Greek text of the reconstructed original four letters.

With regard to the main hypothesis of the book it may be allowed that there is nothing particularly implausible in itself in the idea that a genuine core of Ignatian letters was expanded and interpolated by a forger. Once he has stated this theory, however, Rius-Camps has a completely free hand in identifying and eliminating what he imagines to be the work of the forger. Thus there is nothing to restrict him in raising criticisms against Ignatius' letters and then answering them by cutting out or rewriting the passage concerned. Equally he can separate out features which he regards as characteristic of the forger and label the language in which they are expressed as non-Ignatian. In a sense therefore his theory is bound to 'work', but on the other hand it cannot because of this be said to be proved correct. Yet more problematic than the elimination of supposedly spurious passages is the dissection and recombination of the letters into new units. Rius-Camps might have some hope of convincing his readers if he had produced a revised Greek text of Ignatius which was manifestly superior to the received text and if he carried his readers along with him throughout his argumentation; but in the opinion of the writer of the present article he does neither of these things. The type of argumentation he uses makes the reader sceptical from the start. Thus, after excluding the *Epistle to the Romans*, which he thinks was transmitted separately, he starts by picking out differences between the letters written from Smyrna and those written from Troas which cause him to suspect the latter group. In the first group the writer requests the addressees to pray for the church in Syria, in the second group he asks them to send letters or messengers to the church in Antioch of Syria. The mention of Antioch betrays the hand of a forger—in Rius-Camps's view Ignatius was bishop of Syria, but this was not understood by the forger. Equally suspicious in Rius-Camps's eyes is the fact that when Ignatius refers to deacons he humbly calls them his own fellow servants, σύνδουλοι; these passages have been added by the forger, who thought that Ignatius was a deacon.[1] Also suspicious is the unfulfilled promise of a second letter at the end of *Ephesians*. This has been inserted by the forger to conceal the fact that he has excised the second half of *Ephesians* in order to create the new letter to the Smyrnaeans. Moreover the opening formulas of the letters written from Troas are different from those of the ones written from Smyrna. In the following sections Rius-Camps proceeds to identify what he regards as anomalies in Ignatius' combination of parallelism, repetition, and variation, to strike them out as the work of the forger, and to replace them by his own more logical rearrangement. The details of his argumentation are difficult to follow, not just because of the occasional awkwardnesses of the English translation, but more importantly because they fail to convince. The underlying *naïveté* of approach is shown up if, for instance, one compares the treatment of the opening formulas of the letters with the article on the same subject by H. J. Sieben.[2] The thoroughness with which Rius-Camps goes on to work out the consequences of his rearrangement of the letters, the new picture of Ignatius himself, the motives of the forger and his procedure, and the differences in style between Ignatius and the forger, is impressive. Much interesting material (some of which will be mentioned shortly) is included in the discussion of both general questions and individual points of interpretation. All this fails, however, to compensate for the implausibility of much of the argumentation in the initial diagnosis and proposed

---

[1] Compare, however, Ignatius' reference to the διακονία of the bishop in *Phil.* i, and the rather similar way in which he addresses the Ephesians in *Eph.* iii as his own συνδιδασκαλῖται.

[2] 'Die Ignatianen als Briefe. Einige formkritische Bemerkungen', *Vigiliae Christianae*, xxxii (1978), pp. 1–18.

II

solution of the problems presented by the received text. The new reconstruction remains unproved and unprovable. Professor Joly's approach is a refreshing contrast. His volume is a slim one, and he does not waste words. He carries the reader with him, presenting his argumentation logically and forcefully, often harshly. Even for a reader with little French, his style is more gripping than that of the English translation of Rius-Camps's book. None the less, not all the arguments he uses are convincing, and the most that he achieves is to make a case for the reconsideration of the authenticity of Ignatius' letters and above all of how they fit into the setting of second-century Christianity, in particular in terms of their style and terminology.

Joly's first and strongest argument is one that is used also by Rius-Camps. It concerns the letter of Polycarp to the Philippians. If one denies the authenticity of Ignatius' letters it is necessary to account for the fact that Polycarp appears to refer to them in chapter 13 of his letter. The differences in style and preoccupations between Polycarp's letter and those of Ignatius are so great that it is impossible to ascribe both to the same forger. What can be done, however, is to maintain that chapter 13 is an interpolation inserted into a genuine letter of Polycarp by the forger of Ignatius' letters in order to authenticate his forgery. The main argument in favour of this theory is the fact that Polycarp's remarks in chapter 9 of his letter, where he appeals to the example of Ignatius and other martyrs, seem to imply that he assumes that Ignatius' martyrdom has already taken place, whereas chapter 13 gives the impression that Ignatius had only recently left Philippi and that Polycarp had not yet had news of his fate. A new turn was given to the discussion of the question by P. N. Harrison, who in 1936 published a book[1] in which he maintained that Polycarp's letter is in fact made up of two genuine letters, chapters 1–12 being a later epistle, to which an earlier epistle (chapters 13–14) were accidentally attached. This hypothesis has been widely accepted, although some of those who adopted it have confined the earlier epistle to chapter 13, reattaching chapter 14 to chapters 1–12. Joly, however, argues that the accident assumed by Harrison is highly unlikely. If we imagine the two letters of Polycarp copied one after the other on the same roll or in the same codex, we must explain how the longer one lost its final salutations after chapter 12 and how the shorter one lost its opening greeting before chapter 13. If we prefer to assume the deliberate insertion of the short letter as chapter 13 by a later editor we must supply a motive. Rius-Camps, in arguing the same case, adds that the sentence in chapter 13, 'we have

---

[1] *Polycarp's Two Epistles to the Philippians* (Cambridge, 1936).

sent you Ignatius' epistles . . ., which are subjoined to this letter', implies that what Ignatius' epistles were subjoined to was something longer than just chapter 13 alone. These criticisms of Harrison's thesis would seem to be justified. It we wish to defend the authenticity of chapter 13 of Polycarp's letter, it must be as an original part of the whole letter, not as an accidental or deliberate insertion into a later letter. The unity of the letter was defended by many scholars prior to the appearance of Harrison's book and has been maintained recently by W. R. Schoedel.[1] Much of the argumentation concerning the supposed inconsistency of chapters 9 and 13 centres on detailed points of language and chronology, but the results are inconclusive; the real problem is whether Polycarp's conception of time was sufficiently vague to allow him to speak of Ignatius as a martyr once he had passed out of sight on his journey to martyrdom, or whether he would have been more likely to make careful calculations and to have refrained from such language until Ignatius' death could be safely assumed.

As well as deleting chapter 13 of Polycarp's letter as an interpolation Joly also cuts out the phrase in chapter 1 which refers to the Philippians' hospitality to Ignatius and others on their way through. According to his view there was no reference to martyrs passing through Philippi in Polycarp's original letter and the martyrs Ignatius, Zosimus, and Rufus named in chapter 9 are Philippian martyrs. This interesting theory involves a forced rendering of Polycarp's Greek, which makes it implausible.[2]

One of the arguments used by Harrison for a late dating of the main part of Polycarp's letter was an attempt to apply his anti-heretical polemic to Marcion. This is rejected by Joly, with the exception of one particular point. An anecdote is told by Irenaeus[3] that Polycarp once encountered Marcion and addressed him as the first-born of Satan. In chapter 7 of his letter Polycarp states that whoever perverts the oracles of the Lord according to his own desires and says that there is neither resurrection nor judgement is the first-born of Satan. Joly's argument is that there can be only one first-born of Satan and that therefore if Polycarp applied this term to Marcion he could not have applied it to anyone else. This ignores the fact that Polycarp's use of the term in his

---

[1] *Polycarp, Martyrdom of Polycarp, Fragments of Papias* (New York, 1967), and 'Are the letters of Ignatius of Antioch authentic?', *Religious Studies Review*, vi (1980), pp. 196–201.

[2] Polycarp divides his list of martyrs into two groups by means of ἀλλὰ καί; 'not only in the blessed Ignatius and Zosimus and Rufus, but also in others (i.e.) those from among you and in Paul himself and the rest of the apostles'. If he had wanted to say what Joly wants him to say, he would surely have used a different word order.　　　　　　[3] *Adv. Haer.* III. iii. 4.

II

letter is a generalizing one (it is the last of a string of indefinite clauses with ἄν and the subjunctive and negative μή). When using the term here he could not know that several decades later he might wish to apply it to Marcion, nor is it reasonable to expect that he should have refrained from applying it to Marcion because he had once used it previously in a letter.

As a further argument for a later dating of Polycarp's epistle Joly points to the observation of Helmut Köster[1] that Polycarp appears to have known the Gospels of Matthew and Luke. Köster himself follows Harrison in a later dating for the main part of Polycarp's letter but accepts the authenticity and traditional dating of Ignatius' letters, so that he can draw a contrast between Polycarp as giving evidence of a later state of affairs and Ignatius, whom he regards as showing no knowledge of a written gospel, as reflecting the earlier situation. This judgement is clearly unfavourable to the hypothesis of Joly, who thinks that Ignatius' letters were forged at Symrna after Polycarp's death. If we accept both Ignatius' letters and the whole of Polycarp's letter as authentic, we must regard the divergence between them in this respect as reflecting a difference in background rather than a difference in date.

A type of argument utilized by Joly throughout his book, in discussing both Ignatius and Polycarp, is the citation of parallels between one writing and another, accompanied by the assertion that the writing which he wishes to regard as later is dependent on the other writing. Thus there are parallels between Ignatius and the *Shepherd* of Hermas, supposedly showing that Ignatius depended on Hermas. In the case of the letter of Polycarp there are parallels with *2 Clement* supposedly showing that Polycarp's letter is later than *2 Clement*, and parallels with the letters of Ignatius, supposedly showing that the forger of Ignatius copied Polycarp. One parallel, which involves all three, concerns the quotation of what looks like a variant version of Isaiah lii. 5 in the context of an exhortation to avoid giving offence among the heathen (Ignatius, *Trall.* viii. 2, Polycarp, x. 2–3 and *2 Clement*, xiii; also *Didascalia* iii and *Apostolic Constitutions*, iii. v. 6).[2] This example, which is discussed by van Unnik in an article referred to by Joly,[3] illustrates particularly clearly the possibility that what we are dealing with is not literary dependence but a common oral tradition. Van Unnik suggests that the quotation may come from a lost apocryphal writing

---

[1] *Synoptische Überlieferungen bei den Apostolischen Vätern* (*T.U.* lxv, 1957), p. 122.

[2] Cf. also Rom. ii. 24, 1 Tim. vi. 1, and Titus ii. 5.

[3] W. C. van Unnik, 'Die Rücksicht auf die Reaktion der Nicht-Christen als Motiv in der altchristlichen Paränese', in *Judentum, Urchristentum, Kirche: Festschrift für Joachim Jeremias* (Berlin, 1960), pp. 221–34.

72

and states, 'Wohl war das Wort so bekannt, daß es, wenn irgendwie das Benehmen der Christen den Heiden anstoßgebend sein konnte, verwendet wurde' (pp. 226–7).

A separate chapter is devoted by Joly to the question of Ignatius' links with 4 Maccabees. The parallels are indeed very interesting (they include Stoic terminology and certain features of Ignatius' imagery as well as his enthusiasm for martyrdom), but rather than supporting the theory of a forgery composed in Asia Minor, they can more readily be taken as throwing light on Ignatius' background at Antioch, where the cult of the Maccabean martyrs was established at an early date.[1] Joly uses the important article of O. Perler, 'Das vierte Makkabäerbuch, Ignatius von Antiochien und die ältesten Märtyrerberichte',[2] which discusses not only the evidence for use of 4 Maccabees in Ignatius and other Christian writings but also the influence of Asianic rhetoric on Ignatius' style. Whereas Perler accepts a dating of 4 Maccabees before 70 A.D.,[3] following the argument that it is more likely to have been taken over into Christian use at a period before the split with Judaism, Joly associates himself with the conjecture of Dupont-Sommer, who suggested a date of 117–18 and regarded Ignatius as reflecting the same background.[4] Joly speaks of the parallels between Ignatius and 4 Maccabees as if the author of the letters must have either known 4 Maccabees by heart or worked at leisure in a study with a copy to hand. This is to go much further than Perler does (p. 61, 'Die Stilähnlichkeit vermag . . . die Abhängigkeit . . . keineswegs zu beweisen'; p. 63 (on traces of Stoicism in Ignatius), 'Freilich muss die Quelle nicht notwendig und nur das 4 Makk gewesen sein' (cf. also on Stoic influence, p. 72 n. 1); p. 64 (summarizing), 'dass . . . Ignatius nicht ohne den Einfluss dieser jüdischen Quelle von der gleichen Begeisterung zum Martyrium erfasst wird, weithin die gleichen Gedanken sich zu eigen macht, der gleichen Ausdrucksmittel sich bedient'). The similarities in style and in many of the cases of the use of non-biblical terminology can be explained on the hypothesis that

[1] Cf. E. Bammel, 'Zum jüdischen Märtyrerkult', *Theologische Literaturzeitung*, 1953, pp. 119–6; A. Dupont-Sommer, *Le quatrième livre des Machabées* (Paris, 1939), pp. 67 ff. [2] *Rivista di archeologia cristiana*, xxv (1949), pp. 47–71.
[3] Art. cit., p. 64. He cites eight other scholars for the same view.
[4] Op. cit., pp. 78–85. Dupont-Sommer admits, however, that the text contains no certain allusion to external events (p. 78). Joly also refers for more recent bibliography to R. Renehan, 'The Greek Philosophic Background of Fourth Maccabees', *Rheinisches Museum*, N.F. 115 (1972), pp. 223–8 (who suggests that the author of 4 Maccabees shared a common source with Galen, probably Posidonius). For the dating of the work the latter cites Dupont-Sommer, Nock (probably delivered in Paul's lifetime), Pfeiffer (shortly before Philo), and Hadas (the reign of Caligula).

II

73   IGNATIAN PROBLEMS

Ignatius and the author of 4 Maccabees received a similar rhetorical
education. Certain features, however (above all the striking use of the
term ἀντίψυχον by Ignatius and in the mouths of the Maccabean martyrs),
do indeed suggest that 4 Maccabees was used among the Christians at
Antioch and influenced their ideas and indeed Christian ideas in general
on the subject of martyrdom.

The features of Ignatius' style to which Perler drew attention are
important for what they tell us about his background. Ignatius shows
very little interest in the Old Testament or tendency to imitate its
language. Rather he gives evidence of having received a rhetorical
education. Riesenfeld, in an article taking up some of the points made
by Perler, suggested that, 'Perhaps he had been, before becoming a
Christian or even while he was a Christian, a pleader in a law court at
Antioch, an advocate or a local politician'.[1] Such a theory would not
only tell us why in certain respects Ignatius' vocabulary is more similar to that of the second-century Apologists than to that of the New
Testament.[2] It may also throw light on his peculiar mixture of self-
abasement and authoritarianism. The hypothesis that Ignatius was an
adult convert who rose speedily to leadership in the Christian community
because of the responsible position he had already exercised in secular
life would help to explain why he repeatedly describes himself in relation
to his home community as ἔσχατος αὐτῶν or the like (Eph. xxi. 2, Trall.
xiii. 1, Rom. ix. 2, Smyrn. xi. 1, alluding to Paul's words in I Cor. xv. 8).

An important part in Professor Joly's argumentation is played by the
investigation of Ignatius' vocabulary. One chapter discusses Ignatius'
Christian terminology and lists a number of terms which show the
advanced state of its development: χριστιανισμός, ἡ καθολικὴ ἐκκλησία,
χριστιανός used as an adjective, λιτανεύω with Christ as its object,
ἀποστολικός, αἵρεσις, the way Ignatius uses εὐαγγέλιον, παρουσία, πάθος,
and ὁμιλία. This phenomenon might be taken as providing an indication
of Ignatius' date, if we possessed a large body of Christian literature
deriving from the same milieu. As it is, we only possess a very small

[1] H. Riesenfeld, 'Reflections on the Style and Theology of St. Ignatius of
Antioch', T.U. lxxix (1961), p. 317.
[2] Joly, pp. 61–2, refers to M. P. Brown, The Authentic Writings of Ignatius.
A Study of Linguistic Criteria (Durham, N.C., 1963), for this conclusion. Influence of an Asianic style of rhetoric is found among Christian writers in
developed form in Melito of Sardis and Tertullian. A more primitive specimen
appears in a fragment of a homily preserved in the Codex von der Goltz, which is
discussed by G. Zuntz, J.T.S. xlvii (1946), pp. 71–4 (reprinted in Opuscula
Selecta (Manchester, 1972), pp. 284–90). Zuntz refers for further illustration
of the style in early Christian literature to the anti-Montanist writer Apollonius
quoted by Eusebius and to the anonymous fragment attached to the Epistle to
Diognetus.

proportion of the Christian writings which were produced in the second century, and what we do have derives from a variety of different backgrounds. If Justin stood in the same line of tradition as Ignatius, which he clearly does not, one might be justified in expecting him to show acquaintance with the same technical terms. Conversely it is not surprising that many terms used by Ignatius first reappear in the Martyrdom of Polycarp (Joly pp. 115 ff.), whose author is likely to have known Ignatius' letters. There is nothing improbable in the supposition that Christian terminology developed more quickly at Antioch than elsewhere, indeed Acts xi. 26 suggests that this was the case. None the less there is much of interest in the parallels with other writings to which Joly draws our attention; thus, for example, he finds Ignatius' use of πάθος in a Christian sense paralleled in the *Epistle of Barnabas*, of λιτανεύω in the *Protevangelium Jacobi* and the *Acta Johannis*, of παρουσία in the *Preaching of Peter* (which may also have included a version of the resurrection appearance narrated by Ignatius, *Smyrn.* iii. 2).[1] Parallels with *2 Clement* and Hermas are mentioned elsewhere (pp. 117 and 54–7).

Professor Joly's assertion that Ignatius uses εὐαγγέλιον in the sense of a written gospel rather than the gospel message (pp. 65–7) depends above all on the interpretation of the problematic passage, *Phil.* viii. 2, where Ignatius reports his dispute at Philadelphia with certain opponents who stated ἐὰν μὴ ἐν τοῖς ἀρχείοις εὕρω ἐν τῷ εὐαγγελίῳ οὐ πιστεύω. The interpretation of ἐν τῷ εὐαγγελίῳ has been discussed repeatedly without any satisfactory consensus being reached. An attractively simple solution was suggested to me by Dr. E. Bammel, who proposed emending the text by the deletion of ἐν τῷ εὐαγγελίῳ. Ignatius' opponents are represented as stating, 'If I do not find it in the archives (i.e. the Old Testament), I do not believe it'. ἐν τῷ εὐαγγελίῳ must then be taken as a gloss. It may have been written in an abbreviated form in the margin or as an interlinear addition at the stage at which the different branches of the text diverged, since its case and position vary in the different witnesses. The phrase ἐν τῷ εὐαγγελίῳ is given only by the manuscripts of the uninterpolated version and its Latin translation. The manuscripts of the interpolated version are divided; five of the Greek manuscripts used by Zahn read τοῦ εὐαγγελίου and a sixth τὸ εὐαγγέλιον, together with the Latin translation, which gives a different word order: *si non inuenero euangelium in antiquis*. For the Armenian version Lightfoot records *si . . . non laudatur euangelium*, whereas the Coptic version (cited in the apparatus of the edition of K. Bihlmeyer, *Die Apostolischen Väter*, i (Tübingen, 1924), p. 104) gives οὐ πιστεύω τῷ εὐαγγελίῳ.

[1] Cf. Joly, pp. 53–4; H. Köster, op. cit., pp. 45 ff.

II

75   IGNATIAN PROBLEMS

Another gloss, which has infected only the uninterpolated Greek
text and its Latin translation but which was known also to Timothy
Aelurus, occurs at *Magn.* viii. 2. This is a correction of a credal statement (that Jesus Christ is God's word which came forth from silence),
intended to bring it into line with later orthodoxy. Joly argues that the
supplemented text is the original one, and that Ignatius wrote of Jesus
Christ, ὅς ἐστιν αὐτοῦ λόγος ἀίδιος, οὐκ ἀπὸ σιγῆς προελθών, thereby
intending a criticism of Valentinus. Quite apart from the parallels at
Eph. xv. 2 and xix. 1, which Joly apparently rejects because they use the
word ἡσυχία,[1] it shows a remarkable insensitivity to the flow of Ignatius'
language to suppose that he would distract attention from the force of
his positive affirmation of faith by indulging during the course of it
in an allusive side-hit at an opponent in this way. Even if 'Ignatius'
was in fact a later forger, one might expect that the negative statement
would be followed immediately by a positive one: 'not from silence
but from the Father . . .' Since Joly dates his forged Ignatian letters to
about 165, he can assume that the forger attacks Valentinian teachings.
His chapter on Ignatius and Gnosticism, however, in which he examines
the parallels between Ignatius and Gnostic terminology, leaves wide
open the question it is intended to answer, whether Ignatius reflects
a vague *Vorstufe* of Gnosticism, or an already developed form. If the
author of the letters was acquainted with the fully developed heretical
groups flourishing in the seventh decade of the second century it is
extraordinary that he refrains from attacking any of their characteristic
features and confines himself to a general anti-Docetic and anti-
Judaizing polemic. The accounts of the anti-heretical writers assign an
important part to Antioch in the development of Gnosticism, which
makes it likely that Ignatius would indeed have been in contact with
Gnostic ideas at the date traditionally assigned to him. Menander, a
pupil of Simon Magus, deceived many at Antioch by means of magic,
according to Justin (*1st Apology*, 26), and was followed, according to
Irenaeus (*Adv. Haer.* I. xviii) by Saturninus from Antioch who taught
in Syria, and Basilides who taught in Alexandria in the reign of
Hadrian (cf. also Clement, *Strom.* vii. 17, and Epiphanius, *Panarion*,
23–4). At the same time Cerinthus is represented as teaching in Asia
Minor as a contemporary of St. John (see below). Menander is supposed
to have taught that he himself was the saviour sent by the unknown first
power in opposition to the angels who made the world and to have

---

[1] The idea of the λόγος coming forth from σιγή may have been influenced by
Wisd. xviii. 14–15. On the association of silence with God, cf. H. Chadwick,
'The Silence of Bishops in Ignatius', *Harvard Theological Review*, xliii (1950),
pp. 169–72.

promised immortality by means of baptism (Irenaeus, *Adv. Haer.* I. xvii).[1] Whether a more recognizably Christian Gnosticism of the type represented by Saturninus or Basilides had already developed at the time of Ignatius is uncertain. In any case Ignatius is concerned to give warnings against the infiltration of strange teachings into the Christian communities rather than explicitly to refute any particular rival system of teaching. Particularly striking is the fact that Ignatius shows no interest in arguing against the Gnostic separation of the Old Testament Demiurge from the unknown supreme God revealed by Christ. His emphasis that there is *one* God may indeed show awareness of such teachings (*Magn.* viii. 2; cf. vii. 2, 'one Father'), but at a later date one would expect this to be supplemented by statements that the one God is creator of heaven and earth, both just and good etc. His own links with Gnostic terminology and ideas would seem to be indicative rather of contacts with the milieu from which Gnosticism developed than the result of polemic against fully evolved Gnosticism.

A type of argumentation used by both Joly and Rius-Camps in attempting to prove the inauthenticity of Ignatius' letters is the listing of supposed anomalies in the letters themselves and in the situation which they presuppose. Both authors direct numerous questions against the letters and suppose that because no answer is forthcoming we must be dealing with a forgery. An important misapprehension underlies this type of approach, namely the failure to recognize how extremely limited the surviving evidence of second-century Christianity is. Thus both Joly (p. 101) and Rius-Camps (p. 85) argue that if the Ignatius of whom the seven letters give evidence had really existed, details of his fate and of his correspondence ought to have been described in the writings of Irenaeus, assuming that from Irenaeus' viewpoint Ignatius seemed as central a figure as he does from ours or that Irenaeus ought to have given details of all martyred bishops (why then does he not describe the martyrdom of Telesphorus, bishop of Rome, mentioned *Adv. Haer.* III. iii. 3?). Joly adds that Polycrates of Ephesus ought to have included Ignatius in his list of witnesses in the letter he wrote to Victor of Rome in connection with the Quartodeciman controversy (quoted by Eusebius, *H. E.* v. 24). Whereas some of these questions are simply mistaken or perverse, others may direct our attention to problems which merit further consideration.

Rius-Camps supposes that Irenaeus should have mentioned Ignatius' testimony to confirm his argument on the true apostolic tradition.

---

[1] R. M. Grant, *Gnosticism and Early Christianity*[2] (New York and London, 1966), pp. 93–4, compares Menander's view of baptism with Ignatius' view of the eucharist (*Eph.* xx. 2).

The fact that he does not do so may suggest that Irenaeus has little personal interest in vindicating the claims to orthodoxy of the church of Antioch, but equally it may indicate that he was aware that it was not possible without falsification to draw up a bishop-list for Antioch with the present bishop and Ignatius following in a direct line of succession from St. Peter. The view that Ignatius was the leader of a minority group at Antioch was ably and illuminatingly argued by W. Bauer (although some of the details of Bauer's picture may require correction).[1] An interesting tradition is recorded in the *Apostolic Constitutions*, vii. 46 (ed. F. X. Funk, p. 452), that Peter ordained Evodius as bishop of Antioch and Paul Ignatius. Perhaps this reflects a situation in which a majority group dominated by Jewish Christians looked back to Peter, whereas Ignatius was the leader of a minority Pauline party attempting to win wider acceptance. The usual view that the succession of bishops at Antioch was founded by Peter appears not only in orthodox writers, but also in the anti-Pauline *Clementine Recognitions* which record (x. 71) that a leading citizen Theophilus consecrated the hall of his house as a church and that a throne was set up in it by all the people for Peter.[2]

It may be worth looking more closely at two of the sets of problems against which Joly and Rius-Camps direct questions. They concern the limitations of our collection of Ignatius' letters and Ignatius' position as a condemned prisoner. Professor Joly considers the fact that the interest in Ignatius' letters is confined to a narrow area in Western Asia Minor to be indicative that they were written by a forger working in that district. If Ignatius had really existed, we might have expected letters to have survived addressed to Antioch or to other communities on the route between Antioch and Asia Minor. If his letters were collected by Polycarp, why did Polycarp not bother to get hold of any more? It may be possible to provide an answer to this question by supposing that the initiative for the collection of Ignatius' letters came from Ignatius himself, who conceived the idea of using his stay at Smyrna and Polycarp's co-operation for the composition of a kind of last testament for the Western Asia Minor communities, bringing to bear the authority given him by his forthcoming martyrdom in order to boost the parties friendly to himself in those churches and to supply their bishops with ammunition in their attempts to maintain unity.[3]

[1] *Rechtgläubigkeit und Ketzerei im ältesten Christentum* (Tübingen, 1934), pp. 65 ff.; cf. also pp. 119 ff.

[2] A list of testimonies on Peter at Antioch is given by G. Downey, *A History of Antioch in Syria* (Princeton, 1961), pp. 583–6.

[3] This hypothesis is supported by the self-conscious way in which Ignatius announces the themes of his letters; cf. H. J. Sieben, art. cit., pp. 8 ff.

Such a theory would explain also why the first four letters, written from Smyrna, make a more finished and formal impression than the more personal letters from Troas, the last of which at least (that to Polycarp) may have been completed in some haste. It is not necessary to assume that, because no other letters survive, Ignatius wrote no other letters, but it may be that these were informal notes intended to be supplemented verbally by their carriers, or that they were not intended for this particular collection, or that they revealed distressing details about the divisions at Antioch which made them unsuitable for preservation.

Joly regards the position of Ignatius as a prisoner travelling to Rome to be thrown to the beasts as implausible. He argues that we know of no Christians condemned to beasts before the reign of Marcus Aurelius apart from a vague allusion in the *Shepherd* of Hermas (to which should be added *Epistle to Diognetus*, vii. 7, and perhaps already Heb. xi. 37), and supposes that the one case of which we have details from the reign of Trajan, that of Pliny's procedure in Pontus, is sufficient to form a generalization for that period. The argument *ex silentio*, however, is invalid, particularly since the relevant question is not 'when do we first have evidence of Christians being thrown to beasts?' but 'when did condemned criminals in general begin to be used for this purpose?' For the general practice, including the transport of prisoners from the provinces to Rome, there is no lack of evidence in the early principate.[1] Joly thinks it odd that Ignatius does not mention any companions on his journey to Rome and thus appears to have been the only Christian available at Antioch for sending to be thrown to beasts.[2] This point may throw light on the disputed question whether the troubles in the church at Antioch referred to by Ignatius were internal ones or caused by persecution. Certainly Ignatius' letters give no evidence of a situation of general persecution. Ruis-Camps discusses the matter (pp. 139–42) and concludes, probably correctly, that there had been a public disturbance due to internal discord in the church at Antioch. He suggests that this had attracted the attention of the authorities and that Ignatius had given himself up as responsible (referring to *Rom.* iv. 1, and, more particularly, *Smyrn.* iv. 2, where Ignatius' words can indeed most readily be understood in this way). If this suggestion is correct, Ignatius' appeal to the Romans not to prevent his martyrdom, and in particular

[1] Cf. T. Mommsen, *Römisches Strafrecht* (Leipzig, 1899), pp. 925–8.
[2] It may be that the Christians who have preceded Ignatius from Syria to Rome mentioned at *Rom.* x. i are also destined to be thrown to beasts. Whether these also travelled via Philippi and are to be identified with the Zosimus and Rufus of Polycarp's letter (ix. 1) is uncertain. Ignatius also knows of previous cases when the beasts were not hungry (*Rom.* v. 2).

his words at *Rom.* vi. 2, may reflect the struggle he had already had at Antioch against those attempting to restrain him. It is remarkable that he shows no particular interest in or hostility to the persecuting authorities and appears to have very little idea of what will happen at Rome apart from the encounter with beasts. He is clearly frightened that his own resolve may fail (*Rom.* vii. 1–2), which indicates that he expects an opportunity to recant, and he also fears that the beasts may refuse to perform their task speedily and thoroughly (*Rom.* iv. 2, v. 2). He fears the negative influence of hostile spiritual powers (*Rom.* v. 3, vii. 1; cf. also *Trall.* iv. 2,) and is anxious that the Romans should support him by their prayers (*Rom.* iii. 2, viii. 3) and refrain from attempting to dissuade him from martyrdom. He may fear that they may try to get him released by means of influence or bribery, but the hints to this effect scarcely go so far as to paint an anachronistically powerful picture of the Roman community (as is suggested by Joly, pp. 109–10). His instruction at *Rom.* iv. 2, μᾶλλον κολακεύσατε τὰ θηρία, is completely divorced from reality. A further speculation may be added to that of Rius-Camps concerning Ignatius' arrest. A possible reason for internal disturbances in the church at Antioch could have been Ignatius' own election as bishop. A disputed election might well have caused a split such as must be implied by Ignatius' words at *Smyrn.* xi. 2–3 if we understand them as referring to restoration of peace after internal troubles rather than persecution. Ignatius' voluntary martyrdom would have healed the division and conferred prestige on his own followers.

A number of the problems raised by the two authors in connection with Ignatius are problems arising from our ignorance concerning the Christian communities at the period at which Ignatius is thought to have written. By denying the authenticity of Ignatius' letters one dissociates them from this obscure period without solving the problems themselves. Such problems include the origins of the monarchical epis-copate, the relations between the various Christian writings inside and outside the New Testament with which Ignatius may or may not have been acquainted, and the exact form taken by the heretical tendencies of which some of these writings give evidence. Thus Joly devotes a chapter to the monarchical episcopate, arguing that the position pre-supposed in the Ignatian letters is an anachronism, but giving no explanation for the origin of the institution. He writes as if the only reason for denying Ignatius' dependence on the canonical gospels were a mistaken idea about Ignatius' date, rather than the absence of direct citations in Ignatius and the nature of the parallels which he does show with gospel material.[1] Rius-Camps, on the other hand, by his early

[1] Cf. Köster, op. cit., pp. 24–61, especially p. 25 on the absence of citation

dating of his reduced genuine Ignatius, pushes back the date for the monarchical episcopate as well, though somewhat altering its nature, and he dates Ignatius definitely earlier than John, removing as an interpolation what he regards as the only literal quotation from the Fourth Gospel (p. 207).

Since Ignatius does not give direct citations of New Testament texts, it is impossible to be certain which New Testament writings he was acquainted with. Thus even in the case of St. Paul, whom Ignatius takes as his authority, scholars disputes about which letters he knew.[1] He himself states rather oddly that Paul mentions the Ephesians in every letter (*Eph.* xii. 2),[2] thus showing that he knew a collection of Paul's letters. He self-consciously models himself on Paul[3] and it is by this appeal to Paul that he expects to be accepted at Ephesus (*Eph.* xii. 2) and Rome (*Rom.* iv. 3, where Peter and Paul are mentioned together). Similarly Polycarp takes Paul as his authority when writing to the Philippians (iii. 2 and ix. 1). Lindemann[4] suggests that Ignatius' acquaintance with Paul may be not so much the reflection of an unbroken Pauline tradition at Antioch as rather the result of a recent reintroduction there of Paulinism. The theological influence of Paul on Ignatius is limited to certain themes. Striking is the fact that it is above all the features common to Paul and the Johannine writings that reappear in in Ignatius' thought.[5] That Ignatius shows a strong 'geistige Verwandtschaft' with the Gospel of John is generally agreed, and in this he presumably gives evidence of the influence of 'Johannine' thought on his own theological background. Whether he already used the Fourth Gospel in written form is disputed, since the parallels do not amount to direct quotations.[6] That his links with Johannine ideas derive from his Syrian background (and not from Asia Minor) is suggested by the contrast with Polycarp, who agrees with Ignatius in regarding Paul as his chief authority, but shows no acquaintance with

formulas in Ignatius and the table on pp. 259–60, which gives a comparison between Ignatius and the other apostolic fathers.

[1] His use of 1 Corinthians is the most obvious. For bibliography and various viewpoints cf. A. Lindemann, *Paulus im ältesten Christentum* (Tübingen, 1979), pp. 199 ff., and E. Dassmann, *Der Stachel im Fleisch* (Münster, 1979), pp. 129 ff.

[2] They are in fact mentioned in 1 Cor., Eph., and 1 and 2 Tim.

[3] Cf. the allusions to 1 Cor. xv. 8–10 at *Rom.* ix. 2 and *Smyrn.* xi. 1.

[4] Op. cit., pp. 200, 221, and 397.

[5] Cf. Dassmann, op. cit., pp. 34–45 and 127–8. Whether the Johannine writings show Pauline influence is disputed.

[6] For the 'spiritual affinity', cf. W. von Loewenich, *Das Johannes-Verständnis im zweiten Jahrhundert* (Giessen, 1932), pp. 25 ff. Opinions of various scholars on whether Ignatius used John are listed by V. Corwin, *St. Ignatius and Christianity in Antioch* (Yale, 1960), pp. 70–1.

the Gospel of John. Polycarp may, however, have known the Johannine epistles, or at least 1 John, since he attacks docetism in terms strikingly similar to 1 John iv. 2 f. and 2 John 7.[1] The one of the Synoptic Gospels to which Ignatius shows the closest resemblance is Matthew. There are a number of verbal parallels which can be explained by assuming either that Ignatius knew the First Gospel or that he drew on a tradition used also by the evangelist.[2] The background to the composition of the Gospel of Matthew is described by Vielhauer as follows: 'Die Gemeinde, aus der und in der das MtEv entstanden ist, macht den Eindruck einer gemischten Gemeinde, in der der judenchristliche Teil sich noch nicht völlig von der Synagoge getrennt hat und sich in heftiger Auseinandersetzung mit dem Judentum befindet . . . Manche Anzeichen sprechen dafür, daß ein Teil dieser Gemeinde, vielleicht der heidenchristliche, hinsicht-lich der Verbindlichkeit des Gesetzes liberaler als der andere dachte.'[3] Ignatius' polemic against Judaizers presumably shows acquaintance with communities of this kind.[4]

Rius-Camps devotes a section of his book to Ignatius' polemic against Gnostics and Judaizers (pp. 40–51) and concludes that he attacks two tendencies, not a single type of Judaizing Gnosticism. A similar view was argued independently by P. J. Donahue in an article published in 1978.[5] One of the points which emerge from the attempt to make a distinction between the two groups is the different position of the Judaizers and the Docetics in relation to the communities. Donahue contrasts Ignatius' instruction to the Smyrnaeans (iv. 1) to refrain even from meeting with the Docetics with the fact that at

[1] On Polycarp's use of Paul, cf. Lindemann, op. cit., pp. 221–32; on Polycarp and John, cf. von Loewenich, op. cit., pp. 22–5.

[2] Cf. V. Corwin, op. cit., pp. 67–8. Köster, op. cit., pp. 24–61, argues that, although Ignatius' contacts with Matthew are striking, these are to be explained by his use of Synoptic tradition, and that the dependence on Matt. iii. 15 of *Smyrn.* i. 1 is indirect, coming via a kerygmatic formula. J. Smit Sibinga, 'Ignatius and Matthew', *Novum Testamentum*, vii (1964/5), pp. 263–83, con-cludes that Ignatius used a Matthaean 'special source' in a pre-Matthaean form.

[3] P. Vielhauer, *Geschichte der urchristlichen Literatur* (Berlin, 1975), p. 365.

[4] The combination of 'Johannine' and 'Matthaean' tradition need not be surprising. The *Didache*, a work of a quite different type from Ignatius, which shows contacts with Synoptic tradition particularly of a 'Matthaean' variety, and which is usually assigned to Syria, may preserve traces of influence from a 'Johannine' background in its eucharistic prayers (chapter ix–x); cf. von Loewenich, op. cit., pp. 18–22. Points of contact between 1 John and Matthew are listed by T. W. Manson, *J.T.S.* xlviii (1947), pp. 31–2.

[5] 'Jewish Christianity in Ignatius' Letters', *Vigiliae Christianae*, xxxii (1978), pp. 81–93.

Philadelphia, according to his own account, he held a discussion with representatives of Judaizing tendencies (p. 87). Rius-Camps notes that the terms used in the anti-Judaizing letters are 'slightly gentler' (pp. 50–1). Thus the term αἵρεσις is used only in the anti-Docetic letters (*Eph.* vi. 2 and *Trall.* vi. 1), whereas μερίσαι, μερισμός, and σχίζων are used in the anti-Judaizing letters. It may be possible to maintain a distinction of this kind, though some confusion still remains. In the letter to the Ephesians, a community which Ignatius praises particularly highly and which gave him generous support, sending a five-man delegation to Symrna and arranging for the conveying of his letter to Rome and of his correspondence from Troas back to Smyrna and Philadelphia, the Docetic heretics are attacked as false teachers coming from outside, who are to be avoided like wild beasts (vii–ix). Their teaching is that of the prince of this aeon; they and those who listen to them will go to unquenchable fire (xvi–xvii). In the letter to the Trallians the relation of the Docetics to the community is less clearly specified. They are described as evil off-shoots bearing a deadly fruit (xi) and as offering the Trallians strange fodder, which is heresy, similar to a deadly drug (vi). At Smyrna, a church with which Ignatius was particularly closely linked, it would seem that, despite the fact that the Docetics are characterized as wild beasts in human form and to be avoided (iv and vii), they have succeeded in infiltrating the community and creating a split-off group disobedient to the bishop (vii–viii), although, interestingly, they apparently join the rest of the community in admiration for Ignatius himself (v). In contrast with this, at Philadelphia, where Ignatius' greeting may imply that some presbyters were not 'with the bishop' and whose community he first describes as having suffered not μερισμός but ἀποδιυλισμός (iii. 1), and then later μερισμός after all (vii. 2), representatives of Judaizing tendencies disputed with Ignatius himself (viii) and certain persons, perhaps the same, insulted the deacon Philo from Cilicia and Rheus Agathopus from Syria on their way through Philadelphia to join Ignatius (xi. 1). In opposing these Judaizing tendencies Ignatius is anxious to concede approval of the prophets (v. 2, ix. 2) and priests (ix. 1) as well as to emphasize his own positive teaching. In the Magnesian community too there is a problem of disunity, with certain persons acknowledging the bishop, but doing everything without him (iv). Ignatius finds it necessary to warn against division (vi), against living κατὰ Ἰουδαϊσμόν (viii. 1), and to urge the Magnesians to put off the old leaven (x. 2), as well as showing his own acceptance of the prophets (viii. 2, ix. 2). It is interesting that it is in this letter that he emphasizes that there is *one* God, who revealed himself through his

83   IGNATIAN PROBLEMS

son Jesus Christ (vii. 2, viii. 2), as if to allay fears about his own orthodoxy.

It would seem natural that the chief objection to Judaizing practices would be that they would be likely to cause separatist tendencies within the communities, whereas the teachings of the Docetic heretics appear to be a direct reversal of all that is most meaningful to Ignatius in the Christian message. The distinction between the two groups may not be as simple as this however. Whether or not they were attracted to Docetic views, the Judaizers, like the Docetics, failed to give prime emphasis to the life-giving grace given through the passion and resurrection of Jesus Christ (cf. *Magn.* ix. 1, *Phil.* viii–ix, πιστεύω τῇ χάριτι Ἰησοῦ Χριστοῦ, ὃς λύσει ἀφ' ὑμῶν πάντα δεσμόν . . . ὁ σταυρὸς αὐτοῦ καὶ ὁ θάνατος καὶ ἡ ἀνάστασις καὶ ἡ πίστις ἡ δι' αὐτοῦ, ἐν οἷς θέλω . . . δικαιωθῆναι, and, for the Docetics, *Smyrn.* vi–vii, καὶ τὰ ἐπουράνια . . . ἐὰν μὴ πιστεύσωσιν εἰς τὸ αἷμα Χριστοῦ, κἀκείνοις κρίσις ἐστίν . . . καταμάθετε δὲ τοὺς ἑτεροδοξοῦντας εἰς τὴν χάριν Ἰησοῦ Χριστοῦ τὴν εἰς ἡμᾶς ἐλθοῦσαν). Both groups, Ignatius feels, ought to be persuaded by the prophets (*Smyrn.* v. 1 and vii. 2, *Phil.* viii. 2, γέγραπται), who he knows looked forward to Christ (*Magn.* viii. 2, ix. 2, *Phil.* v. 2,) despite the fact that his own knowledge of the Old Testament is not thorough enough to enable him to dispute successfully with the Philadelphian Judaizers on this question.

It may well be that the two tendencies attacked by Ignatius were not entirely separate. The Docetics may have attempted to infiltrate the Judaizing groups as well as those friendly to Ignatius and they may in turn have picked up ideas from them. Both groups may have spread superfluous 'strange teachings', and there may well have been objectionable features shared by the two groups. In his letter to the Magnesians Ignatius introduces his warning against Judaizing with the words μὴ πλανᾶσθε ταῖς ἑτεροδοξίαις μηδὲ μυθεύμασιν τοῖς παλαιοῖς ἀνωφελέσιν οὖσιν and concludes it with the instruction μὴ ἐμπεσεῖν εἰς τὰ ἄγκιστρα τῆς κενοδοξίας (xi). In the letter to the Philadelphians there is a yet clearer exhortation against the evil teaching of plausible wolves (ii) and evil fodder, which is not the planting of the father (iii). The instruction not to listen to anyone who interprets Judaism (vi. 1) is followed by a warning against the evil arts and snares of the prince of this aeon. The evil fodder mentioned here could well be similar to the strange fodder against which Ignatius warns in his anti-Docetic letter to the Trallians (vi. 1). Some idea of its contents may be given by Ignatius' claim (v) that he could write of τὰ ἐπουράνια if he chose and that he too is able to understand τὰ ἐπουράνια καὶ τὰς τοποθεσίας τὰς ἀγγελικὰς καὶ τὰς συστάσεις τὰς ἀρχοντικάς, ὁρατά τε καὶ ἀόρατα.

84

Ignatius himself no doubt shares with his opponents a background in which magical superstition and speculation about angels and heavenly powers were rife.

Donahue argues that 'the letters of Ignatius are direct evidence for the church at Antioch rather than for the churches of Asia Minor' (art. cit., p. 81), i.e. that Ignatius' anti-heretical attitudes were already formed as a result of his experiences at Antioch. He denies that Ignatius' statement in *Phil.* vi. 1, that it is better to hear Christianity from the circumcised than Judaism from the uncircumcised, must necessarily imply that Ignatius' Judaizing opponents were uncircumcised (p. 89). Instead he envisages a community including both Jewish Christians and 'God-fearing' Gentile converts nurtured in Judaism, who share with the Jewish Christians a reverence for the Law and conviction that it remains binding and take the view that Gentiles can join the church as Gentiles, but occupy a position in it inferior to that of Jews. He argues that 'Ignatius rejects the Jewish Christian distinction between classes of Christians which leads to their refusal to celebrate the Eucharist with Gentiles' (p. 90).

The picture which Donahue paints for Antioch can be supported by the New Testament evidence for its community on the one hand and by what we know of its later history on the other. In Gal. ii. 11 ff. Paul reports that, after the arrival at Antioch of certain persons from James, Peter, the rest of the Jews, and even Barnabas withdrew from holding common meals with the Gentiles. The dominance of the Pauline party there may have been lost. The narrative of Acts only records one visit of Paul there (xviii. 22–3) subsequent to the quarrel with Barnabas described in Acts xv. 36 ff. That influence of a Jewish or Jewish Christian kind remained strong at Antioch is well known and may partly account for the frequent divisions which split the church there in later centuries. The next bishop after Ignatius to have left any writings, Theophilus of Antioch, although he uses John and Paul, is 'in spirit and in content . . . very close to Judaism'.[1] The *Didascalia*, which is thought to have been written in Syria in the early third century and shows close contacts with Ignatius particularly in its view of the ministry, finds it necessary still to direct lengthy polemic against Judaizing tendencies.

In connection with the Judaizing tendencies in Asia Minor it is possible to cite various New Testament references.[2] Of the seven churches

---

[1] According to R. M. Grant, 'The Problem of Theophilus', *Harvard Theological Review*, xliii (1950), pp. 179–96.

[2] For the presence of diaspora Jews in Asia Minor, cf. the references given by E. M. Smallwood, *The Jews under Roman Rule* (Leiden, 1976), p. 121. In Lydia and Phrygia there were Jews who had been brought from Parthia by Antiochus III between 210 and 205 B.C.

addressed in the Apocalypse three coincide with ones addressed by
Ignatius and two of these, Smyrna and Philadelphia, are plagued by
the mysterious 'Synagogue of Satan, of those who say they are Jews
and they are not' (ii. 9 and iii. 9). It seems unlikely, however, that the
Nicolaitans, who figure in the letter to Ephesus (ii. 6) and elsewhere,
have anything to do with Ignatius' Docetic heretics.[1] The opponents
envisaged in the Epistle to the Colossians appear to have combined
'philosophical' speculations (ii. 8) with Judaizing practices in regard to
food, drink, festivals, new moons, sabbaths, and angel-worship (ii.
16 ff.).[2] Reminiscent of Ignatius' Judaizers are the opponents attacked
in 1 Timothy (i. 3–7, iv. 1–3, 7, vi. 3–10 and 20–1). These are envisaged
as threatening the church at Ephesus (i. 34) and as given to myths and
endless genealogies (i. 4, also iv. 7), a phrase which recalls Ignatius,
Magn. viii. 1. Some of them wish to be teachers of the law (i. 7). Their
encratite tendencies are attacked at iv. 1–5. The opponents attacked in
Titus, which purports to give Titus instructions for his ministry on
Crete, are described as including οἱ ἐκ περιτομῆς (i. 10), and as given
to Jewish myths and commands of men (i. 14), and to foolish disputes
and genealogies and strifes and battles about the law (iii. 9 f.). Whether
the opponents of 2 Timothy (which complains that all those in Asia have
turned away from Paul, i. 15) are identical with these seems questionable. μῦθοι are mentioned, however, at 2 Timothy iv. 4.[3] It is interesting
that the letter of Polycarp to the Philippians, which shows parallels at
least with 1 Timothy,[4] attacks only the peripatetic Docetic heretics and
appears unconcerned about Judaizing myths. The Judaizing problems
may have been local ones which presented no danger at Philippi.

The pastoral epistles give no evidence of concern about the Docetic
tendencies which so disturb Ignatius and Polycarp. These tendencies,
however, are attacked in the Johannine epistles. 1 John iv. 2–3 and 2 John
7 represent the denial that Jesus Christ came in the flesh as the teaching

---

[1] They may have been heretics of a libertine variety, whereas Ignatius sees
danger in an over-boastful asceticism (*Polycarp* v. 2).
[2] The Jews are accused of angel worship in early Christian apologetic, cf.
Preaching of Peter, quoted by Clement, *Stromateis*, VI. v. 41 (*G.C.S. Clemens*
vol. ii, p. 452), Aristides, *Apology*, xiv.
[3] The dating of the Pastoral epistles is disputed. von Campenhausen's
suggestion that Polycarp wrote them has not been generally accepted. Some
scholars have regarded 1 Tim. vi. 20 as a reference to Marcion's ἀντιθέσεις,
which would imply a date near the middle of the second century. Others have
regarded them as genuine or as incorporating genuine fragments. In view of this
uncertainty, it seems methodologically unsound to take them as a unity in
arguing about such disputed questions as the evidence they give for heretical
movements or for the development of the Christian ministry.
[4] Cf. Lindemann, op. cit., pp. 223 and 229.

of antichrist. Both in Ignatius and in the Johannine epistles there are two types of Docetism which may be attacked. The simplest conclusion to draw from the Johannine verses just mentioned, from Polycarp, *Philippians*, vii. 1, and from most of Ignatius' anti-Docetic polemic is that the heretical opponents held that Jesus Christ only appeared in the form of a man but was in fact incorporeal. This view is unambiguously attacked at *Smyrn.* ii–iii and v. 2, where Ignatius demonstrates that even after the resurrection Jesus Christ was not a δαιμόνιον ἀσώματον and describes his opponents as not confessing the Lord to be σαρκοφόρος. It is likely to have been an opinion commonly held (it frequently appears in the New Testament apocryphal writings). Irenaeus attributes it to Saturninus, whose followers also, he states, rejected marriage and, for the most part, also the eating of meat (*Adv. Haer.* i. xviii). Certain passages in 1 John and in Ignatius' letter to the Ephesians, however, can more readily be understood as attacking the view ascribed to Cerinthus, which distinguished the heavenly Christ from the man Jesus, son of Joseph and Mary, teaching that the former descended into the latter at his baptism and left again πρὸς τῷ τέλει (Irenaeus, *Adv. Haer.* i. xxi). If the author of 1 John had this doctrine in mind 1 John ii. 22 can be interpreted as condemning those who deny the identity of Jesus and the Christ (cf. also iv. 15 and v. 1 and 5), and the *lectio difficilior* λύει at 1 John iv. 3 can be accepted as meaning 'takes apart', 'separates'.[1] Similarly Ignatius' credal statement at Ephesians vii. 2 can be understood as affirming the unity of a saviour whom his opponents would divide into two, the man Jesus as fleshly, begotten, born of Mary and subject to death and suffering, and the heavenly Christ as spiritual, unbegotten, divine, true life, from God, and impassible. Rather similarly in his letter to Polycarp iii. 2 Ignatius combines two opposed lists of characteristics, including τὸν ἀπαθῆ, τὸν δι' ἡμᾶς παθητόν. Irenaeus states that in Cerinthus' view Jesus suffered and rose, whereas Christ, being spiritual, remained impassible (loc. cit.). Ignatius shows himself particularly anxious always to balance σάρξ and πνεῦμα (cf. *Eph.* viii. 2, x. 3, *Magn.* i. 2, xiii. 2, *Smyrn.* xii. 2, *Polycarp* i. 2, ii. 2). His emphasis on the virgin birth (*Eph.* xviii. 2 f.) may be aimed against the same view. It may be noted that the activity of Christ after his descent into Jesus in Irenaeus' account of Cerinthus' teaching is reminiscent of the Fourth Gospel: 'annuntiasse incognitum patrem et virtutes perfecisse'.

In 1 John ii. 19 the origin of the Docetic heretics attacked as antichrists is described: 'They went out from us but they were not of us;

[1] The witnesses for this reading are discussed by A. von Harnack, *Studien zur Geschichte des Neuen Testaments und der alten Kirche*, i (Berlin, 1931), pp. 132 ff.

for if they had been of us, they would have remained with us'. There are many of them (ii. 18, iv. 1) and they attempt to lead the addressees of the epistle astray (ii. 26). They have gone out into the world as false prophets (iv. 1; cf. also 2 John 7), and the world listens to them (iv. 5), whereas the letter's addressees are hated by the world (iii. 13). 2 John adds that if representatives of the false teachers come to the addressees they are not to be given hospitality. 3 John reveals a situation in which the addressee, Gaius, has given hospitality to brothers who had been sent out apparently on an evangelizing mission to the gentiles, but Diotrephes, who, it appears, regards himself as the leader of Gaius' church, has excommunicated these brothers, abusing the writer of the letter, although he had written to the church. It we take all three letters together a picture emerges of a Johannine group engaging in missionary activity in competition with and less successfully than a Docetic splinter-group which had broken off from it, and at the same time itself attempting to gain admission to a community (communities) which regard it with suspicion. Whether the suspicion has anything to do with the activities of the splinter-group is not stated. Unfortunately it is impossible to date or locate the Johannine epistles with any degree of certainty. A faint light may be cast on the situation by the reflection that the group which produced the Johannine literature and developed in comparative isolation must at some time have entered the 'mainstream church'. 3 John appears to reflect one stage in that process. The Johannine brothers are accepted by the beloved Gaius but excommunicated by Diotrephes, ὁ φιλοπρωτεύων.

Is it possible to construct a coherent picture out of the material so far discussed and in particular out of the fact that Ignatius' letters reveal such a variety of different strands of influence on his background and tendencies to which he is opposed? The portrayal by Donahue of Ignatius' background at Antioch takes into account only the opposition between Jewish and Pauline Christianity. As has been mentioned above, however, it is not certain that there was a continuous tradition of Pauline influence at Antioch. It may be that the background reflected by Ignatius is rather that of a Johannine group attempting to win ground among the Gentile members of a mixed Gentile and Jewish Christian community at Antioch of the type envisaged by Donahue (thus producing the combination of 'Johannine' and 'Matthaean' influences) and that the Pauline influence was a secondary feature. Representatives of Johannine circles may have attempted to enter the 'mainstream' communities on two fronts, firstly in Syria, where one of the results was a combination of Johannine and Jewish Christian elements which was to provide a fertile breeding ground for Gnosticism, and secondly in Asia Minor, where they may have come into contact with groups looking back to Paul and carried back Pauline influences to Syria. If the Docetic heretics attacked by Ignatius had arisen as the result of a split in the Johannine group itself and were attempting to gain ground among the communities in Asia Minor, Ignatius' ferocity against them and his anxiety to affirm his own positive beliefs will be readily comprehensible. In this case his anti-heretical pronouncements will have two aims, firstly to give warnings against the heretics and secondly to make clear his own orthodoxy. It is in accordance with this that his own positive statements of faith vary from letter to letter. In his first letter, that to Ephesus, a centre associated in later tradition with both John and Cerinthus, his affirmations are 'anti-Cerinthian'. In *Magnesians* he is anxious to affirm that Jesus Christ came forth from the one father, and both anti-Judaizing letters declare approval of the prophets. In these two letters he refrains from speaking of Jesus as $\theta\epsilon\delta\varsigma$. His letters written from Troas are those in which phrases appear with a Pauline-sounding emphasis on grace, perhaps reflecting the influence of discussions during his stay at Smyrna (cf. the quotations given above, p. 83 from *Philadelphians* and *Smyrnaeans*). It is by his appeal to Paul that Ignatius expects to be accepted in the churches of Western Asia Minor. In Syria, on the other hand, there may have been strong resistance to the acceptance of Paul as an authority.[1]

The view just suggested provides a convincing background to the hypothesis that the disturbances at Antioch to which Ignatius refers in his letters were caused by internal disputes and not by general persecu-tion. The picture painted by Bauer of the party represented by Ignatius as a minority one struggling to maintain its unity against widespread

---

[1] If the *Epistula Apostolorum* (Hennecke-Schneemelcher *Neutestamentliche Apokryphen*[3], i (Tübingen, 1959), pp. 126 ff.) could be taken as having been written in Syria not long after Ignatius' death it would provide confirmation of the picture suggested here. Despite strong individual differences, this work shows a very similar combination of influences, so that one might, for instance, imagine it to have been produced in the kind of circles to which Ignatius' Johanno-Pauline group was attempting to gain admission. It announces itself as written by the apostles in opposition to the pseudo-apostles Simon and Cerin-thus (1 and 7), emphasizes the virgin birth (3 and 14) and that Jesus put on flesh (21), narrates a resurrection appearance which refutes the idea that Jesus was like a demon or phantom after the resurrection (11–12; cf. Ignatius, *Smyrn.* iii), and discusses the resurrection of the flesh at length (21 ff.). Its apostle list is headed by John (2) and it makes use of all four gospels but particularly heavily of the Gospel of John. Jesus is represented as predicting to the apostles the appearance of Paul and the Gentile mission (31–2) in a manner which suggests that the writer desires to recommend Paul to his readers (cf. von Loewenich, op. cit., pp. 57 ff., Dassmann, op. cit., pp. 261 ff., Vielhauer, op. cit., pp. 683 ff).

competition will be correct.[1] The bishops of the communities addressed by Ignatius in Asia Minor will be the leaders of the Johanno-Pauline groups there, attempting to hold together their flocks in the face of separatist tendencies caused by attraction to Judaizing practices and interest in the teachings of Docetic missionaries. Ignatius, as 'bishop of Syria', will have been chosen as leader of this party in Syria (*Rom.* ii. 2). It may be that the Jewish Christians and those favourable to them at Antioch have such a firm majority that Ignatius does not have the face to call himself the bishop of Antioch. It is to Antioch, however, that he instructs the Smyrnaeans and Philadelphians to send ambassadors once he hears that peace has been restored (*Phil.* x, *Smyrn.* xi, *Polycarp* vii). That churches close to Antioch (perhaps in Cilicia) possess leaders friendly to Ignatius' party in the form of bishops is indicated by his remark at *Phil.* x. 2, that the churches nearest to Antioch have sent bishops and others presbyters and deacons (a piece of information no doubt brought to him by Philo, the deacon from Cilicia, and Rheus Agathopus from Syria). In addition, Ignatius' instruction to Polycarp (viii. 1), that he should write to the churches 'in front' (i.e. between Smyrna and Antioch?) that they should send representatives or letters, would seem to imply the existence of additional communities of a friendly disposition.

The picture of the Ignatian monarchical bishops as the leaders of a Johanno-Pauline party may throw light on the origin of this institution. Joly argues that Ignatius' picture of the monarchical episcopate is anachronistic, but the later its origin is placed the more difficult it becomes to explain. Ignatius gives the first clear evidence, since the possible early parallels which are cited are uncertain. These are the Pastoral epistles, the position of James and his successors at Jerusalem and the angels of the seven churches in the Apocalypse.[2] It is noteworthy that in asserting the authority of the bishop Ignatius nowhere uses the argument of apostolic succession (in contrast to *I Clement*, xlii–xliv). It may be that the institution is a recent one, independent of the

---

[1] Op. cit., pp. 65 ff.

[2] Whether the angels of the seven churches were bishops is questionable. The position of James and his successors at Jerusalem is usually regarded as a special case, but it provided a model which looked very similar to the arrangement of the monarchical episcopate. Hegesippus certainly thought in terms of a succession of monarchical bishops at Jerusalem and was so much dominated by this idea that he projected it onto Corinth and Rome as well (cf. Eusebius' quotations from Hegesippus, above all *H.E.* iv. 21 ff.). 1 Timothy iii. 2 ff. might be taken to imply that there is only one bishop in each community, but since Titus i. 5 ff. suggests rather that the presbyters are envisaged as acting as bishops, this inference is usually rejected. Cf. J. Rohde, *Urchristliche und frühkatholische Ämter* (Berlin, 1976).

presbyter-bishops of which *1 Clement* gives evidence.[1] Of the bishop of Philadelphia Ignatius states that he obtained his ministry 'not from himself, nor through men . . . but in the love of God the father and the Lord Jesus Christ' (*Phil.* i). In a sentence which may perhaps refer at least indirectly to his own choice as bishop, Ignatius states κατὰ θέλημα δὲ κατηξιώθην, οὐκ ἐκ συνειδότος, ἀλλ' ἐκ χάριτος θεοῦ (*Smyrn.* xi. 1). If the bishop was appointed not by men but by God, he must have been selected by spiritual revelation, or by the drawing of lots, or by some kind of miraculous occurrence. Further light may be shed on the matter by the statements of Irenaeus, Clement and Tertullian about the Asia Minor communities.[2]

Irenaeus, who is anxious to affirm the apostolicity and the orthodoxy of the Asia Minor Christianity in which he himself grew up, states of Polycarp that he was not only taught by apostles and associated with many who had seen the Lord, but that he was also ὑπὸ ἀποστόλων κατασταθεὶς εἰς τὴν Ἀσίαν ἐν τῇ ἐν Σμύρνῃ ἐκκλησίᾳ ἐπίσκοπος (*Adv. Haer.* iii. 3. 4). In speaking of 'apostles' here Irenaeus is presumably referring to John. In his letter to Florinus (quoted by Eusebius, *H.E.* v. 20. 4) Irenaeus recalls Polycarp's reminiscences of his intercourse with John and with others who had seen the Lord. After the passage just quoted above he goes on to narrate the story of John and Cerinthus in the bath-house at Ephesus as deriving from Polycarp, and shortly after this states that the church at Ephesus was founded by Paul and that John remained with them until the time of Trajan, so that it is a true witness of the tradition of the apostles. Irenaeus regularly refers to this John as the disciple of the Lord. He clearly intends to imply that he was also an apostle but he nowhere describes him as the apostle or states that he was one of the Twelve or the son of Zebedee. He may hope that his readers will make this assumption (as they usually have), but he himself avoids telling a direct untruth on the matter. Thus in support of the information that the Lord taught when over the age of forty he states that all the presbyters who came together with John, the Lord's disciple, in Asia give evidence that John handed this down to them and

---

[1] Its different character, with the one bishop representing the one God in his overseeing of the community, is emphasised by E. Dassmann, 'Zur Entstehung des Monepiskopats', *Jahrbuch für Antike und Christentum*, xvii (1974), pp. 74–90; cf. also H. Chadwick, art. cit.

[2] In what follows these statements are discussed on the basis of the presupposition that they preserve traditions about a John of Ephesus who was in some way (very likely closely) linked with the circles which produced the Johannine writings (whether he wrote any of them may be left open) and who was not the son of Zebedee but soon came to be confused with him. John is also envisaged as surrounded by 'his bishops' in the Muratorian fragment, see below p. 95.

II

goes on to remark, 'He remained with them until the times of Trajan. Some of them saw not only John but also other apostles and heard the same from them' (*Adv. Haer.* II. xxxiii. 3).

It is presumably the same John to whom Papias of Hierapolis refers, coupling him with Aristion as a disciple of the Lord, as John ὁ πρεσβύτερος in a list which clearly distinguishes him from John the son of Zebedee (quoted by Eusebius, *H.E.* iii. 39). Papias is described by Irenaeus as a hearer of John and companion of Polycarp (*Adv. Haer.* v. xxxiii. 4).[1]

Tertullian gives instructions for the verification of apostolic succession in his *De Praescriptione Haereticorum*, 32. A community which claims to be apostolic must be able to show that its first bishop had apostles or apostolic men as his 'auctor' or 'antecessor'. He goes on to cite as an example the church of Smyrna, which records that Polycarp was placed there by John.

Clement of Alexandria describes the activities of John (whom he identifies with the author of the Apocalypse) in the area round Ephesus (*Quis diues saluetur* 42). After the death of Domitian John came from Patmos to Ephesus and went exhorting the adjacent areas of the gentiles, setting up bishops in some places, organizing whole churches in others, and in others appointing to office by lot (κλῆρον κληρώσων) one person out of those indicated by the Spirit. There is a striking agreement here with what is implied by Ignatius' remarks on the appointment of bishops. The use of lot-drawing need not be surprising. It is paralleled by the account in Acts i. 26 of the appointment of Matthias to make up the number of the apostles. Indication by the Spirit appears in Acts xiii. 2. If Ignatius himself was chosen by lot from a number of candidates selected by the Spirit, this will throw light on the sense of vocation which he shows in his letters, not indeed now to act as bishop at Antioch but to fulfil the more glorious 'lot' of martyrdom. He uses the word κλῆρος in this sense at *Trall.* xii. 3, *Rom.* i. 2 and *Phil.* v. 1, and rather differently at *Eph.* xi. 2, where he expresses the desire for a special association with the Ephesian community, perhaps thereby

[1] In commenting on Papias' distinction of the two Johns (loc. cit.) Eusebius gives the information that there are two tombs or memorials (μνήματα) at Ephesus both said to be John's. These could of course have belonged to two rival groups; they need not necessarily imply that there were two Johns buried at Ephesus. The same statement is made by Dionysius of Alexandria, quoted by Eusebius, *H.E.* vii. 25. A distinction between the two Johns appears also in the bishop-list of the *Apostolic Constitutions* (vii. 46, ed. Funk, pp. 453–4), which states that at Ephesus Paul ordained Timothy and John John. This list, however, shows no acquaintance with Polycarp; for Smyrna it names three bishops, Aristo, Strataeas Loidis filius, and Aristo, perhaps the same as the Aristion mentioned by Papias.

showing his allegiance to a party which centered on Ephesus and was struggling to maintain its position at Antioch.

If we give credence to the tradition that monarchical bishops were introduced into the Asia Minor communities by John as part of a reorganization of the churches in that area, then there is nothing surprising in the fact that the system was not yet in force at Philippi at the time when Polycarp sent his epistle there.[1] What kind of ministry was in operation in the churches of Asia Minor and Syria before the introduction of the monarchical episcopate is an open question. In the case of Asia Minor there is uncertainty over the interpretation of the evidence; the various references to spiritual gifts in the Pauline epistles, including the list headed by apostles, prophets, and teachers in 1 Cor. xii. 28, the address to bishops and deacons in Phil. i. 1, the statement in Acts xiv. 23 that on their return from their first missionary journey Paul and Barnabas elected presbyters for their converts in each church, the mention of presbyters of Ephesus who act as ἐπίσκοποι in Acts xx. 17 ff. (cf. especially xx. 28), the implications of the letters to the seven churches in the Apocalypse, and the dating and interpretation of the Pastoral epistles and the Johannine epistles (if these are assigned to Asia Minor). Further confusion is caused by the fact that the words ἐπίσκοπος, διάκονος, and πρεσβύτερος are not always employed in a technical sense, so that their implications may vary from one community to another. The title presbyter appears to be used in a special sense in 2 and 3 John and in the descriptions by Irenaeus and Papias of John of Ephesus and his circle quoted above.[2]

For Syria the evidence is more sparse. Acts xiii. 1 represents the church at Antioch as led by prophets and teachers. In the *Didache* wandering apostles, prophets, and teachers are an important feature, presbyters remain unmentioned, and the addressees have to be instructed to elect and show respect to a local ministry of bishops and deacons.

Ignatius' ideas on the ministry were presumably formed in Syria, although in his letters he is giving instructions for Asian churches. It is interesting, therefore, that he shows no interest in the idea of a ministry of apostles, prophets, and teachers. In his view apostles are a feature of the past, prophets are Old Testament prophets, and there is only one teacher, Jesus Christ himself (*Eph.* xv. 1, *Magn.* ix). Ignatius' decisiveness on this point is clearly due to his hostility to those corrupters of

---

[1] For a summary of discussion concerning the ἐπίσκοποι greeted together with deacons at the beginning of St. Paul's epistle to the Philippians, cf. J. Rohde, op. cit., pp. 54–6.

[2] Cf. H. von Campenhausen, *Kirchliches Amt und geistliche Vollmacht* (Tübingen, 1953), pp. 132 ff. and 177 ff.

the faith who carry round false teaching (*Eph.* ix. 1, xvi. 2, *Phil.* ii), the evil odour of the teaching of the prince of this aeon (*Eph.* xvii. 1). Teaching is clearly risky (*Eph.* xv. 1) and is allowed without qualification only to the Romans (iii. 1).[1]

A second feature of interest about Ignatius' picture of the ministry is the apparent illogicality in detail of the analogy which he likes to draw between earthly and heavenly hierarchies, with the bishop representing God, the presbyters the college of the apostles, and the deacons entrusted with the ministry of Jesus Christ (*Magn.* vi. I; cf. *Trall.* iii. 1, *Smyrn.* viii. 1, etc.). The same picture reappears in the *Didascalia*, a fact which gives evidence of its currency in Syria. Rius-Camps finds its inconsistency so striking (p. 226, Jesus Christ below the apostles, plural deacons compared with the single figure of Jesus Christ) that he concludes that it was inserted into the Ignatian letters by a forger utilizing the much fuller account of the *Didascalia*. A simpler solution may be to suppose that two separate pictures have been combined. That ἐπίσκοποι and deacons, as officials appointed to perform specific administrative and financial functions, are different in origin from presbyters or elders is apparent and is brought out clearly by Ignatius' picture of presbyters as a collegiate body.[2] Ignatius' analogy can most naturally be understood if one assumes that it reflects the situation of a community in which bishop and deacons were superimposed on a ministry with presbyters only or vice versa, or alternatively the amalgamation of two communities, the one possessing bishop and deacons, the other presbyters alone.[3]

The hypothesis that Ignatius and the bishops whom he addresses in Asia Minor are the leaders of a Johanno-Pauline party presents an obvious difficulty. Why, then, do Ignatius and Polycarp not refer to John

[1] Revelations, however, may be received by the bishop; cf. E. von Dobschütz, *Christian Life in the Primitive Church* (London, 1904), p. 242.

[2] He likes in connection with his comparison of presbyters and apostles to use the term συνέδριον (which does not appear in the other Apostolic Fathers; cf. E. J. Goodspeed, *Index Patristicus* (Leipzig, 1907), *sub voce*): *Magn.* vi. 1, the presbyters compared with the συνέδριον of the apostles; *Trall.* iii. 1, the presbyters as the συνέδριον θεοῦ and σύνδεσμον of the apostles; *Phil.* viii. 1, the Lord forgives those who repent into the unity of God and συνέδριον of the bishop (suggesting that the bishop presides over this body). His corporate view of the apostles recalls that of the various writings ascribed to the twelve apostles, a number of which come from Syria.

[3] Another possibility would be the superimposition of a monarchical bishop on or amalgamation of a monarchically led community with a community possessing presbyter-bishops and deacons. This will be the situation in Asia Minor if we take an early dating for the Pastoral Epistles and follow the most common interpretation of their picture of the ministry. It would be likely to cause particularly strong resentment among the presbyter-bishops.

and his writings in their letters? This difficulty exists in any case, unless we ignore the statements of Irenaeus about John. The strangest fact of all is that Papias of Hierapolis, supposedly a hearer of John, narrated details about the authorship of the Gospels of Mark and Luke, which are reproduced by Eusebius, but said nothing about the authorship of the Fourth Gospel which Eusebius found it appropriate to mention. All that Eusebius has to say is that Papias uses testimonies from the first epistle of John (*H.E.* iii. 39).[1] The simplest conclusion to draw is that Papias did not yet know the Fourth Gospel. One might naturally conclude from the façt that Ignatius shows contacts with the Fourth Gospel and Polycarp does not that it took shape in Syria round about the time that Ignatius wrote his letters or not very long before and was only accepted as authoritative in the churches of Asia Minor subsequently.[2] The earliest statements concerning the authorship of John's Gospel come partly from its opponents and partly from those anxious for its acceptance. Both sides are agreed concerning its late date. Irenaeus states that John, the disciple of the Lord, he who also reclined on his breast, himself published (ἐξέδωκε) the Gospel while staying at Ephesus in Asia (*Adv. Haer.* iii. i. 2). He here identifies John of Ephesus with the beloved disciple of the Gospel (cf. John xiii. 23–5, xix. 26 ff., xix. 35, xx. 2–8, xxi. 20 ff., perhaps also xviii. 15 ff.). His statement that this John published the Gospel at Ephesus may perhaps reveal awareness that it was actually composed elsewhere. The information given by the Gospel itself is rather different.[3] The writer of John xxi. 24, who presumably added an appendix to the Gospel after the death of the beloved disciple, since he refutes a rumour that had spread among the brethren that this disciple would not die, states, 'This is the disciple who gives witness concerning these things and who wrote these things; and we know that his witness is true'. The reference to the disciple's witness appears to take up John xix. 35. If we accept Irenaeus' identification of the beloved disciple with John of Ephesus we must suppose that the Gospel in the form in which it has come down to us was not published by him at Ephesus but introduced in his name at Ephesus after his death. One might deduce from John xxi. 24 that its writer wished to increase the authority of the Gospel by making clear its connection

---

[1] Testimonies on the authorship of the gospels are conveniently collected by K. Aland, *Synopsis Quattuor Evangeliorum* (Stuttgart, 1964), pp. 531 ff. It is difficult to take seriously the story that Papias himself wrote the Gospel at John's dictation (ibid., pp. 532–4, from Cod. Vat. Reg. lat. 14 and Evv. prologi vetustissimi).

[2] It is used in the account of the Martyrdom of Polycarp; cf. von Loewenich, op. cit., pp. 23–4.

[3] Cf. Vielhauer, op. cit., pp. 453 ff.

with a well-known figure, perhaps also to increase the authority of that figure by showing his importance as an eye-witness.[1] It should be added that Irenaeus quotes 1 John and 2 John as the letter of John, the Lord's disciple (*Adv. Haer.* i. ix. 3, iii. xvii. 5 and 8), and that he dates the *Apocalypse* to the end of the reign of Domitian without naming an author (*Adv. Haer.* v. xxx. 3).[2]

The author of the Muratorian fragment appears to be as anxious as Irenaeus to encourage the acceptance of the Fourth Gospel. None the less he avoids explicitly identifying John with the son of Zebedee (contrast 'Johannis ex discipulis' with 'Andreae ex apostolis'). The gospel is interestingly described as a joint effort produced under John's name with the collaboration of his fellow disciples, his bishops, and the apostle Andrew. The author also emphasizes that this John is the some John as the writer of the epistles, who there announces himself as an eyewitness and hearer of the Lord and also as the writer of his marvellous works (1 John i. 1–4).

That the Gospel of John met with considerable opposition in ortho-dox circles because of its use by heretics, particularly by the Valentinians and the Montanists, is well known and is acknowledged by Irenaeus (*Adv. Haer.* iii. xi. 10 and iii. xi. 12 (where he states that the same people reject Paul too)). At an earlier date already its acceptance may have been endangered because of the association of the circles which produced it with the heresy known under the name of Cerinthus. This is indicated by the fact that its opponents ascribed it to Cerinthus (cf. Epiphanius, *Panarion*, 51. 3, probably utilizing Hippolytus,[3] on those who reject both the Gospel and the Apocalypse, ascribing them to Cerinthus). The association with Cerinthus is recognized indirectly by Irenaeus, who narrates the story of John and Cerinthus in the bath-house at Ephesus in order to show John's rejection of Cerinthus and states that John, the Lord's disciple, wished by means of the proclamation of the Gospel to remove the error sown among men by Cerinthus and much earlier

---

[1] Polycrates, bishop of Ephesus, in his letter to Victor of Rome on the Quartodeciman Paschal celebration (quoted by Eusebius, *H.E.* v. 24) states that John rests at Ephesus, listing him after 'Philip of the twelve apostles' and his daughters as Ἰωάννης, ὁ ἐπὶ τὸ στῆθος τοῦ κυρίου ἀναπεσών, ὃς ἐγενήθη ἱερεὺς τὸ πέταλον πεφορεκὼς καὶ μάρτυς καὶ διδάσκαλος. He does not specify what connection he has with the Johannine writings, but his association with the Gospel is implied by the statement that he reclined on the Lord's breast.

[2] Justin, however, whose use of the Fourth Gospel is open to question, ascribes the Apocalypse to John, one of the apostles of Christ (*Dialogue with Trypho*, 81. 12–13, 308A).

[3] On the opposition to John's Gospel cf. T. Zahn, *Geschichte des Neutestament-lichen Kanons*, i (Erlangen, 1888), pp. 220–62; A. Bludau, *Die ersten Gegner der Johannesschriften* (Freiburg, 1925).

by the so-called Nicolaitans (*Adv. Haer.* iii. xi. 7).[1] The details given about Cerinthus in early Christian sources indicate only the tip of an iceberg. The anti-heretical writers find it convenient to organize the early heresies under the names of heresiarchs, but the vaguer picture given by Ignatius of the spreading of obnoxious tendencies may be closer to the truth.

If Ignatius and Polycarp were the leaders of a Johannine party and none the less fail to mention John, the reason may be attributed to the existence of one or more 'Cerinthian' Docetic splinter groups which had broken off from that party and were bringing it into discredit. Evidence for the gravity of the threat presented is provided, as we have seen (above pp. 85–8), both in the Johannine epistles and in Ignatius' letters. It would appear that at the time when Ignatius' letters were written the heretical competition was so strong that it was more tactful not to appeal to John's name at all in the Asia Minor communities. At the same time his letters and the letter of Polycarp give evidence that interest in Paul had been reawakened in these churches, perhaps in connection with the making of contacts further West, where Paul was recognized as an authority together with Peter. If Ignatius' letters were written with the aim of making use of his glory as a martyr in order to gain ground for the Johannine movement in uniting its existing followers and in winning the approval of those outside, then it is understandable that he appeals not to a leader of that movement itself but rather to a recognized authority.[2]

That the movement in its Johanno-Pauline form went on from strength to strength is shown by the fact that within a few generations both the Johannine writings and the institution of the monarchical episcopate

[1] The story told by Clement of Alexandria about John and his disciple who became a brigand chieftain may indicate in mythical form that some disaster resulted from John's unwary choice of followers (*Quis diues saluetur* 42).

[2] The Jewish Christian and anti-Pauline features in Epiphanius' account of Cerinthus (*Panarion* 28), which are usually rejected (cf. for example the detailed discussion of C. Schmidt, *Gespräche Jesu mit seinen Jüngern nach der Auferstehung* (*T.U.* xliii, 1919), pp. 403 ff.), need not be complete nonsense. They may reflect a movement which did indeed show primitive characteristics shared with Jewish Christianity, such as the denial of the virgin birth, and which appealed to those from a Jewish Christian or Judaizing background. In this case it may be part of the stance adopted against it that its opponents take Paul as an authority. Epiphanius records that Cerinthus' school reached its flowering in Asia and Galatia and reports that his followers were divided on the question of the resurrection, some asserting that Christ has not yet risen but rises with everyone (if this is to be made at all consistent with the teaching ascribed to Cerinthus one must read, instead of Christ, the man Jesus), some that corpses will not rise at all. The latter group may have taught a spiritual resurrection. Gaius of Rome accused Cerinthus of a crude millenarianism, a teaching which could be combined with that of Epiphanius' former group.

were generally accepted. Contacts with Rome were furthered by Polycarp's own visit there, described by Irenaeus, *Adv. Haer.* iii. iii. 4, and in his letter to Victor (quoted by Eusebius, *H.E.* v. 24). Whereas at Rome the acceptance of the Johannine writings was disputed and the attack by the anti-Montanist presbyter Gaius had to be refuted by Hippolytus, elsewhere their victory was speedy. In Gaul the churches of Lyons and Vienne had close contacts with Asia and Phrygia, of which ample evidence is given by their letter describing the persecution of 177 (Eusebius, *H.E.* v. 1–2), and by the fact that Irenaeus, Polycarp's disciple, became bishop there. Irenaeus championed the orthodox use of the Fourth Gospel in opposition to its heretical interpretation At Alexandria, on the other hand, the Gospel of John was introduced at an early date by gnostic heretics. This did not, however, prevent its acceptance in the mainstream church there, and Origen wrote a lengthy commentary on John, which included refutations of its exposition by the Valentinian Heracleon.[1] In Africa a champion of John appears in Tertullian, whose openness to influence from the churches of Asia Minor led him to associate himself with the Montanist movement.[2] Ignatius represents an obscure early stage within the complex process which gradually led to the formation and acceptance of the New Testament canon in 'mainstream' churches all over the Roman empire. It is only after attempting to see him within his context that we can either be justified in declaring him incomprehensible or begin to understand him. Joly recognizes the very high value of the evidence which his letters provide for early Christianity and therefore concludes that it is merely the wishful thinking of the pious that prevents their general recognition as a forgery. On the first point he is correct, on the second not.

[1] Clement of Alexandria reflects the influence of a Docetic interpretation of John in citing a tradition, which appears also in the *Acta Johannis*, that, when John touched Jesus' body, his hand met nothing solid; cf. Hennecke–Schneemelcher, ii, p. 126.

[2] Cf. W. Telfer, 'The Origins of Christianity in Africa', *T.U.* lxxix (1961), pp. 512–17, giving various arguments for the hypothesis that the early African church had its chief lines of communication with the East, including the status and number of monarchical bishops there. It is interesting that, apart from the implications of his appeal to Paul, Ignatius' letters give no evidence of this missionary impetus. It may be, however, that the local difficulties which are indicated by Ignatius actually stimulated missionary expansion. Once friendly communities were established overseas, they could give support to the founding groups in the home communities.

III

Justin der Märtyrer

Justin, christlicher Philosoph, Apologet, Lehrer und Märtyrer, hat auch Schriften hinterlassen, von denen drei auf uns gekommen sind: der Dialog mit dem Juden Tryphon und zwei an die römischen Herrscher adressierte Apologien. Diese, zusammen mit seinen Märtyrerakten und einigen Erwähnungen bei späteren Schriftstellern, vor allem bei seinem Schüler Tatian und bei dem Kirchenhistoriker Euseb, bilden die Hauptquellen für sein Leben. Nach seinem eigenen Zeugnis am Anfang der längeren sogenannten ersten Apologie (1) war Justin der Sohn eines gewissen Priscus, Sohn des Bacchius, aus Flavia Neapolis in Palästina. Diese seine Heimatstadt wurde nach dem jüdischen Krieg um 72 n. Chr. vom römischen Kaiser Vespasian in der Nähe der Ruinen des samaritanischen Heiligtums Sichem unterhalb des Berges Garizim begründet. Obwohl er die Samaritaner als sein Volk bezeichnet, gibt sich Justin selbst in seinen Schriften als ein zum Christentum bekehrter Heide zu erkennen. Als er das Christentum kennenlernte, besaß er schon eine philosophische Ausbildung im zeitgenössischen Mittleren Platonismus (Andresen, 1952/53). In der kürzeren sogenannten zweiten Apologie (12) berichtet er, wie er als Anhänger der Lehren Platons die Furchtlosigkeit der Christen angesichts der Todesstrafe beobachtete und davon überzeugt wurde, daß die antichristlichen Verleumdungen falsch sein müßten. In dem in den Märtyrerakten geschilderten Verhör vor dem römischen Stadtpräfekten bekennt Justin, daß er »versucht habe, alle Lehren kennenzulernen, den wahren Lehren der Christen aber seine Zustimmung gegeben« habe (Musurillo, 42f.). Eine ausführlichere Beschreibung seiner geistigen Entwicklung und seiner Bekehrung bringt er in seinem Dialog mit Tryphon (2ff.). Wenn auch manche Einzelheiten dieser Schilderung der literarischen Fiktion zuzuschreiben sind, so gewinnt man doch ein deutliches Bild, wie Philosophie und Christentum sich im Denken Justins zueinander verhalten. Nach der Meinung Justins ist die Philosophie als Zugang zu Gott der höchste Besitz; das Christentum aber ist die einzig zuverlässige Philosophie, während die zeitgenössischen heidnischen Philosophen über die Wahrheit uneinig sind. Er selbst habe begehrt, Philosophenschüler zu werden, und habe sich geraume Zeit einem Stoiker zugesellt, der ihn aber über Gott nicht belehren konnte. Nach weiteren Enttäuschungen bei einem Peripatetiker, der sich als geldbegierig erwies, und einem

Greschat, Martin (Hrsg.), Alte Kirche I (Bd. I der 'Gestalten der Kirchengeschichte') Stuttgart, 1994², s. 51–68.

III

berühmten Pythagoräer, der Vorkenntnisse in Musik, Astronomie und Geometrie verlangte, habe er bei einem hervorragenden Platoniker, der vor kurzem in »unsere Stadt« zugezogen war, große Fortschritte gemacht und hoffte, demnächst Gott sehen zu können. Zu dieser Zeit machte er sich auf den Weg nach einem einsamen Ort unweit des Meeres, um mit den eigenen Gedanken alleine zu sein. In dieser Gegend traf er einen ehrwürdigen, milde aussehenden Greis, der nach einer längeren Unterhaltung über die Philosophie ihm von den vom Geist erfüllten Propheten, ihren Schriften und ihren Weissagungen über Christus erzählte. Nach weiteren Unterweisungen, die Justin nicht berichtet, verschwand der Greis. Justin selbst aber wurde durch Liebe zu den Propheten und zu den Freunden Christi entflammt und entschied sich für diese Philosophie.

Auch nach seiner Bekehrung war die Einstellung Justins dem Platonismus gegenüber durchaus positiv. So behauptet er gegen Ende der zweiten Apologie (13), daß er sich als Christ eifrig bekennt nicht deswegen, weil die Lehren Platons dem Christentum fremd sind, sondern weil sie sich nicht in allem ähneln. In seiner ersten Apologie (20) schreibt er, daß die Christen in mancher Hinsicht den heidnischen Philosophen und Dichtern Ähnliches, in anderer aber in großartigerer und göttlicherer Weise lehren, zudem auch als einzige einen Beweis anbieten. Einige Hauptunterschiede zur heidnischen Philosophie werden im Dialog mit Tryphon vermerkt. Schon am Anfang (Dialog, 1) führt Justin gewisse Einwände, mit denen ein Jude wie Tryphon übereinstimmen würde, vor. Es geht um den Monotheismus, um den Glauben an eine göttliche Vorsehung, die sich nicht nur des Ganzen, sondern auch der Einzelnen annimmt, um den Begriff der Heilsgeschichte (die Philosophen sagen, daß die gleichen Dinge sich immer wiederholen werden) und um die Vorstellungen über die Seele. Diese werden weiter ausgeführt im Bericht über das Gespräch mit dem Greis, der einige platonische Lehren über die Unsterblichkeit der Seele, die Seelenwanderung, ihre Fähigkeit, aus eigener Kraft Gott zu erkennen, und die Ungewordenheit der Seele und der Welt, die Justin sich selbst in den Mund legt, in Frage stellt (Dialog, 3–6). Nach der Meinung des Greises kann die menschliche Seele zwar erkennen, daß Gott existiert und daß Gerechtigkeit und Religion gut sind. Gott selbst kann die menschliche Vernunft aber nicht ohne Ausstattung mit dem Heiligen Geist sehen. Die Seele ist nicht unsterblich, sondern lebt durch Teilnahme am Leben, da Gott will, daß sie lebt. Die Wahrheit haben nicht menschliche Lehrer, sondern nur die Propheten gesehen, die früher als alle Philosophen lebten und mit dem Heiligen Geist erfüllt waren. Sie sagten die Zukunft voraus und verherrlichten den Gott und Vater, Schöpfer aller Dinge, und seinen Sohn Christus. Dies können aber nicht alle verstehen, sondern nur solche, denen Gott und sein Christus die Einsicht schenken.

Nach der Auffassung Justins ist das Christentum also sowohl in Einklang mit den höchsten Bestrebungen der menschlichen Vernunft wie auch eine Offenbarungsreligion. Derselbe Gott, den die Platoniker durch eigene Kraft zu sehen trachten, hat sich durch die Propheten und durch Christus offenbart. Die mittelplatonischen Begriffe über Gott, die Schöpfung und sogar den Logos findet Justin im Christentum wieder. Die Schöpfungslehre, die kosmische Bedeutung des Kreuzes und sogar die Trinitätslehre habe Platon in den Schriften Moses gefunden und in den eigenen Schriften angedeutet (1. Apologie, 59–60). Der Hauptbeweis für die Wahrheit des Christentums besteht aber in der Erfüllung der Weissagungen der Propheten (1. Apologie, 30). Diese werden nicht nur im Dialog mit Tryphon ausführlich zitiert und erläutert, sondern nehmen auch den Mittelteil der ersten Apologie ein (30—53). Er stellt sogar die rhetorische Frage (1. Apologie, 53): »Wie würden wir glauben, daß ein gekreuzigter Mann der Erstgeborene des ungezeugten Gottes ist und selbst das Gericht über das ganze menschliche Geschlecht halten wird, wenn wir nicht Zeugnisse, die vor seiner Ankunft als Mensch über ihn verkündet wurden, vorgefunden und entsprechend erfüllt gesehen hätten?« Solche erfüllten Weissagungen sind in der Verwüstung des Landes der Juden und im Glauben der Heiden aus jedem Volke, sogar unter den in Wagen lebenden Skythen, den Nomaden und den Zeltbewohnern (Dialog, 117), besonders deutlich zu sehen. Die Kraft Gottes zeigt sich in der Lebensumwandlung der bekehrten Christen (1. Apologie, 14), unter denen es nicht nur Philosophen und Gelehrte, sondern auch Ungebildete und Handarbeiter gibt, die bereit sind, für die Lehre Christi zu sterben (1. Apologie, 60; 2. Apologie, 10).

Daß es nicht nur jüdische, sondern auch heidnische Wegbereiter Christi gab und daß Gottes Fürsorge sich auf alle Menschenvölker erstreckt, zeigt Justin in seinen Apologien (vgl. 1. Apologie, 44). Gott hat alle Menschen mit der Fähigkeit, zwischen dem Guten und dem Bösen zu wählen, und mit Samen der Vernunft (d. h. des Logos), die es ihnen ermöglichen, die Wahrheit wenigstens dunkel zu erkennen, ausgestattet (1. Apologie 28, 43–4; 2. Apologie 9,13). Stimmte dies nicht, so wäre die (auch von Philosophen geahnte, 1. Apologie, 8) Lehre von einem Gericht nach diesem Leben nicht vertretbar (1. Apologie, 43). Diese Vernunft oder auch Wort Gottes (Logos), woran alle Menschen Anteil gehabt haben, ist Christus selbst (1. Apologie 5,46). Auch vor seiner menschlichen Geburt hatten die Menschen aller Völker die Möglichkeit, entweder mit oder ohne Vernunft (Logos) zu leben (ebenda; vgl. auch Dialog, 45). So gab es Christen vor Christus, Philosophen, wie Sokrates und Heraklit unter den Griechen, wie auch die Patriarchen und Propheten unter den Juden (1. Apologie, 46; 2. Apologie, 8). In Christus wurde aber das ganze Wort (Logos) Mensch, sodaß die Teilerkenntnisse früherer Zeiten jetzt dadurch überholt sind, daß die Christen an ihm selbst durch seine Gnade teilhaben (2. Apologie, 10,13).

Im Dialog mit Tryphon gibt Justin eine Darstellung seiner eigenen Missionstätigkeit. Als bekehrter Christ trägt er noch den Philosophenmantel, als eine Art Reklame, um seine Bereitschaft zu zeigen, solche Themen wie die göttliche Allmacht und Vorsehung mit allen Entgegenkommenden zu besprechen (Dialog, 1). Im Laufe des Dialogs wird einige Male ausdrücklich Bezug darauf genommen, daß Justin es sich zu seiner Gewohnheit gemacht hat, solche Unterredungen zu führen. So bemerkt Tryphon (Dialog, 50): »Du scheinst durch viele Disputationen mit Vielen über diese Fragen bereit geworden zu sein, auf alles, was man Dich fragt, eine Antwort zu geben.« Später behauptet Justin selbst, daß er nicht nur Tryphon gegenüber, sondern auch mit allen Menschen aus jedem Volk, die dazu willig sind, über diese Themen disputiere und Antwort gebe (Dialog, 64). Auch wenn seine Gesprächspartner sich verstellen, trägt er selbst alles offen und schlicht vor, da er hofft, wie es im Gleichnis vom Säemann geschieht, irgendwo guten Boden zu finden. Wenn er das ihm Anvertraute nicht vergräbt, wird er bei der Wiederkunft seines Herrn nicht verurteilt werden (Dialog, 125; vgl. 1. Apologie, 44). In der Tat, man hat den starken Eindruck, sowohl im Dialog mit Tryphon wie auch in den Apologien die Niederschrift von Disputationsthemen, die Justin öfters in mündlichen Gesprächen wiederholt hat, vor sich zu haben. In den Apologien (die nicht in Dialogform sind) versucht Justin alle möglichen Einwände seiner Gegner vorauszusehen und zu beantworten. So kehren solche Formeln wie: »damit niemand dies oder jenes sage« und »dies kann ich auch erklären« oft wieder. Wegen seiner Offenheit für mögliche Gegenpositionen und seines Wunsches, seine Themen möglichst vollständig und ausführlich zu entwickeln, scheint Justin in Schwierigkeiten bei der schriftlichen Bewältigung und Ordnung seines Stoffes geraten zu sein. Er gibt dem modernen Leser den Eindruck, daß er zwar einen Gesamtplan im Auge hat, daran aber nicht festhält, sondern allzu leicht zu Seitensprüngen sich ableiten läßt. Die Dispositionstechnik Justins hat neuerdings Holfelder (231–251) durch Stichworte wie »gleitende Themenführung«, »assoziative Weiterführung und Variation«, »Unterthemen« und »Einlagen« als bewußt kunstvoll zu verteidigen versucht. Interessanterweise wird als engste Parallele zu dieser Technik der gleitenden Themenführung die Methode des Horaz in seinen von der philosophischen Straßenpredigt (Diatribe) beeinflußten Satiren angeführt (Holfelder, 246 f.). Ein Beispiel eines Themas, das auf den ersten Blick als zufällig eingeführtes Nebenthema erscheint, jedoch im Gesamtplan Justins eine Hauptrolle spielt, ist der Gedankenkomplex, der mit Problemen von Schicksal und Willensfreiheit sich befaßt. Dieses Thema ist für Justin wichtig sowohl als platonische Argumentation gegen den Fatalismus der Stoiker wie auch im Zusammenhang mit den christlichen Lehren über den Sündenfall, die Möglichkeit der Bekehrung und das künftige Gericht. Es wird in der 1. (28, 43–4) und 2. Apologie (7) anscheinend als Abschweifung behandelt, ist aber (nach Holfelder, 60–66) von zentraler Bedeutung für den Aufruf Justins zur Umkehr zum Christentum.

Wanderphilosophen von der Art, wie Justin sich selbst darstellt, waren im römischen Reich seiner Zeit ein bekanntes Phänomen. So erzählt der wohlhabende Sophist und Redner Dio Chrysostomus, der unter dem Kaiser Domitian verbannt wurde und als wandernder Bettler lebte, daß Leute, die ihm begegneten, ihn für einen Philosophen hielten und seine Meinungen über das Gute und das Böse hören wollten; auch forderten sie ihn auf, eine Rede zu halten (Oratio 13,10–12). Besonders die kynischen Philosophen lebten gern als Wanderasketen und pflegten die Kunst der Straßenpredigt (Diatribe). Da die griechische Sprache und Bildungseinrichtungen überall in den Städten der östlichen Hälfte und in manchen Teilen auch des Westens des römischen Reiches verbreitet waren, konnte ein disputierender oder redender Philosoph auf dem Marktplatz einer jeden Stadt eine Schar von Zuhörern anziehen. Justin besaß den nötigen Bildungsgrad, um auf diese Weise als christlicher Philosoph vor der Öffentlichkeit seine Missiontätigkeit auszuüben, während manche andere Christen seiner Zeit es vorzogen, innerhalb der Gemeinden zu wirken oder Frauen und Kinder der großen Haushalte zu missionieren (nach Celsus; vgl. Harnack, 1924, 406 f.). Der Dialog mit Tryphon findet in einer Hafenstadt statt, aus welcher Justin alsbald mit dem Schiff abzureisen beabsichtigt (142). Tryphon gibt sich als ein Hebräer aus der Beschneidung aus, der dem Bar Kochba-Aufstand in Palästina (132–135 n. Chr.) entflohen ist und sich hauptsächlich in Griechenland und Korinth aufhält. Demnach möchte man vermuten, daß die Sprecher des Dialogs sich in Korinth befinden. Der Kirchenhistoriker Euseb aber berichtet, daß der Dialog zu Ephesus gehalten wurde (4, 18,6). Dieser Angabe ist es zu verdanken, daß die Mehrzahl der modernen Lebensschilderungen Justins ihm eine Tätigkeit in Ephesus zuschreiben und sogar oft seine Bekehrung dort lokalisieren (Zahn, 46 ff., argumentiert ausdrücklich dafür). Daß Euseb eine zuverlässige Quelle für seine Behauptung besaß und daß der Dialog überhaupt stattfand (und nicht reine Fiktion ist), ist zwar nicht unmöglich, wenn auch keineswegs sicher. Die Annahme aber, daß Justin zu Ephesus bekehrt wurde, beruht lediglich darauf, daß man die Worte »unsere Stadt« in seiner Schilderung seiner Lehrzeit bei dem Platoniker (Dialog, 2) mit Ephesus identifiziert. Es liegt jedoch näher, an seine Heimatstadt Flavia Neapolis zu denken. Dafür daß Justin als bekehrter Christ in Palästina lebte, spricht seine detaillierte Kenntnis von verschiedenen judenchristlichen Gruppen und deren Verhältnissen zu den Heidenchristen (Dialog, 46–47; Harnack, 1913, 83–90). Auch in seiner Schilderung der christlich-jüdischen Kontroverse im Dialog mit Tryphon vertritt er eine Überlieferung, die auf Palästina zurückgeht. Gewisse Einzelzüge seines Bildes des Judentums gehen spezifisch auf sein samaritanisches Heimatland zurück (Weis). Wenn er in Palästina bekehrt wurde, könnte es sein, daß er aus demselben Grund wie Tryphon das Land verließ. Er berichtet, daß Bar Kochba während des jüdischen Krieges furchtbare Strafen für die Christen verordnete, wenn sie Christus nicht verleugneten und lästerten (1. Apologie, 31), und behauptet, daß die Juden die Christen ermorden würden, wenn die Römer dies nicht verhinderten, und sie auch ermordet haben, so oft sie es konnten (Dialog, 16; vgl. auch 95, 110, 133). Die Märtyrerakten Justins, die in drei Fassungen verschiedener Länge erhalten sind, berichten über das Verhör Justins und seiner Gefährten vor dem römischen

III

Stadtpräfekten Rusticus (Quintus Junius Rusticus), der unter dem Kaiser Marcus
Aurelius zwischen 163 und 168 n. Chr. dieses Amt innehatte. In Beantwortung
der Frage: »Wo kommt Ihr zusammen?«, sagt Justin: »Wo jeder will und kann«,
und gibt dann die Adresse (der Text ist leider verdorben – vielleicht war es in der
Via Tiburtina; vgl. Osborn, 5, Anm. 22), wo er während der ganzen Zeit dieses
seines zweiten Aufenthaltes in Rom gewohnt hat, an. Dies sei der einzige
Versammlungsort, den er kenne. Jedem, der zu ihm kommen wollte, habe er die
Worte der Wahrheit mitgeteilt. Die Gefährten Justins, die zusammen mit ihm
hingerichtet wurden, scheinen seine Schüler gewesen zu sein. Mit einer Aus-
nahme (Liberian) haben sie griechische Namen. Die Frage, ob Justin ihn
bekehrte, beantwortend, sagt Hierax, daß er seit langem Christ ist, während
Paeon und Euelpistus berichten, daß sie das Christentum von ihren Eltern
erhalten haben. Euelpistus fügt hinzu, daß er das Wort Justins gern hörte.
Euelpistus ist Sklave des Kaisers und seine Eltern wohnen in Kappadokien.
Hierax, dessen Eltern tot sind, wurde aus Ikonium in Phrygien entführt.
Justin war also in Rom als Lehrer oder Leiter einer Schule tätig. Daß es solche
christliche Schulen in Rom gab, wissen wir auch aus anderen Quellen. Sie
scheinen zu dieser Zeit eine verhältnismäßig große Unabhängigkeit von der
römischen Kirchenleitung gehabt zu haben (vgl. Harnack, 1924, 365–377). Wo
Justin zwischen und vor seinen zwei Aufenthalten in Rom sich befand, und ob er
Griechenland bzw. Ephesus besuchte, wissen wir nicht. Die Organisation der
Kirche und ihre Amtsträger werden von Justin in seinen erhaltenen Schriften
nicht beschrieben. Nur in seinem sehr wertvollen Bericht über Taufe, Eucharis-
tie und Sonntagsgottesdienst der Christen (1. Apologie, 61–67) erwähnt er den
Vorsteher der Brüder, der das eucharistische Gebet ausspricht, die sonntägliche
Predigt hält und die gesammelten freiwilligen Beiträge zur Unterstützung der
Waisen, Witwen, Kranken, Gefangenen, der auswärtigen Gäste und aller ande-
ren, die bedürftig sind, verwaltet. Er berichtet auch, daß die sogenannten
Diakone die eucharistischen Elemente sowohl zu den Anwesenden wie auch zu
den Abwesenden bringen. Über die Sonntagsgottesdienste sagt er, daß eine
Versammlung aller, die in den Städten oder auf dem Land wohnen, stattfindet.
Wenn er die Verbreitung des Christentums beschreiben will, erklärt er, wie die
zwölf Apostel zu jedem Menschengeschlecht mit dem Wort Gottes von Jerusalem ausgingen (z. B. 1. Apologie, 39).
In den zwei ersten Kapiteln der sogenannten zweiten Apologie beschreibt Justin
gewisse Ereignisse, die vor kurzem in Rom unter dem Stadtpräfekten Urbikus
passiert waren. Der Versuch einer zum Christentum bekehrten Frau, sich von
ihrem unsittlichen heidnischen Mann scheiden zu lassen, hatte dazu geführt, daß
ihr christlicher Lehrer, Ptolemaeus, und zwei bei dem Verhör Anwesende, die
protestierten und sich auch als Christen bekannten, hingerichtet wurden. In
derselben Schrift (3; in der Übersetzung Rauschens, der die Reihenfolge der
Handschrift wiedergibt, 8) erwähnt Justin einen persönlichen Gegner, den

56

kynischen Philosophen Crescens, dessen Nachstellungen er befürchtet. Crescens versucht, dadurch der Volksmenge zu gefallen, daß er die Christen als gottlose Atheisten vor der Öffentlichkeit denunziert. Justin habe mit ihm disputiert und sein Nichtwissen offenbart. Falls diese Disputationen den römischen Herrschern noch nicht berichtet worden sind, erklärt er sich bereit, sie in ihrer Gegenwart zu wiederholen. Auch der Justinschüler Tatian berichtet nach Justins Tod von den Versuchen des Crescens, Justin und ihn selbst zu Tode zu bringen (Oratio, 19).

Die Schriften Justins sind in schlechtem Zustand in einer im Jahre 1364 geschriebenen Pariser Handschrift erhalten (vgl. Harnack, 1958, I,1, 99–100). In der Mitte des Dialogs (74) fehlt ein ganzes Stück, das das Ende des ersten und den Anfang des zweiten Tags des Gesprächs beschrieb. Auch scheint der Anfang des Dialogs zu fehlen. Es muß ursprünglich eine Vorrede an den Empfänger des Dialogs, Marcus Pompeius (der 141 mit Namen und 8 als »liebster« angeredet wird), am Anfang gestanden haben (Zahn, 37 ff.). Die sogenannte zweite Apologie (die in der Handschrift vor der ersten steht) macht den Eindruck, am Anfang verstümmelt zu sein. Während aus den Kapiteln 2, 3 (bzw. 8) und den letzten zwei Kapiteln (14–15) hervorgeht, daß sie, wie die erste, an den römischen Kaiser und seine Kollegen adressiert ist, fängt das jetzige erste Kapitel sehr abrupt mit der Anrede »Römer« an. Mehrere Male im Laufe der zweiten Apologie finden sich Rückverweise auf Themen, die in der ersten Apologie behandelt werden. Man könnte vermuten, daß einige Anfangskapitel, die diese Themen behandelten, verloren gegangen sind. Diese These paßt aber nicht zum Zeugnis Eusebs in seiner Kirchengeschichte. Euseb behauptet, Justin habe zwei Apologien hinterlassen, die eine an Antoninus Pius (Kaiser 138–161), seine Söhne und den römischen Senat, und die zweite an Antoninus Verus (d. h. Marcus Aurelius) adressiert. Er zitiert sowohl aus unserer ersten als auch aus unserer zweiten Apologie mehrere Stücke, die von ihm aber als aus der ersten Apologie stammend bezeichnet werden. Unsere erste Apologie ist mit einer ausführlichen, auch von Euseb zitierten Adresse an Antoninus Pius, seine zwei Adoptivsöhne und den Senat ausgestattet. In den ersten Kapiteln spielt Justin mehrere Male auf den schon in ihren Titeln ausgedrückten Anspruch der Herrscher an, fromm (»pius«) und Philosophen zu sein. Wenn dies stimmt, sollten sie ihr Urteil dementsprechend abgeben. Die zweite Apologie scheint an dieselben Herrscher gerichtet zu sein, da im Kapitel 2 der Kaiser Pius und ein Sohn genannt werden (vielleicht ist der Name des zweiten Sohnes hier im Lauf der Überlieferung ausgefallen) und am Ende des letzten Kapitels der Appell an die Frömmigkeit und Weisheitsliebe der Herrscher deutlich aufgenommen wird. Um diese merkwürdige Sachlage zu erklären, hat man verschiedene Hypothesen erwogen. Meist wird angenommen, daß die von Euseb erwähnte zweite Apologie völlig verlorengegangen ist. Da Euseb unsere zwei Apologien als die erste gekannt hat, hat man gemeint, daß unsere zweite nur ein Anhang oder ein Alternativende zur ersten sei und daß

III

Justin vielleicht die eine Apologie in verschiedenen Ausgaben mit bzw. ohne
Anhang bzw. Alternativende herausgegeben habe. Eine interessante Variation
dieser These wird von Seeberg (2) angeboten. Die einfachste Lösung hingegen ist
diejenige, daß unsere erste und zweite Apologie von Anfang an eine Einheit
bildeten und nur durch eine Umstellung in der handschriftlichen Überlieferung
getrennt wurden (vgl. Holfelder, 52 und 243, Anm. 107). Ein zusätzliches
Problem liegt darin, daß während die äußere Form (vor allem 1. Apologie, 1 und
2. Apologie, 14) voraussetzt, daß Justin seine Schrift(en) wirklich den Herrschern einreichte, sie in ihrer jetzigen Gestalt (gleichviel ob man die zweite
Apologie dazu nimmt oder nicht) wegen ihrer Länge zu diesem Zweck nicht gut
geeignet ist. Eine nähere Datierung ergibt sich aus der Erwähnung (in 1.
Apologie, 29) von Felix, dem Präfekten Ägyptens zwischen 151 und 154. Im
Dialog (120) erwähnt Justin eine schriftliche Mitteilung an den Kaiser, in der er
gesagt habe, daß die Samaritaner irre gehen, indem sie den Magier Simon als Gott
anerkennen. Auf Simon nimmt er in 1. Apologie, 26 und 56, und 2. Apologie, 15
Bezug. So scheint er den Dialog später, aber noch unter demselben Kaiser verfaßt
zu haben.
Justin hat auch Schriften hinterlassen, die nicht mehr erhalten sind. In der
1. Apologie (26), nachdem er Simon den Magier, Menander und Markion
erwähnt hat, berichtet er, daß er ein »Syntagma« gegen alle die Irrlehren, die
entstanden sind, verfaßt habe. Irenaeus bringt ein Zitat aus dem »Syntagma«
gegen Markion, das möglicherweise ein Teil derselben Schrift war. Euseb nennt
die Titel von fünf anderen verlorenen Schriften: »Rede gegen die Griechen« (in
welcher Justin viele Fragen, denen sowohl Christen wie auch Philosophen
nachforschen, ausführlich besprach und die Natur der Dämonen behandelte),
»Elenchos« (Widerlegung, auch gegen die Griechen gerichtet), »Über die
Monarchie Gottes« (wozu er sowohl die heilige Schrift wie auch Bücher der
Griechen heranzog), »Über die Seele« (wieder mit Heranziehung der Meinungen
griechischer Philosophen) und »Psaltes«. Euseb behauptet ferner, daß viele
andere Schriften Justins im Umlauf sind. Zu einer späteren Zeit wurden etliche
unechte Schriften dem Namen Justins untergeschoben. Wie bald dies anfing,
wissen wir nicht. Unter den pseudo-Justinischen Schriften haben die Fragmente
über die Auferstehung am häufigsten Verfechter ihrer Echtheit gefunden (z. B.
Zahn und zuletzt Prigent).
Justin schrieb seine Apologie(n) zu einer Zeit, in welcher das Christentum
sowohl durch Verfolgung stark bedrängt wie durch häretische Spaltungen
geschädigt wurde. Anders als die anderen Apologeten des zweiten Jahrhunderts
nimmt er die Verleumdungen von Menschenfresserei und Hurerei als Grund für
die antichristlichen Vorurteile der Römer und ihrer Herrscher ernst. Im Dialog
(17, 108, 117) beschuldigt er die Juden, diese Verleumdungen verbreitet zu
haben. Sie sind durch falsche Zeugnisse, welche Sklaven christlicher Eigentümer
unter der Folter ablegten, bekräftigt worden (2. Apologie, 12). Justin gibt sogar

58

zu, daß Anhänger häretischer Sekten, die sich Christen nennen, möglicherweise solche Schandtaten wirklich begehen (1. Apologie, 26). Die Herrscher sollten deswegen das Leben eines jeden angeklagten Christen untersuchen und nicht einfach wegen der Bekennung des Namens das Todesurteil aussprechen (1. Apologie, 3 ff.). Bei der Entgegnung auf die Beschuldigung der Gottlosigkeit (1. Apologie 6, 9, 13) wie auch bei einigen anderen Argumenten seiner ersten Apologie scheint Justin einem ähnlichen Schema zu folgen wie mancher andere Apologet (z. B. Athenagoras). Die Rechtfertigung des jüdisch-christlichen Monotheismus gegenüber den heidnischen polytheistischen Religionen wurde in der jüdischen Apologetik ausgearbeitet und von den christlichen Apologeten von dorther geerbt. Schon die heidnischen Philosophen selbst hatten zahlreiche Argumente gegen die gröberen Erscheinungen des Polytheismus (unsittliche Göttermythen, Statuen, Blutopfer, ägyptische Tierverehrung usw.) entwickelt, die von Juden und Christen für ihre eigenen Zwecke übernommen wurden. Neu bei Justin ist im Vergleich mit dem einzigen erhaltenen früheren christlichen Apologeten Aristides (und auch dem anonymen, nicht genau datierbaren Brief an Diognet gegenüber) die Art, wie er die heidnische Religion als Erfindung böser Dämonen behandelt. Diese These hat er nicht selbst erfunden. Sie ließ sich durch Zitate wie Ps. 96,5 (in der Septuagintafassung) belegen (vgl. Dialog, 83) und mit der Lehre des Sündenfalls leicht in Einklang bringen. Die platonischen Philosophen zur Zeit Justins erklärten die heidnischen Kultpraktiken ähnlich, indem sie sie verschiedenen Dämonen zuschrieben (die aber nicht abtrünnig vom höchsten Gott, sondern seine Unterherrscher waren). Anders als Aristides und der Brief an Diognet, welche die Christen als ein neues Volk darstellen, und Athenagoras (der die Propheten nur zweimal kurz erwähnt) verschweigt Justin nicht das enge Verhältnis zwischen Christentum und Judentum, sondern hebt hervor, daß die christliche Religion auf Moses und die Propheten zurückgeht und deswegen älter ist als »alle Schriftsteller, die gelebt haben« (1. Apologie, 23).
Ähnliche Vorurteile wie diejenigen, denen Justin entgegentreten mußte, werden von Minucius Felix in seiner Apologie in Dialogform, dem »Octavius«, geschildert. Dieses Werk erwähnt zweimal eine Rede, die vom römischen Rhetoriker und Schriftsteller Fronto, dem Lateinlehrer des Kaisers Marcus Aurelius und Konsul des Jahres 143, gegen die Christen gehalten wurde. Fronto hat den Verleumdungen der Christen in einer Form, von der Justin (1. Apologie, 26) Kenntnis zeigt, Ausdruck gegeben. Wir wissen nicht, wann (ob vor oder nach dem Märtyrertod Justins) seine Rede gehalten wurde. In der antichristlichen Rede, die Minucius Felix dem heidnischen Sprecher in seinem Dialog in den Mund legt, werden die Christen als eine verschwörerische Geheimsekte geschildert, die das Tageslicht meidet und im Dunkeln zusammentrifft, und deren Gott kraftlos und unfähig ist, seinen Verehrern zu helfen. Die Offenheit, mit der Justin die christlichen Lehren und Kultpraktiken den Heiden vorführt (1. Apologie 3,

6,61 ff.) und die geschichtliche Entwicklung, aus der das Christentum hervorgegangen ist, erläutert (1. Apologie, 30 ff.) gibt dieser Schilderung unrecht. Den Vorwurf, daß der christliche Gott seine Verehrer verfolgt werden läßt, beantwortet er ausdrücklich (2. Apologie, 5). Falls Minucius Felix die Rede Frontos als Quelle heranzog, kann es durchaus sein, daß Justin entweder die Beschuldigungen Frontos selbst oder wenigstens Kritiken allgemeiner Art, die auch Fronto aufnahm, widerspiegelt. Eine solche These wurde von Hubik in einer so übertriebenen Form entwickelt, daß sie wenig Anklang gefunden hat. Der Optimismus, den Justin mit seiner Überzeugung vertritt, daß die Wahrheit und Richtigkeit seiner Sache allen Menschen, die ihrer gottgegebenen Vernunft folgen, deutlich sein müßte, stand in einem krassen Widerspruch zu der feindlichen Gesinnung der römischen Herrscher. Justin weiß die Lage nur dadurch zu erklären, daß die Feinde des Christentums durch böse Dämonen angetrieben werden (1. Apologie 5, 12 und öfter). Demselben Grunde muß es zugeschrieben werden, daß Irrlehrer wie Simon der Magier, Menander und Markion hervorgetreten sind (1. Apologie, 26, 58). Angesichts dieser Begebenheit zeigt sich Justin unbeugsam. Die Christen fürchten den Tod nicht (1. Apologie, 2, 3, 45), wollen aber ihre Richter vor ungerechten Urteilen, die zu deren Bestrafung im künftigen Gericht führen könnten (1. Apologie, 17–18, 45, 68), warnen. Indem er die Hauptschuld den Dämonen zuschiebt, macht Justin es sich leichter, das Gebot der Feindesliebe (zitiert 1. Apologie, 14, 15; Dialog, 35, 85, 96, 133) seinen menschlichen Gegnern gegenüber einzuhalten. Seinen Lesern aber läßt er nur zwei Alternativen offen: entweder die volle Wahrheit des Christentums anzuerkennen oder die Christen als Lästerer der vom Staat verehrten Götter anzusehen. So war seine Apologie nicht gut dazu geeignet, die römischen Herrscher von der Harmlosigkeit der Christen zu überzeugen. Nur für einen Verächter der heidnischen Religion (wie Lukian von Samosata, den Verfasser zahlreicher satirischer Dialoge, der eine spöttische, jedoch nicht rein negative Beschreibung der Christen in seinem »Peregrinus« (11–16) gibt), könnte eine Kompromißlösung (Duldung der Christen als einfältige Narren) annehmbar sein. Justin ist zu redlich, um ernsthaft für eine solche Lösung zu argumentieren (wiewohl er sie auch erwähnt – 1. Apologie, 68). So schreibt er auch viel weniger taktvoll als Athenagoras, der um 177 n. Chr. eine erhaltene Bittschrift an Marcus Aurelius und seinen Sohn Commodus verfaßte. Bei Justin sind Töne des Trotzes und der Herausforderung nicht zu überhören. Es ist sein Stolz und sein ganzes Streben, als Christ erfunden zu werden (2. Apologie, 13). Es mag verboten sein, die Bücher der Propheten zu lesen, er benutze sie aber ohne Angst und biete sie auch zur Einsicht an (1. Apologie, 44). Die Herrscher handeln sowohl gegen ihre eigenen Grundsätze wie auch gegen ihre eigenen Interessen (1. Apologie, 12: »Wenn Ihr wie die Vernunftlosen der üblichen Gewohnheit vor der Wahrheit Vorrang gebt, dann tut, was Ihr könnt...«). Sie betragen sich wie Henker oder Räuber in einer Wüste (ebenda). Die Heiden begehen selbst dieselben Schandtaten, die sie den Christen vorhalten (1. Apologie, 27; 2. Apologie, 12). Die trotzige Seite der Apologetik Justins wurde nach seinem Tode in aggressiver Weise von seinem Schüler Tatian in seiner »Rede gegen die Griechen« weitergeführt. Gegen Ende der Regierungszeit des Marcus Aurelius wurden mehrere christliche Apologien verfaßt – nicht nur die erhaltenen Werke von Athenagoras und Tatian, sondern auch verloren gegangene Schriften der kleinasiatischen Apologeten, Apollinarius von Hierapolis, Melito von Sardis und Miltiades. Die Rechtsstellung der Christen blieb dieselbe. Wenn man als Christ vor einem römischen Statthalter oder dem römischen Stadtpräfekten angeklagt wurde und nicht bereit war, zu widerrufen, konnte man die Todesstrafe erwarten.

Als Irrlehrer, die durch magische Künste viele verführt haben, nennt Justin die Samaritaner Simon den Magier und dessen Schüler Menander (1. Apologie, 26, 56; 2. Apologie, 15). Die größte Sorge hat ihm aber Markion bereitet. Er klagt (1. Apologie, 26 und 58), daß Markion viele aus jedem Volk irregeführt hat. Viele glauben ihm, als ob er allein die Wahrheit verstünde, und spotten über Justin, obwohl sie für das, was sie sagen, keinen Beweis haben. Sie werden gegen alle Vernunft wie Lämmer von einem Wolf weggerissen. Markion lehrt, daß es einen anderen Gott gebe, der größer sei als der Schöpfer des Weltalls, und dementsprechend auch einen anderen Gottessohn. In der Tat hätte der Gegensatz zwischen Justin und Markion kaum größer sein können. Markion hat die zwei Ecksäulen, auf denen Justin seinen Glauben gründete, verworfen: die Identität des höchsten transzendentalen Gottes der Philosophen mit dem von den Propheten verkündeten Schöpfergott wie seines Wortes oder Logos mit Christus, und zweitens den Schriftbeweis, daß die Weissagungen der Propheten im Leben Christi und in der Ausbreitung seiner Botschaft erfüllt worden sind. Im Dialog 35 bringt Justin eine Liste häretischer Sekten, die sich Christen nennen, aber in ihren Worten und Taten Gott lästern (Markianer, Valentinianer, Basilidianer und Satornilianer). Er tröstet sich damit, daß Christus solche Pseudopropheten vorausgesagt hatte. An einer späteren Stelle (Dialog 80) spricht er von den verschiedenen christlichen Auffassungen über die Auferstehung. Er selbst erwartet zusammen mit anderen rechtgläubigen Christen, daß nach der Auferstehung des Fleisches Jerusalem wiederaufgebaut werden wird und daß die Gerechten tausend Jahre dort verbringen werden. Erst danach wird die allgemeine Auferstehung und das Gericht aller Menschen stattfinden (81). Viele aber, die reinen und frommen Glaubens sind, teilen diese Erwartung nicht. Die Häretiker hingegen, die den Gott Abrahams lästern, verneinen die Auferstehung der Toten und behaupten, daß sogleich beim Tod ihre Seelen in den Himmel aufgenommen werden.

Im Dialog 47 erklärt Justin seine eigene Haltung gegenüber denjenigen Juden, die nach ihrer Bekehrung zum Christentum das Gesetz Moses weiter beobachten wollen. Wenn solche Judenchristen bereit sind, mit anderen Christen zusammen zu leben, ohne sie zur Beschneidung, Sabbatbeobachtung usw. zu zwingen,

dann sollte man sich ihnen als Brüdern in allem zugesellen. Diejenigen Judenchristen aber, die die Heidenchristen entweder zur Gesetzesbeobachtung zwingen oder sie von der Gemeinschaft ausschließen, erkennt er nicht an. Die Heidenchristen, die von solchen Judenchristen zur Gesetzesbeobachtung überredet worden sind, werden vielleicht gerettet werden, diejenigen aber, die zum Judentum übertreten und Christus verleugnen, nicht. So wie Justin es schildert, ist noch keine feste Trennmauer zwischen Judenchristen und Heidenchristen errichtet worden. Bald wurde es anders, und die Judenchristen wurden als Häretiker angesehen. Schon Justin selbst räumt ein, daß manche Christen nicht bereit sind, gesetzestreue Judenchristen in ihre Gemeinschaft aufzunehmen.
Im Dialog 49 äußert Tryphon die Meinung, daß diejenigen, die sagen, Christus sei ein Mensch gewesen, der als Messias auserwählt wurde, plausibler reden, als Justin selbst, der die Präexistenz Christi behauptet. Justin würde gerne Tryphon, wenn nicht zu seiner eigenen Auffassung, dann doch wenigstens zu der Annahme Jesu als Messias überreden. Er gibt zu, daß einige (Christen oder Judenchristen – der Text ist unsicher) Jesus als Messias anerkennen, aber für einen »Menschen aus Menschen« halten (48). Seinen eigenen Glauben an die Präexistenz Christi als Gott findet er durch die Heilige Schrift bestätigt. Erstens wird Christus in mehreren prophetischen Weissagungen Gott genannt (36 ff.), und zweitens spricht die Schrift von einem zweiten Gott, der Moses und den Patriarchen erschien. Dieser zweite Gott dient dem Vater des Alls als Bote oder Engel (das griechische Wort für Engel bedeutet Bote) und als Apostel und wird auch selbst Herr genannt (Dialog, 58, 1. Apologie, 63). Die Juden irren, indem sie den Sohn mit dem Vater gleichsetzen und nicht erkennen, daß der Vater des Alls einen Sohn hat (1. Apologie, 63). Die These, daß die Gotteserscheinungen im Alten Testament vom Sohn Gottes berichten, dient nicht nur als Beweis für die Präexistenz Christi, sondern bietet auch eine Lösung für das Problem des anthropomorphen Gottesbildes in diesen Schriften. Im Dialog 127 betont Justin, daß der unaussprechbare Vater und Herr des Alls nicht an einer Stelle der Erde erscheinen würde, da er sich nicht hin und her bewegt und nicht örtlich begrenzt ist. Vor allen Geschöpfen hat Gott eine worthafte Kraft aus sich selbst und durch seinen Willen erzeugt, ohne selbst dadurch eine Verminderung zu erfahren. Ähnliches geschieht, wenn wir ein Wort aussprechen oder wenn aus einer Fackel eine zweite Fackel entzündet wird (Dialog, 61). Dieser Sohn oder Wort Gottes ist zahlenmäßig ein anderer, vollbringt aber immer den Willen des Vaters (Dialog, 56, 128–9). Er ist nicht, wie manche sagen möchten, lediglich eine vom Vater untrennbare Kraft, die nach dem Willen des Vaters aus ihm entspringt und in ihn zurückkehrt. Dieses Wort, Weisheit, Kraft und Herrlichkeit Gottes spricht über seine eigene Erzeugung in Sprüche 8,21–36 (Dialog, 61).
Sowohl in seiner Geschichtstheologie wie in seiner Logoslehre hat Justin schon vorhandene christliche und jüdische Auffassungen durch seine Offenheit der griechischen Philosophie gegenüber bereichert, ohne die überlieferten christli-

chen Lehren preiszugeben. Gewisse Kritiken am Alten Testament, die zu der Ablehnung des Schöpfergottes durch die Häretiker führten, läßt er aber deutlich erkennen. Nach dem wörtlichen Verständnis der jüdischen Lehrer ist das alttestamentliche Gottesbild anthropomorph (Dialog, 114). Die Begrenzung der Bestimmungen der Beschneidung und des Gesetzes auf ein Volk und auf bestimmte Zeiten, welche Justin als durch die Sündhaftigkeit und Härte der Juden veranlaßt erklärt, könnte zu der Annahme führen, der Gott des Gesetzes sei nicht derselbe Gott, der dieselbe Gerechtigkeit von allen Menschenvölkern zu allen Zeiten verlangt (Dialog, 23, 30). Wenn im Alten Testament Gott Fragen stellt (wie Genesis 3,9 und 4,9), darf man dies nicht als ein Zeichen seiner Unwissenheit ansehen (Dialog, 99). Aus dem Genesisbericht über die Schöpfung der Menschen geht hervor, daß Gott mit einem Anderen redet, den Justin mit dem Logos gleichsetzt. Gewisse jüdische Häretiker meinen aber, daß Gott hier Engel anredet, oder sogar daß Engel den menschlichen Leib schufen (Dialog, 62). Justins eigenes Bild des Schöpfungsprozesses, nämlich daß Gott die Welt aus formloser Materie erschuf, entspricht sowohl seinem eigenen Verständnis der Lehre Platons (1. Apologie, 59; vgl. 1. Apologie, 10) wie auch der Aussage von Weisheit 11,17. Darin, daß die von Justin abgelehnten christlichen Häretiker einen anderen Gott über dem Schöpfergott einführten, Justin aber den präexistenten Gottessohn als einen zweiten Gott unter ihm ansah, besitzen die zwei Systeme eine gewisse Ähnlichkeit. Beide haben sich von der stoischen Lehre einer der Schöpfung innewohnenden göttlichen Kraft zugunsten des platonischen transzendentalen Gottesbegriffes abgewandt (vgl. 2. Apologie, 7). Nach dem platonischen Schema konnte man leicht eine oder mehrere vermittelnde Kräfte zwischen Gott und die Welt   einschieben. Manche Platoniker und Pythagoräer des zweiten Jahrhunderts haben die sichtbare Welt durchaus negativ betrachtet (z. B. Numenius von Apamea in Syrien). Solchen dualistischen Tendenzen folgend, haben christliche Irrlehrer die der Stoa und der jüdischen und christlichen Missionspredigt gemeinsame Lehre von der in der Ordnung und Harmonie der Schöpfung sich widerspiegelnden Güte der göttlichen Vorsehung preisgegeben und den Schöpfergott als einen Stümper erklärt. Zwischen dem höchsten Gott und dem niedrigen Schöpfergott haben sie mehrere Hypostasen oder Abstraktionen eingeschoben. In diesen häretischen (gnostischen) Systemen wurde Christus als ein Bote oder Erlöser aus der himmlischen Welt angesehen. Justin dagegen spielt mit seiner Beibehaltung der biblischen Schöpfungslehre und seiner Ausarbeitung der Logoslehre als Alternative zum Adoptianismus judenchristlicher Kreise und zur Hypostasenlehre der Gnostiker eine Hauptrolle in der Entwicklung der großkirchlichen Theologie.
So stark das persönliche Gepräge der Schriften Justins auch ist, so wichtig ist er auch als Vertreter und Bewahrer älterer Überlieferungen. Sowohl in der Heidenpredigt wie auch in der Rechtfertigung des christlichen Glaubens gegenüber den Juden hat er von älteren Richtlinien ausgehen können. Die erste Apologie macht

den Eindruck, ähnliche Stoffe zu enthalten, wie sie auch im katechetischen Unterricht der neubekehrten Christen vorgetragen wurden. So bringt Justin (1. Apologie, 14–17) eine Übersicht der Lehraussprüche Christi und (31–53) eine Darstellung des Lebens Christi anhand der Weissagungen der Propheten. Seine Hauptargumente im Dialog mit Tryphon, nämlich daß das Gesetz Moses durch Christus, das neue Gesetz, und durch den neuen Bund überholt worden ist, daß die Christen das neue geistige Israel sind, daß die Propheten einen ersten Advent Christi im Leiden und einen zweiten in Herrlichkeit voraussagten, daß die Leiden und das Kreuz Christi und der christliche Kult im Alten Testament symbolhaft angedeutet sind, daß die Schrift neben dem Schöpfer aller Dinge von einem zweiten Gott und Herrn spricht und dessen Menschwerden und Geburt durch eine Jungfrau voraussagt, daß die Gnadengaben des Geistes nach der Himmelfahrt Christi bei den Juden aufgehört haben und auf die Christen übergegangen sind: alle diese Vorstellungen hat er nicht selbst erst erfunden. Es wird meist angenommen, daß Justin für seinen Schriftbeweis im Dialog und in der ersten Apologie (31–53) eine ältere Testimoniensammlung bzw. Testimoniensammlungen benutzte, die auch bei anderen christlichen Schriftstellern Spuren hinterlassen haben. Auf diese Weise lassen sich verschiedene Ungereimtheiten wie Mischzitate, abweichende Zitate und falsche Quellenangaben (die teilweise auch anderswo auftauchen) am leichtesten erklären. Es kann natürlich auch sein, daß Justin mündlich überlieferte exegetische Traditionen weitergibt. Als Justin seine christliche Ausbildung erhielt und selbst lehrte, hatte das Neue Testament noch nicht feste Form angenommen. Für ihn sind es die Schriften der Propheten, die als Heilige Schrift anzusehen sind. Die prophetischen Weissagungen nimmt er sogar als Hauptquelle für das Leben Christi und die Ausbreitung seiner Botschaft. Als Hauptautorität daneben gelten eher die Lehren Jesu selbst als die Schriften, die darüber berichten. Die einzige neutestamentliche Schrift, die Justin mit Verfassernamen erwähnt, ist die Offenbarung des Johannes (Dialog, 81). In der ersten Apologie spricht er zweimal von Evangelien. Die Apostel haben die Einsetzungsworte der Eucharistie in den von ihnen verfaßten Erinnerungen (»Apomnemoneumata«), die Evangelien genannt werden, überliefert (1. Apologie, 66). Im christlichen Sonntagsgottesdienst werden die Erinnerungen der Apostel und die Schriften der Propheten vorgelesen (1. Apologie, 67; eine indirekte Erwähnung gibt es auch in 1. Apologie, 33). Im Dialog sind »das sogenannte Evangelium« (von Tryphon schon gelesen, 10; vgl. 18) und das Evangelium (100), aber auch die Erinnerungen der Apostel (100–107 mehrere Male; vgl. auch 88) als Quelle für die Lehre und Taten Jesu genannt. Am ausführlichsten spricht Justin Dialog 103 von den Erinnerungen, »die, wie ich sage, von seinen Aposteln und denjenigen, die ihnen folgten, zusammengestellt wurden«. Ob Justin (Dialog, 106) mit den Worten »in seinen Erinnerungen«, kurz nachdem er Petrus genannt hat, auf Erinnerungen Petri hinweisen will, ist unsicher.

In seinem Bericht über die Lehren Christi (in 1. Apologie, 14 ff.) und in seinen Zitaten im Dialog bringt Justin Mischtexte, deren Wortlaut teilweise eigentümlich und teilweise aus verschiedenen Stellen der synoptischen Evangelien kombiniert ist. In seinen Angaben über das Leben Jesu erzählt Justin meist Einzelheiten, die sich in den synoptischen Evangelien belegen lassen, einige Male aber auch außerkanonische Überlieferungen (wie die Berichte über die Geburt Jesu in einer Grotte und über das Aufflammen eines Feuers im Jordan bei seiner Taufe, Dialog, 78 und 88). Es wird allgemein anerkannt, daß Justin unsere synoptischen Evangelien benutzte, auch wenn er zusätzlich von anderen Quellen beeinflußt wurde. Seine abweichenden Zitate sind nicht ausschließlich durch freie Umgestaltung oder Gedächtnisirrungen zu erklären, da in manchen Fällen dieselben Abweichungen sich auch anderswo belegen lassen (z. B. bei Klemens von Alexandrien und in den Pseudo-Klementinen). So hat man verschiedene Möglichkeiten erwogen. Hat Justin eine Evangelienharmonie benutzt, ähnlich derjenigen, die von seinem Schüler Tatian hergestellt wurde (Diese neuerdings modisch gewordene These wurde von Strecker zurückgewiesen)? Ließ er sich durch eine Sammlung von Herrenworten beeinflussen, die zum Zwecke des katechetischen Unterrichts mündlich überliefert wurde? Hat er vielleicht eine sehr altertümliche schriftliche Logiensammlung gekannt, die sogar hinter unseren synoptischen Evangelien steht, oder ein judenchristliches Evangelium als Quelle herangezogen? Der Grund, warum solche Fragen immer auf verschiedene Weise beantwortet wurden, ist wohl, daß die Wissenschaftler mit jeweils verschiedenen vorgefaßten Meinungen über den allgemeinen Zusammenhang an sie herangegangen sind. So weichen die Meinungen darüber voneinander ab, welche Rolle die mündliche gegenüber der schriftlichen Überlieferung spielte, und dementsprechend, welchen Platz unsere synoptischen Evangelien in einer Entwicklung einnahmen, die auch zur Bildung apokrypher Evangelien führte. Falls Justin seine christliche Ausbildung in Palästina erhielt, gewinnt die These an Wahrscheinlichkeit, daß er dort eine nicht mehr erhaltene Quelle (bzw. Quellen) kannte, und erst später während seiner Reisen in Gemeinden kam, wo die synoptischen Evangelien gebraucht wurden. Zu dieser christlichen Ausbildung scheinen auch das Johannesevangelium und die Paulusbriefe nicht gehört zu haben. Justin erwähnt Paulus nie – am häufigsten spricht er von den Aposteln als Zwölfergruppe, die von Jerusalem aus die christliche Verkündigung ausbreiteten. Weder aus Paulus noch aus dem Johannesevangelium und den Johannesbriefen bringt er Zitate. In beiden Fällen gibt es aber Parallelen und Berührungen, die Anlaß geben, seine Kenntnis dieser Schriften anzunehmen (vgl. z. B. Osborn, 135–138). Daß er von ihnen gewußt hat, als er in Rom als christlicher Lehrer tätig war, ist kaum zu leugnen. Ob die Parallelen auf direkte Benutzung, auf indirekte Bekanntschaft oder auf gemeinsame frühere Überlieferungen zurückgehen, bedürfte einer gründlichen Untersuchung. Seine Logoslehre verdankt Justin wohl nicht dem Johannesevangelium selbst, sondern einem Bereich jüdischer bzw. christlicher Spekulation, von dem aus sie auch nach dorthin gelangt ist. Obwohl die erhaltenen Werke Justins nicht an christliche Leser adressiert sind, wurden sie in christlichen Kreisen geschätzt und überliefert. Die an die römischen Herrscher gerichtete(n) Apologie(n) dient bzw. dienen nicht nur als eine nützliche Sammlung christlicher Argumente gegen die Verfolgung und als Entgegnungen auf heidnische Einwände, sondern auch als Ruf zur Bekehrung und Einführung in das Christentum für interessierte Heiden bzw. neu Hinzugewonnene. Man möchte vermuten, daß Marcus Pompeius, der Empfänger des Dialogs, ein Heide war, der sich für das Christentum interessierte und über dessen Verhältnis zum Judentum informiert werden wollte. Im zweiten Jahrhundert war das Judentum in der heidnischen Welt eine viel bekanntere Erscheinung als das Christentum. Die Christen mußten bereit sein, ihren Konvertiten zu erklären, warum sie sich vom Judentum getrennt hatten. Sowohl die Apologie(n) wie auch der Dialog konnten den Schülern Justins als nützliche Handbücher im Gespräch mit Außenstehenden und mit Neubekehrten dienen. Die Tatsache, daß der Bericht über sein Martyrium nach seinem Tod verfaßt und erhalten wurde, zeigt, daß die Erinnerung an Justin wach blieb. Er wurde von späteren christlichen Schriftstellern, wie zum Beispiel Tatian, Irenaeus (der ihn zitiert), Tertullian und Hippolyt mit Anerkennung erwähnt (vgl. Harnack, 1958, I, 1, 100 ff.), wahrscheinlich auch benutzt. Apologeten und Missionare wie Justin müssen im zweiten und dritten Jahrhundert den Hauptbeitrag zur Verbreitung des Christentums unter dem gebildeten Mittelstand geleistet haben. Wie ein dem Christentum feindlich gesinnter Heide auf die Argumente Justins in seiner Apologie (oder wenigstens auf sehr ähnliche Argumente) reagierte, sieht man aus der gegen die Christen gerichteten Schrift des Celsus (Andresen, 1955, 308–400). In späteren Jahrhunderten hat Justin wenig Einfluß gehabt. Anders als so überragende Gestalten wie etwa Origenes oder Augustin hatte er weder begeisterte Anhänger noch passionierte Gegner. Seine Schriften besaßen wohl hauptsächlich antiquarisches Interesse. Wie schon erwähnt wurde, hat man mehrere unechte Schriften seinem Namen (als Hauptvertreter der frühchristlichen Apologetik) unterschoben. In der Neuzeit ist er mancherlei Kritik ausgesetzt worden. Man braucht nur die Haupteinflüsse auf sein Denken aufzuzählen, um zu sehen, daß die Schwerpunkte seiner Theologie anderswo liegen, als dies im Protestantismus der Fall ist. Vom Standpunkt der späteren Orthodoxie aus gesehen, läßt sich an seinen Aussagen zu den Problemen, die in den trinitarischen Kontroversen des vierten und den Pelagianischen Streitigkeiten des fünften Jahrhunderts erörtert wurden, manches aussetzen. Einen Überblick über die Beurteilung Justins bis in die Neuzeit bringt von Engelhardt (1–70; vgl. auch Seeberg, 4 ff.).

Für uns steht Justin als Einzelfigur zwischen den apostolischen Vätern und Irenäus. Wenn es andere ihm ähnliche Lehrer gab (was an sich wahrscheinlich ist), so sind ihre Schriften verloren gegangen. In Justin kommt der platonische Einfluß (der nach ihm in der christlichen Theologie herrschend war) zum ersten Mal deutlich zum Ausdruck. In den christlichen Schriften vor Justin (z. B. im ersten Klemensbrief) merkt man eher einen wohl schon durch das hellenistische Judentum vermittelten stoischen Einfluß. Justin ist der einzige christliche Schriftsteller vor dem Ende des zweiten Jahrhunderts, dessen erhaltene Werke von einer philosophischen Ausbildung zeugen und zudem den Versuch darstellen, das Gesamtbild einer christlichen Weltanschauung zu geben. Die Apologeten Aristides, Athenagoras, Tatian und Theophilus sind in der Thematik ihrer erhaltenen Schriften sehr beschränkt. Von der einst reichen kleinasiatischen christlichen Literatur des zweiten Jahrhunderts besitzen wir kaum mehr als Bruchstücke und Titel. Mehrere begabte Christen dieser Zeit, die (wie Basilides oder Valentinus und dessen Schüler) ihren Glauben zu einem umfassenden System auszubilden versuchten, sind Leiter eigener Sekten geworden, die von der Großkirche nicht anerkannt wurden. Justin dagegen hat es vermocht, seine Offenheit zur heidnischen Philosophie mit der Bewährung des ihm überlieferten Glaubensguts auf eine Weise zu verbinden, die ihm auch spätere Achtung gewann.

Als Persönlichkeit macht Justin durch seine Redlichkeit und Tapferkeit einen durchaus positiven Eindruck. Er ist seinem eigenen am Anfang der (ersten) Apologie (2) ausgesprochenen Motto treu geblieben: »Derjenige, der die Wahrheit liebt, sollte auf jede Weise, sogar vor seinem eigenen Leben, es sich zum Vorsatz machen, selbst dann, wenn der Tod angedroht wird, das Gerechte zu sagen und zu tun.«

Quellen

Musurillo, H.: The Acts of the Christian Martyrs. Oxford 1972.
Otto, J. C. Th. [Hg.]: Corpus Apologetarum Christianorum Saeculi Secundi. Bd. 1, Teil 1 und Teil 2. 3. Aufl. Jena 1876–1879.

Übersetzungen

Rauschen, G. u. a.: Frühchristliche Apologeten und Märtyrerakten. Bd. 1, München 1913.
Häuser, P.: Des Heiligen Philosophen und Märtyrers Justinus Dialog mit dem Juden Tryphon. München 1917.

Darstellungen

Altaner, B.: Patrologie. 8. Aufl. Freiburg 1978, 65–71.
Andresen, C.: Justin und der mittlere Platonismus. In: Zeitschrift für die Neutestamentliche

III

Wissenschaft 44 (1952/53), 157–195. Unveränderter Abdruck in: Der Mittelplatonismus. Darmstadt 1981, 319–368.

Andresen, C.: Logos und Nomos. Berlin 1955.

Campenhausen, H. von: Die griechischen Kirchenväter. 5. Aufl. Stuttgart 1982, 14–23.

Chadwick, H.: Early Christian Thought and the Classical Tradition. Oxford 1966.

Engelhardt, M. von: Das Christentum Justins des Märtyrers. Erlangen 1878.

Freudenberger, R.: Die Acta Justini als historisches Dokument. In: Humanitas-Christianitas. Walther von Loewenich zum 65. Geburtstag. Witten 1968, 24–31.

Harnack, A. von: Geschichte der altchristlichen Literatur bis Eusebius. 2 Bde., 2. Aufl. Leipzig 1958. Bd. 1: Die Überlieferung und der Bestand. Bd. 2: Die Chronologie.

Harnack, A. von: Die Mission und Ausbreitung des Christentums in den ersten drei Jahrhunderten. 4. Aufl. Leipzig 1924.

Harnack, A. von: Juden und Judenchristentum in Justins Dialog mit Trypho. In: Texte und Untersuchungen, Bd. 39,1. Leipzig 1913, 47–98.

Holfelder, H.: Εὐσέβεια καὶ φιλοσοφία. Literarische Einheit und politischer Kontext von Justins Apologie. In: Zeitschrift für die Neutestamentliche Wissenschaft 68 (1977), 48–66; 231–251.

Hubik, K.: Die Apologien des Hl. Justinus des Philosophen und Märtyrers. Wien 1912.

Osborn, E. F.: Justin Martyr. Tübingen 1973.

Prigent, P.: Justin et l'Ancien Testament. Paris 1964.

Seeberg, B.: Die Geschichtstheologie Justins des Märtyrers. In: Zeitschrift für Kirchengeschichte 58 (1939), 1–81.

Strecker, G.: Eine Evangelienharmonie bei Justin? In: New Testament Studies 24 (1978), 297–316.

Studer, B.: Der apologetische Ansatz zur Logos-Christologie Justins des Märtyrers. In: Richter, A. M. [Hg.]: Kerygma und Logos. Festschrift für Carl Andresen zum 70. Geburtstag. Göttingen 1979, 435–448.

Weis, P. R.: Some Samaritanisms of Justin Martyr. In: Journal of Theological Studies 45 (1944), 199–205.

Zahn, Th. von: Studien zu Justinus Martyr. In: Zeitschrift für Kirchengeschichte 8 (1886), 1–84.

IV

Herakleon

Leben

Herakleon war ein Hauptvertreter der valentinianischen Gnosis. Seine Wirkungszeit lag in der zweiten Hälfte des zweiten Jahrhunderts. Clemens Alexandrinus (Str. IV,9) nennt ihn den berühmtesten Vertreter der Schule Valentins. Nach Origenes (Comm. in Joh. II,8) galt er als Schüler Valentins. Hippolyt (haer. VI,35,5-6) berichtet, daß die valentinianische Schule wegen einer Auseinandersetzung darüber, ob der Leib Jesu pneumatisch oder psychisch gewesen sei, sich in eine anatolische und eine italische Schule spaltete; als Vertreter der italischen Schule nennt er Herakleon und Ptolemaeus. Am Anfang seines Berichts über die Valentinianer spricht Hippolyt von "Valentin und Herakleon und Ptolemaeus und deren ganzer Schule" (haer. VI,29.1). Irenäus erwähnt ihn nicht in seiner Schilderung der Schüler Valentins (haer. I,11-12), sondern nur einmal nebenbei zusammen mit Ptolemaeus (haer. II,4,1). Bei Ps. Tertullian, haer. 4, wird Herakleon nach Valentin, Ptolemaeus und Secundus aufgeführt, und seine Lehre dadurch charakterisiert, daß er, statt von der Syzygie Bythos und Sige, von einem ursprünglichen Monas sprach, aus welchem die ersten zwei und dann die anderen Äonen entstanden. Einen solchen Lehrunterschied unter den Valentinianern nennt auch Hippolyt (haer. VI, 29), ohne Namen der Vertreter der beiden Richtungen anzugeben. Nach Epiphanius (haer. 36) gab es eine Schule der Herakleoniter. Aus Origenes kann man schließen, daß Gnostiker, die sich auf Herakleon beriefen, sich zu seiner Zeit in Alexandrien befanden. Er spricht von οἱ ἀπ' αὐτοῦ (22.11, 44.15-16 Brooke) und οἱ ἀπὸ τῆς γνώμης αὐτοῦ (23.10) und gibt als Veranlassung für seine eigene Johannesauslegung die Tatsache an, daß Heterodoxe, welche Gnosis beanspruchen, vielbändige Abhandlungen, die die evangelischen und apostolischen Worte zu erklären versprechen (V,8), besitzen und damit die Wißbegierigen mangels reiner Nahrung verführen. Die Exegesen Herakleons,

2

die Origenes in seinem Kommentar anführt, müssen wohl aus einer solchen Abhandlung stammen. Ob man aus den Erwähnungen bei Clemens und Origenes auf eine persönliche Tätigkeit Herakleons in Alexandrien schließen sollte, ist zweifelhaft.

Werke

Im Johanneskommentar des Origenes sind 48 Fragmente der Johannesexegese Herakleons erhalten. Das Werk Herakleons, aus dem Origenes zitiert, nennt er ὑπομνήματα (4.11). Ob darin das ganze Johannesevangelium ausgelegt wurde, ist unsicher. Aus dem Johanneskommentar des Origenes besitzen wir die Bücher I-II, VI, X, XIII, XIX-XX, XXVIII und XXXII zu Johannes 1,1-7; 1,19-29; 2,12-25; 4,13-54; 8,19-53; 11,39-57 und 13,2-33. Er erwähnt Herakleon erst in II,14 zu Joh 1,3 und nicht mehr in den Büchern XXVIII und XXXII, sonst öfters, aber ohne den vollen Wortlaut in seinen Berichten anzugeben. Man hat den Eindruck, daß die Exegese Herakleons nicht sehr ausführlich war. Origenes beschreibt seine Erklärungen zu Joh 1,21ff als "recht wenig und nicht wissenschaftlich durchforscht" (4.10ff) und erwähnt, daß er zu Joh 4,32 und Joh 8,12ff nichts sagte (29 und 41). Preuschen (Ausgabe ciii) vermutet, daß das Werk aus knappgefaßten Glossen, ähnlich den Hypotyposen des Clemens, bestand. Zwei weitere Fragmente (49-50; ob aus derselben Schrift ist unsicher) sind in den Eclogae Propheticae und den Stromateis von Clemens Alexandrinus erhalten. Im ersten erwähnt Clemens nach einem Mt 3,11 bzw. Lk 3,16 lose entsprechenden Zitat eine Bemerkung Herakleons über die Feuertaufe. Im zweiten führt er einen langen Auszug über das Bekenntnis und die Verleugnung vor den Menschen bzw. im Leben und Glauben als Exegese Herakleons zu den Versen Lukas 12,8-11 bzw. Mt 10,32-33 an (τοῦτον ἐξηγούμενος τὸν τόπον ...). Das Fragment 51 stammt aus Photius, der eine Herakleon und seinen Schülern zugeschriebene Meinung zu Joh 1,17 verneint. Dies könnte möglicherweise auf ein verlorenes Buch des Johanneskommentars des Origenes zurückgehen (nach Salmon 898; Preuschen, art. Valentinus, 410).

Exegese

Herakleon ist der erste Schriftsteller, von dem eine zusammenhängende Exegese einer neutestamentlichen Schrift erhalten ist. Vermutlich wurde die großkirchliche Exegese von der valentinianischen stark beeinflußt. Die

Methoden des Origenes sind nicht grundsätzlich verschieden von denjenigen
Herakleons. Für beide findet sich in den biblischen Erzählungen sowohl ein
Bericht über Ereignisse, die wirklich geschehen sind, wie auch die
symbolhafte Andeutung höherer Wahrheiten, die sich in den Geschehnissen
dieser Welt widerspiegeln und durch den biblischen Wortlaut
durchschimmern. Die Erzählungen des Evangeliums werden als
Schilderungen der Begegnungen Christi mit den verschiedenen
Menschentypen und des darin sich vollziehenden Übergangs aus dem
vergänglichen Reich des Demiurgen aufgefaßt. Herakleon hat durchaus einen
Sinn für geschichtliche Entwicklung (vgl. 20.9-17, 22.15-21, 4-8;
Gottesverehrung der Menschen vor dem Gesetz und der Heiden, der Juden
unter dem Gesetz, Ausbreitung des Heils und des Logos in die bewohnte Welt
von Judaea aus). Origenes zitiert oft seine Auslegungen auf der "einfachen"
geschichtlichen Ebene (z.B. 30.2, 32.1-2, 39.1, 42.1), manchmal mit
Anerkennung (z.B. 5.61-3, 6.9-11, 8.21-27, 20.3-6), wie auch
Alternativauslegungen auf einfachen und symbolischen Ebenen (8.24f, 18.15-
17). Einige symbolische Auslegungen lobt er auch (8.28-32, 17.12-14, 25-29).
Die darin von Herakleon angewendeten Methoden sind Origenes nicht fremd.
Biblische Ortsnamen, Menschen und Menschengruppen werden symbolisch
verstanden, manchmal doppelschichtig. So sind die Juden nicht nur
Psychiker, die den Demiurgen anbeten, sondern auch εἰκόνες τῶν ἐν τῷ
πληρώματι (22.9-11). Jerusalem bezeichnet den "psychikos Topos", der
selbst Bild des (himmlischen) Jerusalem ist (13.1-4; vgl. auch 12 und 38.2-7).
Herakleon benutzt gern Zahlensymbolik (16.3-10, 18.22-5, 40.45-7).
    Origenes kritisiert die Exegese Herakleons als nicht systematisch genug
und deswegen gezwungen oder willkürlich. Er setzt Worte hinzu, die im
Evangelium nicht da sind (1.10,17, 13.25-6, 17.36-7), unterläßt es, den
Parallelstellen in den anderen Evangelien (11.7f) oder der Geschichte (16.4)
nachzuforschen. Er unterscheidet zwar den biblischen Sprachgebrauch
hinsichtlich der Bezeichnung "Kind" (46.16-28), nicht aber die verschiedenen
Bedeutungen des Wortes "Tod" (40.59-63). Auch wenn er manchmal genaue
Beobachtungen macht (wie z. B. über Präpositionen, 1.24-6, vgl. 50.17-19),
stützt er seine Aussagen nicht durch Beweise, Beispiele oder gründliche
Untersuchungen.
    Vor allem geht die Kritik des Origenes von den grundsätzlichen
Unterschieden zwischen der heterodoxen Lehre und derjenigen der
Großkirche aus. Hier ergeben sich Schwierigkeiten (auch für die moderne
Forschung), weil in der Exegese Herakleons, obwohl manche Einzelheiten
sich nur vom Valentinianismus her verstehen lassen, doch kein
valentinianischer Mythos geschildert wird und auch die Dreinaturenlehre
nicht voll konsequent zum Ausdruck kommt. So spricht Origenes nur im
allgemeinen von der μυθοποιία der Häretiker (II 24, II 28, XX 33) oder der

4

Schüler Herakleons (18.31-2, 23.10-14), und klagt, daß Herakleon selbst seine Meinung nicht deutlich ausspricht (2.3-5, 35.18-20). Er bietet oft selbst Erklärungen zu den Aussagen Herakleons an. Ähnlich greift er die Dreinaturenlehre im allgemeinen an, findet die Aussagen Herakleons dazu widersprüchlich, und freut sich, wenn er 44.14-17 endlich schließen kann, daß Herakleon, gleich seinen Schülern, diese Lehre doch vertritt. (Weil Origenes selbst meint, daß alle λογικά, einschließlich des Teufels, gleich geschaffen wurden und daß alle gerettet werden, unterscheidet sich seine eigene Lehre auf jeden Fall grundsätzlich von derjenigen Herakleons.) Ein eindeutiger Lehrunterschied ist es, daß Herakleon den Gott der Großkirche, den Demiurgen, auf einen niedrigeren Rang herabstuft. Was aber die Bewertung des Alten Testaments angeht, gibt es nur einen Gradunterschied, da auch Origenes das wörtliche Verständnis desselben für überholt hält (vgl. 17.1-12, 20-25, 22.8-14).

Die Theologie Herakleons ist nicht nur durch Johannes sondern auch durch Paulus beeinflußt. In den erhaltenen Fragmenten zitiert er aus dem Alten Testament, den Evangelien und den Paulusbriefen (einschließlich Heb).

Lehre

Aus den erhaltenen Fragmenten Herakleons läßt sich kein vollständiges valentinianisches Lehrsystem rekonstruieren. Sie behandeln z.B. weder die valentinianische Äonenlehre noch den Fall der Sophia. Die früheren Forscher haben anhand der Angaben und der Systemschilderungen der Häresiologen, deren Quellen sie analysiert haben, versucht, Herakleon in ein allgemeines Entwicklungsbild der valentinianischen Gnosis einzufügen und das vermeintlich von ihm vorausgesetzte System etwa mit dem anonymen System bei Hippolyt (haer. VI,29-34) oder dem ptolemäischen System bei Irenäus (haer. I,1-10) gleichzusetzen (vgl. Leisegang 2270). Der Fund der Nag Hammadi-Schriften hat nicht nur neuen Stoff für die Forschung der Entwicklung des Valentinianismus geliefert, sondern die Methodik der früheren Anläufe in Frage gestellt. Es hat sich gezeigt, daß der Versuch, eine Klassifizierung der gnostischen Schriften und Schriftsteller in nach ihren Gründern genannten Schulen mit festen Lehrsystemen vorzunehmen, überhaupt verfehlt ist (vgl. z.B. Wisse). Bei dem Valentinianismus ist es unsicher, ob man an eine Entwicklung aus einem einfachen Frühstadium zu immer komplizierteren Systemen oder umgekehrt an eine Rechristianisierung früherer Systeme denken sollte oder ob beide Alternativen nicht eine Übervereinfachung darstellen würden (vgl. die Beiträge von Stead, Quispel und Wilson in *The Rediscovery of Gnosticism* I). Daß die Johannesexegese

Herakleons zwar die Grundzüge eines valentinianischen Systems voraussetzt, es aber vermeidet, Einzelheiten des Mythos zu erwähnen, ist wohl als Absicht des Verfassers, nicht als Zufall der Erhaltung, anzusehen. Ob dies aber zeigt, daß Herakleon durch sein Johannesstudium christlicher wurde (vgl. Colpe, 105 Anm. 30), daß die Johannesexegese als exoterisch gemeint war oder nur die "kosmische" Reichweite des Evangeliums auslegen sollte (vgl. Pagels, 19,47), oder daß er überhaupt in einer nur losen Beziehung zu diesem Mythos stand (vgl. Stead, 93), ist fraglich. Unter den Nag Hammadi-Schriften zeigt der Tractatus Tripartitus (Nag Hammadi Cod. I 5, früher I 4), der ein monistisches System, in welchem Sophia durch den Logos ersetzt wird, schildert, gewisse Parallelen zu Herakleon, welche dazu führten, seinen Verfasser bzw. den Verfasser seiner Vorlage mit Herakleon zu identifizieren oder als aus der Schule Herakleons stammend anzusehen (vgl. Colpe 105 Anm. 30 und 119 Anm. 84, der eine religions- und kirchengeschichtliche Neueinordnung des Herakleon aufgrund einer computergerechten Textbearbeitung der Herakleon-Fragmente von Ch. Elsas ankündigt). Diese Hypothesen haben wenig Einfluß auf die neuere Forschung ausgeübt, die sich eher auf den philosophischen Hintergrund der Theologie des Tractatus Tripartitus (z.B. Perkins, Thomassen) und auf die Anthropologie und Soteriologie Herakleons konzentriert hat (z.B. Langerbeck, Pagels, Mühlenberg, Aland, Devoti). Mehrere Einzelheiten der Lehre Herakleons sind in der Forschung umstritten: z. B. ob er in der Auslegung der Geschichte der Samaritanerin den Sophiamythos andeuten will, wie der "Menschensohn über dem Topos" zu erklären ist (35.14-15), ob die geretteten Psychiker ein anderes Endziel als die Pneumatiker haben (wie 13.10-12 anscheinend vorausgesetzt wird), ob die drei Menschenklassen schon bei der Schöpfung festgelegt wurden oder ineinander übergehen können bzw. erst in der Begegnung mit dem Heiland zum Vorschein kommen. Vielleicht tastet Herakleon selbst nur nach einer Antwort zu solchen Fragen.

In den erhaltenen Fragmenten erwähnt Herakleon Gott, den Vater der Wahrheit, der Pneuma ist (20.16, 24.1-4), den Demiurgen, den von den Juden angebeteten Schöpfer und Gesetzgeber, dem auch das Gericht übergeben ist, der wie ein kleiner König vom Gesamtkönig eingesetzt über ein kleines und vergängliches Reich herrscht (20.11-17, 48, 40.1-6), und den Teufel, der ein Teil der ganzen Materie (ὕλη) ist und dessen Natur aus Irrtum und Unwissenheit besteht (20.7-8, 47.4-12). Der Kosmos und was in ihm ist, wurde durch den Logos geschaffen, nicht aber der Äon oder was im Äon ist, da dies vor dem Logos entstand (1). Die Pneumatiker oder die pneumatische Kirche, die auch als ἐκλογή bezeichnet wird (37), sind von derselben Natur wie der Vater, nämlich Pneuma, und beten ihn in Wahrheit an (24). Das dem Vater Verwandte (οἰκεῖον) ist aber in der tiefen Materie des Irrtums verlorengegangen (23), ähnlich wie die Hurerei der Samaritanerin mit sechs

IV

6

Männern ihre Verstrickung in die Schlechtigkeit der Materie andeutet (18.23-
7). Deswegen hilft der Herr nicht nur der Berufung (κλῆσις), welche ohne
Pneuma ist, sondern auch den Pneumatikern, indem er durch das Kreuz und
durch die Kraft und Wirkung des Heiligen Geistes alle Schlechtigkeit vertilgt
und die Kirche (ἐκκλησία), nicht mehr als eine Höhle von Räubern und
Kaufleuten, sondern als das Haus seines Vaters bereitet (13). Weil das Ende
des Gesetzes der Tod ist, hat der Demiurg den Heiland gebeten, zur Hilfe
seines Sohnes (d.h. des psychischen Menschen, 40.28, 45-7), der in
Unwissenheit und Sünden war, aus der Größe (μέγεθος) herabzusteigen (40;
8.28-38). Nach der Heilung des Sohnes des Demiurgen, dessen Natur es ist,
durch Werke und Sinneswahrnehmung überzeugt zu werden, nicht aber dem
Wort zu glauben (40.21-3), berichten die Engel des Demiurgen, daß er nicht
mehr Unpassendes tut (40.37-45). Die Samaritanerin (Pneumatikerin)
begegnet dem Heiland mit dem ihrer Natur entsprechenden Glauben (17.30-
32) und wird von ihm aufgefordert, ihren Mann, d.h. ihr Pleroma oder ihren
Paargenossen (σύζυγος) aus dem Pleroma zu rufen, damit sie vom Heiland
die Kraft, die Einigung und die Verschmelzung mit ihrem Pleroma
bekommen könnte (18.3-15). Nach der Begegnung mit dem Heiland kehrt die
Samaritanerin in die Welt zurück, um "der Berufung" (κλῆσις) die Parusie
des Christus zu verkündigen. "Denn die Psyche wird von dem Pneuma dem
Heiland zugeführt" (27.1-9). Die Gesprächspartner Jesu in Joh 8,44 sind nach
46.9f gefallene Psychiker. Die Psychiker, welche von Natur aus die
Möglichkeit haben, nach Vorsatz (θέσει) Söhne Gottes zu heißen, können
auch nach Vorsatz Söhne des Teufels werden, indem sie seine Begierden
lieben und tun und dadurch ihm gleich werden (46.10-16, 36-8). Diejenigen,
in denen Jesu Wort keinen Platz findet, sind ungeeignet entweder κατ'
οὐσίαν oder κατὰ γνώμην (43.3-4). Die Worte "aus dem Vater, dem
Teufel" werden als ἐκ τῆς οὐσίας des Teufels erklärt (44.5f). Choiker, die
von Natur Söhne des Teufels sind, werden nur einmal ausdrücklich erwähnt
(46.10-1; nach Langerbeck 69 Interpretation des Origenes; dagegen Aland
177 Anm. 63). Die Seele ist fähig, gerettet zu werden, nicht aber unsterblich
(40.12f). Der Untergang der nicht von dem Heiland geretteten Menschen (und
Engel) des Demiurgen wird 40.49-57 und 46.23-8 durch Schriftzitate
erläutert, die endzeitliche Hochzeit 12.5-6 und 38.3 erwähnt, aber nicht
eingehend geschildert. Von dem Besätwerden der Seelen, ihrem Heranreifen
und ihrer Ernte handeln Fr. 2 und 32-6 (vgl. auch 16.4-10). Der
Menschensohn über dem τόπος sät, der Heiland, der auch selbst
Menschensohn ist, erntet und schickt als Schnitter die Engel, jeden auf die
eigene Seele (36.14-18). In der Gegenwart wird sowohl gesät wie auch
geerntet (35.10-11; 32.11). Bei der Rettung und Wiederherstellung der

Geernteten wird der Logos auf ihnen ruhen (34.1-5). Der Tempel ist Bild
sowohl der Kirche (13) wie auch des Heilands selbst (16.4-10).

Quellen

A.E. Brooke, The Fragments of Heracleon, TaS 1.4 (1891)
E. Preuschen, Origenes: Johanneskommentar, GCS, Leipzig 1903
Werner Foerster, Die Gnosis, Zürich/Stuttgart, I 1969, 214-240 (Ausw.; dt.)

Literatur

B. Aland, Erwählungstheologie und Menschenklassenlehre. Die Theologie
des Herakleon als Schlüssel zum Verständnis der christlichen Gnosis?　Nag
Hammadi Studies 8 (1977) 148-181. — G. Bareille, Art. Héracléon: DThC
6,2 (1947) 2198-2205. — C. Barth, Die Interpretation des Neuen Testaments
in der Valentinianischen Gnosis, TU 37.3 (1911). — C. Blanc, Le
Commentaire de Héracléon sur Jean 4 et 8, Aug. 15 (1975) 81-124. —
Dieselbe, Origène Commentaire sur Saint Jean, SC 120 (1966), 157 (1970),
222 (1975), 290 (1982). — Carsten Colpe, Heidnische, jüdische und
christliche Überlieferung in den Schriften aus Nag Hammadi VIII, JAC 22
(1979) 98-122. — D. Devoti, Antropologia e storia della salvezza in
Eracleone, MAST 2 (1978) 3-83. — Eugène de Faye, Gnostiques et
gnosticisme, Paris ²1925. — Werner Foerster, Von Valentin zu Herakleon:
Untersuchungen über die Quellen und die Entwicklung der valentinianischen
Gnosis, Gießen 1928, ZNW Beiheft 7. — Wolf-Dieter Hauschild, Gottes
Geist und der Mensch, München 1972. — Y. Janssens, Héracléon.
Commentaire sur l'évangile selon saint Jean, Muséon 72 (1959) 101-151,
277-299. — Dieselbe, Episode de la Samaritaine chez Héracléon, Sacra
Pagina II, BEThL 13 (1959). — H. Langerbeck, Aufs. zur Gnosis. Hg. v.
Hermann Dörries, 1967 (AAWG.PH 69) 38-82. — H. Leisegang, Art.
Valentinus: PRE ²7 (1948) 2269-2270. — W. von Loewenich, Das Johannes-
Verständnis im zweiten Jahrhundert, ZNW Beiheft 13, Gießen 1932. — J.
Mouson, La Théologie de Héracléon (diss.), Leuven 1949. — Derselbe, Jean-
Baptiste dans les fragments d'Héracléon, EThL 30 (1954) 301-22. —
Ekkehard Mühlenberg, Wieviel Erlösungen kennt der Gnostiker Herakleon?
ZNW 66 (1975) 170-93. — Elaine H. Pagels, A Valentinian Interpretation of
Baptism and Eucharist, HThR 65 (1972) 153-69. — Dieselbe, The
Valentinian Claim to Esoteric Exegesis of Romans as Basis for

8

Anthropological Theory, Vig Chr 26 (1972) 241-258. — Dieselbe, The Johannine Gospel in Gnostic Exegesis: Heracleon's Commentary on John, New York 1973. — Pheme Perkins, Logos Christologies in the Nag Hammadi Codices, Vig Chr 35 (1981) 379-96. — E. Preuschen, Art. Valentinus, Gnostiker, und seine Schule: RE 20 (1908) 409-411. — H.-Ch. Puech und G. Quispel, Le Quatrième Écrit gnostique du Codex Jung, Vig Chr 9 (1955) 65-102. — The Rediscovery of Gnosticism. I The School of Valentinus, hg. Bentley Layton, SHR 41 (1980). — Francois-M.-M. Sagnard, La Gnose Valentinienne et le Témoignage de Saint Irénée, EPhM 36, Paris 1947. — George Salmon, Art. Heracleon: DCB 2 (1880) 897-901. — Manlio Simonetti, Eracleone e Origene, Vetera Christianorum 3 (1966) 111-141, 4 (1967) 23-64. — G.C. Stead, The Valentinian Myth of Sophia, JThS, NS 20 (1969) 75-104. — Einar Thomassen, The Structure of the Transcendent World in the Tripartite Tractate, Vig Chr 34 (1980) 358-75. — Tractatus Tripartitus, hg. R. Kasser u.a., Bern 1973-5. — Walter Völker, Herakleons Stellung in seiner Zeit im Licht seiner Schriftauslegung, diss., Halle 1922. — Frederik Wisse, The Nag Hammadi Library and the Heresiologists, Vig Chr 25 (1971) 205-223.

V

THE STATE OF PLAY WITH REGARD TO
HIPPOLYTUS AND THE *CONTRA NOETUM*

In a recent book on Hippolytus Josef Frickel[1] reviews the problems connected with his person and writings and attempts to refute arguments that two of the most important works, the *Elenchos* and the *Contra Noetum,* are not by the same author. Since little of the recent discussion on Hippolytus has been conducted in English, it may be useful to provide more extended comments.

Frickel writes as an advocate rather than as an impartial umpire and his arguments in the introductory part of the book (pp.1-122) can be followed better if one is aware that they are aiming at the identification of (1) the mysterious writer Hippolytus mentioned by Eusebius as having 'presided over a Church somewhere', by Jerome and Theodoret as bishop and martyr, and in a catena extract from Apollinarius as well as in other Greek sources from the late sixth century onwards (including manuscripts of his own writings) as bishop of Rome and (2) the martyr Hippolytus venerated at Rome and celebrated in verse by pope Damasus and Prudentius, as well as (3) the author of an Easter table for A.D.222-333 and other writings inscribed on the throne of the famous statue discovered not far from Hippolytus' catacomb in 1551, restored as a portrait of Hippolytus and now positioned at the entrance to the Vatican library with (4) the opponent of pope Callistus who reveals himself so frankly in the *Elenchos.* For those who disagree some passages will look like special pleading, but this need not mean that Frickel's case is wrong. The separation, championed most notably by Nautin from 1947 onwards[2] and by contributors to the volume *Ricerche su Ippolito,*[3] between the anonymous Roman schismatic author of the *Elenchos* and of works listed on the statue[4] and Eusebius' bishop Hippolytus author of exegetical writings has a certain superficial plausibility, but the two authors are linked by Eusebius' attribution to Hippolytus of what is clearly the same Easter table as the one on the statue as well as by points of contact in the writings themselves.

Frickel makes much of the argument that the puzzling nature of the early testimonies on Hippolytus is to be explained by the assumption that their authors knew the full facts but were embarrassed by them. I would agree that such embarrassment and probably also some confusion is likely to lie behind the omissions in the testimonies — it is instructive to compare the case of Novatian, whose schism (being fully publicized at the time of its inception and also long perpetuated) was familiar to later Greek historians, but whose writings (in Latin) were preserved under the names of Tertullian and Cyprian. Given that Eusebius had more knowledge than he reveals, are we to suppose that he remained silent about Hippolytus' schism because he was reluctant to give a negative report about an admired writer, or are those scholars correct who have maintained that the author of the *Elenchos* (who claims to share in high-priesthood and the power to expel sinners from the Church, but does not state explicitly that he regards himself as

rightful bishop of Rome) was not in schism after all?[5]
With regard to the evidence from the writings themselves, it would have been helpful if Frickel had printed the list from the statue for comparison with Eusebius' and Jerome's lists (the summaries on pp.68 and 76, nn.212 and 230, diverge) and stated clearly which works or parts of works are transmitted under Hippolytus' name and which not. May it be that his later works were circulated anonymously after the reconciliation of his followers with the Church at Rome?

Points in the first part of the book which I find implausible include the attempt to salvage the speculation (of Wendel [1937/8], cf.pp.81ff. and nn.206 and 252) that the statue was put up in honour of Julius Africanus in the library he organized for Severus Alexander in the Pantheon, despite the discovery by Guarducci (1974/5) that the statue was originally a female one. Surely the hypothesis is to be preferred that the inscription on this reused statue, perhaps now interpreted as a personification, was made on the orders of a wealthy admirer or patron of Hippolytus (cf.p.87 n.267) — perhaps even of the Severina to whom one of the works in the list on the statue was addressed.

Frickel translates the puzzling item in lines 21-22 of the list of writings on the statue ωδαι (ε)ις πασας τας γρα | φας as 'Oden zu allen Schriften' and regards it as referring to Hippolytus' exegetical works (pp.84-5). Lightfoot, taking the title at its face value, had been stimulated to attempt a retroversion of the Muratorian fragment into iambic trimeters![6] It is surely preferable[7] to read it as two entries, 'Odes' and 'On all the Scriptures', the latter entry summarizing the exegetical works not already listed. The list itself is not very expertly executed, squeezed into rather an unfortunate position on one of the back corners of the throne, the sides being occupied by the Easter table.[8] The spacing of lines 5-8 may perhaps betray uncertainty about where one title ends and the next begins and in lines 14 and 18 letters have been forgotten and added.

A further implausibility occurs in the treatment of Damasus' epigram and its assignment of Hippolytus to the schism of Novatian ('Hippolytus fertur. . .| presbyter in scisma semper mansisse Nouati'; pp.23ff.). Damasus uses the name 'Novatus' (the form used by Eusebius) instead of 'Novatianus' not as a 'vage Formulierung' in order to indicate 'eine nur geistige Verbindung zwischen Hippolyt und Novatian', nor with reference to an Alexandrian (or indeed Carthaginian) Novatus,[9] but simply because it is impossible to accommodate the longer name within the hexameter verses he employs.

On pp.110-111 Frickel states the correct conclusion that the central question concerning Hippolytus is whether the division among the transmitted writings into a more exegetical and pastoral group and a more scientifically orientated group is so radical as to exclude the possibility of a single author. He uses the fact that there has been some disagreement about the exact delimitation of the two groups as an argument against such a radical division. In the second and longer part of the book (pp.123-300) he contributes to a solution by means of the examination and comparison of *Elenchos* Book X and the *Contra Noetum*, which contain parallel expositions of the true teaching but exhibit striking differences in style and doctrine. In this he takes up the first part of a challenge by Nautin[10] to refute his own demonstration that the two pairs of writings, *Elenchos* and *Contra Noetum* and *Chronicle* and the *Commentary on Daniel*, cannot be by the same author.

The choice of the *Contra Noetum* introduces major additional complications.[11] The majority of scholars, including Nautin, have identified the surviving text (which is preserved in a single manuscript of the twelfth or thirteenth century under the title 'Homily of Hippolytus archbishop of Rome and martyr against the heresy of a certain Noetus') as the final part of a lost treatise listed by Eusebius and Jerome as Hippolytus' *Against all Heresies* and described by Photius (*Bibliotheca* 121) as Hippolytus' *Syntagma against 32 Heresies* (perhaps the same as the earlier less detailed refutation referred to in the preface of the *Elenchos*). Many have followed Lipsius in the hypothesis that this lost treatise was the joint source of Pseudo-Tertullian, Epiphanius, and Philastrius in their works against heresy. Others have regarded the *Contra Noetum* as part, or the main part, of a homily or a treatise against the Monarchians (this was the view initially favoured by Harnack). A further complication is the fact that a long quotation corresponding to a passage near the end of the transmitted text but with much simpler wording is reproduced by Theodoret in his *Eranistes* as from Hippolytus' interpretation of Psalm 2 and in a collection of testimonies (derived from Theodoret) which is preserved in Latin translation appended to Pope Gelasius' treatise *De duabus naturis*.

The internal arguments for regarding the *Contra Noetum* as a homily or part of a homily are the recurring form of address ἀδελφοί (once μακάριοι ὅδελφοί) and the clearly homiletic character of the last section. The main evidence that opening sentences or sections referring to or dealing with other heresies have been lost is the fact that the transmitted text starts with the words 'Certain others are introducing a different teaching': Ἕτεροί τινες ἑτέραν διδασκαλίαν παρεισάγουσιν. R. Butterworth translates this as 'Certain strangers are introducing a strange teaching' but that would require some such wording as Ξένοι τινὲς καινὴν διδασκαλίαν παρεισάγουσιν. In addition there are references back in the course of the work to the fact that 'Noetus *too* has now been refuted', to 'the truth against which all these great heresies have arisen', and to 'Valentinus, Marcion, Cerinthus and all their rubbish'. A comparison between the one-sided scriptural interpretation of the Noetians and that of Theodotus implies that the heresy of Theodotus has already been treated.

The *Contra Noetum* has generally been thought to be earlier than the *Elenchos* (the heresy attacked is less developed than that ascribed by Hippolytus himself to Callistus and by Tertullian to Praxeas),[12] but Nautin dated it later. A number of scholars have suspected the text of containing later interpolations, regarding the Trinitarian theology as suspiciously far advanced. Richard, who in other respects has championed the unity of Hippolytus, came round to the view that it is the work of 'a mediocre writer of the fourth century'.[13] Frickel himself in an earlier paper[14] had taken it to be 'post-Hippolytan' (cf.p.195 n.587).

Frickel's answer to the problem of the differences between the expositions of true teaching in *Elenchos* Book X and the *Contra Noetum* is to emphasize the different setting and addressees of the two versions. The proof of antiquity and demonstration of truth in *Elenchos* X, he argues,[15] are a shortened version of corresponding sections of the lost *De universo*, which is referred to in *Elenchos* X.32.4 (cf. also X.5.2, where the author states that he has often given this demonstration before). Frickel shows that there is a new apologetic orientation in Book X and that the addressees envisaged are now mankind in general (X.31.6, 33.13,34.1). For this reason the demonstration of truth is not a doctrinal exposition for Christians but a philosophically orientated presentation of Christian truth for educated pagans, necessarily different therefore from that in the *Contra Noetum*.

The *Contra Noetum* Frickel assigns to the situation described in *Elenchos* IX.11-12. The author is replying to accusations of ditheism, defying the authority of his opponents and, without naming them explicitly, is attacking them as followers of Noetus. Frickel even goes so far as to identify our text as the accusation against Callistus before the Churches referred to in *Elenchos* IX.12.15, sent round, he suggests, to other Churches with an accompanying letter. He follows Butterworth in regarding the *Contra Noetum* as an independent work, but rightly rejects his idea that the opening sentence can be viewed simply as a rhetorical device. He suggests therefore that there was a brief mention of other heresies in the accompanying letter (pp.205-6 and 209). With regard to Epiphanius' chapter on the

198

Noetians in *Panarion* 57 Frickel argues that Epiphanius copied not the *Contra Noetum* but a different, earlier and less technical version, which formed the end of Hippolytus' lost *Syntagma*.[16]

In countering the various arguments put forward by Nautin against common authorship Frickel attempts to show that the difference is due in most cases to the different aims of the two works. Thus with regard to the difference in Trinitarian theology Frickel argues that Trinitarian formulas would have been out of place in the demonstration of truth presented for pagans in the *Elenchos,* but that the fact that they do not appear here, or indeed in the *Commentary on Daniel, Antichrist* or *Benedictions of Isaac, Jacob and Moses,* need not mean that the author was unaware of the Holy Spirit. The abundance of references to the Holy Spirit in the *Contra Noetum* he explains as caused by Hippolytus' desire here to show that his own faith is in accordance with the baptismal formula. He follows Nautin in rejecting the hypothesis of later interpolations, but does admit that there is an anti-Apollinarian interpolation in chapter 17 (p.254 n.728). In a short section on stylistic arguments Frickel takes the line that these are only useful when employed positively (to demonstrate common authorship) and he shows up a few errors in the previous use of such criteria.

Where does all this lead to? The majority of readers of Frickel's book may well agree that the external evidence can be satisfactorily explained on the hypothesis that there was only one, Roman Hippolytus. What is now required is more detailed examination of the surviving writings and fragments. Frickel has made interesting use of the plausible theory that Hippolytus reused his own material in successive writings and has provided some illuminating discussion of the *Elenchos* and the *Contra Noetum.* The selection of the *Contra Noetum,* however, as a key writing in the argument for unity of authorship is likely to provoke further dispute. One may for example agree with Frickel that the other writings are by a single author and still reject the *Contra Noetum* (or our text of the *Contra Noetum*) as not by Hippolytus.[17] Even if one accepts the arguments for an association of the *Contra Noetum* with Hippolytus, suspicion must remain regarding the state of the surviving text. Its preservation in a single manuscript as a piece of special doctrinal interest with its beginning broken off is not such as to inspire confidence. Frickel's argumentation for the hypothesis that Epiphanius preserves evidence for a lost version is important.[18] It is a pity that he was only able to give a brief summary of the detailed comparison he had undertaken (cf. p.177 n.526). In any case, however, the theory requires testing with reference to Epiphanius' style and treatment of his sources elsewhere and to the development of Trinitarian terminology.

Over the decades the debates concerning Hippolytus have produced a substantial quantity of literature. It is not the case that this discussion has been sterile or that the earlier arguments are now all outdated or outworn. Contributions whose main conclusions provoked disagreement have none the less often provided important new insights. Frickel is to be thanked for mastering so much of the earlier argumentation and for providing so stimulating an introduction. His exploration of the darkness surrounding Hippolytus, well structured and neatly arranged in short sections, has something of the excitement of a detective story, and the irony of Hippolytus' fate — torn apart like his namesake in Greek mythology not only according to the later legend of his martyrdom but also in the scattering of his works and the fragmentation of his reputation, remembered as a martyr in the West and as a writer in the East, even his statue broken up and reconstituted from different sources — is brought out in a lively manner.

Notes

1 *Das Dunkel um Hippolyt von Rom. Ein Lösungsversuch: Die Schriften Elenchos und Contra Noetum* (= *Grazer Theologische Studien* 13 (Graz, 1988), pp.325, one plate; no price given.

2 Pierre Nautin, *Hippolyte et Josipe* (Paris 1947).

3 = *Studia Ephemeridis 'Augustinianum'* 13 (Rome 1977); reviewed by G.C. Stead in *JThS*, NS 30 (1979), pp.549ff.

4 Nautin named this anonymous author Josipe because of the attribution of one of his works, the *De universo*, to Josephus.

5 Cf. p.93, n.287 and D.L. Powell, 'The Schism of Hippolytus', *T.U.* 115 (1975), pp.449-456.

6 *The Apostolic Fathers I, ii:Clement* (London 1890), pp.405-413.

7 This possibility is mentioned but rejected by Lightfoot, ibid., p.412.

8 Cf. the photographs, transliteration and description in M. Guarducci, *Epigrafia greca,* 4 (Rome 1978), pp.535-545.

9 Although it must be admitted that Jerome, *De viris illustribus* 70, does confuse Novatian and the Carthaginian Novatus.

10 *Lettres et écrivains chrétiens* (Paris 1961), pp.179-188.

11 There is a useful account of earlier controversy in the introduction to the edition of R. Butterworth, *Hippolytus of Rome: Contra Noetum* (London 1977).

12 In *Ricerche su Ippolito* Simonetti argued for a date prior to Tertullian's *Adversus Praxean.*

13 *Dictionnaire de spiritualité* 7 (1969) col.533.

14 *Ricerche su Ippolito,* pp.137-9.

15 He here rejects an earlier theory of his own (cf. p.127) and follows an idea of Botte (cf. p.102).

16 He ignores the problem that the brief summaries of pseudo-Tertullian on Praxeas and Philastrius on the Noetians are closer to the *Contra Noetum* than to Epiphanius.

17 This is the position taken by Capelle, *Recherches de théologie ancienne et médiévale* 17 (1950), p.148, by Richard, loc. cit., and by Marcovich, *Theologische Realenzyklopädie* 15 (1986), p.382.

18 Capelle had argued the same with regard to the opening part of Epiphanius' account, *Revue Bénédictine* 38 (1926), pp.321-330, and Richard that Theodoret's extract gives the original wording, *Mélanges de science religieuse* 10 (1953), pp.177ff.

VI

Peacemaking and Religious Tolerance in the Early Church[1]

This paper is not concerned with the relations of early Christians with other religions - neither with the complexities of their attitudes towards Judaism, nor with their intolerance towards pagan religion, which they regarded as the worship of wicked demons who stirred up persecution in response to the Christian refusal of participation.[2] Instead I shall be using the two topics indicated in the title to give a very general picture of the pre-Constantinian church. I shall be mentioning not only intolerance within Christianity but also various kinds of tolerance - these may be labelled as active tolerance, social and moral tolerance, passive tolerance and retrospective tolerance.

In studying the history of the early church one might easily gain the impression that the main occupation of early Christians was the conflict against heresy. In a movement so torn by disagreements the search for peacemaking and religious tolerance might seem to have little prospect of success. If tendencies towards tolerance had not existed however, there would have been nothing to halt the process of fragmentation into ever smaller schismatic groups. In fact the forces which succeeded in holding together or reuniting the diverging currents were sufficiently strong that near the end of the second century Celsus in his attack on Christianity was able to make a clear distinction between what he calls the 'great church' or the 'church of the multitude' and the various heretical groups

---

[1] This paper (the colloquial style of which I have not altered) started life as a contribution to the conference of the Pauleios Hetaireia Historikon Meleton held at Kavalla in 1986, and was later given in an expanded version as a lecture to the Theological Faculty of the University of Erlangen (in German) and as a paper to the Senior Patristic Seminar at Cambridge. I am grateful for the comments received on all these occasions. I would like to dedicate it to my father, N. G. L. Hammond.

[2] Christian apologists occasionally use the argument that toleration should be extended to Christianity on the grounds that different people worship different gods (thus Athenagoras, *Legatio* 1, Tertullian, *Apology* 24.5, and Dionysius of Alexandria in the account of his hearing before Aemilian in Eusebius, H.E. VII.xi.8), but the view that different approaches can be equally valid (as stated later by Symmachus in his famous plea for the restoration of the Altar of Victory) is logically incompatible with the picture of pagan religion as demon-worship, a picture which was powerfully reinforced by the experience of persecution. On religious freedom and religious coercion in the ancient world cf. B. Kötting, *Religionsfreiheit und Toleranz im Altertum* (Opladen 1977, a lecture held before the Rheinisch-Westfälische Akademie der Wissenschaften in Düsseldorf).

(Origen, *Contra Celsum* V.59 and 61 end).[3] When Constantine was converted there seems to have been no doubt that it would be to this 'great church' that he would show his favour and not to one of the other competing Christian sects. In an edict against heretics he forbade heretical assemblies and urged them to come over to the catholic church (Eusebius, *Vita Constantini* III.64-5).

In the course of the rapid spread of Christianity in the Roman empire and to the East of it during the early centuries A.D. there naturally arose differences with regard to practice, belief and also the writings valued by the groups concerned. Such differences were tolerated, as long as they remained unnoticed. When unacceptable disagreements became apparent, the offending teachings, teachers, groups or writings were rejected by the church leaders in their own sermons and writings. In this way the 'great church' took shape during the course of the first two centuries by means of deliberate self-differentiation over against other groups and through the contacts between communities which accepted common guide lines.[4]

The process of self-differentiation, i.e. of the conscious rejection of unacceptable views and hence of religious intolerance over against teachings regarded as heretical, occupies a central position in our sources, because these sources reflect the interests of the great writers and church leaders in the main centres of early Christianity. In the small communities and among simple church members however it may have been different. If we follow the picture given in Eusebius' Church History our impression will be yet more distorted. According to Eusebius the Christian message spread over the whole world already in the time of the apostles and crowded churches arose in every city and every village honouring God with true piety (H.E. II.3). Only after the apostolic period did the demonically instigated attacks of heretics attempt to corrupt the virgin church (III.32.7-8, IV.7.1ff.). In fact however the organisation of the great church together with its claims for authority and conscious rejection of heretical errors only developed and extended itself gradually. In the light of hindsight when one looked back from the vantage point of the Constantinian age, it was possible to claim as catholic all Christians who were not explicitly labelled as members of heretical sects. There is a sense in which this attitude to earlier Christian history seen from the point of view of Eusebius can be labelled retrospective tolerance. I shall return to it later.

The main part of this paper I would like to divide according to three topics: firstly the active religious tolerance which resulted in the great church becoming

---

[3] Celsus' attack is quoted by Origen in his reply in his *Contra Celsum.* I suspect that Celsus may have obtained some of his information on Christian sects from a mainstream Christian informant.

[4] Cf. R. A. Markus, *Christianity in the Roman World* (London 1974) 61-4.

ever greater rather than ever more fragmented; secondly the passive religious tolerance which simply ignored differences in belief; and thirdly the activity of individual church leaders who attempted to promote tolerance or effect reconciliation.

The first detailed description of the great church and its claims is given in the earliest surviving antiheretical work, that written by Irenaeus bishop of Lyons in the last quarter of the second century. One might perhaps describe Irenaeus as the architect of the great church. According to Irenaeus this church is spread throughout the whole world, but has received and preserved the same faith everywhere from the apostles and their successors. He implies that he would be able to give succession lists for all the churches, but in fact limits himself to just one bishops' list for Rome going back to Peter and Paul and to the information that his own teacher Polycarp was appointed by apostles as bishop of Smyrna, and that the church founded by Paul at Ephesus, where John lived until the time of Trajan, is a true witness to the apostolic tradition (*Adversus Haereses* III.2-4).[5]   In the choice of these three churches, on the one hand Rome and on the other the Asiatic churches Smyrna and Ephesus, may be seen Irenaeus' attempt to hold together two different streams within the great church. As I shall be mentioning again shortly there were tensions between the Roman church and the Christians of Asia Minor, which Irenaeus tried to reconcile. Irenaeus is also aware that the church is not in fact entirely uniform everywhere, and that so far from all the apostles having been active in all the churches, it was different apostles that bequeathed the heritage of their preaching to different churches. Thus he writes that Matthew wrote his gospel among the Hebrews, whereas Peter and Paul preached at Rome. After their death the preaching of Peter was written down by Mark and that of Paul by Luke. Subsequently John, the disciple of the Lord, published his gospel when he was at Ephesus (*Adv. Haer.* III.1.2 = III.1 Mass.). Thus Irenaeus attempts to fit a church organisation with at least two divergent centres and several different traditions within an ideal picture of a universal apostolic church.[6]

A feature of this apostolic church is the acceptance of a New Testament canon substantially the same as ours, characterised by the use of four gospels - neither more nor less. Such a canon represents the combination of different streams. Irenaeus seems scarcely aware that tolerance was once necessary to recognise both Paul and Peter as common founders of the church, although he does know of Jewish Christians who reject Paul and only use the Gospel of

---

5 The references are to the edition of W. W. Harvey (Cambridge 1857).

6 It is interesting to contrast with this the idea that all twelve apostles taught exactly the same as found in the attribution to the twelve of various writings, such as the Epistula Apostolorum and the Didascalia and even the composition of the creed; cf. W. Bauer in E. Hennecke and W Schneemelcher, *Neutestamentliche Apokryphen* 2 (Tübingen 1964) 17.

Matthew, as well as of Marcionites who use only Paul and an abbreviated Gospel of Luke (*Adv. Haer.* III.11.10 and I.22 = III.11.6 and I.26.2 Mass.). A faint memory of the earlier situation is preserved in a much later writing, the Apostolic Constitutions. This work gives bishops' lists according to which separate successors were appointed by Peter and Paul at Antioch and Rome, at Antioch Euodius by Peter and Ignatius by Paul, at Rome Linus by Paul and Clement by Peter. Similarly it states that at Ephesus Timothy was appointed by Paul and John by the apostle John (Book VII.46). With respect to the canon the main problem for Irenaeus is to win acceptance for the Gospel of John - as we know from other sources there were disputes at Rome in which Gaius acted as spokesman of a group which rejected the fourth Gospel and the Apocalypse as heretical forgeries.[7] For Irenaeus the defense of the Gospel of John was part of the championing of his own Asiatic tradition and hence of the fusing of the Roman and Asiatic streams that was necessary to his ideal picture of a universal apostolic Christianity.

The claim to belong to a universal church founded by the apostles and faithfully transmitting apostolic doctrine naturally exercised great attraction. Thus Tertullian in Africa and Origen at Alexandria give descriptions of the rule of faith entrusted by the apostles to the universal church similar to that of Irenaeus.[8] This picture was also important for missionary preaching.[9] The prophets had foretold that the heathen in every land would be converted.[10] The fact that this had actually happened manifested the divine power contained in the Christian message.[11] It is comprehensible that individual Christians, Christian communities and even groups of communities were prepared to tolerate tensions and disagreements rather than to separate themselves off from a church that could make such a claim.

The reason however that Celsus used the term 'great church' and 'those of the multitude' (οἱ ἀπὸ τοῦ πλήθους)[12] was not the geographical extension of this variety of Christianity but rather the fact that it included the most members from the common people. When Celsus complains that Christians only preach to the uneducated, fools, manual workers, slaves, women and children and

---

[7] Cf. Theodor Zahn, *Geschichte des Neutestamentlichen Kanons* (Erlangen 1888-92) I.i,220-62; I.ii,967-991; W. von Loewenich, *Das Johannes-Verständnis im zweiten Jahrhundert* (Giessen 1932) 140-141.

[8] Tertullian, *De Praescriptione Haereticorum* 13.20-21, *Adversus Marcionem* IV.5, Origen, *De Principiis* praef. 3ff.

[9] A. von Harnack, *Die Mission und Ausbreitung des Christentums in den ersten drei Jahrhunderten* (Leipzig 1924) 529ff., quotes general claims about the spread of Christianity from the Pauline epistles onwards.

[10] So for example Justin, *I Apology* 31,32,40,53, *Dialogue with Trypho* 52-3,117,121.

[11] Cf. e.g. Origen, *De Principiis* IV.1.

[12] See above p.1.

that none of the educated believe the Christian message, he is no doubt thinking c
the 'great church' (Origen, *Contra Celsum* III.18,44,50,55,59,73). Where h
explicitly speaks of the great church, he asserts that its members accept as true th
account of creation in Genesis even with respect to the six days (V.59). Christian
imagine that God has a body in the same form as the human body and hope to se
him after death with the eyes of the flesh (VII.27), though he does admit that ther
are some intelligent Christians who attempt to explain the biblical storie
allegorically (I.27, IV.38ff.). That the church did indeed contain more uneducate
than educated members is admitted by Origen in his reply to Celsus (I.27) - bot
he and other apologists report with pride on the conversion of simple folk to
virtuous way of life as a sign of the divine power contained in the Christia
gospel.[13] Similarly we hear quite a bit about the charitable activities within th
great church, activities which required a number of widows, orphans and othe
impoverished persons as recipients and at least a few rich Christians a
benefactors.[14] Such a composition of the communities however demanded
certain degree of tolerance on both sides, if the rich and educated members wer
not to despise the uneducated poor and the latter were not to regard the former wit
suspicion.

    Above all tensions were liable to arise not so much directly between ric
and poor as between the bishops of the communities and the wealthy Christia
benefactors and educated teachers, whose influence could be seen as posing
threat. Examples range from Ignatius' warnings against listening to outsid
teachers to the instructions in the Didascalia Apostolorum aimed at bringin
almsgiving under the control of the bishop.[15] It can perhaps be regarded as a sig
of tolerance that such wealthy and educated Christians did not simply leave th
great church en masse in the face of episcopal attempts to restrict the independen
of their activities.

    At Alexandria the writings of Clement give a most interesting picture of th
gulf in educational level and in prosperity within the Christian communit
Clement writes that the majority of believers are afraid of Greek philosophy an
shut their ears towards it (*Stromateis* VI.x.80; VI.xi.89). Some say that on
should limit oneself to what is necessary, others that philosophy is evil. Cleme
himself values philosophical education very highly and aims to use correctly th

---

[13] Athenagoras, *Legatio* 11.4, Justin *2 Apology* 10, *1 Apology* 60, Tatian, *Oratio* 33.

[14] Cf. e.g. Harnack, op. cit., 111-220, M. Hengel, *Eigentum und Reichtum in der frühen Kirc*
(Stuttgart 1973), 124 (E.T. *Property and Riches in the Early Church* (Philadelphia 1974)),
M. Grant, *Early Christianity and Society* (London 1978). The role of wealthy Christians
benefactors of the communities and their teachers is attractively portrayed in the apocryphal Ac
of Peter.

[15] IX, ed. R. H. Connolly (Oxford 1929) 88-9. L. Wm. Countryman, *The Rich Christi*
(New York 1980) is illuminating on this.

tudies wrongly used by heretics (*Stromateis* I.i.18; VI.x.83.), but his own
writings are addressed to readers who are both highly educated and also extremely
wealthy (*Paedagogus* II and III). These wealthy Christians have difficulty in
fitting in to the community. When they hear that a camel can more easily pass
through the eye of a needle than a rich man enter the kingdom of God, some fall
into despair, while others think they have to throw away all their possessions
Quis diues salvetur 2 and 11). Of the other members of the community some
treat the wealthy with impudence and others, who are avaricious, attempt to flatter
them (3). Clement recommends the rich Christian to use his wealth to collect a
whole army of holy old men, orphans, widows and men who will pray for him
and give him advice and support (34-5). He should also select a venerable
Christian as a kind of private teacher or domestic chaplain (41). We remember that
Origen, as a gifted Christian teacher, enjoyed the patronage of a wealthy
Alexandrian lady, who held mixed assemblies of heretics and main-stream
Christians at her house, and later of Ambrose, whom he himself converted from
Valentinianism (Eusebius, H.E. VI.2.12-14 and 18.1 and 23.1-2).

In view of the degree of independence recommended by Clement to the
wealthy and educated Christians and, on the other side, the suspicious attitude of
the Christian majority with regard to philosophy, one can regard it as a victory of
religious tolerance that Clement and Origen remained loyal to the great church.
Whether Clement left Alexandria only because of the persecutions or rather
because of tensions with bishop Demetrius is uncertain.[16] Origen was still able
after his break with Demetrius to remain active as a Christian presbyter under the
protection of the bishops of Caesarea and Jerusalem. We hear that the bishops of
Palestine, Arabia, Phoenicia and Achaea refused their assent to a letter sent round
from Alexandria, but not of any resulting schism.[17]

The great church merited this appellation not only because of geographical
extension and as the church of the multitude but also because while respecting the
practice of asceticism it refrained from demanding it of all its members. Together
with this went a certain moral tolerance shown in the readiness to receive back
repentant sinners. This attitude is represented by Hermas and Dionysius of
Corinth in the second century and the Roman bishops Callistus and Cornelius in
the third. It was the schismatic rigorists, Hippolytus and Novatian, and the
founders of ascetic sects, such as Saturninus and Marcion, who showed
themselves intolerant. Within the great church ascetics like Origen could live in

---

6 Pierre Nautin thinks the latter - *Lettres et Écrivains chrétiens* (Paris 1961) 118 and 140. A.
M. Ritter, 'Klemens von Alexandrien' in ed. M. Greschat, *Gestalten der Kirchengeschichte* I
Stuttgart 1984) 122, regards it as possible.

7 Jerome, *Epistle* 33.5; 84.10 - has history perhaps drawn a veil over what followed?

mutual toleration with Christians of secular lifestyle. Although the imposition o
the requirement of celibacy on all baptised Christians was rejected as heretical by
church leaders, none the less apocryphal writings like the Acts of Paul and the
Acts of Peter which represent the preaching of sexual continence as the heart of the
Christian gospel were read and treasured widely.[18] Similarly writings with a
docetic Christology, such as the Acts of John, were widely read.

This brings me to my second main point. In many respects there was
tolerance in the pre-Constantinian church for the simple reason that it remained
unnoticed that there were differences in the beliefs of individual Christians, o
Christian communities and even of whole regions. It was only certain prominen
individual leaders and writers who concerned themselves with antiheretica
polemic. This means that one can maintain the thesis that the active intolerance o
which we hear so much from our sources was only the exception to a genera
phenomenon that one could label as 'passive tolerance'.

Within the individual communities teachers arriving from elsewhere could
join the church and collect groups of disciples, as was done at Rome in the second
century not only by Justin, but also by Valentinus, Cerdo and Marcion.[19] Even
if they split off from the community contemporary writers call such group
'schools' (σχολή or διδασκαλεῖον), as if they were philosophica
schools.[20] Origen gives a 'tolerant' account of the rise of heresy in his Contra
Celsum (III.12-13), where he compares the sects in Christianity with those i
medicine and philosophy and in Judaeism.[21]. At Alexandria there were member
of the church who continued to visit heretical teachers as late as the third century
as we learn from a letter of Dionysius of Alexandria, reporting on the procedur
taken by his predecessor Heraclas with regard to such persons (Eusebius, H.E
VII.7.4) Except when these teachers or their hearers were reported and cros
questioned it was not so easy to expose them. The antiheretical writings c
Irenaeus, Tertullian and Hippolytus make it clear that heretics, in particular the
Valentinians, did not openly confess their allegiance to their special teachings c
their supposed founders but instead remained on the fringe of the Christia
community and spread their teachings secretly among individual church membe
(cf. e.g. Irenaeus, Adversus Haereses III.15.2). Tertullian states explicitly tha
the Valentinians of his time refused to acknowledge this label, kept quiet abou

---

[18] Cf. H. Strathmann und P. Keseling, 'Askese II', Reallexikon für Antike und Christentum
(Stuttgart 1950) 758ff.;   H. Chadwick, 'Enkrateia', Reallexikon für Antike und Christentum
(Stuttgart 1962) 343-365.
[19] Irenaeus, Adversus Haereses III.4.2, quoted in Eusebius, H.E. IV.11.1; Tertullian, D
Praescriptione Haereticorum 30).
[20] Hippolytus, Refutatio IX.12.20-6, Contra Noetum I, Rhodo in Eusebius, H.E. V.13.4.
[21] So also Clement, Stromateis VII.xv.89.3.

their characteristic teachings and claimed to hold the same belief as the great church (*Adversus Valentinianos* 1-4; cf. Irenaeus, *Adversus Haereses* proem.). It is for this reason that the antiheretical writers are so concerned to expose the different groups, to equip them with names and a genealogy and to reveal and ridicule their myths and other heretical ideas. On the other side Gnostics such as the Valentinians could show tolerance towards the great church, because they regarded themselves as a superior level of spiritual Christians and the simple Christians as a lower group of 'psychics' who could expect a lower kind of salvation in their own way.[22] One group of heretics described by Hippolytus (*Ref.* VIII.1ff.) under the label 'Docetae' is supposed even to have taught that there were thirty different ways of seeing Jesus represented by thirty sects corresponding to thirty different types of soul.[23]

If heretics could easily conceal themselves within the individual communities it could happen yet more easily that different communities or groups of communities harboured divergent beliefs. Eduard Schwartz wrote of the pre-Constantinian church that it 'formed only an ideal unity, but in outward form consisted of a number of autonomous communities under bishops'.[24] The later hierarchical organisation under the bishops of the larger cities and under metropolitan bishops was not yet systematised. It was not the case that the bishops of the more important churches kept the surrounding communities under tight control. We only know of a few cases of their interfering. I shall mention one example now and a few more later.

Sometime around the turn to the third century Serapion bishop of Antioch visited the church of Rhossus, a town about thirty miles distant (Eusebius, H.E. VI.12.2ff.). When he became aware of a disagreement among the Christians there caused by the fact that some of them used the Gospel of Peter, he said that they should go on reading it. Only later, after he had received further reports and read the book himself, did he notice that it was not entirely orthodox. As a result of this he wrote a work about it addressed to the Christians of Rhossus and promised another visit. In this case it is interesting to note that Serapion did not interfere on his own initiative but because a disagreement had arisen within the church of Rhossus. In more distant communities there may well have been all sorts of unorthodox writings and ideas circulating.

When Constantine came forward as patron of the catholic church, it was natural that membership of that church should be claimed by all those Christians and Christian communities who did not wish to label themselves explicitly as

---

22 The book of K. Koschorke, *Die Polemik der Gnostiker gegen das kirchliche Christentum* (Leiden 1978) is revealing on the relations of Gnostics with the main-stream church.

23 Cf. Koschorke, op. cit., 189ff.

24 *Kaiser Constantin und die christliche Kirche* 2 (Leipzig 1936), 72-3, cf. 28-30.

heretics or schismatics. Eusebius narrates in his Life of Constantine (III.6) that
for the Council of Nicaea there assembled numerous bishops who were most
widely separated from one another in mind, body, country and place of origin and
race, and that they formed as it were a vast garland of priests, composed of a
variety of the choicest flowers. One notices how attracted he was by the idea of
unity in diversity. A large number of the individual churches enumerated on the
surviving bishops' lists for the council appear here for the first time.[25] We can by
no means be certain that all were previously uniform in their teachings or in close
contact with the main centres of the great church. Rather it seems probable that
some may have represented syncretistic tendencies and used heretical writings. In
any case Constantine wished for inner peace and harmony within the church, as he
emphasised in his opening speech (Eusebius,*Vita Constantini* III.12). When the
arriving bishops began to accuse each other and to hand him writings containing
mutual accusations, he is reported to have burnt them and to have told the bishops
to entrust their disagreements to divine judgement and to relinquish their
quarrelsome tendencies (Rufinus, H.E. X.2).

The edict against heretics that I mentioned at the beginning had the effect
that a great influx came into the catholic church. Eusebius reports that some came
over dishonestly and through fear, others with conviction and rejoicing, and that
the bishops tested those who had previously been heretics and only let them in
after a period of probation, whereas schismatics were received straight away (*Vita
Constantini* III.66). It is obvious that such an influx will have had results for the
composition and the self-understanding of the catholic church. Firstly very varied
traditions were now brought within the compass of the one church. I would think
that this is one of the reasons for the flourishing of the monastic movement in the
fourth century. Secondly it was now felt to be important to see one's own past as
catholic. In a certain sense one can see these developments as favourable to
religious tolerance, even if the picture was different for obstinate heretics. In this
way certain earlier writings and writers were accepted within the catholic church
that had not previously belonged to it, for example the Pseudo-Clementines or the
Syrian writer Bardesanes, whom Eusebius depicts as a converted Valentinian
(H.E. IV.30).

In the last part of this paper I will give a few individual examples of church
leaders attempting to promote tolerance or to make peace. The first example takes
us back to Irenaeus.

When the Quartodeciman controversy towards the end of the second
century led to bishop Victor of Rome attempting to excommunicate the churches of
all Asia together with the neighbouring churches, Irenaeus wrote a famous letter
pleading for mutual toleration. The bishops of Rome prior to Victor, writes

---

[25] Cf. e.g. Harnack, op. cit.

Irenaeus, had communicated with Quartodeciman visitors to Rome and had preserved the peace of the whole church. There were also differences in the observance of the fast going back to much earlier predecessors who had been prepared to tolerate disagreement and live at peace. He uses the paradoxical formulation that 'the disagreement in the fast confirms the agreement in the faith'. Eusebius only quotes Irenaeus' letter but he states that others too wrote exhorting Victor to think of peace and neighbourly unity and love (H.E. V.24.9-18).

This episode has an interesting postscript in the church history of Socrates.[26] Socrates describes the so-called 'indifferent canon' of the Novatianists, according to which a difference with regard to the celebration of Easter is not sufficient reason for separation from the church. He then mentions the events in the time of Victor and Irenaeus' letter and also Constantine's letter on the decision of the Council of Nicaea about the celebration of Easter. Socrates himself emphasises that there are many different customs in the churches of different regions and that such disagreements go back to apostolic times. Those who agree in belief vary in their customs. He gives a detailed list of such differences in customs, including ones concerning the length and nature of the fast before Easter, the times and character of religious assemblies, clerical celibacy and penitential practice. He cites the report on the apostolic council in Acts 15 in order to show that Christians are free from bondage to formal observances.[27]

Irenaeus acted as a peacemaker also in connexion with discussions about the Montanist movement - under Eleutherus, the predecessor of Victor, he carried a letter of the Christians in Gaul to Rome in which they gave their judgement on the matter (Eusebius, H.E. V.3.4 - 4.2). Eusebius describes this judgement as cautious and most orthodox, and narrates that the martyrs wrote letters both to Eleutherus and to the brethren in Asia and Phrygia in which they pleaded for the peace of the churches. One might guess that, although these letters are unlikely to have pronounced unqualified recognition for the Montanist prophecy, they will probably have come out against any excommunication of the Montanist prophets and their followers. We find Irenaeus using hard words against those who make void the gifts of the spirit, reject the Gospel of John because of the promise of the Paraclete, and cast out the grace of prophecy from the church (*Adversus Haereses* III.11.12 = III.11.9 Mass.).

Elsewhere in the West the Montanist movement at first met with toleration. In Africa the Passion of Saints Perpetua and Felicitas is full of enthusiasm for the

---

[26] H.E.V.21; there is a corresponding passage also in Sozomen, H.E.VII.18-19).

[27] In fact variety in belief could be tolerated also, if the belief was not regarded as central. An obvious example from the early period is Justin's report on the different views with regard to chiliasm (*Dial.* 80). On the variety of eschatological teaching in the early church cf. Charles E. Hill, *Regnum Caelorum. Patterns of Future Hope in Early Christianity* (Oxford 1993).

new prophecy but none the less continued to be valued in the main-stream church. The writings of Tertullian continued to be read, despite his open championship of Montanism. Perhaps the division on the grounds of his recognition of the Paraclete mentioned by Tertullian in the first chapter of his work against Praxeas was a separation from his side only, without any corresponding excommunication from the side of the church.

With regard to Tertullian's claim that a Roman bishop was on the point of recognising Montanist prophecy and had already composed letters of peace but was deterred by Praxeas' slanders against the Montanists and citation of decisions of earlier Roman bishops, it is normally assumed that these earlier Roman decisions condemned Montanism - but it could be, I would suggest, that the bishops in question had simply refused to give their recognition to the new prophecy, since this would have led to a break with its opponents.

In the middle of the third century occurred an episode somewhat similar to the Quartodeciman controversy. Because of a disagreement about heretical baptism bishop Stephen of Rome excommunicated Cyprian of Carthage, and also the bishops in Cilicia, Cappadocia, Galatia and the neighbouring provinces, who agreed with Cyprian (Eusebius, H.E. VII.5.3-4). The Roman attitude was intolerant towards Cyprian and the others but more tolerant towards heretics in that it recognised their baptism, accepted members of heretical groups into the community without rebaptising them and even cited in defense of heretics the verse Phil.i.18: 'in every way, whether in pretense or in truth, Christ is preached'.[28] Cyprian on the other hand took the view that each bishop should form his own judgement on such matters and that a difference of opinion ought not to lead to excommunication.[29] Firmilian states that there are many other differences too in the churches of the different regions which have not necessitated a separation from unity. The Roman claim to have preserved the tradition of the apostles in all things is shown to be false by the fact that the customs at Rome are not in every respect the same as those at Jerusalem .[30]

As peacemaker in this quarrel Dionysius of Alexandria played a role reminiscent of Irenaeus earlier. He wrote to Stephen and to his successor Xystus, also to two Roman presbyters, Philemon and Dionysius (who was later bishop), and although he himself agreed with the Roman practice, he emphasised that the African custom of rebaptising heretics was not new but corresponded to the decisions of earlier episcopal councils (Eusebius, H.E. VII.7.5; cf.VII.5.5). According to a Syriac fragment of the letter to Stephen he gave the opinion that one

---

[28] This is reported by Firmilian in Cyprian, Ep. 75.20.
[29] Ep. 69.17, preface to 7th Council of Carthage.
[30] Firmilian in Cyprian, Ep. 75.6.

should leave the decision to the bishop concerned.[31] Dionysius had also attempted earlier to act as a peacemaker in the Novatianist schism and had written various letters with this aim including one to Novatian, stating that schism is worse that idolatry and urging him to bring back his followers into the church (Eusebius, H.E. VI.45).

It would be possible to include examples of peacemaking councils and debates, but it is a question of interpretation to what extent such gatherings really were intended to promote tolerance.   Debates could be used to force to submission, refute or expose and excommunicate heretics (as happened in the case of Paul of Samosata), or for the representatives of two irreconcileable parties each to display his arguments before an audience. Bishops gathered in councils in order to make joint decisions, not so much with a view to reconciling opposing sides or reaching a compromise.

I will only mention two such gatherings, where it is at least possible to see the main aim as conciliatory. The first is the debate of which we have a partial record in the Dialogue of Origen with Heraclides. Doctrinal disagreements had arisen in Heraclides' church and the whole community had assembled together with bishops from elsewhere and the issues had been discussed and clarified. Although Heraclides was, as it were, under trial, the tone of the debate is polite and restrained. Eusebius possessed the record of a similar gathering at which Beryllus bishop of Bostra was won back to orthodoxy by the arguments of Origen (Eusebius, H.E. VI.33; cf. 37).

My second example is the debate held by Dionysius of Alexandria with the presbyters and teachers of the nome of Arsinoe in Egypt, where the prevalence of chiliastic doctrines was giving rise to dissensions. According to Dionysius' own account (Eusebius, H.E. VII.24) the debate was a most pacific affair, lasting three days, with honest and conscientious discussion of the disputed questions and difficulties and readiness of those involved to change their opinions if proved wrong, and ending with the leader of the chiliasts and a number of his followers being won over.[32]

To conclude - I have argued that religious tolerance of both active and passive varieties was necessary for the pre-Constantinian church to develop into a universal church. Of the great writers I have mentioned the two bishops Irenaeus and Dionysius were active as peacemakers in attempting to heal or alleviate threatening schisms between Rome and the churches of other provinces. The others are only regarded as members of the great church by virtue of some

---

[31] Ed. Ch. L. Feltoe (Cambridge 1904) 47-8.

[32] This episode is sympathetically described by R. Lane Fox, *Pagans and Christians* (Harmondsworth 1986) 265.

VI

13 PEACEMAKING AND TOLERANCE

measure of retrospective tolerance. The Roman presbyters, Hippolytus and Novatian, both went into schism. Tertullian became a Montanist. Cyprian was excommunicated by a Roman bishop. Clement perhaps had difficulties with the bishop of Alexandria, Origen was excommunicated. None the less it is these great figures that give us our picture of the church of that period. It is their writings that are preserved and were valued by later ages. The will to turn the ideal picture of a universal church into reality was strong enough to win over the intellectual élite and to cover over certain splits in the developing organisation of the catholic church.

VII

DIE EINHEIT DES GLAUBENS UND DIE MANNIGFALTIGKEIT DER BRÄUCHE IN DER CHRISTLICHEN ÜBERLIEFERUNG NACH IRENÄUS

Dem Grundsatz, dass die Kirchen in aller Welt ihren Glauben durch Überlieferung, d.h. 'traditio' oder παράδοσις, von den Aposteln erhalten haben, hat Irenäus in seiner Abwehr gegen die Häretiker grundlegenden Ausdruck gegeben [1]. Dass er in der Ausprägung dieses Gedankens eine Schlüsselstellung einnimmt, ist wohlbekannt. Während die Valentiner vor Valentin und die Marcioniten vor Marcion überhaupt nicht existierten, so behauptet er, vielmehr, während die verschiedenen Häretiker ihre Überlieferungen von Simon Magus herleiten, haben die Apostel den wahren Glauben sowohl in den Schriften der Evangelien überliefert wie auch den Leitern der von ihnen begründeten Kirchen, vor allem der Kirche Roms und denjenigen von Smyrna und Ephesus in Kleinasien anvertraut [2]. Hauptinhalt dieser Überlieferung ist der Glaube an den einen Schöpfergott und den einen Christus, seinen Sohn [3].

---

[1] *Adv. Haer.* II, 8, 1; III, praef. ff. (hg. W. W. Harvey, Cambridge 1857).
[2] III, 4, 2; III, praef.; III, 1-3. Für Rom war Irenäus in der Lage, eine Successionsliste von den Aposteln bis zu seiner eigenen Zeit zu zitieren. Über die kleinasiatischen Kirchen behauptet er nur, dass Polykarp von Aposteln unterrichtet und als Bischof von Smyrna eingesetzt wurde, ohne seine dortigen Nachfolger zu nennen. Für die Kirche in Ephesus, die von Paulus gegründet wurde und Johannes bis zur Zeit Trajans beherbergte, nennt er hier überhaupt keine Bischöfe; vgl. auch II, 33, 3, wo er von dem Zeugnis der kleinasiatischen Presbyter, die Johannes und andere Apostel gesehen hatten, redet. Die Bischofslisten in den *Apostolischen Konstitutionen* VII, 46 kennen Polykarp nicht und bringen einen doppelten Anfang für Ephesus (Timotheus von Paulus und Johannes von Johannes eingesetzt).
[3] II, 8, 1; III, 1, 2.

Wie muss also Irenäus die drohende Kirchenspaltung geschmerzt haben, als in dem Osterstreit der römische Bischof Viktor wegen eines Unterschieds in der christlichen Praxis versuchte, die Kirchen Kleinasiens zusammen mit den Nachbarkirchen aus der Gemeinschaft auszuschliessen [4].

In seinem von Euseb zitierten Mahnbrief an Viktor bringt Irenäus in prägnanter Form zum Ausdruck, dass die Tatsache, dass die Vorgänger der jetzt streitenden Parteien trotz unterschiedlicher Praxisüberlieferungen bezüglich des Tages des Osterfestes und der Dauer des vorösterlichen Fastens miteinander den kirchlichen Frieden bewahrt hatten, als Bestätigung des einen gemeinsamen Glaubens anzusehen sei. « Der Unterschied des Fastens », so schreibt er « bestätigt die Einheit des Glaubens »: ἡ διαφωνία τῆς νηστείας τὴν ὁμόνοιαν τῆς πίστεως συνίστησιν [5]. Dass es nicht um eine neue Einführung in der Osterpraxis sondern um verschiedene Überlieferungen ging, wird sowohl in der Rahmenerzählung Eusebs wie auch in den von ihm zitierten Briefen herausgestellt. Besonders wichtig bei dem Brief des Irenäus ist es, dass er in seiner klaren Unterscheidung zwischen Praxis und Glauben sich von den streitenden Bischöfen Viktor und Polykrates bewusst abhebt. So schreibt Polykrates in seinem Brief an Viktor, dass die kleinasiatischen Kirchenführer in ihrer Beobachtung des vierzehnten Tages des Passahs der Regel des Glaubens gefolgt sind: κατὰ τὸν κανόνα τῆς πίστεως ἀκολουθοῦντες. [6]. Nach dem Bericht Eusebs war es wegen ihrer

---

[4] Euseb, *H.E.* V, 24, 9. Zum Osterstreit vgl. H. von Campenhausen, *Urchristliches und Altkirchliches*, Tübingen 1979, S. 300-330, mit der dort S. 301 Anm. 3 angegebenen Literatur. Es wird meist angenommen, dass die Briefe der Bischöfe und Bischofskonzilien, die Euseb *H.E.* V, 23, 2-4 anführt, von Viktor von Rom angefordert wurden, nachdem am Rom wegen quartadezimanischer Christen aus Kleinasien Auseinandersetzungen ausgebrochen waren (der von Euseb, *H.E.* V, 15 und V, 20, 1 erwähnte abgefallene römische Presbyter Blastos, der einen Brief von Irenäus περὶ σχίσματος erhielt, war nach Pseudo-Tertullian, *Adv. Haer.* VIII, 1, ein Quartadezimaner). Nach der Meinung aber von P. Nautin, *Lettres et Écrivains chrétiens*, Paris 1961, S. 36-38, 65-91, fing der Streit dadurch an, dass die (von Euseb nicht erwähnten) kleinasiatischen Gegner des Polykrates ihn bei Viktor anklagten. Diese These hat Einiges für sich. Die kleinasiatischen Überlieferungen waren wahrscheinlich nicht einheitlich. Für die kleinasiatischen Auseinandersetzungen über das Passah zur Zeit des Melito von Sardis siehe Euseb, *H.E.* V, 26, 3, Clemens Alexandrinus, *De Pascha* (Fragmente), hg. O. Stählin, GCS *Clemens* III, 1909, S. 216 ff., Apollinaris von Hierapolis, *De Pascha* (Fragmente) in *Chronicon Paschale*, PG 92, 80C-81A; vgl. dazu hg. S.G. Hall, *Melito of Sardis, On Pascha*, Oxford 1979, S. xxiv-xxvi.
[5] Euseb, *H E.* V, 24, 13.
[6] Euseb, *H.E.* V, 24, 6.

VII

Heterodoxie, dass Viktor die sich widersetzenden Kirchen aus der Gemeinschaft ausschloss: ὡς ἂν ἑτεροδοξούσας [7]. Die Frage könnte sich ergeben, ob die Apostel zwar einen einheitlichen Glauben aber unterschiedliche Bräuche den von ihnen begründeten Kirchen überlieferten. Irenäus sagt dies nicht ausdrücklich. In dem von Euseb zitierten Teil seines Briefes schreibt er, dass Polykarp [das quartadezimanische Passahfest] zusammen mit dem Herrenjünger Johannes und den anderen ihm bekannten Aposteln gefeiert hatte [8], während Aniket von Rom der Gewohnheit der Presbyter, die vor ihm waren, folgen zu müssen meinte [9], sowie auch dass die Mannigfaltigkeit der Bräuche bezüglich der Fastenzeit schon lange vor seiner eigenen Zeit entstanden war. Er schreibt aber die Verantwortung für diese Mannigfaltigkeit einem Mangel an Genauigkeit bei den Vorgängern zu [10]. So versucht er nicht, einen Streitpunkt daraus zu machen, ob die eine oder die andere Überlieferung als apostolisch zu bezeichnen sei [11], sondern mahnt, dass man trotz des Unterschieds den Frieden bewahren sollte.

In der Rahmenerzählung Eusebs wird die Frage der Apostolizität hervorgehoben. Die quartadezimanische Praxis beschreibt er als

---

[7] Euseb, *H.E.* V, 24, 9.
[8] Euseb, *H.E.* V, 24, 16. Irenäus spricht nur von τηρεῖν und μὴ τηρεῖν. Nach dem Zusammenhang in der Rahmenerzählung Eusebs zu beurteilen, ist τὴν ἡμέραν bzw. τὴν ἡμέραν τῆς τεσσαρεσκαιδεκάτης τοῦ πάσχα, wie im Brief des Polykrates, V, 24, 6, als Objekt zu τηρεῖν zu ergänzen; vgl. auch den Anfang des ersten Zitats aus dem Irenäusbrief (Euseb, *H.E.* V, 24, 12): οὐδὲ γὰρ μόνον περὶ τῆς ἡμέρας ἐστὶν ἡ ἀμφισβήτησις. Nach einer anderen Deutung der Worte des Irenäus war es das vorösterliche Fasten, welches Polykarp gehalten, Anicet aber nicht gehalten hatte; vgl. von Campenhausen, *art. cit.*
[9] Euseb, *H.E.* V, 24, 16.
[10] Euseb, *H.E.* V, 24, 12-13: καὶ τοιαύτη μὲν ποικιλία τῶν ἐπιτηρούντων οὐ νῦν ἐφ᾽ ἡμῶν γεγονυῖα, ἀλλὰ καὶ πολὺ πρότερον ἐπὶ τῶν πρὸ ἡμῶν, τῶν παρὰ τὸ ἀκριβές, ὡς εἰκός, κρατούντων τὴν καθ᾽ ἁπλότητα καὶ ἰδιωτισμὸν συνήθειαν εἰς τὸ μετέπειτα πεποιηκότων. Diesen nicht ganz leichten Satz übersetzt von Campenhausen: « Und diese Unterschiede zwischen denen, die 'die Fasten' halten, sind nicht erst jetzt zu unserer Zeit aufgekommen, sondern schon viel eher unter den Früheren, die offenbar ohne besondere Sorgfalt nach ihrer Einfalt und 'lokalen' Besonderung die 'jeweilige' Gewohnheit festhielten und für die folgenden 'Generationen' begründeten » (*art. cit.*, S. 305-6; vgl. auch S. 306 Anm. 16 und 18).
[11] Vgl. auch Eusebs Zusammenfassung des Briefes, *H.E.* V, 24, 11: ὡς μὴ ἀποκόπτοι ὅλας ἐκκλησίας θεοῦ ἀρχαίου ἔθους παράδοσιν ἐπιτηρούσας. Polykrates selbst, der behauptet, dass Philippus und seine Töchter, Johannes, der am Brust des Herrn lag, Polykarp, und verschiedene andere den vierzehnten Tag beobachteten, spricht nicht von einer apostolischen Überlieferung, sondern nur von der Überlieferung seiner eigenen Verwandten, von denen sieben Bischöfe waren.

VII

aus einer älteren Überlieferung herrührend[12], die Sitte aber, dass man erst am Tage der Auferstehung die Fastenzeit beende, schreibt er einer apostolischen Überlieferung zu[13]. Euseb erwähnt auch, dass die versammelten Bischöfe Palästinas in ihrem Brief die Überlieferung, welche sie bezüglich des Passahs durch Sukzession von den Aposteln erhalten hatten, ausführlich behandelten[14]. Die Friedfertigkeit des Irenäus blieb nicht ohne Nachwirkung. In der zweiten Hälfte dieses Beitrags werde ich einige spätere Äusserungen zum selben Thema erwähnen. Denselben Grundssatz wie Irenäus, dass man nicht wegen Unterschieden in den überlieferten Bräuchen die Kirchengemeinschaft auflösen sollte, wiederholte Firmilian, Bischof von Cäsarea in Kappadozien in einem Brief, den er an Cyprian zur Zeit des Streits über die Ketzertaufe richtete. Er behauptet, dass es in den verschiedenen Provinzen viele Unterschiede gibt, ohne dass man deswegen die Einheit der katholischen Kirche gespalten habe[15]. Interessant ist es, dass er seine Ablehnung der Apostolizität der römischen Praxis dadurch unterstützt, dass er sich auf die Unterschiede zwischen Rom und Jerusalem beruft. Dass man nicht in jeder Hinsicht in Rom die ursprünglichen Überlieferungen bewahre, werde dadurch bewiesen, dass bezüglich des Osterfestes und vieler anderer religiöser Bräuche nicht alles dort in gleicher Weise wie in Jerusalem beobachtet werde[16].

Dieses Argument wird nicht in den erhaltenen Briefen Cyprians vorweggenommen, während Firmilian sonst viele Aussagen Cyprians wiederholt. So verneinen beide, dass die römische Praxis, bekehrte Häretiker ohne Taufe aufzunehmen, auf apostolische Überlieferung

---

[12] Euseb, *H.E.* V, 23, 1: ὡς ἐκ παραδόσεως ἀρχαιοτέρας; vgl. auch V, 24, 1.
[13] Euseb, *H.E.* V, 23, 1: ἐξ ἀποστολικῆς παραδόσεως. In dieser und gewissen anderen Hinsichten stellt Euseb den Tatbestand falsch dar (nach B. Lohse, *Das Passafest der Quartadecimaner*, Gütersloh 1953, S. 134). R. M. Grant, *Eusebius as Church Historian*, Oxford 1980, S. 166-167, erwägt die These, dass Euseb seinen Bericht über den Osterstreit nach dem Konzil von Nicäa dahin gehend änderte, dass er die Einigkeit der nichtasiatischen Kirchen auf eine Weise betonte, die der Wahrheit nicht entsprach.
[14] Euseb, *H.E.* V, 25, 1: περὶ τῆς κατελθούσης εἰς αὐτοὺς ἐκ διαδοχῆς τῶν ἀποστόλων περὶ τοῦ πάσχα παραδόσεως πλεῖστα διειληφότες.
[15] Cyprian, *ep.* 75, 6: «in ceteris quoque plurimis prouinciis multa pro locorum et hominum diuersitate uariantur, nec tamen propter hoc ab ecclesiae catholicae pace atque unitate aliquando discessum est».
[16] Ebda: «eos autem qui Romae sunt non ea in omnibus obseruare quae sint ab origine tradita et frustra apostolorum auctoritatem praetendere scire quis etiam inde potest, quod circa celebrandos dies Paschae et circa multa alia diuinae rei sacramenta uideat esse apud illos aliquas diuersitates nec obseruari illic omnia aequaliter quae Hierosolymis obseruantur».

beruhen könne. Die Apostel können zu dieser Frage keine Regel festgelegt haben, weil das Problem der von Ketzern getauften Konvertiten damals noch nicht existierte [17]. Sie ziehen es vor, diese Überlieferung als menschliche Überlieferung bzw. als eine Sitte zu bezeichnen, die man am liebsten aufgeben sollte [18]. Als apostolische Überlieferung sehen sie dagegen das Prinzip, dass es nur *eine* Taufe und *eine* Kirche geben könne, an. Dadurch werde die eigene Sitte, bekehrte Häretiker zu taufen, als richtig erwiesen. Cyprian mahnt zur Rückkehr zur Quelle der Überlieferung [19], während Firmilian behauptet, selbst die 'Sitte der Wahrheit' vom Anfang an bewahrt zu haben [20]. Man müsse aber auch diejenigen respektieren, die es nicht über sich bringen können, die andere Sitte abzulegen [21].

Es wäre interessant zu wissen, woher Firmilian sich über die unterschiedlichen Bräuche in Rom und Jerusalem informiert hatte. Hat er Einzelheiten über den Osterstreit gewusst? [22]. Wurden solche Unterschiede schon zur Zeit jenes Streites erwähnt? [23].

---

[17] Cyprian, *ep.* 75, 5; 74, 1-2.
[18] Cyprian, *ep.* 75, 6; 74, 3: « humana traditio »; 75, 19: « quis tam uanus sit ut ueritati consuetudinem praeferat...? »; 74, 9: « consuetudo sine ueritate uetustas erroris est »; 73, 13: « frustra quidam ... consuetudinem nobis opponunt »; 73, 23: « non tamen quia aliquando erratum est, ideo semper errandum est ».
[19] Cyprian, *ep.* 74, 10-11: « si ad diuinae traditionis caput et originem reuertamur »; « ad originem dominicam et ad euangelicam adque apostolicam traditionem reuertamur »; 73, 13, 15: « ad euangelicam auctoritatem adque ad apostolicam traditionem ... reuertamur ».
[20] Cyprian, *ep.* 75, 19: « ceterum nos ... consuetudini Romanorum consuetudinem sed ueritatis opponimus, ab initio hoc tenentes quod a Christo et ab apostolis traditum est, nec meminimus hoc apud nos aliquando coepisse... ».
[21] Cyprian, *ep.* 72, 3; 73, 26.
[22] Bei seinen Besuchen in Judäa (Euseb, *H.E.* VI, 27, 1) hätte er mündliche Berichte erhalten oder die Briefsammlungen in den dortigen Bibliotheken einsehen können. Nach der Meinung von P. Nautin, *op. cit.*, S. 87-9, gehörten die von Euseb erwähnten bzw. zitierten Briefe zwei Sammlungen an, die Polykrates und seine kleinasiatischen Gegner nach Jerusalem sandten. Nautin denkt, dass der Brief der palästinensischen Bischöfe an diese Gegner des Polykrates (nicht, wie sonst angenommen wird, an Viktor von Rom) gerichtet war. Es hätten aber auf verschiedene Weise solche Briefsammlungen eine weitere Verbreitung finden können. Die palästinensischen Bischöfe selbst geben im zitierten Teil ihres Briefes Anweisungen, dass Abschriften an alle Gemeinden verschickt werden sollen. Der Brief des Irenäus an Viktor war noch im achten Jahrhundert bekannt; vgl. M. Richard, *La lettre de saint Irénée au pape Victor*, in *Zeitschrift für die neutestamentliche Wissenschaft* 56 (1965) 261 und 274.
[23] Abgesehen von den von Irenäus beschriebenen Unterschieden bezüglich der Fastenzeit und den von Apollinaris und Clemens erwähnten Auseinandersetzungen bezüglich der Chronologie der Evangelienberichte, ist est kaum anzunehmen, dass alle nichtquartadezimanischen Christen zur Zeit des Osterstreits das Fest am selben Tag feierten. Nach der These von Karl Holl, *Ein Bruchstück aus einem bisher unbekannten Brief des Epiphanius*, in *Gesammelte*

Die anderen Äusserungen zur Mannigfaltigkeit der christlichen Bräuche, die ich hier anführen werde, nehmen ausdrücklich Bezug auf den von Euseb zitierten Brief des Irenäus.

Der Kirchenhistoriker Sokrates bringt eine sehr interessante Erörterung der unterschiedlichen christlichen Bräuche in Anschluss an seinen Bericht über den sogenannten 'indifferenten Kanon' der Novatianer[24]. Er erzählt, wie eine Versammlung der novatianischen Bischöfe diesen Kanon beschlossen hatte, wonach ein Unterschied bezüglich des Passahfestes kein genügender Grund zur Kirchentrennung sei[25]. Dieses Urteil wird in dem Kanon dadurch begründet, dass auch die Alten, die den Aposteln nah waren, trotz Uneinigkeit über die Feier des Passahs miteinander Gemeinschaft hielten[26]. In seiner Behandlung der Passahbräuche erwähnt Sokrates die Vorgänge zur Zeit Viktors und den Brief des Irenäus[27], sowie den Brief Konstantins, in dem er die Beschlüsse des nizänischen Konzils über die Feier des Osterfestes berichtete[28].

Obwohl nach Sokrates die Quartadezimaner sich auf eine Überlieferung des Apostels Johannes, die Römer aber und die anderen westlichen Kirchen sich auf eine Überlieferung der Apostel Petrus und Paulus beriefen, behauptet er, dass weder die einen noch die

---

Aufsätze zur Kirchengeschichte II, Tübingen 1928, S. 214-216 (mit der M. Richard, *La Question pascale au IIe siècle*, in *L'Orient syrien* 6 (1961) 184-188, und W. Huber, *Passa und Ostern*, Berlin 1969, S. 49-55, übereinstimmen) wurde die Ostersonntagsfeier zuerst nach dem zweiten jüdischen Krieg in der neuen heidenchristlichen Gemeinde Jerusalems eingeführt. Wie aus dem von Euseb zitierten Teil des Briefes der palästinensischen Bischöfe hervorgeht, pflegten diese, Briefe mit denjenigen in Alexandrien zu wechseln, um eine Übereinstimmung bezüglich des Tags zu erzielen (*H.E.* V, 25). Als man in Rom und Alexandrien Ostertafeln herstellte, unterschieden sie sich in der Weise von einander, dass der Ostersonntag in Alexandrien nicht vor dem 15ten Tag des Mondmonats, in Rom aber nicht vor dem 16ten Tag fallen darf; vgl. Holl, *art. cit.*, S. 218-9, Huber, *op. cit.*, S. 52-3; E. Schwartz, *Christliche und jüdische Ostertafeln*, in *Abhandlungen der K. Gesellschaft der Wissenschaften zu Göttingen*, Philol.-Hist. Kl., N.F. 8, 6 (1905) S. 8-9 und 30-31.

[24] *H.E.* V, 21-22 (hg. W. Bright, Oxford 1878, S. 235-244).

[25] *H.E.* V, 21, hg. Bright, S. 236: μὴ ἀξιόλογον εἶναι αἰτίαν πρὸς χωρισμὸν τῆς ἐκκλησίας τὴν διαφωνίαν τῆς ἑορτῆς. Zu dieser Synode vgl. W. Huber, *op. cit.*, S. 80; H. J. Vogt, *Coetus Sanctorum: Der Kirchenbegriff des Novatian und die Geschichte seiner Sonderkirche*, Bonn 1968, S. 245.

[26] Hg. Bright, S. 236: καὶ γὰρ τοὺς ἀρχαίους καὶ τοὺς ἐγγὺς τῶν ἀποστόλων, διαφωνοῦντας περὶ ταύτης τῆς ἑορτῆς κοινωνεῖν τε ἀλλήλοις, καὶ μηδαμῶς διαφέρεσθαι.

[27] Er bringt eine Zusammenfassung des Briefs und einen Hinweis auf seine Quelle in der Kirchengeschichte Eusebs (*H.E.* V, 22, hg. Bright, S. 238).

[28] Hg. Bright, S. 238-9; zu den hier von Sokrates skizzierten Kontroversen über das Osterfest, die dem Konzil vorausgingen, vgl. F. Daunoy, *La question pascale au concile de Nicée*, in *Échos d'Orient* 24 (1925) 428 ff.

anderen einen schriftlichen Beweis erbringen können[29]. Nach seiner eigenen Meinung haben die Apostel selbst keine Regel über Ostern und die anderen christlichen Feste hinterlassen. Weil aber die Menschen sich zur Zeit der Feste gern entspannen, sind bei den verschiedenen Christen in den einzelnen Gegenden verschiedene Sitten und Bräuche durch die Gewohnheit entstanden[30].

Diejenigen, welche denselben Glauben halten, unterscheiden sich hinsichtlich der Sitten[31]. Er bringt eine Liste mit reichlichen Beispielen solcher Sittenunterschiede, welche unter anderem das vorösterliche Fasten, die Zeiten und die Ordnung des Gottesdienstes, das klerikale Zölibat und die Bussdisziplin betreffen. Er hält die jeweiligen Kirchenleiter verantwortlich für die Einführung der unterschiedlichen Bräuche. Dadurch, dass deren Nachfolger solche Bräuche als Regel weitergaben, sind sie zu Überlieferungen geworden[32]. Es entstanden aber schon im apostolischen Zeitalter viele Unterschiede bezüglich solcher Bräuche, was den Aposteln selbst nicht unbekannt war[33]. Es ist ein wichtiges Anliegen des Sokrates zu zeigen, dass die Apostel die Christen vom Joch der Beobachtung von Zeremonien, Tagen und Speisevorschriften sowie der Streitigkeiten darüber befreien wollten.

In einem entsprechenden Abschnitt in der Kirchengeschichte des Sozomenos[34] wird wieder der Entschluss, trotz unterschiedlicher Bräuche bei Übereinstimmung in den Hauptpunkten des Glaubens die Kirchengemeinschaft zu bewahren, als eine sehr weise Lösung gelobt. Sozomenos schreibt diese Lösung des Osterstreites irrigerweise den Parteien um Viktor und Polykarp zu[35], bejaht sie aber umso kräftiger[36]. Es ist nicht möglich, so schreibt er, dieselben Überlieferungen in allen Kirchen zu finden, wenngleich sie desselben Glaubens sind[37]. Nachdem er Beispiele zitiert hat, schliesst er mit der Bemerkung, dass diejenigen, die mit verschiedenen Bräuchen aufgewachsen sind, es für sündhaft halten, diese aufzugeben. Dazu

---

[29] Hg. Bright, S. 239.
[30] Hg. Bright, S. 238.
[31] Hg. Bright, S. 240.
[32] Hg. Bright, S. 242.
[33] Hg. Bright, S. 242; er zitiert den Brief des apostolischen Konzils aus der Apostelgeschichte 15, 23.
[34] *H.E.* VII, 18-19, hg. J. Bidez, GCS 50, S. 327-332.
[35] Derselbe Fehler findet sich schon bei Epiphanius, *Panarion, haer.* 70, 9, hg. K. Holl, GCS *Epiphanius* III, S. 242.15.
[36] *H.E.* VII, 19, 1, hg. Bidez, S. 330.
[37] *H.E.* VII, 19, 2, hg. Bidez, S. 330.

VII

werden sie durch Ehrfurcht vor den Stiftern dieser Überlieferungen oder deren Nachfolgern bestimmt [38].

Wir haben Beispiele für einen sicheren oder wahrscheinlichen Einfluss des Briefes des Irenäus bei Firmilian, den novatianischen Bischöfen, Sokrates und Sozomenos bemerkt — und, nicht zu vergessen, auch bei Euseb, der selbst den Brief mit Zustimmung zitiert [39]. Die Bejahung des Grundsatzes, dass man bei gemeinsamem Glauben eine abweichende Osterpraxis nicht als Grund der Kirchentrennung ansehen sollte, ist bei den drei Kirchenhistorikern insofern überraschend, als sie selbst die römische Osterpraxis gegen judaisierende Kritiker unterstützten und mit dem Versuch des nizänischen Konzils, eine einheitliche Osterfeier einzuführen, übereinstimmten [40]. In der Tat, das Argument, dass Bräuche und Feste für Christen weniger wichtig als die Einheit der Kirche sind, ist zweischneidig. Man kann es benutzen, sowohl um Einheit in Vielfalt zu empfehlen wie auch um eine widerstrebende Minderheit zu mahnen, ihre eigenen Bräuche aufzugeben und sich der Mehrheit anzuschliessen [41]. Die Feststellung, dass Christen vom Joch des jüdischen Zeremonialgesetzes frei und dass solche Bräuche nur Schatten und Abbilder sind, geht auf das Neue Testament zurück [42], aber Sokrates zeigt in seiner Behauptung dieses Prinzips vor allem den Einfluss des Origenes, den er auch ausdrücklich zitiert [43]. Auch Euseb in seiner

---

[38] H.E. VII, 19, 12, hg. Bidez, S. 332.

[39] Er lobt Irenäus als einen Friedenstifter H.E. V, 24, 18.

[40] Vgl. Euseb, Vita Constantini III, 5; III, 14; III, 16-20 (den Brief Konstantins) und das Fragment seiner Konstantin gewidmeten Schrift De Solemnitate Paschali 8 (PG 24, 701C-704A), wo er erzählt, dass die Bischöfe des Ostens, um Einheit zu erzielen, nachgaben; Sokrates, H.E. V, 22, hg. Bright, S. 239; I, 8, S. 12-13; Sozomen, H.E. I, 16, hg. Bidez, S. 36.1ff. Während Konstantin in seinem Brief an die Kirchen (Euseb, Vita Constantini III, 18) und Sokrates (H.E. V, 22, S. 237) sich gegen die Nachahmung der Sitte der Juden richten, versucht Sozomen zu zeigen, dass die judaisierenden Christen doch nicht der Praxis der alten Juden folgen (H.E. VII, 18, 7-10, S. 328.9-26; vgl. Anatolius in Euseb, H.E. VII, 32, 16-18).

[41] So z.B. Chrysostomus, In eos qui Pascha ieiunant. Adversus Judaeos III (PG 48, 861 ff.): vgl. 3 (864), 5 (869): die Eintracht ist wichtiger als die Beobachtung von Tagen; 4 (866-7): Paulus bzw. Christus befreite den Christen von solcher Beobachtung; 6 (871): οὐδὲ γὰρ ἡ Ἐκκλησία χρόνων ἀκρίβειαν οἶδεν.

[42] Sokrates zitiert u.a. Gal. 4, 10; 4, 21; 5, 1; 5, 13; Col. 2, 16-17 (H.E. V, 22, S. 237, vgl. auch S. 244); vgl. Origenes, Contra Celsum II, 2-3, hg. P. Koetschau, GCS Origenes I, S. 128.17 ff., mit Zitaten von Hbr. 8, 5; 10, 1; Col. 2, 16-17 und Gal. 4, 21-24; Hom. Lev. X.2, hg. W. A. Baehrens, GCS Origenes VI, S. 443.18-24, mit Zitaten von Hbr. 8,5; 1 Cor. 5, 7 und Gal. 4, 9-10; Comm. ser. Mt. 79, hg. E. Klostermann, GCS Origenes XI, S. 189.15 ff., gegen diejenigen, die das jüdische Passah deswegen feiern wollen, weil Jesus dies tat.

[43] H.E. V, 22, S. 241.

VII

De Solemnitate Paschali folgt Origenes in seiner geistigen Auslegung der Bedeutung des Passahfestes und in der noch weiter zurückreichenden Anschauung, dass der wahre Christ immer Passah feiern sollte[44]. Die Frage, ob die Apostel unterschiedliche Regeln überliefert haben, wird von Cyprian und Firmilian bezüglich der Ketzertaufe und von Sokrates bezüglich des Osterfestes ausdrücklich verneint. Euseb und Sozomenos bestreiten die Ansprüche der beiden Parteien im Osterfeststreit nicht, was aber die unterschiedlichen Bräuche im allgemeinen angeht, so neigt Sozomenos, ähnlich wie Sokrates und schon Irenäus selbst, dazu, sie als menschliche, d.h. nichtapostolische Überlieferungen anzusehen.

Die Briefe Cyprians über die Ketzertaufe hat Augustin in seiner *De Baptismo contra Donatistas* besprochen. Die Donatisten beriefen sich auf Cyprians Ablehnung der schismatischen Taufe, während Augustin hervorhob, dass Cyprian die Liebe, den Frieden und die Einheit der Kirche an die erste Stelle setzte[45]. Damals, schreibt er, wurde der Meinungsunterschied geduldet, weil noch kein Beschluss eines allgemeinen Konzils vorlag[46]. Er hält aber die Gewohnheit, bekehrte Ketzer ohne Taufe aufzunehmen, für eine apostolische Überlieferung[47]. Das, woran die ganze Kirche immer festgehalten hat, so schreibt er, wird mit Recht als eine apostolische Überlieferung angesehen[48]. Viele Sitten der universalen Kirche werden als Vorschriften der Apostel angesehen, obwohl sie weder in ihren Schriften noch durch spätere Konzile festgelegt sind[49].

---

[44] *De Solemnitate Paschali* 1-2, 7 (PG 24, 694A-696C, 701AB); vgl. Origenes, *Contra Celsum* VIII, 22, GCS *Origenes* II, S. 239.20-24, zusammen mit den von H. Chadwick, *Origen: Contra Celsum*, Cambridge 1953, S. 467 Anm. 5 aus Clemens Alexandrinus und Philo zitierten Parallelstellen; Origenes, *Comm. ser. Mt.* 79, GCS *Origenes* XI, 189.15 ff.; *Comm. Jn.* X, 13 ff., hg. E. Preuschen, GCS *Origenes* IV S. 183.7 ff. Ähnliches findet sich im Galaterbriefkommentar II, 5 zu *Gal.* 4, 10-11 des Hieronymus, der offensichtlich hier die verlorene Erklärung des Origenes ausschöpft (PL 26, 377A-378C: « omnes dies aequales esse »). Vgl. auch W. Rordorf, *Der Sonntag*, Zürich 1962, S. 104.
[45] Z. B. *De Baptismo* II, 1, 2; II, 7, 12; III, 1, 1; V, 4, 4; V, 17, 22; V, 25, 36, hg. M. Petschenig, CSEL 51, 176.24 ff., 186.25-26, 196.22 ff., 266.14-15, 280.5 ff., 292.4-7.
[46] *Op. cit.* IV, 9, 12; V, 25, 36; VII, 54, 103, CSEL, 51, 236.12-16, 292, 7-9, 374.24-375.4.
[47] *Op. cit.* II, 7, 12, vgl. II, 8, 13; II, 9, 14; IV, 6, 9; V, 23, 31, CSEL 51, 186.27 ff., 188.27 f., 189.19, 232.7-9, 289. 11-14.
[48] « Quod uniuersa tenet ecclesia nec conciliis institutum, sed semper retentum est, non nisi auctoritate apostolica traditum rectissime creditur », *op. cit.* IV, 24, 31, CSEL 51, 259.2-4.
[49] *Op. cit.* II, 7, 12; V, 23, 31, CSEL 51, 187.4-6, 289.13-16.

VII

Anders als die früheren hier behandelten Kirchenväter macht
Augustin in seiner Behandlung der verschiedenen kirchlichen Sitten
und Bräuche in den verschiedenen Gegenden in seiner *Epistula* 54
einen festen Unterschied zwischen den nur örtlichen Gewohnheiten
und denjenigen der universalen Kirche [50]. Christus hat uns seinem
sanftem Joch unterworfen und sein neues Volk an nur wenige
Sakramente gebunden [51]. Man sollte an solchen Bräuchen, die in der
Schrift empfohlen oder in der ganzen Welt überliefert, d.h. von den
Aposteln selbst oder von allgemeinen Konzilen verordnet sind, fest-
halten [52]. Was die örtlichen Bräuche angeht, so ist es besser, die
Unterschiede zu dulden und sich anzupassen, als Anstoss oder
Streitigkeiten zu erregen [53].

Schliessen wir mit einem Vergleich der griechischen Aussagen
zum Osterstreit und der lateinischen Aussagen zum Streit über die
Ketzertaufe. Die Griechen, Irenäus, Sokrates und Sozomenos, bringen
interessante Überlegungen zur Entstehung der unterschiedlichen
Sitten bzw. Überlieferungen in den verschiedenen Kirchen. Sie
behaupten nicht ausdrücklich, dass die eigene Überlieferung apostolisch, diejenige der Gegner aber dies nicht sei [54]. Es gibt eine wichtige
Strömung, die verneint, dass die Apostel Regeln über Bräuche
hinterlassen wollten. Bei den Lateinern, Cyprian und Augustin,
finden sich wichtige Aussagen zu dem Grundsatz, nach dem die
Entscheidung einer strittigen Frage zu treffen sei. Cyprian ruft zur
Rückkehr zur Quelle der Überlieferung in der Heiligen Schrift,
Augustin versucht festzustellen, nach welchen Kriterien Bräuche als
apostolisch bezeichnet werden dürfen.

---

[50] Dieser Brief wird von Professor François Decret in seinem Beitrag
behandelt, siehe unten S. 407-411.

[51] *Ep.* 54, 1, 1, hg. A. Goldbacher, CSEL 34, 159.5-9.

[52] *Op. cit.* 54, 1, 1, vgl. *ep.* 55, 19, 35, und, zum christlichen Passahfest,
ep. 54, 9, 16 und 15, 27, CSEL 34, 159.10-160.3, 210.2-4, 187.1 ff., 200.8-18. In
ähnlicher Weise beruft er sich schon in *De Baptismo* VII, 1, 1, CSEL 51, 341.
14-18 auf die « prisca consuetudo » und « concilii plenarii auctoritas », erkennt
aber in II, 3, 4, CSEL 51, 178.11 ff., der Heiligen Schrift die höchste Autorität an.

[53] *Ep.* 54, 2 ,2 ff., CSEL 51, 160 ff.; so schon in dem von Augustin
zitierten Rat des Ambrosius, 2, 3, CSEL 51, 161.1 ff.

[54] Die von Epiphanius beschriebenen Audianer konnten aber für ihre
Osterpraxis auf eine schriftliche Regel der Apostel hinweisen; *Panarion, haer.*
70, 10, GCS *Epiphanius* III, S. 242.23 ff.; vgl. *Didaskalia* 21.

VIII

DIE BEKEHRUNG DERJENIGEN, DIE SCHON CHRISTEN SIND [1]

Das Erlebnis der Bekehrung steht so sehr im Mittelpunkt des christlichen Lebens, dass sich für diejenigen, die von Kindesbeinen an Christen sind, ein Problem ergibt. Sollen sie ohne die Erfahrung der Bekehrung durchs Leben gehen oder gibt es für sie etwas Vergleichbares?

Um eine Antwort auf diese Frage zu finden, ist es zunächst nötig, sich darüber zu vergewissern, welche Arten von Bekehrungserfahrung es gibt. Im Mittelpunkt der Bekehrung steht die Übertragung der Verbundenheit von einer Religion zu einer anderen. Der Heide, der zum Christentum übertritt, verwirft den Kult der heidnischen Götter und gibt sich dem Dienst des christlichen Gottes hin. Damit in Zusammenhang stehen zwei Elemente, ein verstandesmässiges und ein ethisches. Der Hinzutretende nimmt die Wahrheit der christlichen Lehre an und unternimmt es, nach ihr zu leben. Beides wird in Justins Beschreibung der Taufe (I *Apol.* 61) zum Ausdruck gebracht. Die Taufkandidaten werden beschrieben als solche, « die sich überzeugt haben und glauben, dass das, was wir lehren und sagen, wahr ist und versprechen, dass sie dementsprechend leben können ». Im Ritus der Taufe, die Erleuchtung oder φωτισμός genannt wird, wie Justin berichtet, erhält der Konvertit Erleuchtung, seine Sünden werden vergeben und er wird zu einem neuen Leben geboren.

---

1. Diese Ausführungen wurden beim *XV Incontro di Studiosi dell'Antichità Cristiana* in Rom am 8. Mai 1986 vorgetragen. Ich bin den Professoren Kannengiesser und Studer für Hinweise in der Diskussion dankbar. Sie werden in den Anmerkungen 2, 4 und 10 berücksichtigt.

VIII

In den Beschreibungen einzelner Bekehrungen mag der eine oder der andere Zug die Oberhand haben. In Justins Schilderung seiner eigenen Bekehrung im *Dial.* 8 wird die verstandesmässige Seite in der Annahme des Christentums zusammen mit der Entzündung einer Liebesglut in seiner Seele betont. Schon vor der Bekehrung war es ihm in seinem philosophischen Studieren auf die Gotteserkenntnis angekommen. Nichts davon ist erkennbar, dass es etwa das Gewicht von Sünden gewesen sei, von denen er in der Bekehrung Befreiung gefunden habe. Cyprian gibt in seinem Werk *An Donatus* (3-4) ein ganz anderes Bild von seiner Bekehrung. Er beschreibt sich als einen, der in die schlechten Gepflogenheiten seines früheren Lebens verstrickt und durch die Taufe zu einem neuen Leben der Tugend geboren war, einem Leben, das er zuvor nicht für möglich gehalten hätte. Die Erleuchtung mit dem Geist bei der Taufe bewirkt bei ihm viel mehr eine Änderung des Lebenswandels als eine neue Dimension der Erkenntnis.[2] Ein zweiter Unterschied zwischen Justin und Cyprian liegt in dem Zeitpunkt der neuen Erfahrung. Cyprian beschreibt den Augenblick der Taufe, Justin dagegen den Zeitpunkt der geistigen Überzeugung durch das Christentum — er ist zugleich der Höhepunkt seines philosophischen Suchens und fand ohne Zweifel nach einer angemessenen Zeit in der Taufe als einer weiteren Stufe seiner christlichen Entwicklung seine Fortsetzung.

Im Heidentum ist das Phänomen der Bekehrung viel mehr im philosophischen als im religiösen Bereich bekannt. In keinem von beiden war die Ableugnung einer etwaigen früheren Zugehörigkeit gefordert. Wohl aber brachte die philosophische wie die christliche Bindung es mit sich, dass eine geistige Annahme und eine sittliche Erneuerung erforderlich waren. Anders als bei den Christen brauchte der Philosophenjünger keine Aufnahmezeremonie durchzumachen, wohl aber konnte er seine Bekehrung wie die Christen als das Erfahrnis eines Augenblicks, in dem er von der Dunkelheit des Irrtums

---

[2] Bei der Diskussion wies Professor Studer auf die Möglichkeit hin, dass ein Unterschied im Taufritus den Unterschied in der Einstellung von Justin und Cyprian bestimmt haben könnte. Justins Beschreibung der Taufe ist aber nur summarisch, sodass man keine Sicherheit über die Einzelheiten des ihm bekannten Taufritus gewinnen kann. Es mögen aber vielleicht zeitliche und örtliche Unterschiede in der Taufauffassung zu dieser Verschiedenheit beigetragen haben. Nach Karl Baus, *Von der Urgemeinde zur frühchristlichen Grosskirche* [Handbuch der Kirchengeschichte I], Freiburg 1963, S. 320, kam im Katechumenat Nordafrikas der moralisch-asketischen Erziehung des Bewerber das grössere Gewicht gegenüber der Einführung in das Glaubenswissen zu. Zu der Frage der Entwicklung des Taufritus und der Taufauffassung vgl. hg. K.F. Müller und W. Blankenburg, *Leiturgia*, Bnd. 5: *Der Taufgottesdienst*, Kassel 1970.

und der Sünde erwacht war, ansehen — oder aber er konnte sie als
Ergebnis eines längeren und wiederholten Prozesses der Erneuerung
und Veränderung erleben.[3]
    Wie steht es denn nun um den Christen, der schon von christli-
chen Eltern abstammte und für den also kein Bekehrungserlebnis
möglich war? Gab es für ihn Ersatzerfahrungen? Gewiss, er konnte
in schwere Sünde verfallen und zu Busse genötigt sein — ein Prozess,
der demjenigen der sittlichen Bekehrung, die sich in Reue, Vergebung
und Beginn eines neuen Lebens in der Taufe ereignet, jedenfalls
ähnlich war.[4] Mir ist allerdings unbekannt, dass solche Busse bei
als Christen Geborenen häufiger war als bei erwachsenen Konvertiten. Eine andere Möglichkeit war der Übertritt zu einer häretischen
Sekte — allem Anschein nach haben die Führer der gnostischen Beweg-
ungen im 2. Jahrhundert viele ihrer Konvertiten aus der Grosskirche
herübergezogen.[5] Auch ist wohlbekannt, dass die Bekehrungserfahrung in der Gnosis eine grosse Rolle spielte. So wird sie im *Evangelium
Veritatis* als eine Erleuchtung beschrieben, ähnlich dem Erwachen
aus unruhigem Schlaf oder dem Zustand der Trunkenheit, als eine
Abkehr aus Irrtum und Unwissenheit mit dem Ziele der Rückkehr
zum eigentlichen Sein und zum Vater.
    Beide Vorgänge wären freilich recht extrem. Statt nach der
Taufe in Sünden zu fallen und zur Busse genötigt zu sein, wie es
z.B. im Falle der Kinder des christlichen Propheten Hermas, der,
wie es scheint, seine Kinder getauft, aber nicht vor Sünden bewahrt
hatte, verlangt wurde,[6] legte es sich nahe, die Taufe aufzuschieben,
bis man selbst dazu bereit war, sie als eine Handlung der Hingabe
und Selbstverpflichtung auf sich zu nehmen. Solch ein Aufschub
der Taufe wird von Tertullian in seinem Werk *De bapt.* 18 mit
Nachdruck anempfohlen. Im 4. Jahrhundert, als es einen besonders
starken Zugang von erwachsenen Konvertiten gab, war es auch bei
christlichen Eltern üblich, die Taufe ihrer Kinder aufzuschieben.

---

    [3] Vgl. A.D. Nock, *Conversion*, Oxford 1933, S. 179-186; ders., art. *Bekehrung*
RACh 2 (1954) 107.
    [4] Etwas anders, weil sie nicht als eine einmalige Erfahrung angesehen
wird, ist die innere Reue und Busse, zu der jeder Christ z.B. zu Beginn
der Fastenzeit aufgefordert wird (vgl. dazu die den Beginn der Fastenzeit
anzeigenden Festbriefe des Athanasius an die ägyptischen Kirchen). Der Aufruf
zu einer solchen moralischen Umkehr ist natürlich von der Bibel her wohlbekannt.
    [5] Vgl. G. Bardy, *La Conversion au Christianisme durant les premiers siècles*,
Paris 1949, S. 308 ff. Er zitiert Irenaeus, *Adv. haer.* I, *praef.;* Tertullian, *Praescr.*
4, 1-6; *Adv. Valentinianos* I.
    [6] Hermas, *Vis.* II, 2-3.

Diese Handlungsweise ist uns aus einer Anzahl von berühmten Fällen bekannt, darunter den kappadozischen Vätern, Johannes Chrysostomus, Ambrosius und Hieronymus. Mit dieser Entwicklung hängt die folgende Praxis zusammen: es wurde üblich, die Aufnahme als Katechumene der Kirche von der Vorbereitung zur Taufe zu trennen.[7] Aus Augustins *Bekenntnissen* (I, 11) ist bekannt, dass er schon als Säugling (*ab utero matris meae*) mit dem Ritus der Bezeichnung mit dem Kreuz und des Salzens mit Salz als Katechumene zugelassen worden war,[8] obwohl es seiner Mutter Absicht war, die Taufe selbst aufzuschieben.

Basilius von Caesarea mag als Beispiel für einen Sohn aus einer bekannten und frommen christlichen Familie, der seine Taufe hinausschob und nach empfangener christlichen Erziehung die Erfahrung der Bekehrung als schon Erwachsener hatte, angeführt werden. Er beschreibt die eigene Bekehrung in *ep.* 223 (PG 32, 824) als ein Erwachen aus tiefem Schlaf zu dem wunderbaren Licht der evangelischen Wahrheit. Nachdem er seinen bisherigen Lebensweg bedauert und um Hilfe für die Besserung seines Charakters gebetet hatte, wurde er durch die Anweisungen in den Evangelien, das Eigentum wegzugeben und mit den Hungernden zu teilen, ins Herz getroffen. Nach dem, was sein Bruder Gregor von Nyssa berichtet, fand diese Bekehrung des Basilius unter dem Einfluss seiner älteren Schwester Makrina statt (*Vita Macrinae*, PG 46, 966 C). Sie weist auch auf einen anderen Zug hin, der in den uns bekannten Beispielen des 4. Jahrhunderts sehr geläufig war: die gleichzeitige Bekehrung zur asketischen Lebensweise. Die Entscheidung zur Taufe und zu einem asketischen Leben wurde in manchen Fällen zur selben Zeit getroffen. In anderen Fällen mochte ein Christ, der bereits getauft war, danach die Bekehrung zu einem asketischen Leben erleben. Dieser letztere Fall war bei Antonius gegeben, dessen fromme Kindheit und Bekehrung zur Weggabe seines Eigentums im Alter von etwa achtzehn oder zwanzig Jahren von Athanasius in seinem Leben des Antonius beschrieben wird. Die Erfahrung des Antonius war nach der Beschreibung des Athanasius eine direkte und zur Tat schreitende Antwort auf die Aufforderung der Bibel. Nichts lässt darauf schliessen, dass es in seinem früheren Leben etwas gab, was der Busse oder

---

[7] Vgl. K. Baus u. E. Ewig, *Die Reichskirche nach Konstantin dem Grossen* [Handbuch der Kirchengeschichte II/1], Freiburg 1973, S 304-5; F. van der Meer, *Augustine the Bishop*, London 1961, S. 353 ff.; A. Stenzel, *Die Taufe*, Innsbruck 1958, S. 171 ff.

[8] Vgl. G. Bonner, *St. Augustine of Hippo: Life and Controversies*, London 1963, S. 38-9.

der Leugnung früherer Irrtümer bedurfte. Dagegen ist es bei Basilius so, dass er, obwohl er eigentlich immer Christ gewesen war, seine Bekehrung im Stil einer Busse, moralischen Erneuerung und geistigen Erleuchtung beschreibt. Jeder von beiden zieht dieselbe Folgerung aus demselben biblischen Text (*Mt.* 19, 21), nämlich, dass nur derjenige, der seine Habe verkauft und den Armen gibt, vollkommen werden kann, aber in der Selbstbeschreibung des Basilius wird diese Erkenntnis durch die auch sonst geläufigen Merkmale einer Bekehrung gekennzeichnet.[9]

Viele andere Beispiele für eine Bekehrung zu asketischem Leben im Zuge der von Antonius angefachten Bewegung könnten gegeben werden.[10] Statt dessen kehre ich in die früheren Zeiten zurück, in denen die Mehrzahl der uns bekannten herausragenden Persönlichkeiten als Erwachsene zum Christentum bekehrt wurden. Der bekannteste frühchristliche Schriftsteller, von dem es bezeugt ist, dass er als Christ erzogen wurde und der darum die Gelegenheit der Bekehrung als Erwachsener verfehlt hat, ist Origenes.[11] Euseb berichtet in seiner Beschreibung des Lebens des Origenes über zwei Ereignisse, die als Wendepunkte angesehen werden können (H. E, VI, 2, 2ff. und 12f.; 3, 8ff.), das Erlebnis der Inhaftierung und des Blutopfers seines Vaters, als Origenes sechzehn Jahre alt war, und die eigene, einige Jahre später gefallene Entscheidung, den Unterricht heidnischer Literatur aufzugeben und seine heidnischen Bücher zu verkaufen, um sich ganz dem christlichen katechetischen Unterricht hinzugeben. Das letztere Ereignis mag man als eine Bekehrung zu asketischem Leben beschreiben.[12] Dem ist jedoch hinzuzufügen, dass sein früheres

---

[9] Es überrascht nicht, wenn die Reue über das frühere Leben in einer Selbstbeschreibung eine grössere Rolle spielt als in der Biographie eines Heiligen. Es wäre interessant, der Frage nachzugehen, inwiefern das Auftauchen derselben Motive in Bekehrungsbeschreibungen durch literarische Abhängigkeit verursacht wird. Dabei ist zu beachten, dass nicht nur die Beschreibung sondern auch die Erfahrung selbst durch ein literarisches Vorbild beeinflusst worden sein kann.

[10] Auch im Mittelalter gibt es wichtige Beispiele wie etwa die Bekehrung von Gertrud der Grossen oder von Teresa von Avila.

[11] Die Apologeten, Justin, Tatian und Theophilus berichten, dass sie als Erwachsene bekehrt wurden. Dasselbe scheint auch bei Klemens von Alexandrien und Tertullian der Fall gewesen zu sein, obwohl sie keine diesbezüglichen Berichte hinterlassen haben. Bei Polykarp, der bis zu seinem Tod 86 Jahre lang Christus gedient hatte, und Irenaeus, der Polykarp in seiner Jugend gehört hatte, liegt es nahe zu vermuten, dass sie als Christen erzogen wurden. Falls es stimmt, dass der Vater Marcions Bischof von Sinope war, wird Marcion vermutlich als Christ aufgewachsen sein.

[12] So wird es von P. Nautin bezeichnet, der es nach dem Jahre 211 datiert, *Origène: sa vie et son oeuvre*, Paris 1977, S. 417, vgl. S. 39-41, 363-5.

Leben durch völlige Hingabe an das Christentum bereits gekennzeichnet war. Nach dem Bericht des Euseb (H. E. VI, 2, 6-11; 3, 3-7) zeigte Origenes in seiner Knabenzeit einen Eifer für das Studium der Heiligen Schrift, der über die Massen war, und plagte seinen Vater mit altklugen Fragen über deren Bedeutung; und die Zeit vor dem Verkauf der heidnischen Bücher war durch Tapferkeit, die sich in der Gemeinschaft mit den Märtyrern und dem ununterbrochenen Weitergehen des katechetischen Unterrichts während der Verfolgung ausdrückte, bestimmt.

Es mag daher interessant sein, einen kurzen Blick auf die Bemerkungen des Origenes zum Thema Bekehrung zu werfen, um zu sehen, ob sie auch auf eine Erfahrung wie es seine eigene war, Bezug nehmen. Die Schrift c. *Celsum* wird als Beispiel genommen werden, da Origenes in diesem Werk, durch die Angriffe des Celsus auf die christliche Mission und insbesondere auf den christlichen Appell an Sünder und einfache Menschen dazu veranlasst wird, auf diese Fragen einzugehen. Celsus verspottet die christlichen Lehrer und behauptet, dass sie auf Glauben statt auf Vernunft vertrauen und nur Sünder und ungebildete Leute bekehren wollen. Dagegen verteidigt Origenes die christliche Mission damit, dass er die Konvertiten und die Typen der Bekehrung in verschiedene Kategorien einteilt und mit philosophischen Bekehrungen vergleicht. Während Celsus bezweifelt, dass eine Bekehrung von verstockten Sündern möglich sei, weist Origenes darauf hin, dass sich Beispiele dieser Art nicht nur im Christentum sondern sogar aus den Bekehrungen zur Philosophie erheben lassen.[13] Die christliche Lehre ist sowohl in der Lage, einen Wechsel im Leben derjenigen, die zuvor lax, feige und schlecht waren, zu bewirken, wie auch solche, die bereits ein Gespür für das Gute haben, für sich zu gewinnen (III, 65-8). Ebenso ist das Christentum in der Lage, sowohl die einfachen Geister, die auf Glauben allein vertrauen, wie auch diejenigen, die verstandesmässigen Argumenten nachgehen können, zu bekehren. Die ersteren werden durch ihren Glauben an Belohnungen und Strafen nach dem Tod zur sittlichen Besserung veranlasst.[14] Sie geben durch die Veränderung,

---

[13] Origenes kennt natürlich auch eine moralische Umkehr, die nicht mit der Bekehrung von Heidentum zum Christentum verbunden ist. Das Wort ἐπιστροφή kann sowohl dies bezeichnen, wie auch im Zusammenhang der Bekehrung zum Christentum verwendet werden. Was mit diesem Begriff in *2 Cor.* 3, 16 gemeint wird, erklärt Origenes in *hom. Ex.* XII, 2. Wenn er von Bekehrung spricht, benutzt Origenes auch Worte wie προτρέπειν, μεταβάλλειν, μεταποιεῖν, wie auch μετάνοια, βελτίωσις und διόρθωσις.

[14] Nicht nur die Lehre eines jenseitigen Gerichts sondern auch diejenige, dass Gott alles, was wir sagen, tun und denken, sieht, ist zur sittlichen Besserung der Mehrzahl der Menschen wirksam (IV, 53).

VIII

die sich in ihrem Leben vollzieht, Zeugnis für das Walten der
göttlichen Vorsehung im Erfolg des Evangeliums (I, 9; V, 16).[15]
   In Beantwortung der Aufforderung des Celsus, die Christen
sollten eher dem Verstand als allein dem Glauben folgen, führt
Origenes wieder einen Vergleich mit der Philosophie durch. *De
facto* entscheiden diejenigen, die sich für eine philosophische Schule
im Unterschied zu einer anderen erklären, irrational; sie tun es,
ohne zuvor in eine ins Einzelne gehende Prüfung der Beweisgründe
aller Schulen eingetreten zu sein (I, 10). Viel besser als das Vertrauen
in den menschlichen Begründer einer philosophischen Richtung ist
die Handlung des Christen, der sein Vertrauen auf den höchsten
Gott setzt (I, 11). Origenes betont allerdings, dass es für diejenigen,
die dazu in der Lage sind und die die Gelegenheit dazu haben,
wünschenswert ist, sich von den praktischen Geschäften des Lebens
abzukehren und der Philosophie hinzugeben, damit sie nach rationaler
Durchprüfung mit Vernunft und Weisheit die christlichen Lehren
bejahen können (I, 9-10; I, 13).[16]
   Es ist deutlich, dass der zum Christentum Bekehrte, der zuvor
eine Bekehrung zur Philosophie durchgemacht hatte, ein Mann wie
Justin oder die Konvertiten, die Origenes selbst unter den Adepten
der Philosopie in Alexandrien machte, eine weit weniger dramatische
Bekehrungserfahrung durchlief als ein verstockter Sünder. Ein
solcher wird ein Leben philosophischer Bemühung und sittlicher
Ertüchtigung sowohl vor wie nach der Bekehrung geführt haben,
dies aber als Christ, wie Origenes betont, unter der helfenden Hand
Gottes. Die Seele des Menschen, der tugendhaft leben will, oder
bereits einen Fortschritt gemacht hat oder schon tugendhaft lebt,
wird angefüllt mit oder hat anteil am Geist Gottes (IV, 5).[17] Der

---

[15] Im Gegensatz zu den philosophischen Bekehrungen ist im Falle des
Christentums die schnelle Verbreitung der Mission und die grosse Zahl der
aus sündigem Leben Bekehrten ein Zeichen der göttlichen Kraft; vgl. auch
c. Celsum I, 26-7, I, 43; I, 46; I, 62; II, 29, II, 44; III, 29; III, 68; IV, 4-5; V, 62;
VI, 2; VI, 11; VIII, 43; VIII, 47; *Princ.* IV, 1, 1-2.
[16] Vgl. auch III, 38, wo Origenes sagt, dass der Glaube an Jesus, wie der
Glaube im allgemeinen, in den meisten Fällen sozusagen eine Frage des Glücks
(weil er von der Erziehung abhängt), und nur bei ganz wenigen Menschen
rational durchgeprüft sei.
[17] Die Frage des Zusammenhangs von Geistempfang, Bekehrung und Taufe
bei Origenes wird behandelt von W.-D. Hauschild, *Gottes Geist und der Mensch*,
München 1972, S. 99ff. Er schliesst (S. 105), dass der Gottesgeist nicht durch
die Taufe vermittelt wird, sondern durch den « neuen Lebenswandel, welcher
in der Bekehrung beginnt, in der Taufe von Gott akzeptiert wird und sich
in einem ständigen Prozess sittlicher Bemühungen fortsetzen muss ». Origenes
spricht auch von dem bösen Geist bzw. bösen Geistern, die vor der Bekehrung
dem Menschen innewohnen; vgl. Hauschild, S. 109-113; *hom. Ex* VIII, 4 (GCS

göttliche Logos wurde als ein Arzt zu Sündern gesandt und als ein Lehrer göttlicher Mysterien zu denjenigen, die schon rein sind und nicht mehr sündigen (III, 62). Die Christen rufen Sünder dazu auf, Worte zu hören, die sie lehren, nicht mehr zu sündigen; und diejenigen, die schon Fortschritt machen und durch den Logos gereinigt sind, rufen sie zu Erkenntnis und Verstehen der tieferen geistigen Wahrheiten (III, 59).[18]

Wir haben gesehen: Origenes kennt nicht nur eine dramatische Bekehrungserfahrung, bei der der Wechsel so gross ist, dass völlige Diskontinuität zur Vergangenheit besteht, sondern ebenso die Möglichkeit eines kontinuierlichen geistigen und sittlichen Fortschritts,[19] bei dem die Entscheidung für das Christentum nur eine Stufe darstellt. Die letztere Erfahrung wird wohl in der Mehrzahl der Fälle der Erfahrung desjenigen, der schon als Christ erzogen ist, gemässer sein. Das wirft aber nur indirekt ein Licht auf die Ansicht des Origenes über die Erfahrung derer, die eine christliche Erziehung hatten, und lässt die Frage offen, ob er an eine Art Ersatzbekehrungserfahrung bei ihnen dachte. Es mag jedoch sein, dass wir darüber etwas in seinen Bemerkungen über die Entwicklung des Kindes erfahren. Eine kurze Zusammenfassung über diesen Gegenstand findet sich in einem Papyrusauszug aus Origenes Erklärung von *Rom.* 3, 9-18. Einige unter den Griechen, sagt Origenes, haben gut dargelegt, dass es notwendig ist, dass zur selben Zeit, da die Vernunft (λόγος) ihre volle Entwicklung erzielt, die Sünde auf der Bildfläche erscheint, und dass nur nach einer gewissen Zeit durch Bemühung und Fleiss die Sünde beseitigt wird und Tugend in Erscheinung tritt.[20] Diese Ansicht ist stoisch.[21] Origenes entwickelt

---

VI, 225. 12 ff., 226. 22 ff.). Nach *c. Celsum* V, 57 werden diejenigen, welche an Jesu Auferstehung glauben und beachtenswerte Frucht des Glaubens in einem gesunden Lebenswandel und Umkehr (μεταβολή) aus der Flut der Laster aufzeigen, in ihrer Bekehrung zu Gott (ἐπιστροφή, hier offensichtlich als Prozess verstanden) von helfenden Engeln begleitet.

[18] Es können dies durchaus zwei Stadien in der Entwicklung desselben Konvertiten sein, wie an der eben zitierten Stelle; vgl. auch *hom. Jer.* V, 15 (der wörtliche Sinn der Schrift ist nützlich für das erste Stadium der Entwicklung).

[19] Über die Stadien eines solchen Fortschrittes (προκοπή) vgl. auch III, 71; IV, 16; IV, 64; VI, 2; *hom. Jer.* V, 10 (die moralische Umkehr braucht Zeit), IV, 6 (es gehört Bibelstudium dazu); *com. Ct. prol.* GCS VIII, 79. 5-21; das erste Stadium ist die moralische Besserung, das zweite die Absage zur Welt, das dritte die Schau der Dinge, die unsichtbar und ewig sind, *com. Ct.* I (GCS VIII, 102. 28ff.).

[20] Καὶ Ἑλλήνων δέ τινες οὐ κακῶς ἀπεφήναντο ὅτι ἀναγκαῖόν ἐστιν ἐν τῷ λογικῷ καὶ θνητῷ γένει ἅμα τῇ συμπληρώσει τοῦ λόγου πρότερον ὑποστῆναι τὴν κακίαν, εἶτα χρόνῳ ἐξ ἐπιμελείας καὶ προσοχῆς ταύτην μὲν ἀνασκευάζεσθαι, τὴν δὲ ἀρετὴν ὑφίστασθαι, hg. J. Schérer, *Le Commentaire d'Origène sur Romé. III. 5-V. 7* (Kairo 1957) 136; vgl. 137 Anm. 13.

sie an anderen Stellen in grösserer Ausführlichkeit. Die Freiheit
kleiner Kinder von Leidenschaften wird in seinem Kommentar zu
Mt. 18, 1-6 dargelegt an Hand des Wortes, dass es nötig sei, wie ein
Kind zu werden, um ins Himmelreich einzutreten. Ein Kind, in dem
die Verstandesfähigkeiten (λόγος) noch nicht ausgebildet sind, ist
durch keine Leidenschaften (πάθη) angezogen (*com. Mt.* XIII, 16).[22]
Paulus spricht von dieser vorrationalen Stufe, wenn er sagt, dass
die Sünde ohne das Gesetz tot war — so erklärt Origenes zu *Rom.*
7, 8 (die Stelle ist auf Griechisch in Katenenauszügen erhalten).[23]
Jedermann lebte ohne Gesetz, als er als Kind nicht vom Verstand
bestimmt war. Als aber seine Verstandeskräfte (λόγος) ausgebildet wurden, da wurde er des Gebotes, das ihm sagt, was er tun und was er lassen soll, gewahr, und die Sünde wurde lebendig. Es ist, sagt Origenes,
für die menschliche Seele unmöglich, nicht unter den Einfluss von
Leidenschaften zu geraten, selbst dann, wenn sie späterhin durch
Bemühung den Zustand einer Leidenschaftslosigkeit erreicht.[24] Die
Stufen der Entwicklung sind in *c. Celsum* IV, 64 zusammengefasst,
wo Origenes erklärt, dass es mit dem menschlichen Verstand,
Vernunft und Handlungen nicht immer gleichmässig bestellt ist.
Zu einer Zeit hat er die Fähigkeit zu rationalem Denken (λόγος)
noch nicht erworben, zu einer anderen hat er Sünde (κακία)
zusammen mit dem Logos in sich aufgenommen und seine Sünde hat
sich mehr oder weniger ausgedehnt, zu einer dritten hat er sich
zur Tugend bekehrt und macht darin grösseren oder geringeren
Fortschritt; und manchmal kommt es vor, dass er die Tugend selbst
durch längere oder kürzere Betrachtung erreicht.[25] Nach dieser
Auffassung von der Entwicklung des Menschen ist wenigstens eine

---

[21] Vgl. Max Pohlenz, *Die Stoa. Geschichte einer geistigen Bewegung,*
Göttingen 1948, S. 56, 118-9, 147; SVF IV, Index unter νόμος, λόγος, ἔννοια, πάθος,
ἐπιθυμία, παιδίον usw. Zum Begriff des moralischen Fortschritts in der stoischen
Philosophie vgl. die Hinweise bei E. Bickel, *Fiunt, non nascuntur christiani,*
in *Pisciculi. Studien zur Religion und Kultur des Altertums F.J. Dölger ...
dargeboten,* Münster 1939, S. 54-61.
[22] Diese Stelle des Matthäuskommentars zitiert SVF III, 477, S. 127-8.
[23] XXXIX, hg. A. Ramsbotham, JTS 14 (1912) 14; vgl. auch S. 11. 34 ff.
[24] XXXVIII, hg. Ramsbotham, JTS 14 (1912) 13.
[25] Zu diesem Thema vgl. auch *com. Io.* I, 37 (GCS IV, 48. 4-11 18-21)
(zu *Io.* 15, 22: diejenigen, in denen der Logos noch nicht voll entwickelt ist,
haben keine Sünde, diejenigen aber sind der Sünde unterworfen, die schon
Anteil haben am Logos, aber gegen die Einsichten [ἔννοιαι], aus denen der
Logos in uns voll entwickelt wird, handeln) und XX, (GCS IV, 344. 15-19)
(jedermann, in dem der Logos ausgebildet ist, wird entweder Kind Gottes
oder Kind des Teufels, weil er entweder sündigt oder nicht sündigt) *hom. Ex.*
IV, 8 (GCS VI, 181. 6ff.), *com. Rom.* I, 176ff., 190ff., 241f., 334ff., 370ff.; II, 11f.,
43ff.

Bekehrung sittlicher Art für jeden Menschen notwendig, da ja die Sünde in einer bestimmten lebensgeschichtlichen Stunde in Erscheinung tritt und ihr dann widerstanden werden muss. Nach den Stoikern, denen Origenes folgt, erreicht die Vernunft ihre volle Entwicklung im Alter von 14 Jahren.[26] Wenn wir geneigt sind anzunehmen, dass Origenes selbst erfuhr, was er beschrieb, dann müssen wir diese Erfahrung in eine Zeit datieren, die vor dem Martyrium seines Vaters liegt.

---

[26] Vgl. Pohlenz, *Die Stoa*, S. 56 und 119; SVF I, 149, S. 404.

IX

THE FAREWELL DISCOURSE IN PATRISTIC EXEGESIS*

ABSTRACT
Survey of patristic exegesis of the Gospel of John with special reference to the Farewell Discourse

T he task of this contribution would be a clear cut one if the Patristic exegetes commented on the problem of the Farewell Discourse as a literary form or considered its meaning and message as a whole, but in fact they make scarcely any comments of this kind. Their approach is rather to consider the text of John verse by verse or paragraph by paragraph and most of them do not even seem to notice that anything special starts with the beginning of the discourse.

There would of course be plenty to say about the exegesis of the Fourth Gospel as a whole, since, after an initial period when its use by the church and even its authorship had to be defended against attacks, it played a major role in the development of Christian theology.[1] It was not only the favourite gospel of the Gnostics but also championed by anti-Gnostic writers. One of Irenaeus' main aims in his work Against Heresy was to argue for an orthodox understanding of John against the Valentinians,[2] and Origen was similarly motivated in embarking on his own Commentary on John.[3] Texts from the Gospel of John, both from inside and outside the Farewell Discourse, were basic to the Christian understanding of Christ from earliest times. One only needs to glance at the lists of

---

* Due to technical reasons it was decided to keep the reference system of this article as originally presented, and not to adapt it to the norms followed by *Neotestamentica*.

[1] On the early use of the Gospel of John cf W von Loewenich, *Das Johannes-Verständnis im zweiten Jahrhundert*, Giessen 1932, and J N Sanders, *The Fourth Gospel in the Early Church*, Cambridge 1943. On patristic exegesis of John in general cf Maurice F Wiles, *The Spiritual Gospel: The Interpretation of the Fourth Gospel in the Early Church*, Cambridge 1960. A bibliography (by no means exhaustive) on Patristic biblical exegesis book by book and verse by verse is provided by Hermann Josef Sieben, *Exegesis Patrum*, Rome 1983.

[2] Cf W von Loewenich, *op cit*, pp 115-141.

[3] See below p 196.

quotations in the Biblia Patristica[4] to see how commonly Christian writers quoted the Johannine ἐγώ εἰμι texts, including Jn 14:6 and 15:1ff. From the third century onwards Johannine verses were used as proof texts in Trinitarian and Christological controversies[5] as well as providing the basis for the doctrine of the procession of the Holy Spirit.[6] It is possible therefore to examine Johannine exegesis in various ways: for example from the point of view of its influence on doctrine, or by looking at key themes and concepts, or at the Patristic understanding of particular episodes. Thus Maurice Wiles in his book The Spiritual Gospel not only considers Christological interpretations but also looks at the concepts of spirit, truth, life, light, world, judgement, glory, knowledge, faith, vision of God, and Logos in Johannine exegesis,[7] and includes a chapter on the Patristic understanding of the main signs in the Gospel, one of which is the washing of the disciples' feet in Jn 13.[8]

Since nearly all patristic writings make use of and quote the Bible it is possible to consider exegesis in a more general way in relation to early Christian writers as a whole, or to limit oneself to exegetical works in a strict sense. In this paper the narrower of these approaches will be taken, concentrating particularly on the period up to and including Origen but also drawing a few illustrations from later commentaries and homilies, and an attempt will be made to give a picture of some of the methods used by the patristic exegetes and the kind of problems they looked at. Examples will be taken from the setting of the Farewell Discourse as well as the discourse itself.

The earliest full scale New Testament patristic commentary[9] was that of Origen on John, which he started while living at Alexandria before 232, and continued on and off during the following decades after his move to Caesarea.[10] Only a

---

[4] Biblia Patristica: *Index des Citations et Allusions Bibliques dans la Littérature Patristique*, Paris 1975ff.

[5] Cf T E Pollard, *Johannine Christology and the Early Church*, Cambridge 1970.

[6] Cf Anthony Casurella, *The Johannine Paraclete in the Church Fathers*, Tübingen 1983.

[7] The treatment of such concepts in the Fathers can now be studied more easily with the aid of G W H Lampe, *A Patristic Greek Lexicon*, Oxford 1961, the Biblia Patristica, and modern computer aids.

[8] Wiles, *op cit*. In addition Sieben, *op cit* pp 87-8, lists no less than six contributions on this episode.

[9] Jerome speaks of a Gospel Commentary by Theophilus of Antioch, but this (if it ever existed) is not preserved; cf J Quasten, *Patrology*, Vol 1, Utrecht-Antwerp 1950, pp 238-9. No doubt homilies were preached on the Gospel readings during Christian worship before the time of Origen, but the earliest such Gospel homilies to survive are those of Origen on Luke in the Latin translation of Jerome; on the practice of such exegetical sermons cf Pierre Nautin, *Origène: sa vie et son oeuvre*, Paris 1977, pp 389-401).

[10] E Preuschen in the introduction to his edition, *GCS Origenes 4*, Leipzig 1903, pp lxxviii ff, dates the surviving books between about 218/9 and 235-7; Nautin, *Origène*, pp 377-80, prefers a later dating between 231 and 248.

IX

few books of this lengthy work survive.[11] The last of these is Book 32, which expounds Jn 13:2-33 and thus includes the beginning of the Farewell Discourse. It is uncertain whether the work went any further. It may be that Origen only wrote short notes on the rest of John.[12]

After Origen's Commentary on John we do not hear of any further commentators on the Fourth Gospel until we reach three fourth-century exegetes, Theodore of Heraclea, Apollinarius of Laodicea and Didymus the Blind. In all three cases the original commentaries are lost but extracts are preserved in catena manuscripts.[13] Theodore, bishop of Heraclea near Constantinople, was a leader of the Arian party under Constantine and Constantius, and is regarded as a representative of the Antiochene school of exegesis. Apollinarius, bishop of Laodicea in Syria from about 360 onwards, was a supporter of Athanasius in the Arian controversy, but ended his life in schism because of his heretical Christological teachings. Didymus the Blind, who died aged eighty-five in about 398, was the head of the catechetical school at Alexandria and an admirer of Origen.

Fully preserved in Greek is a set of 88 homilies on John by John Chrysostom, probably delivered in about 391 when he was a presbyter at Antioch.[14] Chrysostom's friend Theodore, who was also a priest at Antioch before becoming bishop of Mopsuestia in Cilicia from 392-428, composed a Commentary on John, which survives in a Syriac translation together with fragments of the original Greek.[15] We also have most of Cyril of Alexandria's lengthy Commentary on John,[16] written sometime before 429. Finally, standing outside the main stream of Greek exegesis, there are 124 homilies on John by Augustine, the first 54 preached at Hippo in 413, and the remaining ones composed later, probably in 418.[17]

Whereas the early Christian commentators on the Old Testament could look

[1] Books 1-2, 6, 10, 13, 19-20, 28 and 32 (on John 1:1-7; 1:19-29; 2:12-25; 4:13-54; 8:19-3; 11:39-57 and 13:2-33), also some extracts in the Philocalia and in catenae.
[2] This is the view of Nautin, op cit, pp 242-3. The list of Origen's works in Jerome, Epistle 33, includes 32 books on John and also the item 'In partes quasdam Iohannis excerptorum liber I'. We have three fragments on Jn 14:3; 17:11 and 20:25, but these may come from a lost book of excerpts on selected passages in John. Origen refers back to his exposition of Jn 19:18 in his later Commentary on Matthew, but without specifying what work it was in. Cf Nautin, op cit, pp 242-3.
[3] These have been edited by Joseph Reuss, Johannes-Kommentare aus der griechischen Kirche = Texte und Untersuchungen 89 (Berlin 1966).
[4] Migne PG 59
[5] Syriac translation, ed and translated into Latin by J -M Vosté, Theodori Mops Comm in v Iohannis Apostoli, Paris and Louvaine 1940 (= Corpus Scriptorum Christianorum Orientalium, Scriptores Syri, Ser 4.3). Greek fragments in R Devreesse, Essai sur Théodore de Mopsueste = Studi e Testi 141, Vatican 1948, pp 305-419.
[6] Ed P E Pusey, Cyrilli Archiepiscopi Alexandrini in D Joannis Evangelium, Oxford 1872.
[7] Ed D R Willems, Corpus Christianorum Ser Lat 36 (Turnhout, 1954).

back to the work of Jewish predecessors,[18] for the New Testament there were no such models. The commentaries of pagan scholars on Classical literature provided a model for Christian exegetes with regard to methods and general principles of interpretation,[19] but that is not the same as having predecessors who had actually commented on the same writings. Thus Origen had no Jewish predecessors for his New Testament commentaries, but he did however have Gnostic predecessors. He wrote his commentary for his wealthy friend and patron Ambrose, whom he had converted from Valentinian Gnosticism,[20] and in the preface to Book 5 he explains that he has undertaken the work because of the dearth of orthodox exegetes and the fact that heretics claiming to possess gnosis circulate exegetical treatises in many volumes expounding the words of the Gospels and apostolic writings.[21] These heretical commentaries are lost, with the exception of parts of an exposition of John by the Valentinian Gnostic Heracleon, which Origen himself quotes and refutes in his own commentary.[22] Heracleon's expositions of the individual verses were clearly very much briefer than those of Origen, and Origen criticises him as insufficiently systematic and thorough. Heracleon regards the events narrated in the Gospel as symbolising higher truths, and Origen follows him in this approach, while attacking Gnostic features contrary to orthodoxy such as the relegation of the creator god of the Old Testament to an inferior level and the division of mankind into predetermined categories. We do not know whether Heracleon's work included the Farewell Discourse, since the last comment from it which Origen quotes is on Jn 8:50. It could be that by the time Origen reached the later books of his own commentary he was no longer

---

[18] Cf Ed P R Ackroyd and C F Evans, *The Cambridge History of the Bible*, vol 1 (Cambridge 1970), sections 8 and 12-14; W Horbury, '*Old Testament Interpretation in the Writings of the Church Fathers*' in ed M J Mulder and H Sysling, Mikra (Compendia Rerum Iudaicarum ad N T ii.i, Assen and Philadelphia, 1988), especially p 733 note 17 and pp 770-776; and N R M de Lange, *Origen and the Jews*, Cambridge 1976. On Origen's references to his predecessors cf A von Harnack, *Der Kirchengeschichtliche Ertrag der exegetischen Arbeiten des Origenes*, 1 Teil (=Texte und Untersuchungen 42.3 Leipzig 1918) pp 22-30, and 2 Teil (=Texte und Untersuchungen 42.4, Leipzig 1919) pp 10-34.

[19] Cf Bernhard Neuschäfer, *Origenes als Philologe*, Basel 1987, and Christoph Schäublin, *Untersuchungen zu Methoden und Herkunft der antiochenischen Exegese*, Köln/Bonn 1974.

[20] Cf his Commentary on John 5.8, ed Preuschen, p 105.16-19, and Eusebius, *HE*.6.18. Ambrose provided him with shorthand writers and copyists for his commentaries; cf Eusebius, *HE* 6.23.

[21] Cf Commentary on John 5.8, ed Preuschen, p 105.4ff. The heretics Origen refers to may have been followers of Heracleon, since he speaks more than once of οἱ ἀπ ' αὐτοῦ and οἱ ἀπὸ τῆς γνώμης αὐτοῦ.

[22] There is a separate edition by A E Brooke, *The Fragments of Heracleon*, Cambridge 1891. On his exegesis cf Elaine H Pagels, *The Johannine Gospel in Gnostic Exegesis: Heracleon's Commentary on John*, New York 1973.

interested in refuting Heracleon.

Heracleon's comments on John may have been in a similar form to a lost work of Clement of Alexandria, his Hypotyposes.[23] According to the description by the church historian Eusebius[24] this work contained concise expositions of all the biblical writings. It will therefore have included notes on John, but all we possess is a statement quoted by Eusebius[25] characterising John's gospel as a spiritual gospel written to complement the outward account given in the other three gospels. Some idea of what Clement said on various Johannine themes is given by his notes on the first and second Johannine epistles, which are preserved in Latin translation.[26]

I will give one example of a comment of Clement's which illustrates his opposition to the Gnostic use of John. After quoting 1 Jn 5:19, one of the Johannine verses which appear to take a negative attitude to the world, he puts the question: 'Surely the world and all that is in the world is said to be the creation of God and "very good"?'[27] His solution is that by the word 'world' John means the people who live in a worldly manner following their desires.[28] Later on Origen develops this approach to the problem in much more extensive discussions of the meaning and usage of the Greek word κόσμος.[29] The definition of the meaning of words plays a very important role in Origen's exegesis and he draws for it on both pagan definitions of terms and his own extensive knowledge of biblical usage. The modern reader wishing to check on patristic understanding of Johannine terms will find Lampe's *Patristic Lexicon* a very useful reference book.[30]

The example I have just quoted from Clement illustrates an approach that is both early and frequent in patristic exegesis, that of the presentation of a problem followed by a proposed solution.[31] The problems considered may be clashes

---

[23] This is the view taken by Preuschen in his introduction to his edition of Origen on John, p ciii. A similar brief form of exegesis was included by Origen in his early lost work, the Stromateis, cf Nautin, *op cit*, p 294.

[24] *HE* 6.14.1. The surviving fragments are printed by O Stählin in his edition of Clement, *GCS Clemens* 3, Leipzig 1909, pp 195-215. On this work cf also C Duckworth and E Osborn, 'Clement of Alexandria's *Hypotyposeis:* a French eighteenth-century sighting', *Journal of Theological Studies*, NS 36 (1985), pp 67-83.

[25] *HE 6.14.5-7.*

[26] Ed Stählin, pp 209-215; cf also Stählin's introduction, pp xlff.

[27] Ed Stählin, p 213.1-11, commenting on 1 Jn 2:13-17.

[28] Ed Stählin, pp 213.24-5 and 214.30-31, commenting on 1 Jn 3:1b and 5:19. A similar interpretation is given by Theodore of Heraclea on Jn 14:17: κόσμον ὧδε λέγει τοὺς κοσμικοὺς ἀνθρώπους... (ed Reuss, fragment 262, p 134).

[29] Cf the section on the concept in Wiles, *op cit*, pp 76-9; also Lampe, *Patristic Lexicon*, s *.

[30] See above note 7.

[31] Cf G Bardy, 'La Littérature patristique des "Quaestiones et responsiones" sur l' Écriture sainte', *Revue Biblique* 41 (1932), pp 210-236, 341-369 and 515-537, and 42

IX

between Old and New Testament verses, such as the heretic Marcion listed in his work the *Antitheses*, or they may be clashes between the Gospels,[32] or other exegetical puzzles. The disagreements between the Gospels were felt by Origen to be so irreconcilable on a literal level that he states that anyone who examines these discrepancies carefully will become dizzy and either give up regarding all four gospels as truly valid and select one at random, or conclude that their truth is not to be sought at a literal level.[33] The former approach had been taken by Marcion, who selected Luke, and by certain Jewish Christians or Ebionites, who confined themselves to Matthew. Later on the discrepancies in the Gospel narratives were used in pagan attacks on Christianity, in particular the lost attack of Porphyry *Against the Christians*, written in the late 3rd century.[34] In order to meet such difficulties the church historian Eusebius of Caesarea not only wrote a reply to Porphyry, but also a work called *Gospel Questions and Solutions*, in which he discussed the disagreements between the gospel accounts of Christ's birth and resurrection.[35] It is also Eusebius who informs us of a much earlier pair of writings in the same genre, by Tatian and his pupil Rhodo, who had been taught by Tatian at Rome in the latter part of the 2nd century. According to Eusebius[36] Rhodo reported that Tatian had composed a book of problems setting out obscurities in the biblical writings and Rhodo himself had promised to provide solutions to these problems in a writing of his own. We do not know whether Johannine problems were included, but Tatian must have become very much aware of the disagreements between John and the synoptics in composing his own Gospel harmony.

The discussion of problems with proposed solutions plays an important role in Origen's Commentary on John. In order to show the type of problems that might be raised I will give two examples from the short section which survives on the Farewell Discourse.

The first example illustrates Origen's distinction between a simple or literal sense of scripture and a deeper sense and the way he attempts to achieve a harmony between verses drawn from different parts of the Bible, and the second is a

(1933) 14-30, 211-229 and 328-352; Helmut Merkel, *Die Widersprüche zwischen den Evangelien*, Tübingen 1971, pp 122ff, and 'Frühchristliche Autoren über Johannes und die Synoptiker', paper presented to Colloquium Biblicum Lovaniense XXXIX, 7-9 August 1990.
[32] On the concern felt by Christian readers about these discrepancies cf Merkel, *op cit*, pp 32-4.
[33] Commentary on John 10:3, p 173.25-32.
[34] Cf Robert L Wilken, *The Christians as the Romans saw them*, Yale 1984, pp 144-147 Merkel, *op cit*, pp 8-31. Celsus was less detailed in his criticism; cf Merkel, *op cit*, pp 9-13.
[35] Migne PG 22.879ff; cf Merkel, *op cit*, pp 130-146, Bardy, art cit, pp 228-236.
[36] Eusebius *HE* 5.13.8. Eusebius' information comes from a lost work of Rhodo against the heresy of Marcion (*HE* 5.13.1).

case of a contradiction which had puzzled his predecessors so much that they had posited a textual corruption.[37] Here again Origen distinguishes between a simple and a deeper sense and offers solutions at both levels.

In expounding Jesus' words about his imminent departure in Jn 13:33 Origen states[38] that the literal sense is clear, since Jesus is about to be arrested, led off to Annas and Pilate, and crucified, and then to spend three days and three nights in the heart of the earth. Yet according to the deeper sense one might question whether he will not still be with his disciples. His promises to be with his disciples in Mt 18:20 and 28:20 mean that he can be with them without being physically present. The fact however that the disciples are going to be scandalised and scattered, as prophesied in Mt 26:31, shows that they will no longer be worthy for him to be with them. A possible objection, that Jesus is even with those who do not know him, based on Jn 1:26 ('He whom you do not know is standing in the midst of you') is refuted by drawing a distinction between the promises of the former verses and the statement made in the latter one, and Origen then adds that even if Jesus was not with the disciples, none the less they were going to seek him, as is shown by Peter's bitter weeping after his denial.

Going on to the second half of Jn 13:33 Origen contrasts Jesus' earlier words to the Jews in 8:21 with his words to the disciples here, since he promises that the disciples will see him again shortly (in Jn 16:16f). He suggests that the Greek word ἄρτι at the end of verse 33 conveys this distinction, and that Jesus is saying to the disciples, 'Where I am going, you cannot come now'. He then points out a difficulty with the literal interpretation of the warning to the Jews. In saying to the Jews, 'Where I am going, you cannot come', Jesus cannot be referring to his own death and descent to Hades, since the Jews too would die. One might offer the answer that Jesus will be in the paradise of God, where the disciples will later follow him, and the Jews not. Connected with this however is a major problem. How can the prophesy in Mt 12:40, that the Son of Man will spend three days and three nights in the heart of the earth be reconciled with Jesus' promise to the robber in Luke 23:43, saying, 'Today you will be with me in the paradise of God'? Certain persons, says Origen, have been so upset by this disagreement that they have dared to conjecture that the words in Luke were added to the Gospel by forgers. Origen himself suggests two solutions — one according to the simpler sense that Jesus perhaps first restored the robber to Paradise and then descended to the heart of the earth, and one according to the deeper sense according to which the word 'today' in Luke refers to the whole of the present age.[39]

---

37 Origen makes few references to his predecessors (apart from Heracleon) in the Commentary on John; cf A von Harnack, *Der kirchengeschichtliche Ertrag der exegetischen Arbeiten des Origenes 2* =Texte und Untersuchungen 42.4 (Leipzig 1919), p 28.
38 Commentary on John 32.30, ed Preuschen, p 477.6ff.
39 In his Commentary on Matthew XII.3 (ed E Klostermann, *GCS Origenes 10*, Leipzig

If problems of the kind just mentioned were disputed by Origen's predecessors, then one might expect the major differences between John and the Synoptics to have received considerable attention. In fact these disagreements were one of the reasons for early opposition to John,[40] and we can see an attempt to meet them in Clement's characterisation of John as the spiritual gospel that I have already referred to. This approach is expanded by Origen, for whom John's words are greater and more perfect, since he lay on Jesus' breast and has clearly revealed his divinity.[41] The reason that John fails to narrate either Jesus' temptation by the devil or his agony in the garden of Gethsemane is, in Origen's view, that the other evangelists give an exposition rather according to Jesus' human nature and John according to his divine nature.[42] Because of this spiritual approach, John may sometimes neglect strict chronological sequence.[43] Thus in the context of the Farewell Discourse it is in order to direct his readers' attention to the spiritual significance of the washing of the disciples' feet that John ignores the normal order of washing before a meal and instead describes Jesus as rising from the meal for this purpose.[44]

A rather different approach to John's divergences from the Synoptics is taken by Theodore of Mopsuestia, who regards John as having deliberately aimed to avoid repetition of what the other evangelists had related, except where this is unavoidable in order to produce a continuous narrative. He makes this comment at the beginning of his exposition of John 13, perhaps referring particularly to John's omission of the institution of the eucharist, and he goes on to remark that John's account of Jesus' deeds and words to his disciples before his passion, which are not recorded by the other evangelists, are intended to show that the Saviour knew of his impending passion and freely chose it.[45]

To return to the question of the attacks made on John's Gospel at an early

---

1935, pp 72.33-73.3) Origen only mentions the 'simpler' interpretation.

[40] A prominent opponent of both the Gospel and the Apocalypse was Gaius, who wrote against the Montanists under Zephyrinus, bishop of Rome. Hippolytus wrote in refutation of him and it is likely that his arguments were reused by Epiphanius, who himself writes against opponents of John, to whom he gives the label ἄλογοι. Epiphanius refutes objections based on the divergences of John from the other gospels, Panarion haer 51.2.4ff, ed Karl Holl, *GCS Epiphanius 2*, Leipzig 1922, pp 251ff.

[41] Commentary on John 1.4, ed Preuschen p 8.8-10; cf also the exposition of John 13:23 and 25 at Book 32.20 and 25, p 460.28ff (on the authorship of the Gospel) and p 461.24ff. (John 'reclined on the Word and rested in higher mysteries.')

[42] Commentary on Matthew, Comm Ser p 210. A similar comment is made by Apollinarius on Jn 18:1-4, Fragment 132, ed Reuss, p 53.

[43] He says the same of all four evangelists, Commentary on John 10.5, ed Preuschen, p 175.7-20.

[44] Commentary on John 32.2, ed Preuschen, p 426.29-427.7.

[45] Book 6, ed Vosté, p 180.26ff.

date, we learn from Irenaeus[46] that certain opponents of the Montanist prophetic movement rejected the Gospel of John because of Jesus' promise of the Paraclete in the Farewell Discourse. It seems that the Montanists claimed that this promise was only fulfilled in the prophecy of Montanus, through whom the Paraclete spoke. It is interesting therefore to find that the comments on John 14, 16 and 26 of the early fourth-century exegete Theodore of Heraclea contain quite fierce polemic against the Montanists and their assertion that the Paraclete was only sent after a delay of 230 years.[47] A similar claim made later by Mani, the founder of Manichaeism, was similarly refuted by the fourth-century anti-Manichaean writer, Hegemonius.[48] Another problem was the fact that the title Paraclete is applied to Jesus himself in 1 Jn 2:1.[49] This led Origen to distinguish between two meanings of the word παράκλητος, 'intercessor' as applied to Jesus and 'comforter' as applied to the Spirit,[50] whereas Theodore of Mopsuestia takes Paraclete as used of the Spirit to mean 'teacher', deriving this from the other statements about the Spirit in the Farewell Discourse.[51]

An early dispute concerned with the Gospel of John centered on its dating of the Last Supper and crucifixion. Was the Last Supper itself the Passover meal, as seems to be the case in the Synoptic Gospels, or was it the evening before the Passover, as in John? A number of lost second-century writings entitled On the Passover apparently dealt with this subject. Eusebius mentions two books by Melito of Sardis On the Passover, which referred to a major disputation at Laodicea in Asia Minor about the question,[52] and he states that a work with the same title by Clement of Alexandria was composed because of Melito's writing.[53] Contemporary with Melito was Apollinarius of Hierapolis, who also wrote

---

[46] *Adversus Haereses* III.xi.12, ed W W Harvey, Cambridge 1857, Vol 2, p 51. The passage is wrongly explained in Harvey's footnotes.

[47] Ed Reuss, Fragments 260-1 and 271-2, on Jn 14:15-16 and 26, pp 133-4 and 136; cf Casurella, op cit pp 41 and 73, n116. With regard to the timing, Reuss prints μετὰ διακόσιά που καὶ τριάκοντα ἔτη in fragment 260 and μετὰ σ ΄λ΄ ἔτη in fragment 261 (= 230 years, wrongly translated by Casurella, op cit p41 as 'after two-to-three hundred years'). In fact 130 years would be more accurate.

[48] *Acta Archelai 31*, ed *GCS 16*, p 44. Cf Casurella, *op cit* p 39.

[49] This is noted by Clement in the Latin translation of his *Hypotyposes* on 1 Jn 2:1, ed Stählin, p 211.12ff.

[50] *De Principiis* 2.7.4, ed P Koetschau, *GCS Origenes 5*, Berlin 1913, pp 151-2; cf Casurella, *op cit*, pp 4-5.

[51] In his exposition of Jn 14:15-16, ed Vosté, p 194.19; ed Devreesse, fragment 16, p 391.12-13. For other comments on the meaning of Paraclete cf Casurella, *op cit*, p 44 and Lampe, *Patristic Lexicon* sv.

[52] *HE* 4.26.2-3. If Eusebius' information is correct, this must have been a different work from the surviving homily with this title. Cf S G Hall, *Melito of Sardis, On Pascha and fragments*, Oxford 1979, pp xix-xxi and xxv-xxvi, for discussion of the varying views which have been taken on this and related questions.

[53] *HE* 4.26.4

IX

on the subject. A surviving fragment from Apollinarius' On the Passover[54] complains of the contentious ignorance of those who assert that Jesus ate the Passover lamb with his disciples on the 14th of the month and interpret Matthew to mean this, thus producing a view discordant with the Law and a conflict between the Gospels. A second fragment shows that Apollinarius himself thought that Jesus was crucified on the 14th of the month at the same time as the sacrifice of the Paschal lambs.[55] He must therefore have offered an alternative explanation of Matthew's gospel, fitting it to the Johannine timing. A rather longer fragment survives from Clement's lost work,[56] taking the same line and referring to Mt 26:17 and Jn 18:28. Clement harmonises the gospel accounts by dating the last supper to the 13th, which he describes as the day when the sanctification of unleavened bread and the preparation of the festival took place. For this reason, he says, John appropriately writes that the disciples had their feet washed by the Lord as if in preparation. The Lord suffered on the following day, being himself the paschal lamb sacrificed by the Jews. Further arguments for the Johannine timing appear in the fourth-century exegete Apollinarius of Laodicea in Syria. The words in Jn 13:1 'Before the festival of the Passover' show that the Last Supper was the preparation of the Passover, not the Passover meal itself. The 'first day of unleavened bread' in Mt 26:17 means 'the day before the unleavened bread' and Jesus' words in Lk 22:15-16 show his sympathy for the disciples, who will spend the festival in grief.[57]

Those exegetes who follow the synoptic timing are left with the problem of

---

[54] Preserved in the Chronicon Paschale, Migne PG 92.80C-81A.

[55] The dispute was probably connected with the Quartodeciman Easter celebration, but I do not think it is possible to separate Quartodecimans and their opponents neatly into supportors of John versus supporters of the Synoptic chronology or vice versa. As is shown below, non-Quartodeciman fathers are divided in this respect. A view of the Quartodeciman celebration as a Christian Passover different in character from the Passover of the Jews is compatible with the Johannine chronology, and Polycrates of Ephesus in his letter to Victor of Rome (in Eusebius, *HE* 5.24.3) states that John, who lay on the Lord's breast, as well as other 'luminaries' of the Asian churches, including Melito, followed the Quartodeciman practice. On the other hand supporters of the Synoptic chronology could claim that, if Jesus celebrated the Jewish Passover before his Passion, then Christians should do so too; Origen refers to this argument and describes it as 'falling into Ebionism' in his Commentary on Matthew, Comm Ser 79, ed E Klostermann, *GCS Origenes 11*, Leipzig 1933, p 189.15ff.

[56] Ed Stählin, pp 216-7.

[57] Fragment 131 on Mt 26:20 and 130 on Mt 26:17-18, ed J Reuss, *Matthäus-Kommentare aus der griechischen Kirche*, Texte und Untersuchungen 61, Berlin 1957, pp 44-5. Hippolytus (On the Holy Passover Fragments 5-6, ed G N Bonwetsch and H Achelis, *GCS Hippolytus 1*, Leipzig 1897, p 270) and Peter of Alexandria (Migne, PG 18.520A) also argue against the view that Jesus ate the Passover at the Last Supper. According to Epiphanius, *Panarion haer* 30.22.4-5 (ed Karl Holl, *GCS Epiphanius 1*, Leipzig 1915, p 363), the Ebionites altered Lk 22:15 to μὴ ἐπιθυμίᾳ ἐπεθύμησα κρέας τοῦτο τὸ Πάσχα φαγεῖν μεθ' ὑμῶν in order to show Jesus' rejection of meat-eating.

explaining that of John. According to Eusebius of Caesarea[58] Jesus ate the Passover on the first day of unleavened bread with his disciples, thus instituting the new Christian Passover celebrated every Sunday at the Eucharist, whereas the Jews ate their Passover on the wrong day, the 15th of the month.[59] Similarly John Chrysostom explains John 18:28 as showing that the Jews were so zealous in their desire to kill Jesus that, having managed to catch him unexpectedly, they chose to neglect the Passover and celebrate it on a different day. Jesus himself had not neglected the correct time of the Passover.[60]

A quite different tradition about the timing of the Last Supper is preserved in the Didascalia, a Syrian church order of the third century.[61] According to this Jesus ate the Passover with his disciples on the Tuesday, three days before his crucifixion on Friday. The writer of the Didascalia harmonises this with the timing of the crucifixion on the 14th by adding the explanation that the Jews had decided to celebrate the Passover early, on the 11th of the month, in order to be able to arrest Jesus without disturbance.

A very interesting harmonisation between the Synoptic and Johannine accounts of the Last Supper and Farewell Discourse appears in Tatian's *Diatessaron*.[62] This divides off Jn 13:1-20 with the account of the footwashing as a separate supper taking place 'before the feast of the Passover',[63] then inserts the

---

[58] *De Solemnitate Paschali 9 and 12*, Migne PG 24.704A-B and 705B-C.

[59] No full discussion of the problem by Origen (whom Eusebius often follows) is preserved. In his Commentary on Matthew the catena fragments (Fragments 520.3-5, 526.6-7 and 552.6-8, ed Klostermann, *GCS Origenes 12*, Leipzig 1941, pp 213, 215 and 226) appear to favour the Johannine chronology, but the Latin translation (if the words are taken at their surface meaning) the Synoptic identification of the Last Supper with the Passover (Comm Ser 80, 82, ed Klostermann, pp 191.20 and 194.7-9 and 21-25). For further references to relevant comments in both Origen and other fathers, cf Lampe, *Patristic Lexicon*, art. πάσχα. Cf also, for Origen's views about the Passover, *Origène, Sur la Pâque*, ed O Guéraud and P Nautin, Paris 1979, with Nautin's introduction, pp 96ff.

[60] Homily on Matthew 84, 799E-800A, ed F Field, Vol 2, Cambridge 1839, p 487. Chrysostom takes a different approach in his Homily on John 83.3 on Jn 18:28, Migne, PG 59.452 (top of column).

[61] Ed R H Connolly, *Didascalia Apostolorum*, Oxford 1929, pp 188-9. Traces of the same tradition are found also in Epiphanius, Victorinus of Pettau and certain persons opposed by Theodoret; cf Annie Jaubert, *The Date of the Last Supper*, New York 1965, pp 69-80, and 'Une discussion patristique sur la chronologie de la Passion', *Recherches de science religieuse* 54 (1966), pp 407-410.

[62] On Tatian's *Diatessaron* cf Merken, op cit, pp 68ff; Bruce M Metzger, *The Early Versions of the New Testament*, Oxford 1977, pp 10-36; William L Peterson in Helmut Koester, *Ancient Christian Gospels*, London and Philadelphia 1990, pp 403-430. In what follows I give references to the English translation of the Arabic version by Hope W Hogg, *Ante-Nicene Fathers* Vol X, Grand Rapids 1980 (reprint), pp 33ff, and to the Latin version in ed E Ranke, *Codex Fuldensis*, Marburg and Leipzig 1868.

[63] Arabic 44.11ff, p 111-112; Latin 155, p 136.25ff.

IX

pericope from the Synoptic Gospels about the preparation for the Passover,[64] followed by the Last Supper itself. The account of the Last Supper contains firstly Jesus' words from Lk 22:15-16,[65] secondly the prophecy of Judas' betrayal including the question by the beloved disciple and Judas' exit,[66] thirdly Jesus' words in Jn 13:31-32,[67] fourthly the institution of the Eucharist from the Synoptics,[68] fifthly a composite account of the prophecy of Peter's denial including Jn 13:33-8,[69] and lastly the first part of the Farewell Discourse from Jn 14:1-31a.[70] There then follow Jesus' instructions from Lk 22:35-39 up to the departure for the Mount of Olives, into which the words 'Arise, let us go hence' from Jn 14:31b have been inserted.[71] After this follows the rest of the Farewell Discourse to Jn 17:26.[72] It is interesting to note the dominant position of John's Gospel in this part of the *Diatessaron*. The arrangement chosen has the advantage of respecting the statement of timing given in Jn 13:1, while combining the main part of the last Supper with the Synoptic account, and it also provides a suitable context for the otherwise puzzling exhortation in Jn 14:31b.

One might expect that exegetes would have some kind of harmonisation of the Gospel narratives in mind even when they are not explicitly attempting to construct a harmony. Thus the detail from John 13:30 that Judas immediately went out can be used as a supplement to the Synoptics, in order to show that he was absent from the institution of the Eucharist. Apollinarius of Laodicea refers to it for this purpose,[73] and the detail is emphasised in a rather odd harmonisation of the gospel accounts in the *Apostolic Constitutions*. In this account the prophecy of the betrayal including the question by the beloved disciple and Jesus' answer is assigned to a separate supper preceding Judas' exit to bargain with the priests, and the Last Supper starts with the eating of the Passover, then Judas' receipt of the sop and his departure, and after this the prophecy of Peter's denial and the institution of the Eucharist ('Judas not being present with us').[74] Chrysostom however takes a different line, emphasising that Jesus even allowed Judas to partake in the sacred mysteries.[75] and Augustine explicitly states that the

---

[64] Arabic 44.34ff, p 112; Latin 156, p 137.21ff.
[65] Arabic 44.41ff, p 112; Latin 156. p 137.32ff.
[66] Arabic 44.44ff, p 112; Latin 156, p 138.1ff.
[67] Arabic 45.10ff, p 112; Latin 156, p 138.27ff.
[68] Arabic 45.12ff, p 112f; Latin 157, p 138.30ff.
[69] Arabic 45.17ff, p 113; Latin 157, p 139.3ff.
[70] Arabic 45.29-46.11, p 113f; Latin 158, p 139.28-141.9.
[71] Arabic 46.12-16, p 114; Latin 159, p 141.10-23.
[72] Arabic 46.17-47.44, pp 114-117; Latin 160, pp 141.24-146.4.
[73] Fragment 133 on Mt 26:26, ed Reuss, p 46.
[74] Book 5.14, ed P A de Lagarde, *Constitutiones Apostolorum*, Leipzig 1862, pp 141-2.
[75] Homily on Matthew 82, ed Field, Vol 2, p 460.

institution of the Eucharist took place before Judas received the sop and went out.[76]

With regard to the puzzling verse Jn 14:31b the patristic commentators take the exhortation to depart as following on from the announcement that the ruler of the world is coming, and debate about Jesus' purpose. Apollinarius of Laodicea[77] states that this is not a matter of retreat but of Jesus' giving himself up willingly, since Jesus goes to a place where he will be recognised by the betrayer. John Chrysostom[78] on the other hand supposes that Jesus is acting out of consideration for the disciples, who are now becoming uneasy about the expected arrival of Judas, and that he is therefore taking them to a different place, where they can listen without fear to the lofty doctrines he is about to deliver to them. Differently yet again, Theodore of Mopsuestia[79] takes the continuation of the discourse as showing that Jesus did not go out, and understands Jesus' words 'Let us go hence' as a reference to his own impending death. Finally Cyril[80] elaborates on this interpretation as a reference to Jesus' departure from this corruptible world to the incorruptibility of heavenly life and an exhortation to his followers to do the same. He describes the literal interpretation referring to departure to the place where Jesus would be arrested[81] as the common and well-worn one.

At the beginning of this paper it was stated that the patristic exegetes make only very brief and occasional comments about the Farewell Discourse as a whole. I will conclude by mentioning some of these comments, taking them in reverse chronological order. Augustine, characteristically, is more inclined than most to take a general overview of several chapters at a time. He does therefore at several points in his sermons on John draw his hearers' attention to this great and lengthy discourse delivered by Jesus to his disciples before his passion as being his last words, after the departure from the banquet of him who would betray him. He makes these comments at the beginning of the discourse at Jn 13:31,[82] at its end at Jn 18:1,[83] and also at the transition to the prayer at the beginning of Jn 17.[84] With regard to the prayer itself Augustine remarks that Jesus could have prayed silently, but that his purpose in it was also to teach his disciples and sub-

---

[76] Homily on John 62.3, ed D R Willems, *Corpus Christianorum Ser Lat 36* (Turnhout, 1954), p 484.

[77] Fragment 111 on Jn 14:31, ed Reuss, p 45.

[78] Homily on John 76.1, Migne, PG 59.410-411.

[79] Ed Vosté, p 200.21-27; Greek fragment on Jn 14:31, ed Devreesse, p 395.9-12.

[80] Book 10.1, ed Pusey, p 531.21ff.

[81] This is the interpretation followed by Augustine, *Tractatus in Iohannem* 79.2, ed D R Willems, *Corpus Christianorum Ser Lat 36* (Turnhout, 1954), p 527.40-41.

[82] *Tractatus* 62.6, and 63.1, pp 485-6.

[83] *Tractatus* 112.1, pp 633.

[84] *Tractatus* 104.1, p 601.

sequent readers of the Gospel.[85] Similarly, but more briefly, Theodore notes the beginning and end of the discourse,[86] and includes a brief summary at Jn 16:33, pointing out that Jesus' prayer in chapter 17 only has the form of a prayer.[87] Cyril too selects the same points for generalising comments,[88] but Chrysostom misses these opportunities, choosing instead Jn 13:33 to state that Jesus is now embarking on sad words, setting things before the disciples which they would forget, but which the Spirit would recall to them.[89] No general comments of this kind by Origen are preserved, but the introduction and conclusion to Book 32 of his commentary indicate a central theme of his exegesis of Jn 13. Jesus is about to depart, the disciples wish to follow, they wish to confess him, but they are not yet able, because the Holy Spirit has not yet come.[90] They are still little children, no longer slaves, but not yet brothers of Christ.[91] They are still progressing as pilgrims along the path of the Gospel on which Jesus leads the way like the pillar of fiery cloud in the wilderness. Origen regards himself as journeying along the same path in his own task of scriptural interpretation.[92]

WORKS REFERRED TO

Patristic Commentaries and Homilies on John

Third century:
Origen, Commentary on John, ed E Preuschen *GCS Origenes 4*, Leipzig 1903. Books 1-2, 6, 10, 13, 19-20, 28 and 32 (on John 1:1-7; 1:19-29; 2:12-25; 4:13-54; 8:19-53; 11:39-57 and 13:2-33) and some extracts are preserved.

Fourth century:
Theodore of Heraclea, Apollinarius of Laodicea, Didymus the Blind — all three wrote commentaries which are lost but from which extracts have been preserved in catena manuscripts edited by Joseph Reuss, *Johannes-Kommentare aus der griechischen Kirche* = Texte und Untersuchungen 89 (Berlin 1966).

Late fourth and early fifth century:
John Chrysostom, Homilies on John, Migne PG 59.
Theodore of Mopsuestia, Commentary on John, preserved in Syriac translation, ed and translated into Latin by J -M Vosté, *Theodori Mops Comm in Ev Iohannis Apostoli*,

---

[85] *Tractatus* 104.2, p 602.
[86] Ed Vosté, pp 186.28-30 and 231.15.
[87] Ed Vosté, pp 218.30-219.11; fragment on Jn 17:1, ed Devreesse, p 403.25-6. So too Chrysostom, Homily 80 on Jn 17:1 (Migne, PG 59.433): οὐδὲ εὐχὴν ὁ εὐαγγελιστὴς τὸ πρᾶγμα καλεῖ κ.τ.λ., and Homily 83 on Jn 18:1 (Migne, PG 59.447): οὐκ εὐχὴ ἦν, ἀλλὰ λαλία διὰ τοὺς μαθητὰς γινομένη.
[88] Books 9 and 11, ed Pusey, Vol 2, pp 376.28ff and 658.1ff and Vol 3, pp 14f.
[89] Homily 72, Migne, PG 59.393.
[90] 32.32, ed Preuschen, p 480.13-21.
[91] 32.30, ed Preuschen, p 476.16-477.4.
[92] 32.1, ed Preuschen, p 425.1-17

Paris and Louvaine 1940 (=Corpus Scriptorum Christianorum Orientalium, Scriptores Syri, Ser 4.3). Greek fragments in R Devreesse, *Essai sur Théodore de Mopsueste* = Studi e Testi 141, Vatican 1948, pp 305-419.
Cyril of Alexandria, Commentary on John, ed P E Pusey, *Cyrilli Archiepiscopi Alexandrini in D Joannis Evangelium*, Oxford 1872.
Augustine, Homilies on John, ed D R Willems, *Corpus Christianorum Ser Lat 36* (Turnhout, 1954).

Secondary Literature
Biblia Patristica: *Index des Citation et Allusions Bibliques dans la Littérature Patristique*, Paris 1975ff.
G W H Lampe, *A Patristic Greek Lexicon*, Oxford 1961.
Hermann Josef Sieben, *Exegesis Patrum*, Rome 1983 (=bibliography on Patristic biblical exegesis book by book and verse by verse).
Maurice F Wiles, *The Spiritual Gospel: The Interpretation of the Fourth Gospel in the Early Church*, Cambridge 1960
J N Sanders, *The Fourth Gospel in the Early Church*, Cambridge 1943
W von Loewenich, *Das Johannes-Verständnis im zweiten Jahrhundert*, Giessen 1932
Harold Smith, *Ante-Nicene Exegesis of the Gospels*, Vols 1-6, London 1925-1929 (extracts from early Christian writers in translation).
G Bardy, 'La Littérature patristique des "Quaestiones et responsiones" sur l' Écriture sainte', *Revue Biblique* 41 (1932), pp 210-236, 341-369 and 515-537, and 42 (1933) 14-30, 211-229 and 328-352.
Anthony Casurella, *The Johannine Paraclete in the Church Fathers*, Tübingen 1983.
Helmut Merkel, *Die Widersprüche zwischen den Evangelien*, Tübingen 1971.

X

DIE HEXAPLA DES ORIGENES:
DIE *HEBRAICA UERITAS* IM STREIT DER MEINUNGEN

Die christliche Kirche hat als ihr Altes Testament eine Büchersammlung vom Judentum geerbt, die in zwei verschiedenen Formen existiert, deren beide eine göttliche Autorität beanspruchen — die hebräische Bibel und die Septuaginta. Das frühe griechisch sprechende Christentum wurde bald in seinen Auseinandersetzungen mit jüdischen Gegnern mit dem Problem der grossen Unterschiede im Text und Kanon konfrontiert, stand diesen aber hilflos gegenüber, bis Origenes mit seiner Hexapla die wissenschaftliche Grundlage zum Vergleich der beiden Fassungen schuf. Die Frage, worauf Origenes mit dieser Arbeit abzielte, ob er vielleicht dadurch die Priorität des hebräischen Textes gegenüber der Septuaginta anerkennen oder nur seinen Inhalt feststellen wollte, ist oft erörtert worden [1]. Wir werden vielleicht einen neuen Zugang zu dieser Frage gewinnen können, wenn wir die Aussagen des Origenes in den Zusammenhang anderer frühchristlichen Äusserungen zum selben Problem stellen. Ich werde mit den christlichen Zeitgenossen und Vorgängern des Origenes anfangen und dann zu der späteren Einschätzung seiner Hexapla bis zur Zeit des Hieronymus übergehen.

In seinem berühmten Brief an Africanus bringt Origenes eine Verteidigung der kirchlichen Benutzung der Septuaginta,

---

[1] Vgl. z. B. P. Wendland, *Zur ältesten Geschichte der Bibel in der Kirche*, in ZNW 1 (1900) 272-4; P. Nautin, *Origène: Sa vie et son oeuvre*, Paris 1977, S. 344-53; D. Barthélemy, *Origène et le texte de l'Ancien Testament*, in *Études d'histoire du texte de l'Ancien Testament*, Göttingen 1978, S. 203-217; S. P. Brock, *Origen's aims as a Textual Critic of the Old Testament*, in *Studia Patristica X* [TU 107], Berlin 1970, S. 215-8; N. de Lange, *Origen and the Jews*, Cambridge 1976, S. 49ff.; und (am gründlichsten) G. Sgherri, *Sulla valutazione origeniana dei LXX*, in *Biblica* 58 (1977) 1-28.

126

die von seinen späteren Lesern sehr geschätzt wurde. Africanus
hatte Origenes getadelt, weil er in einer öffentlichen Diskussion
die Geschichte Susannas zitiert hatte, die nur auf griechisch
überliefert ist und sich im jüdischen Danielbuch nicht befindet.[2] Es ist wahrscheinlich, dass diejenigen, die wie Africanus
die hebräische Bibel zum Massstab nahmen, in der Minderheit waren gegenüber den anderen Kritikern, welche Origenes
seine allzu grosse Hochschätzung des hebräischen Textes vor-
warfen[3]. Auf jeden Fall nimmt Origenes in seiner Antwort
die Gelegenheit wahr, um gegenüber beiden Gruppen von
Kritikern seine eigene Stellung deutlich zu machen. Er schreibt,
das er keine Mühe gescheut habe, um die kirchlichen Exemplare
des Alten Testaments mit denjenigen der Juden zu vergleichen,
sich aber umsomehr der Septuaginta zugewandt habe, um
denjenigen keinen Anlass zu geben, die behaupten möchten,
er entwerte die kirchliche Münze[4]. Die Vorsehung habe allen
Kirchen Christi in den Heiligen Schriften Erbauung gegeben,
und es wäre nicht das Richtige zu meinen, man müsse diese
verwerfen und von den Juden sich unverfälschte Exemplare
erbeten[5].

---

[2] Brief des Africanus an Origenes 2, 5, 7, hg. N. de Lange, SCh
302, Paris 1983, S. 514-520.

[3] Vgl. Nautin, *op. cit.*, 345-7. Nach Nautin (loc. cit. und SCh 232,
Paris 1976, S. 46-9, 117) hat Origenes die bekannte Septuagintalesart
von *Jer.* 15, 10 (ὠφέλησα usw.) in seiner *hom. Jer.* XIV, 3 darum ausgelegt,
weil man ihn wegen seiner Bevorzugung der mit dem hebräischen Text
übereinstimmenden Lesart (ὠφέληοα usw.) in der vorangehenden Homilie
(XV, 5) getadelt hatte. In der Homilie XV, 5 beschreibt Origenes die
Lesart der meisten Septuagintahandschriften als ein γραφικὸν ἁμάρτημα,
in der Homilie XIV, 3 als τὸ καθημαξευμένον καὶ φερόμενον ἐν ταῖς ἐκκλησίαις,
behauptet aber auch hier weiterhin, man dürfe τὸ ἀπὸ τῶν Ἑβραϊκῶν γραφῶν
nicht unerklärt lassen (hg. E. Klostermann, GCS *Origenes* III, 129.13
und 107.24-9). Hat Nautin recht mit dieser These, so möchte man
vermuten, dass Origenes bei seinen späteren textkritischen Äusserungen
in dieser Homilienreihe die Argumente derselben Kritiker im Auge hat
(*hom. Jer.* XVI, 5 und 10, XX, 5, GCS III, 137 14-17; 138.27; 141.15-18;
184.23-8; vgl. unten Anmerkung 23). Nach Nautin wurden die Jeremia-
homilien um 242 und der Brief an Africanus um 249/250 verfasst (*op.
cit.* 182 und 411, SCh 232, 21; vgl. auch de Lange, SCh 302, 498-501, der den
Brief um 248/250 datiert).

[4] *Ep. ad Africanum* 9, SCh 302, 534: ἵνα μή τι παραχαράττειν δοκοίη-
μεν ταῖς ὑπὸ τὸν οὐρανὸν ἐκκλησίαις, καὶ προφάσεις διδῶμεν τοῖς ζητοῦσιν
ἀφορμὰς, ἐθέλουσι τοὺς ἐν μέσῳ συκοφαντεῖν...

[5] *Ibid.* 8, SCh 302, 532: ἡ πρόνοια, ἐν ἁγίαις γραφαῖς δεδωκυῖα πάσαις
ταῖς χριστοῦ ἐκκλησίαις οἰκοδομήν...

Bei den Aussagen des Origenes muss man unterscheiden, ob er einzelne Varianten im Text des Alten Testaments erörtert, oder feststellen will, welche Teile als kanonisch gelten sollen. Was den Kanon angeht, so berichtet Origenes darüber, welche Bücher bei den Juden zum Alten Testament gehören, benutzt aber selbst auch die nur von der Kirche anerkannten Bücher [6]. Das Problem der handschriftlichen Abweichungen sowohl im Neuen wie auch im Alten Testament erwähnt Origenes in *com. Mt.* XV, 14. Um zwischen den Varianten der Septuagintahandschriften eine Entscheidung zu treffen, benutze er als Kriterium das Zeugnis der anderen Übersetzungen aus dem Hebräischen [7]. Im Brief an Africanus geht es hauptsächlich um ein drittes Problem, nämlich um diejenigen Stellen im Alten Testament, wo die Septuaginta gegenüber dem hebräischen Text ein Plus oder ein Minus aufweist. Stellen der ersten Art hat Origenes in seiner Hexapla mit einem Obelus bezeichnet, während er die Lücken in der Septuaginta entsprechend dem hebräischen Text aus den anderen Übersetzungen ausgefüllt und mit Asterisken versehen hat. Dies dient der Information und, nach seiner Aussage im Brief an Africanus, dem Dialog mit den Juden, welche die Heidenchristen auslachen, wenn sie sich als über die jüdische Bibel unwissend zeigen [8].

Diejenigen Kritiker, die wie Africanus die Geschichte von Susanna verwerfen, werden von Origenes auch in der ersten Levitikushomilie erwähnt und mit Leuten identifiziert, die seine eigene allegorische Bibelauslegung ablehnen [9]. In der-

---

[6] Vgl. z.B. *ep. Afric.* 19, SCh 302, 562, wo er feststellt, dass die Hebräer die Bücher Tobit und Judith nicht benutzen und auch nicht unter den Apokryphen auf Hebräisch besitzen. In *com. Ps.* 1-25 bringt er eine Liste der 22 kanonischen Bücher (ἐνδιαθήκους βίβλους) nach hebräischer Überlieferung (von Euseb, HE VI, 25, zitiert). Vgl. de Lange, *Origen and the Jews*, S. 52ff., und J. Ruwet, *Les « Antilegomena » dans les oeuvres d'Origène* (II), in *Biblica* 24 (1943) 18-42.

[7] Hg. E. Klostermann, GCS *Origenes* X (1935), 387.28-388.17. In der Tat war die Hexapla ihm auch ein Hilfsmittel, um den Text des Alten Testaments zu verstehen; vgl. Nautin, *op. cit.*, 351-2, und Sgherri, *art. cit.*, 23-4, 27.

[8] *Ep. Afric.* 7, 9, SCh 302, 530-2, 534; *Com. Mt.* XV, 14, GCS X, 388.17-30.

[9] *Hom. Lev.* I, 1, hg. W. A. Baehrens, GCS *Origenes* VI (1920) 281.

X

selben Homilienreihe klagt er über Christen, die das, was sie
gestern von den Juden gelernt haben, heute in der Kirche
vorbringen [10]. Anderswo berücksichtigt Origenes die Möglichkeit, das seine Leser sich auf die von den Juden anerkannten
Schriften und Schriftteile beschränken, ohne sich gegen diesen
Standpunkt zu äussern. So in seiner Schrift *Vom Gebet*:
nachdem er aus einem im Hebräischen fehlenden Teil des Da-
nielbuches und aus Tobit Beispiele des Gebets zitiert hat,
schreibt er, dass er andere Beispiele geben wird, weil er die
Stelle im Danielbuch obelisiert hatte, und weil 'die aus der
Beschneidung' das Tobitbuch als unkanonisch ablehnen [11]. In
seinem Matthäuskommentar schreibt Origenes nach einem
Zitat aus der Susannageschichte, dass er weiss, dass diese
Stelle im Hebräischen fehlt, dass er sie aber benutzt, weil sie
in den Kirchen anerkannt wird [12]. In einem von Hieronymus
übersetzten Auszug aus einer Frühschrift, den *Stromateis*,
scheint Origenes geneigt, sich denjenigen anzuschliessen, welche sagen, man soll die Susannageschichte nur dann anerkennen, wenn man nachweisen kann, dass ihre Ursprache
hebräisch war [13].

---

[10] *Hom. Lev.* V, 8, GCS VI, 349.4-5. Vgl. dazu de Lange, *Origen and the Jews*, S. 86f.
[11] 14.4, hg. P. Koetschau, GCS *Origenes* II (1899) 331.27-332.5. ὠβέλισαν ist wohl ein Fehler für ὠβελίσαμεν oder ὠβέλισα. Anerkennung bei den Juden erwähnt Origenes als Kriterium auch im Falle der Bücher Enochs (*hom. Num.* XXVIII, 2, hg. W. A. Baehrens, GCS *Origenes* VII [1921] 282.6-11: *quia libelli ipsi non uidentur apud Hebraeos in auctoritate haberi ...*), die er in *De principiis* ohne Vorbehalt zitiert, aber in *Contra Celsum* V, 54 (hg. P. Koetschau, GCS *Origenes* II [1899] 58.16-17) als nicht von den Kirchen anerkannt beschreibt (ἐν ταῖς ἐκκλησίαις οὐ πάνυ φέρεται ὡς θεῖα) ; vgl. Ruwet, *art. cit.*, S. 48-50, und unten Anm. 29.
[12] *Com. Mt. ser.* 61, hg. E. Klostermann, GCS *Origenes* XI (1933) 140.18-20.
[13] Hieronymus, *com. Dan.* zu *Dan.* 13, 54-9, CCL 75A, 948-9; vgl. auch CCL 75A, 950 zu *Dan.* 14, 17 (den einzigen Auszug zu der Geschichte von Bel). Es kann sein, dass Hieronymus, der keine wörtliche Übersetzung verspricht (*ponam breuiter quid Origenes ... dixerit*, CCL 75A, 945), durch seine Vorliebe für die *hebraica ueritas* sowohl in seiner Auswahl der Auszüge wie auch im Wortlaut seiner Wiedergabe bestimmt wird. Vgl. die ausführliche Erörterung von J. Ruwet, *art. cit.*, S. 21-42, sowie Sgherri, *art. cit.*, S. 20, Anm. 57, und de Lange, SCh 302, 488-93 zu den Aussagen des Origenes über die Susannageschichte. Als Origenes den Africanusbrief schrieb, sah er das Wortspiel in *Dan.* 13, 58-9 nicht mehr als Gegenanzeige gegen die Annahme einer Übersetzung aus dem He-bräischen an (18, SCh 302, 558-60).

Dass Origenes in seinem Africanusbrief diejenigen Kritiker, die sich vor jedem Eingriff in den Text der Septuaginta fürchten, beruhigen will, selbst aber eine Mittelstellung einnimmt, sieht man, wenn man seine Aussagen zum christlichen und jüdischen Bibeltext mit denjenigen seiner kirchlichen Vorgänger vergleicht. Auf der|einen Seite erkennt er die Septuaginta als das kirchliche Alte Testament ohne Vorbehalt an, auf der anderen Seite aber begründet er diese Anerkennung einfach mit der Tatsache, dass die Septuaginta von den Kirchen benutzt wird, und auf sein Vertrauen in die göttliche Vorsehung. Wenn dagegen Irenäus die Autorität der Septuaginta behaupten will, argumentiert er in einer ganz anderen Weise [14]. Irenäus erzählt die Geschichte, das die siebzig von Ptolemäus beauftragten Ältesten ihre göttliche Inspiration dadurch bewiesen, dass sie getrennt übersetzten aber alle den gleichen Wortlaut hervorbrachten. Diejenigen also, die jetzt zu einer viel späteren Zeit andere Übersetzungen anfertigen wollen, werden nach Irenäus als unverschämt und tollkühn erwiesen. Ausserdem behauptet Irenäus, dass die Verkündigung der Apostel mit der Septuagintaübersetzung übereinstimmt.

Die Geschichte von der wunderbaren Simultanübersetzung der Septuaginta kommt schon bei Philo vor und wird auch von Klemens Alexandrinus wiederholt [15]. Origenes wird sie also sicher gekannt haben. Er wird aber auch gewusst haben, dass der Aristeasbrief und Josephus [16] solch ein Wunder nicht erzählen. Was die Benutzung der Septuaginta bei den Aposteln angeht, so hat er die Quellen der alttestamentlichen Zitate im Neuen Testament studiert und wusste, dass nicht immer der Wortlaut der Septuaginta dort wiedergegeben wird [17]. Die

---

[14] *Adv. haer.* III, 24-25 (= Mass. III.xxi.2-3).
[15] Philo, *Vita Mosis* II, 37ff.; Klemens, *Strom.* I, 22, 148; auch bei Pseudo-Justin, *Cohortatio ad Graecos* 13, und dem Dialog von Timotheus und Aquila, hg. F. C. Conybeare, *Anecdota Oxoniensia*, Oxford 1898, S. 90-92, fol. 117 und 119. Vgl. P. Benoit, *L'inspiration des Septante d'après les Pères*, in *L'homme devant Dieu: Mélanges offerts au Père Henri de Lubac* I, Paris 1963, S. 169ff., der weitere rabbinische und patristische Überlieferungen zu diesem Thema bespricht.
[16] *Ant.* XIII. 103-109.
[17] Vgl. Sgherri, *art. cit.*, S. 25-6; C. P. Hammond Bammel, *Der Römerbrieftext des Rufin und seine Origenes-Übersetzung*, Freiburg 1985, S. 234-8.

130

Kritik an den neueren Übersetzungen, von der Irenäus und andere kirchlichen Schriftsteller bestimmt sind, liegt Origenes fern. Nach Origenes ist Aquila derjenige der Übersetzer, der bestrebt war, den hebräischen Text mit der grössten Genauigkeit wiederzugeben[18], während Symmachus klarer und einleuchtender übersetzt (σαφέστερον)[19]. Zwar nicht im Brief an Africanus aber in anderen Schriften gesteht Origenes, dass wegen des höheren Alters der Septuagintaübersetzung ihre Handschriften eher Verderbnissen ausgesetzt worden sind als diejenigen der anderen Ausgaben[20]. Deswegen ist es möglich, dass sie Varianten und Fehler aufweisen, die durch Heranziehung der neueren Übersetzungen geheilt werden können[21]. Andere Unterschiede mögen auf die hebräische Vorlage der Septuaginta zurückgehen[22], oder auf absichtliche Änderungen aufseiten der Übersetzer[23]. An zwei auf lateinisch erhaltenen

---

[18] Vgl. *ep. Afric.* 4, SCh 302, 526; *Philocalie* 14, hg. J. A. Robinson, Cambridge 1893, S. 68.27-9.

[19] Vgl. *Sel. in Ps.* 4, 1 und 5, PG 12, 1133 und 1145; Sgherri, *art. cit.*, S. 21.

[20] *Com. Io.* VI, 41, hg. E. Preuschen, GCS *Origenes* IV (1903) 150. Die Namen werden fehlerhaft geschrieben in den griechischen Abschriften nicht nur der Evangelien sondern auch des Gesetzes und der Propheten, ὡς ἠκριβώσαμεν ἀπὸ ῾Εβραίων μαθόντες, καὶ τοῖς ἀντιγράφοις αὐτῶν τὰ ἡμέτερα συγκρίναντες, μαρτυρηθεῖσιν ὑπὸ τῶν μηδέπω διαστραφεισῶν ἐκδόσεων ᾿Ακύλου καὶ Θεοδοτίωνος καὶ Συμμάχου. Es können aber auch Fehler in den hebräischen Handschriften vorkommen; vgl. Sgherri, *art. cit.*, S. 13-14.

[21] Vgl. oben Anm. 3, und Sgherri, *art. cit.*, S. 8-11. Zu der Auslassung des Wortes πρῶτον in *Jer.* 16, 18 bemerkt Origenes: τὸ » πρῶτον « εἴτε μὴ νοήσαντες ἐξεῖλάν τινες τῶν γεγραμμένα εἴτε καὶ οἰκονομήσαντες ἐξελεῖν οἱ ῾Εβδομήκοντα, θεὸς ἂν εἰδείη (*hom. Jer.* XVI, GCS III, 137.13ff.).

[22] *Sel. in Ps.* 3, 8 (PG 12, 1129B): Εἰκὸς οὖν, ὥς τινες ῾Εβραίων λέγουσι, τὰ ἀρχαῖα ἀντίγραφα ἑτέρως ἐσχηκέναι, ἢ τὸ εὐτελὲς περιϊστάμενους τοὺς ῾Εβδομήκοντα τῆς λέξεως, τετολμηκέναι ἀντὶ τοῦ « σιαγόνα » ποιῆσαι « ματαίως ». *Sel. in Ezech.* 7, 27 (PG 13, 796A): τὸ, ὁ βασιλεὺς πενθήσει, συνήθως ἱστόρηται, τάχα διὰ τὸν Σωτῆρα οὐκ ἂν νομισθέντα πενθεῖν, οὐχ ἑρμηνευσάντων τῶν ῾Εβδομήκοντα τὸ ῥητὸν, ἢ μὴ εὑρηκότων τότε ἐν τῷ ῾Εβραϊκῷ τὴν λέξιν. Vgl. Nautin, *op. cit.*, S. 353, Sgherri, *art. cit.*, S. 13, Anm. 37, und *A proposito di Origene e la lingua ebraica*, in *Augustinianum* 14 (1974) 252, Anm. 74.

[23] Vgl. die beiden eben zitierten Bemerkungen. Origenes benutzt manchmal den Terminus οἰκονομία in einem solchen Zusammenhang; vgl. oben Anm. 21 und *Sel. in Ps.* 2, 12 (PG 12, 1116D): ὑποπτεύομεν μήποτε ἢ κατ᾿ οἰκονομίαν προσέθηκαν τοῦτο, ἢ τὰ ἀντίγραφα ἡμάρτηται. Africanusbrief

X

Stellen spricht Origenes von einer Überwachung der Übersetzungsarbeit durch die Vorsehung bzw. durch den Heiligen Geist[24].

Nach den Vorgängern des Origenes, insbesondere nach Justin, haben die Juden zum Zweck der antichristlichen Polemik die Septuagintaübersetzung getadelt, haben selbst versucht, anders zu übersetzen, und den Text geändert und verstümmelt[25]. Im Dialog von Timotheus und Aquila wird die Beschuldigung wiedergegeben, dass der Bibelübersetzer Aquila die Schrift verfälschte, indem er Weissagungen über Christus nicht nur in seiner eigenen griechischen Ausgabe sondern sogar aus dem hebräischen Text entfernte[26]. Solche Anklagen gegen den jüdischen Bibeltext liegen Origenes fern[27], er bringt

---

SCh 302, 560: καὶ γὰρ ἐπ' ἄλλων πολλῶν ἔστιν εὑρεῖν οἰκονομικῶς τινα ὑπὸ τῶν ἑρμηνευσάντων ἐκδεδομένα. Vgl. auch Barthélemy, *art. cit.*, S. 214-5 (258-9). Vielleicht haben schon Zeitgenossen des Origenes argumentiert, dass Änderungen in der Septuagintaübersetzung beabsichtigt und deswegen den Lesarten des hebräischen Textes vorzuziehen seien; vgl. oben Anm. 3, *hom.* Jer. XVI, 5 (zitiert oben Anm. 21) und XX, 5 (GCS III, 184.23ff.): παρὰ μὲν ἡμῖν, ὡς οἱ Ἑβδομήκοντα παραδεδώκασιν οὐκ οἶδ' ὅ τι σκοπήσαντες...
 [24] Hom. Jer. II, 4 (von Hieronymus übersetzt; hg. W. A. Baehrens, GCS *Origenes* VIII [1925] 294.9-15): *dispensatio prouidentiae, etiamsi non magnopere curauit, ut disertitudinem, quae in Graeco sermone laudatur, Graece interpretando sequeretur, curauit tamen ea quae significantia sunt exhibere et differentiam eorum explanare dilucide his qui scripturas diligentissime perscrutantur. Com. Ct.* I (GCS VIII, 100.29-101.7): *nos Septuaginta interpretum scripta per omnia custodimus, certi quod Spiritus sanctus mysteriorum formas obtectas esse uoluit in scripturis diuinis...* Vgl. Benoit, *art. cit.* S. 179, Sgherri, *art. cit.*, S. 14-15. In den Kapiteln über die göttliche Eingebung der heiligen Schrift in *De principiis* IV macht Origenes keinen Unterschied zwischen hebräischem Text und Septuaginta. Dieselbe göttliche Kraft, die in und durch die ursprüngliche Fassung wirkt, kann dies nicht weniger durch eine Übersetzung erreichen. Vgl. auch die oben Anm. 5 zitierte Stelle aus dem Africanusbrief.
 [25] Justin, *Dialog mit Tryphon* 68, 71ff., 84. Justin zitiert Texte, die nach seiner Aussage die Juden entfernt (zwei jetzt als unecht angesehene Texte und Jer. 11, 19), verstümmelt (*Ps.* 95, 10) oder anders übersetzt (*Is.* 7, 14) haben.
 [26] Dialog von Timotheus und Aquila, hg. Conybeare, S. 89-92, fol. 115v, fol. 118v-119. Das Datum der Quelle oder Quellen dieses Teils der Schrift und deswegen auch der Anklage ist unsicher.
 [27] Nach dem Katenenauszug 318 zu *Mt.* 14, 10 (hg. Klostermann, GCS *Origenes* XII [1941] 140), auf welche Stelle H. Bietenhard, *Caesarea, Origenes und die Juden*, Stuttgart 1974, S. 51, Anm. 2, als parallel zu

132

aber eine verwandte Beschuldigung gegen die Ältesten und die Leiter der Juden, nämlich dass sie solche Schriften bzw. Schriftstellen, welche von ihren eigenen Missetaten berichteten, entfernt und geheimgehalten haben [28]. Er kommt auf diese These nicht nur wegen der Susannageschichte sondern auch wegen der Stellen im Neuen Testament, die über Verbrechen gegen die Propheten berichten, die in den kanonischen Büchern des Alten Testaments nicht beschrieben aber teilweise in apokryphen Schriften noch überliefert sind. Zum Beispiel die Überlieferung, dass der Prophet Jesaia entzweigesägt wurde, befindet sich in einer apokryphen Schrift, welche die Juden vielleicht absichtlich mit unpassenden Worten interpoliert haben, um dadurch die ganze Schrift als unglaubwürdig erscheinen zu lassen [29]. Im Matthäuskommentar erwähnt Origenes die Möglichkeit, dass die Juden aus antichristlichen Absichten bestimmte apokryphe Schriften gefälscht hätten [30].

---

den Justinstellen hinweist, besitzen die Juden die Prophezeiungen in einem toten und enthaupteten (ἀποτετμημένας) Zustand, weil sie das Haupt, d.h. Christus, nicht haben. Dies bezieht sich aber auf das verstümmelte Schriftverständnis der Juden, nicht auf deren Text. Nach Hieronymus (com. Is. 3 zu 6, 9-10, CCL 73, 92, 49-54) hat Origenes gegen die These, dass die Juden ihre Bücher verfälscht haben, im achten Buch seines Isaiaskommentars argumentiert, dass der Herr und die Apostel ein solches Verbrechen nicht verschwiegen hätten; vgl. Sgherri, art. cit., S. 20 Anm. 61.

[28] Brief an Africanus, SCh 302, 542-550. Ein ähnliches Urteil über die Susannageschichte bringt Hippolyt, Danielkommentar 14, GCS Hippolytus I (1897) 23.

[29] Op. cit., S. 13, SCh 302, 542-4; vgl. zum selben Problem Com. Mt. ser. 28, GCS XI, 49.19-51.22. Origenes hat sich viel mit dem Problem der apokryphen jüdischen Schriften und ihrer Benutzung im Neuen Testament beschäftigt. Seine erhaltenen Aussagen darüber hat A. v. Harnack, Der kirchengeschichtliche Ertrag der exegetischen Arbeiten des Origenes, Leipzig I [TU 42.3], 1918, S. 17ff. und II [TU 42.4], 1919, S. 42ff. gesammelt. Vgl. dazu auch Bietenhard, op. cit., S. 30ff., 48, 51 (der aber 31 oben und 37 Anm. 117 Harnack, TU 42.3, S. 17 falsch abschreibt). Origenes äussert sich gegen Leute, die gewisse neutestamentliche Schriften ablehnen, weil sie jüdische Apokryphen zitieren (com. Mt. ser. 28 und 117, GCS XI, 51 und 250), meint aber, es wäre gefährlich, solche Apokryphen, deren Lektüre weder unter den Juden noch in der Kirche überliefert ist, deswegen anerkennen zu wollen, weil sie im Neuen Testament zitiert werden (com. Ct., prol., GCS VIII, 87.24-88.10).

[30] Com. Mt. ser. 28, GCS XI, 51.13-14: Iudaeos, qui forte ad destructionem ueritatis scripturarum nostrarum quaedam finxerunt confirmantes dogmata falsa. Vgl. J. Ruwet, Les Apocryphes dans les oeuvres d'Origène II, in Biblica 25 (1944) 311-334.

Nach dem Tod des Origenes erfreute sich seine Hexaplaarbeit weiterhin einer grossen Berühmtheit. Der hexaplarische Septuagintatext wurde abgeschrieben und verbreitet — vor allem durch Pamphilus und Euseb [31] — und Berichte über die verschiedenen Lesarten der anderen Hexaplaspalten wurden in Kommentaren und Glossensammlungen wiedergegeben [32]. Nicht alle Berichterstatter oder Benutzer der Hexapla waren aber von rein wissenschaftlichen Erwägungen bestimmt, sondern viele wurden in ihren Äusserungen durch ihre Stellungnahme sowohl zur Person des Origenes selbst wie auch zur Konkurrenz zwischen Septuaginta und *hebraica ueritas* beeinflusst. Ich werde mich auf fünf Beispiele beschränken.

Euseb von Cäsarea bringt in seinem Bericht über die Hexapla in der Kirchengeschichte (VI, 16-17) seine Bewunderung des grossen Fleisses des Origenes zum Ausdruck. Er hat sich um die Verbreitung des hexaplarischen Septuagintatextes bemüht [33] und zitiert Lesarten aus den Hexaplaspalten in seinen eigenen exegetischen Schriften. Er ist durchaus bereit, solche Lesarten zu loben und zu bevorzugen [34]. Inwiefern diese Lesarten und seine Beurteilung derselben aus den entsprechenden Kommentaren des Origenes übernommen sind, können wir in den wenigsten Fällen feststellen [35], weil keine Kommentare des Origenes zum Alten Testament in ihrer ursprünglichen Form erhalten sind [36]. Ähnlich wie Origenes erkennt Euseb die Septuaginta als Bibel der Kirche an. Seine stärkste Befürwortung der Überlegenheit der Septuaginta findet sich in

---

[31] Vgl. H. Dörrie, *Zur Geschichte der Septuaginta im Jahrhundert Konstantins*, ZNW 39 (1940) 57-110, insb. 69-70; Nautin, *op. cit.*, S. 353ff.

[32] Solche Berichte sind teilweise in Katenenhandschriften erhalten; vgl. G. Dorival, *L'apport des chaînes exégétiques grecques à une réédition des Hexaples d'Origène*, in *Revue d'histoire des textes* 4 (1974) 45-74.

[33] Vgl. z.B. H. B. Swete, *Introduction to the Old Testament in Greek*, Cambridge 1900, S. 76-8.

[34] Vgl. z.B. D. S. Wallace-Hadrill, *Eusebius of Caesarea*, London 1960, S. 62ff., 84ff.; hg. J. Ziegler, GCS *Eusebius* IX, Jesaiakommentar (1975), S. xxxviii-xli und Namenregister 443-4.

[35] Vgl. aber Ziegler, *op. cit.*, S. xxxi ff.; D. Barthélemy, *Eusèbe, la Septante et « les autres »*, in *Études d'histoire du texte de l'Ancien Testament*, Göttingen 1978, S. 179ff.

[36] Rufins Übersetzung des Hoheliedkommentars lässt fast alle textkritische Bemerkungen des Origenes aus; vgl. Bammel, *op. cit.*, S. 232.

X

134

dem in armenischer Übersetzung erhaltenen ersten Teil der
Chronik. Dort behauptet er, dass die Septuaginta-Übersetzung
aus einer alten und fehlerlosen hebräischen Vorlage übersetzt
und die Bibel der Kirche Christi sei, welche « auch unseres
Heilandes Apostel und Jünger von Anbeginn an zu gebrauchen
überliefert haben»[37]. Anlass zu dieser Behauptung gibt ihm
die Feststellung, dass hinsichtlich der Chronologie der Pa-
triarchenleben Unterschiede zwischen dem hebräischen Text
und der Septuaginta bestehen, in denen die Septuaginta teilweise durch den samaritanischen Pentateuch unterstützt wird.
Euseb erklärt diese Sachlage dadurch, dass die Juden den
hebräischen Text verfälscht haben, um ihrer eigenen Sitte der
frühen Eheschliessung Unterstützung zu geben[38]. Wenn er
aber hier eine Fälschung im hebräischen Text voraussetzt, so
gibt er anderswo zu, dass die siebzig Ältesten manchmal undeutlich übersetzt und sogar messianische Prophezeiungen
verdunkelt haben, welche in den anderen Ausgaben deutlicher
wiedergegeben werden — dies haben sie mit Absicht getan,
weil sie in einer vorchristlichen Zeit die Bibel für Heiden
herausgaben[39]. Durch solche Beobachtungen, die mit aller
Wahrscheinlichkeit auf Origenes zurückgehen[40], werden die
früheren Anklagen gegen die Juden auf den Kopf gestellt.

---

[37] GCS *Eusebius* V (1911) 45, und für den griechischen Text die
Ausgabe von A. Schoene, Berlin 1875, I, S. 96: πανταχόθεν τοιγαροῦν τῆς
τῶν ο‘ ἑρμηνείας ἐκ παλαιᾶς, ὡς ἔοικε, καὶ ἀδιαστρόφου Ἑβραίων γραφῆς
μεταβεβλῆσθαι συνισταμένης, εἰκότως ταύτῃ καὶ ἡμεῖς κεχρήμεθα κατὰ τὴν
παροῦσαν χρονογραφίαν, ὅτε μάλιστα καὶ ἡ καθ’ ὅλης οἰκουμένης ἡπλωμένη
Χριστοῦ ἐκκλησία ταύτῃ μόνῃ προσέχει τῶν τοῦ σωτῆρος ἡμῶν ἀποστόλων
τε καὶ μαθητῶν ἀρχῆθεν ταύτῃ χρῆσθαι παραδεδωκότων. Vgl. auch *Dem. ev.*
proem., 35-6, GCS *Eusebius* VI (1913) 209-10. In *Praep. ev.* VIII, 1ff, GCS
Eusebius VIII, 1 (1954) 419ff. bringt Euseb einen sachlichen Bericht
über die Entstehung der Septuaginta mit Zitaten aus dem Aristeasbrief.
Er sieht die Übersetzung als das Werk der göttlichen Vorsehung an:
τῆς θεόθεν οἰκονομηθείσης ἑρμηνείας.
[38] Op. cit. 37ff., insb. 40 und 44. Auch Origenes hat den samaritanischen Pentateuch benutzt; vgl. F. Field, *Origenis Hexaplorum quae
supersunt* I, Oxford 1875, S. lxxxiiff.; H. B. Swete, *Introduction to the
Old Testament in Greek*, Cambridge 1900, S. 437, N. de Lange, *Origen
and the Jews*, S. 37, E. Tov, *Die griechischen Bibelübersetzungen*, in
Aufstieg und Niedergang der römischen Welt II, 20, Berlin 1987, S. 185.
[39] *Com. Ps.* 86, 6, PG 23, 1049B-C; *Eclogae Propheticae* II, 5, PG
22, 1097Dff.
[40] Nach Barthélemy, *art. cit.*, S. 184-187; vgl. die oben Anm. 24
zitierte Stelle aus dem Hoheliedkommentar.

X

Einen grossen Streit über den relativen Wert der Septuaginta und des hebräischen Textes hat Hieronymus mit seiner neuen Bibelübersetzung hervorgerufen [41]. Bevor ich aber zu Hieronymus komme, werde ich einen älteren Zeitgenossen und einen Gegner erwähnen [42]. Mit Epiphanius hat Hieronymus sich in den letzten Jahren des vierten Jahrhunderts in der Polemik gegen den Orige-

---

[41] Die Bewertung der Septuaginta in der frühchristlichen Kirche ist oft erörtert worden. Vgl. die Testimoniensammlung in hg. Paul Wendland, *Aristeae ad Philocratem Epistula cum ceteris de origine versionis LXX interpretum testimoniis*, Leipzig 1900, S. 85ff.; Paul Wendland, *art. cit.* (oben Anm. 1); Benoit, *art. cit.*, (oben Anm. 15); Heinrich Karpp, «*Prophet*» *oder* «*Dolmetscher*»?, in *Festschrift für Günther Dehn*, Neukirchen 1957, S. 103-117; D. Barthélemy, *La place de la Septante dans l'Église*, in *Études d'histoire du texte de l'Ancien Testament*, S. 111-126 (auch zum Problem des Kanons).

[42] Sowohl Hieronymus selbst wie auch vor ihm die lateinischen Väter Hilarius und Ambrosius haben in exegetischen Werken textkritische Einzelheiten aus den Kommentaren des Origenes übernommen. Vgl. über die Benutzung des Origenes im allgemeinen Émile Goffinet, *L'utilisation d'Origène dans le Commentaire des Psaumes de Saint Hilaire de Poitiers*, Louvain 1965; H. J. Auf der Maur, *Das Psalmenverständnis des Ambrosius von Mailand*, Leiden 1977, und (zu Hieronymus) Pierre Courcelle, *Les Lettres grecques en Occident*, Paris 1948, S. 88-100, Nautin, *op. cit.*, S. 326ff. Den Bericht des Hilarius über die siebzig Ältesten, welche er als Nachfolger der siebzig Ältesten, denen Moses geheime Lehren anvertraute, und deswegen als fähig, die Doppeldeutigkeiten der hebräischen Sprache richtig zu interpretieren, ansieht (während die späteren Übersetzer, die diese geheime Überlieferung nicht kannten, Fehler verbreiteten), und sein Urteil über die Autorität der Septuagintaübersetzung hängt er an einer aus Origenes geschöpften Beobachtung zu *Ps* 2 an (*Tractatus super Psalmos*, hg. A. Zingerle, CSEL 22 [1891] 37ff.); vgl. Goffinet, *op. cit.*, S. 53: Paulus zitierte diesen Psalm (*Act.* 13, 33) als den ersten Psalm; er tat dies aber, weil er hier Hebräern predigte und deswegen der Gewohnheit der Hebräer folgte, CSEL 22, 40.11-20, vgl. 9.18ff. und Goffinet, *op. cit.* 26 ff. Die textkritische Bemerkung des Ambrosius über einen Zusatz der Septuaginta in *Gn* 1, 9 findet sich auch bei Basilius (*Hexaemeron*, PG 29, 88D-89A), nicht aber das Urteil dazu (*Exameron* III.5, hg. K. Schenkl, CSEL 32.1 [1896] 73.1ff.: *nos non putamus absurdum id quod perhibetur additum, etiamsi ceteris interpretibus uel ueritas doceatur subpetere uel auctoritas; multa enim non otiose a septuaginta uiris Hebraicae lectioni addita et adiuncta comperimus*). Hexaplalesarten zitiert Ambrosius häufig in seiner Psalmauslegung, diejenigen des Aquila oft mit der Bezeichnung *pulchre* (vgl. die Verzeichnisse in CSEL 62 [1913] 537 und CSEL 64 [1919] 421-2, 438-9). Zu *Ps.* 118, 67 begründet er seine Bevorzugung einer Lesart der Septuaginta mit den Worten: *quia septuaginta uirorum sententias magis sequitur ecclesia et hic sensus est planior et nihil offensionis admittit* (CSEL 64 [1919] 196.16ff.).

nismus verbündet. Was den Bibeltext angeht, so waren sie nicht derselben Meinung. Epiphanius sieht die Septuagintaübersetzung als die einzig wahre Fassung des griechischen Alten Testamentes an. Wie er in seinem *Liber de mensuris et ponderibus* vom Jahre 392 berichtet, haben die zweiundsiebzig Ältesten unter dem Einfluss des Heiligen Geistes getrennt arbeitend in vollem Einklang übersetzt. Wo Zusätze oder Auslassungen nötig waren, sind alle auf gleiche Weise mit dem Text verfahren. So liege die Wahrheit bei ihnen und nicht bei den drei soviel späteren jüdischen Übersetzern, welche sich zum Judentum jeweils vom Christentum, Samaritanertum und Marcionitismus abgekehrt hätten und sich durch polemische Zwecke bestimmen liessen [43]. In seinem Bericht über die Hexapla ist Epiphanius bestrebt zu zeigen, dass auch Origenes den Vorrang der Septuaginta anerkannte und dass er nur der Information halber gewisse Stellen mit Obelisken bezeichnete und andere mit Asterisken hinzusetzte. Origenes habe die von den zweiundsiebzig Ältesten hinzugesetzten Stellen nicht entfernt, weil er von ihrer Notwendigkeit wusste [44]. Bei der Anfertigung der Hexapla habe er die Septuagintaübersetzung wegen ihrer Genauigkeit in die Mittelspalte gestellt, um dadurch die anderen Übersetzungen zu beiden Seiten widerlegen zu können [45]. Die Hexapla sei das Einzige, was Origenes an nützlichen Dingen gemacht habe [46].

---

[43] *De mensuris et ponderibus* 19 und 14ff., PG 43.265A-B, 261D (Aquila griff die Septuaginta an und änderte die Zeugnisse über Christus), 264C (Symmachus wollte die samaritanischen Übersetzungen verdrehen), 264 D (Theodotion, sich im Zorn von der Irrlehre Marcions abwendend, ist zum Judentum übergetreten und hat das Meiste im Einklang mit der Septuagintaübersetzung herausgegeben, weil er mit dieser Fassung vertraut war). Der Bericht über Aquila ist mit demjenigen im Dialog von Timotheus und Aquila eng verwandt.
[44] 17, PG 43, 265B; vgl. auch 2-3, PG 43, 237Bff. insb. 240C-D: Origenes habe die von den siebzig Dolmetschern als überflüssig ausgelassenen Wörter mit Asterisken hinzugesetzt, um zu verhindern, dass die Juden und Samaritaner die Heiligen Schriften der Kirchen angreifen.
[45] 19, PG 43.269A. Nach Nautin, *op. cit.*, S. 321, hat Epiphanius diese Erklärung vielleicht schon in der Apologie von Pamphilus und Euseb vorgefunden.
[46] 7 und 19, PG 43, 248A und 269A.

In den durch die neue Übersetzung des Hieronymus aus-
gelösten Streitigkeiten über die Autorität der hebräischen
Bibel werden die vielen anonymen Gegner, über die Hieronymus so oft klagt, für uns vor allem in den Werken Rufins
und Augustins erkennbar. Rufin nimmt zu diesem Thema nur
einmal ausdrücklich das Wort, nämlich in seiner *Apologie
gegen Hieronymus* II, 36-41 [47]. Hier macht er seinen eigenen
Standpunkt sehr deutlich. Nach der Ansicht Rufins ist Hieronymus in seinem Unternehmen dabei, die Stimme des Heiligen Geistes und das Erbe der Apostel zu entweihen. Die
wunderbare Simultanübersetzung der Septuaginta wurde durch
den Heiligen Geist inspiriert. Sie sei von den Aposteln der
Kirche übergeben. Wenn diese gemeint hätten, dass die Septuaginta fehlerhaft sei und dass die Wahrheit bei den Juden
liege, so hätten sie schon damals für die nötige Korrektur
gesorgt. Wenn Hieronymus sich jetzt nach vierhundert Jahren
die Wahrheit von den Juden erbitte und ganze Teile der Bibel,
wie etwa die Geschichte Susannas, ausmerze, so gebe er den
Eindruck, dass die Kirche während dieser ganzen Zeit im
Irrtum gewesen sei, und mache dadurch die Christen den
Heiden gegenüber lächerlich. Hieronymus dürfe sich nicht auf
den Vorgang des Origenes in der Hexapla berufen, erstens
weil er Origenes sonst verdammt, und zweitens weil die Absicht des Origenes eine ganz andere war. Origenes habe die
Heilige Schrift nicht ändern wollen, sondern er habe über
die von den Juden benutzten Übersetzungen informiert, indem
er durch die kritischen Zeichen deutlich machte, welche Teile
bei den Juden fehlen oder hinzugesetzt worden sind. Ausserdem
habe Origenes gezeigt, dass die Stellen in der Schrift, die
undeutlich scheinen, in der Tat voller geistiger Geheimnisse
seien.

Bei seiner Erklärung der Absichten des Origenes in der
Hexapla kam Rufin der Brief an Africanus sehr gelegen. Dies
sieht man aus der Stelle in seiner Übersetzung der Kirchengeschichte Eusebs, wo Euseb den Africanusbrief erwähnt.
Während Euseb nur berichtet, dass Origenes eine sehr aus-

---

[47] Hg. M. Simonetti, CCL 20 (1961) 111-116.

138

führliche Antwort an Africanus gegeben habe, fügt Rufin eine eigene Zusammenfassung des Inhalts hinzu. Origenes ant-worte in glänzender Weise und behaupte, man dürfe keines-wegs den Erfindungen und Fälschungen der Juden zuhören, sondern nur das in der Heiligen Schrift für wahr halten, was die siebzig Dolmetscher übersetzt haben, weil dies durch die Autorität der Apostel bestätigt sei [48]. In seiner Übersetzung von Eusebs Bericht über die Hexapla macht Rufin einige kleine Änderungen, die seine eigene Geringschätzung der jüdischen Fassungen zum Ausdruck bringen, und fügt eine Erklärung der verschiedenen Hexaplaspalten hinzu. Während Euseb schreibt, dass Origenes die ursprünglichen, bei den Juden sich befindenden Schriften in hebräischen Buchstaben sich zu eigen machte und dass er die Ausgaben der anderen Übersetzer abgesehen von der Septuaginta aufspürte, lässt Rufin das Wort « ursprünglich » (πρωτότυπος) aus und schreibt, dass Origenes erkennen wollte, welcher Art Sachen bei den Juden in he-bräischen Buchstaben gelesen werden, und wie gross die Ab-weichungen der Ausgaben der anderen Übersetzer seien [49].

Auch in seinen Übersetzungen der Werke des Origenes bemüht sich Rufin, seine eigenen Ansichten über den Vorrang der Septuaginta zu unterstützen. Bei einer Untersuchung der textkritischen Bemerkungen in Rufins Übersetzung des Rö-merbriefkommentars wurde es deutlich, dass Rufin die An-gaben des Origenes über Lesarten von Aquila, Symmachus und Theodotion auslässt und mit Vorliebe nur diejenigen Bemerk-ungen wiedergibt, die zum Lob der Septuaginta dienen oder Anlass zu antijüdischer Polemik geben [50]. In derselben Über-setzung versucht Rufin zu zeigen, dass Paulus in seinen alttestamentlichen Zitaten nicht dem hebräischen Text folgt, sondern entweder die Septuagintaübersetzung zitiert oder selbst frei formuliert. Hiermit treibt Rufin stillschweigend Polemik gegen Hieronymus, der das Gegenteil behauptete, nämlich dass die Apostel und Evangelisten bei Unterschieden

---

[48] VI, 31, hg. Th. Mommsen, GCS *Eusebius* II (1908) 585.27ff.
[49] VI, 16, GCS II, 552.26ff.; 555.1ff.
[50] Bammel, *op. cit.* (oben Anm. 17), S. 231ff.

zwischen dem hebräischen Text und der Septuaginta das Hebräische bevorzugen[51].

Hieronymus selbst hat Aussagen zu unserem Thema in
grosser Fülle hinterlassen[52]. Ich werde versuchen, Einiges, was
für seine Bewertung der Hexapla des Origenes wichtig ist,
zusammenzufassen. In seiner Frühzeit hat Hieronymus als
Anhänger des Origenes[53] ähnlich wie Euseb die Hexapla voller
Bewunderung angesehen und sich seiner Kenntnis derselben
gerühmt. Im Tituskommentar schreibt er, dass man wegen
dieser Arbeit den Spott der Juden nicht mehr zu fürchten
brauche. Er habe sich selbst bemüht, die aus der Bibliothek
in Caesarea abgeschriebenen Bücher des Alten Gesetzes anhand
der Hexapla zu korrigieren[54].

Das Vorwort zu seinem Buch über hebräische Fragen[55]
schrieb Hieronymus zu einer Zeit, als er Origenes noch gern
offen lobte (trotz der Angriffe seiner Gegner), aber den Vor-

---

[51] *Op. cit.*, S. 234ff. Vgl. auch unten 140 und 145. Hieronymus hatte
Rufin aufgefordert: *ostendat aliquid scriptum esse in Nouo Instrumento
de Septuaginta interpretibus quod in hebraico non habetur (Apologie
gegen Rufin* II, 34, CCL 79 [1982] 72).
[52] Seine Aussagen sind oft erörtert worden. Vgl. die oben Anm.
41 aufgeführten Aufsätze, P. W. Skehan, *St. Jerome and the Canon
of the Holy Scriptures*, in hg. F. X. Murphy, *A Monument to Saint
Jerome*, New York 1952, S. 259-287, und Colette Estin, *Saint Jérôme,
de la traduction inspirée à la traduction relativiste*, in *Revue Biblique*
88 (1981) 199-215. Über die Werke des Hieronymus und deren Datierung
vgl. F. Cavallera, *Saint Jérôme, sa vie et son œuvre*, Louvain-Paris
1922; P. Nautin, *Études de chronologie hiéronymienne*, in *Revue des
Études Augustiniennes* 18 (1972) 209-218; 19 (1973) 69-86; 20 (1974) 251-
284; ders., art. *Hieronymus*, TRE XV, 304-315; J. N. D. Kelly, *Jerome:
His Life, Writings, and Controversies*, London 1975.
[53] Zu den Aussagen des Hieronymus über Origenes vgl. Cavallera,
op. cit., II, S. 115-127.
[54] PL 26, 595B. Über diese Behauptung vgl. Nautin, *Origène*, S.
328-331. Seine Freude an der Hexapla hatte Hieronymus schon im
Vorwort zu seiner Übersetzung der Chronik des Euseb zum Ausdruck
gebracht (hg. R. Helm, GCS *Eusebius* VII [1956] 3f.).
[55] CCL 72 (1959) 1-2. Auch in seinem Werk *De viris illustribus*,
welches er kurz vor dem Ausbruch der origenistischen Streitigkeiten
im Jahre 393 verfasste, zollt Hieronymus den Leistungen des Origenes
sowohl in seiner Meisterung der hebräischen Sprache und in seiner
Hexapla wie auch sonst noch das höchste Lob (54). Im Abschnitt über
seine eigene Arbeit aber (135) erwähnt er schon seine Übersetzung des
Alten Testaments aus dem Hebräischen (TU 14, 32-3, 56). Vgl. auch das
Vorwort zu seinem *com. Mich.* II (CCL 76 [1969] 473).

rang der *hebraica ueritas* schon anerkannt hatte. Er nimmt
hier den grossen Origenes als Vorbild für sein Vorhaben, die
Fehler in den griechischen und lateinischen Exemplaren des
Alten Testaments anhand der hebräischen Bibel zu korrigieren.
Origenes wurde ja auch getadelt, weil er in seinen Kommentaren die Wahrheit des Hebräischen anerkannte. Die siebzig
Ältesten haben manchmal, vor allem bezüglich der Prophezeiungen Christi, die Geheimnisse der Heiligen Schrift nicht
deutlich ans Licht bringen wollen, weil sie für einen Heiden
arbeiteten und den Eindruck des Ditheismus zu vermeiden
versuchten. Zudem bringen die Evangelisten, der Heiland selbst
und der Apostel Paulus viele Zitate, die nicht in den Exemplaren der Kirche stehen. Die siebzig Ältesten haben nach
Josephus ohnehin nur den Pentateuch übersetzt. Diese Bücher
stünden dem hebräischen Text näher.

Bei seiner Arbeit am Text des Alten Testaments hatte
Hieronymus mit einer Neubearbeitung angefangen, in der er
die Methoden des Origenes in der Septuagintaspalte der Hexapla nachahmte. In den erhaltenen Vorworten zu einzelnen
Büchern erwähnt er Origenes nicht, erklärt aber seine Benutzung der aus der Hexapla übernommenen kritischen Zeichen. Er klagt über die vielen Fehler der griechischen und
lateinischen Handschriften, schreibt diese aber der Nachlässig-
keit der Schreiber zu, nicht den siebzig Ältesten, welche er
hier noch als vom Heiligen Geist erfüllt beschreibt [56].

Einblick in die Methoden des Hieronymus bei seiner
Neubearbeitung anhand der Hexapla gibt sein späterer Brief
an die Gothen Sunnia und Fretela, welche ihm eine Fragenliste
über die Unterschiede zwischen den Lesarten seiner Psalmen-
bearbeitung und denjenigen des griechischen Textes zugesandt
hatten [57]. Aus demselben Brief wird es deutlich, dass er hier

---

[56] *Praef. in libr. Paralipomenon iuxta LXX interpretes*, PL 29.401-4,
insb. 402A: *nec hoc Septuaginta Interpretibus, qui Spiritu sancto pleni
ea quae uera fuerant transtulerunt, sed scriptorum culpae ascribendum...*;
404A über die Zusätze der Septuaginta: *Ubi uero obelus ... praeposita est,
illic signatur quid Septuaginta Interpretes addiderint, uel ob decoris
gratiam, uel ob Spiritus sancti auctoritatem, licet in Hebraeis uoluminibus non legatur;* vgl. auch *praef. in libr. Job, praef. in libr. Psalmo-
rum, praef. in libros Salomonis*, PL 29, 61-2, 117-120, 403-4.
[57] *Ep.* 106, hg. I. Hilberg, CSEL 55 (1912) 247ff.

bestrebt ist, den hexaplarischen Septuagintatext seinen Lesern zu empfehlen. Er erklärt, dass man zwischen der (von Sunnia und Fretela benutzten) κοινή oder *communis editio* der Septuaginta, welche die im Lauf der Überlieferung korrumpierte alte Ausgabe sei (κοινή *pro locis et temporibus et pro uoluntate scriptorum uetus corrupta editio est*), und derjenigen, die in der Hexapla stehe und die er selbst übersetzt habe, welche in den Büchern der Gelehrten unverdorben und rein erhalten worden sei (*quae in eruditorum libris incorrupta et inmaculata septuaginta interpretum translatio reseruatur*), unterscheiden müsse. Die *communis editio* werde von vielen die lukianische genannt [58]. Bei der Behandlung einzelner Lesarten spricht er oft in diesem Brief, alsob die Septuaginta mit dem hexaplarischen Septuagintatext identisch sei [59]. Als er den Brief schrieb, hatte er schon mit der Übersetzung aus dem Hebräischen begonnen [60]. In einer Bemerkung zu *Ps.* 73, 8 macht er einen Unterschied bezüglich der Benutzung der beiden Fassungen: beim Gesang in der Kirche sollte man dem Text der Septuaginta folgen, aber die Gelehrten müssen die Lesarten der *hebraica ueritas* kennen [61].

Aus den Aussagen, die Hieronymus in *ep.* 106 wie auch anderswo [62] macht, erhellt, dass es im griechischen Bereich

---

[58] CSEL 55, 249.9-15, 248.22.

[59] Er tut dies auch dort, wo er über die Zusätze, die aus der Übersetzung Theodotions übernommen und mit Asterisken bezeichnet sind, redet und indem er den hebräischen Text als Massstab nimmt. Nur 253.21-3 (zu *Ps.* 17, 47) macht er einen Unterschied zwischen den Zusätzen und der Arbeit der siebzig Dolmetscher selbst. Gleich danach (253.23-254.6 zu *Ps.* 17, 48) behauptet er, man müsse die Fehler der Septuaginta zugeben und korrigieren (*si quid uel transferentis festinatione uel scribentium uitio deprauatum est, simpliciter confiteri et emendare debemus*).

[60] CSEL 55, 289.18.

[61] CSEL 55, 270.1ff.

[62] Vgl. *praef. in Quatuor Evangelia*, PL 29, 527B: *eos codices, quos a Luciano et Hesychio nuncupatos, paucorum hominum asserit peruersa contentio: quibus utique nec in ueteri Instrumento post Septuaginta Interpretes emendare quid licuit ...; De Viris Illustribus* 77 (TU 14, 41-2): *Lucianus ... tantum in Scripturarum studio laborauit, ut usque nunc quaedam exemplaria Scripturarum Lucianea nuncupentur; praef. in libr. Paralipomenon*, PL 28, 1324B - 1325A: *Alexandria et Aegyptus in Septuaginta suis Hesychium laudat auctorem. Constantinopolis usque Antiochiam Luciani martyris exemplaria probat. Mediae inter has*

X

lauf waren, Konkurrenz gab. Sein Freund Epiphanius gehörte
zu den Verteidigern des hexaplarischen Septuagintatextes und
brachte dies in seinem *De mensuris et ponderibus* vom Jahre
392 deutlich zum Ausdruck. Weil Hieronymus sich bei dieser
Gruppe nicht unbeliebt machen wollte, sind seine Aussagen
über die Septuaginta uneinheitlich, je nach dem wann und an
wen er schreibt. Manches Mal verschweigt er seine immer
grösser werdenden Zweifel, in anderen Schriften äussert er
sich jedoch deutlich darüber. Bei der Bevorzugung des hexaplarischen Septuagintatextes konnte er für Lesarten, die mit
dem hebräischen Text übereinstimmten, sich einsetzen, ohne
die siebzig Dolmetscher offen anzugreifen [63].

Als die Streitigkeit über Origenes im Jahre 393 offen
ausbrach, hatte Hieronymus schon mehrere Bücher des Alten
Testaments aus dem Hebräischen übersetzt. Er war zu dieser
Zeit auf zwei Fronten der Kritik ausgesetzt. Seine Vorliebe
für die *hebraica ueritas* war denjenigen anstössig, welche wie
Epiphanius und Rufin die Septuaginta als das Werk des
Heiligen Geistes ansahen [64], während er wegen seiner früheren
Begeisterung für Origenes sehr leicht selbst als Anhänger der
origenistischen Irrlehren hätte angegriffen werden können.
Kein Wunder also, dass er sich den Gegnern des Origenes
anschloss. Er hat Origenes weiterhin als Textkritiker und
Exegeten bewundert [65], war aber mit der Zeit immer mehr
geneigt, seine eigene Übersetzung aus dem Hebräischen als
der Hexaplaarbeit des Origenes überlegen anzusehen.

---

*prouinciae Palaestinos codices legunt, quos ab Origene elaboratos Euse-
bius et Pamphilus uulgauerunt; totusque orbis hac inter se trifaria
uarietate compugnat.* Vgl. H. Dörrie, *art. cit.* (oben Anm. 31), der die
Zeugnisse über Lukian bespricht und zu folgendem Schluss kommt
(85): « Es hat, wohl im Anfang des V. Jhs., ein recht erbitterter Kon-
kurrenzkampf zwischen der Bibel des Origenes und einer anderen,
die unter Lukians Namen ging, stattgefunden ».
   [63] So schreibt er in seiner *praef. in libros Salomonis iuxta LXX
interpretes,* alsob durch die hexaplarische Bearbeitung der Septuagintatext wiederhergestellt sei (PL 29, 403-4: *tres libros Salomonis ... ueteri
Septuaginta interpretum auctoritati reddidi*).
   [64] Er wurde natürlich im Westen auch von denjenigen angegriffen,
die keine Änderungen im vertrauten Wortlaut der altlateinischen Bibelübersetzungen dulden wollten.
   [65] Vgl. Cavallera, *loc. cit.* (oben Anm. 52-3).

X

Über seine Beweggründe, Ziele und die Kritik, die ihm
begegnete, berichtet Hieronymus in den Vorworten zu seinen
Übersetzungen. Nach dem an Sophronius gerichteten Vorwort
zu der Psalmenübersetzung hat er damit eine Aufforderung
dieses Mannes befolgt [66]. Sophronius habe in einer Auseinandersetzung mit einem Juden Psalmstellen aus der Septuaginta
zitiert, die von diesem als vom hebräischen Text abweichend
abgelehnt wurden; er (Sophronius) werde selbst durch die
verschiedenen Lesarten der Übersetzer (d.h. wohl Aquila, Symmachus und Theodotion) verwirrt und wolle sich auf die Übersetzung bzw. das Urteil des Hieronymus verlassen. Er habe
versprochen, die Übersetzung des Hieronymus ins Griechische
zu übersetzen [67]. Hieronymus fürchtet, dass er sich dadurch
die Kritik der Griechen zuziehen werde, verteidigt sich aber
schon im Voraus, indem er verneint, dass er seine Vorgänger
(die Septuaginta) tadeln will, an seine eigene Neubearbeitung
nach dem hexaplarischen Septuagintatext erinnert, und den
Unterschied zwischen dem Vorlesen der Psalmen in der Kirche
und der Auseinandersetzung mit Juden betont.

Im Vorwort zur Übersetzung des Propheten Isaias [68] erwähnt Hieronymus wieder die Kritik, die er erwartet. Er
bittet die Leser, sie sollten ihn so lesen, wie die Griechen
nach den siebzig Dolmetschern auch Aquila, Symmachus und
Theodotion lesen *uel ob studium doctrinae suae uel ut Septuaginta magis ex collatione eorum intelligant*. Sein Zweck sei,

---

[66] PL 28, 1123-1128. Nach P. Jay, *La datation des premières traductions de l'Ancien Testament sur l'hébreu par saint Jérôme*, in *Revue
des Études augustiniennes* 28 (1982) 208-212, hat Hieronymus seine ersten
Übersetzungen in der Reihenfolge *Ps., Proph., Sam., Reg., Job* herausgegeben. Eine abweichende Datierung bringt Nautin, TRE XV, 309-310,
der auch meint, dass Hieronymus gar nicht aus dem Hebräischen
übersetzte, sondern einfach anhand einer hexaplarischen Septuaginta-
handschrift arbeitete (ebda). Über die Psalmenbearbeitungen des Hieronymus vgl. Colette Estin, *Les traductions du Psautier* in hg. J. Fon-
taine und C. Pietri, *Le monde latin antique et la Bible*, Paris 1985,
S. 77-88.
[67] Diese Übersetzung zusammen mit einer Übersetzung der Prophe-
tenübersetzung des Hieronymus wird angeführt im Kapitel über Sophronius in *De viris illustribus* 134, TU 14, 55.
[68] PL 28, 771-4. Ähnlich im *Prologus galeatus* klagt er über die
Kritiker und behauptet, es sei nicht seine Absicht, die alten Übersetzer
zu tadeln (*praef. in libros Sam. et Malachim*, PL 28, 557A, 558A).

X

144

dass die Juden nicht mehr die Kirchen wegen der Fehlerhaftig-
keit ihrer Schriften verspotten. Er bemerkt, dass die siebzig
Dolmetscher die Prophezeiungen Christi und der Kirche nicht
deutlich wiedergegeben haben. Sie haben, wie er meint, die
Geheimnisse des Glaubens nicht deutlich an die Heiden ver-
raten wollen.

Im Vorwort zur Übersetzung des Buches Hiob vergleicht
Hieronymus seine eigene Arbeit mit der Hexapla des Origenes.
Seinen Kritikern wirft er vor, es sei inkonsequent, den Hexa-
platext anzunehmen, der ja durch seine Hinzufügungen unter
Asterisken zeige, dass die alte Übersetzung Vieles auslässt, und
dann seine eigene neue Übersetzung zu verwerfen[69]. Er habe
gearbeitet, nicht um die alte Übersetzung   zu tadeln, sondern
um die Undeutlichkeiten, Lücken und Schreibfehler darin durch
die eigene Übersetzung zum Vorschein zu bringen[70]. Wenn
unter den Griechen die Übersetzungen des Juden Aquilas und
der judaisierenden Häretiker Symmachus und Theodotion, die
viele Geheimnisse des Heilands auf trügerische Weise verhehlt
haben, in der Hexapla in den Kirchen gelesen und von kirchlichen Kommentatoren ausgelegt werden, so sollte er, ein Christ,
der sowohl die Septuaginta wie auch den hebräischen Text ins
Lateinische übersetzt habe, nicht kritisiert werden[71].

In seinen späteren Vorworten wiederholt Hieronymus
diese Argumente und setzt neue hinzu. Die Übersetzung der
siebzig Dolmetscher sei nicht rein überliefert sondern werde
in den verschiedenen Gegenden in verschiedenen verdorbenen
Exemplaren gelesen[72]. Origenes habe nicht nur die vier Ausgaben gesammelt, sondern sogar die Ausgabe Theodotions in
diejenige der Septuaginta hineingemischt[73]. Wenn die Griechen

---

[69] PL 28, 1079-80; vgl. *ep.* 57, 11 (CSEL 54, 523) wo er erklärt, dass
man die Auslassungen der Septuaginta entweder anhand der Asterisken
oder durch den Vergleich seiner eigenen Übersetzung mit der alten
erkennen könne.
[70] PL 28, 1082A: *ut ea, quae in illa aut obscura sunt, aut omissa, aut
certe scriptorum uitio deprauata, manifestiora nostra interpretatione
fierent.*
[71] PL 28, 1082B-1084A.
[72] *Praef. in libr. Paralip.*, PL 28, 1323B-1325A; vgl. *praef. in Ezram*,
PL 28, 1403B-1404A.
[73] *Praef. in libr. Paralip.*, PL 28, 1325A; vgl. *praef. in Pentateuchum*,
PL 28, 148A-149A: *Origenis me studium prouocauit.*

das, was die Siebzig nicht kannten, in den Kirchen lesen, warum erkennen die Lateiner Hieronymus nicht an, der ohne die alte Ausgabe zu verderben, eine neue hergestellt habe?[74] Seine eigene Übersetzung sei viel billiger und leichter abzuschreiben als die Hexapla. Auch wenn man die Hexapla besitze, wisse man ohne Kenntnis der hebräischen Sprache immer noch nicht, welche Fassung die richtige sei[75]. Die Arbeit des Hieronymus könne dort herangezogen werden, wo die alten Exemplare Varianten aufweisen[76]. Die Apostel zeigen, dass Hieronymus in seiner Bevorzugung des hebräischen Textes recht habe, da sie ja im Neuen Testament Stellen nach dem Hebräischen zitieren, die nicht in der Septuaginta stehen[77]. Die Geschichte der Simultanübersetzung sei eine Lüge. Die siebzig Ältesten seien Dolmetscher gewesen, nicht Propheten[78]. Sie haben die Texte, welche die Trinitätslehre bezeugten, geändert oder verschwiegen, weil sie für den monotheistischen Heidenkönig Ptolemaeus schrieben[79]. Er wolle sie nicht verdammen, sie haben aber vor der Ankunft Christi gearbeitet und, was sie nicht kannten, haben sie undeutlich wiedergegeben. Hiero-

---

[74] *Praef. in libr. Paralip.*, PL 28, 1325A-B; vgl. *praef. in Ezram*, PL 28, 1404B, *praef. in libr. Jos.*, PL 28, 464A: warum bewundern seine Kritiker Origenes und Euseb, die alle Ausgaben ähnlich kommentieren?

[75] *Praef. in Ezram*, PL 28, 1404B-1405A. Er kritisiert hier einen Griechen, der neulich solche Unkenntnis gezeigt habe. Nach seiner *Apologie gegen Rufin* II, 34 ist dies Apollinaris (CCL 79, 71.15-20).

[76] *Praef. in libr. Jos.*, PL 28, 463A.

[77] *Praef. in libr. Paralip.*, PL 28, 1325B-1326A; *praef. in Pent.*, PL 28, 149A-150A; *praef. in Ezram*, PL 28, 1404A; *praef. in libr. Jos.*, PL 28, 464A. Er beruft sich auf sein Werk *De optimo genere interpretandi* (*ep.* 57, 7ff., CSEL 54, 512ff.), wo er Zitate im Neuen Testament angeführt hatte, die dem Wortlaut der Septuaginta nicht genau folgen (und meist auch nicht demjenigen des hebräischen Textes). In diesem Werk (11, CSEL 54, 523.12-13) hatte er behauptet, dass die Apostel die Septuaginta dort benutzten, wo sie vom hebräischen Text nicht abweicht; vgl. *Apologie gegen Rufin* II, 34 (CCL 79, 71.21 - 72.40).

[78] *Praef. in Pent.*, PL 28, 150A - 151A; vgl. *praef. in libr. Paralip.*, PL 28, 1325A: *septuaginta cellulas, quae uulgo sine auctore iactantur; ep.* 57, 7 (CSEL 54, 515.1-9): wenn die Siebzig *Os.* 11,1 anders übersetzt haben als im hebräischen Text steht, so müsse man ihnen als Menschen verzeihen.

[79] *Praef. in Pent.*, PL 28, 150A. Vgl. auch oben S. 133-134 und Barthélemy, *art. cit.* (oben Anm. 35), der die Äußerungen Eusebs und des Hieronymus über absichtliche Änderungen und Unklarheit auf seiten der Septuaginta bespricht.

146

nymus selbst habe nach der Auferstehung geschrieben und habe besser wiedergegeben, was er besser verstand [80]. Geben wir dem heiligen Augustin das letzte Wort [81]. Um das Jahr 395 schrieb Augustin einen Brief an Hieronymus, in dem er ihn bat, mit der Arbeit der Bibelübersetzung sich nicht weiter abzugeben, ausser wenn er, wie in seiner frühen Hiobübersetzung, die kritischen Zeichen hinzusetzen wollte, um die Unterschiede zur Septuaginta deutlich zu machen. Es könne in den hebräischen Exemplaren sich kaum noch etwas finden, was die früheren Übersetzer nicht bemerkt hätten [82]. Dieser Brief erreichte Hieronymus nicht, aber etwa acht Jahre später kam Augustin auf dasselbe Thema zurück in seiner *ep.* 71 [83], der er eine Abschrift des früheren Briefes beilegte. Hier schreibt er, dass er es lieber haben würde, wenn Hieronymus die Septuaginta ins Lateinische übersetzen würde. Er verstehe nicht, warum Hieronymus nach seiner Hiobübersetzung aus dem Griechischen mit Asterisken und Obelisken noch eine zweite Übersetzung aus dem Hebräischen ohne solche Zeichen angefertigt habe. Wenn die Fassung aus dem Hebräischen in den lateinischen Kirchen gelesen wird, so werden Unterschiede zu den griechischen Kirchen entstehen. Bei Abweichungen von den bekannten Lesarten gebe es kaum die Möglichkeit nachzuprüfen, ob Hieronymus recht habe oder

---

[80] *Praef. in Pent.*, PL 28, 151A-B.

[81] Ein Nachklang der griechischen Polemik gegen Hieronymus findet sich im Bericht des Photius (*Bibliothek* 177, hg. R. Henry, II, Paris 1960, S. 177) über ein Werk Theodors von Mopsuestia *Gegen diejenigen, welche behaupten, dass die Menschen von Natur und nicht durch Wahl sündigen.* Der Leiter dieser Häretiker habe die Septuagintaübersetzung sowie diejenigen des Symmachus und Aquilas und der anderen verworfen und habe sich angemasst, mit Hilfe von gewissen knechtischen Juden eine eigene neue anzufertigen, obwohl es ihm an der nötigen Vorbereitung zu solcher Arbeit gefehlt hätte.

[82] *ep.* 28, 2 (= Hieronymus, *ep.* 56, 2), in der Separatausgabe des Briefwechsels mit Vorwort von J. Schmid, SS. *Eusebii Hieronymi et Aurelii Augustini Epistulae mutuae*, Bonn 1930, S. 28.5-29.14. Vgl. zu dem Briefwechsel im allgemeinen D. De Bruyne, *La correspondance échangée entre Augustin et Jérôme*, in ZNW 31 (1932) 233-248. Augustins Beurteilung der Septuaginta in seinen Briefen an Hieronymus bespricht G. Jouassard, *Réflexions sur la position de saint Augustin relativement aux Septante dans sa discussion avec saint Jérôme*, in *Revue des Études Augustiniennes* 2 (1956) 93-99.

[83] Augustin, *ep.* 71 = Hieronymus, *ep.* 104, hg. Schmid, S. 41-4.

nicht, während man die Lesarten des griechischen Textes sehr
leicht nachsehen könne[84]. Überhaupt möchte er gern wissen,
warum es so viele Unterschiede zwischen den hebräischen
Handschriften und den Septuagintahandschriften gebe. In seiner Antwort auf diesen Brief[85] wirft Hieronymus Augustin
vor, dass er die Septuagintaübersetzung nicht in ihrer reinen
Form lese, sondern nach dem Text, den Origenes mit Obelisken
und Asterisken verfälscht habe — Origenes habe nämlich Zusätze aus der Ausgabe des Theodotion, eines Juden und Gottes-
lästerers, hinzugefügt. Augustin sollte entweder diese Zusätze
ausradieren, wenn er die Septuaginta bewundert, oder der
Übersetzung des Christen, Hieronymus, folgen. Er selbst habe
die alte Fassung nicht abzuschaffen versucht, sondern er habe
die Texte, welche von den Juden ausgelassen oder verfälscht
seien, ans Licht bringen wollen, damit die Christen wissen
können, was die hebräische Wahrheit enthält. Niemand brauche
seine Übersetzung zu lesen, wenn er es nicht mag. In seiner
Antwort, in der er sich hauptsächlich mit anderen Fragen
befasst, begrüsst Augustin[86] diese Begründung der Übersetzung
aus dem Hebräischen, fragt aber, welche Juden der Texte
verfälscht haben, die vorchristlichen, die vor dem Geburt
Christi übersetzten, oder die späteren, von denen man meinen
könnte, sie hätten die Weissagungen über den christlichen
Glauben entfernt oder verfälscht. Er bittet Hieronymus, ihm
ein Exemplar seiner Übersetzung der Septuaginta zu senden.
Dass er dagegen war, dass die Übersetzung aus dem Hebräischen in den Kirchen gelesen werde, hatte darin seinen
Grund, dass er das Volk, das an die Septuaginta gewöhnt sei,
nicht durch Neuerungen gestört sehen wollte.

---

[84] Hieronymus hatte den Benutzern seiner Übersetzungen vorgeschlagen, sie möchten bei Unterschieden gegenüber den bekannten griechischen und lateinischen Lesarten irgendeinen Juden befragen (z.B.
praef. in libros Sam. et Malachim, PL 28, 558A; *praef. in Ezram*, PL
28, 1404AB). Als man aber in Oea diesem Rat folgte, haben die um
ihre Meinung befragten Juden sich zustimmend zur griechischen und
lateinischen Fassung geäussert (Augustin, *ep.* 71, 5, hg. Schmid, S. 42.29-
43.7; Hieronymus antwortet darauf in seiner *ep.* 112.21-2 = Augustin,
ep. 75.21-2, hg. Schmid, S. 71.16-73.2).
[85] Augustin, *ep.* 75.19ff. = Hieronymus, *ep.* 112.19ff., hg. Schmid,
S. 68.26ff.
[86] Augustin, *ep.* 82.34-5 = Hieronymus, *ep.* 116.34-5, hg. Schmid,
S. 92.25-93.18.

Seine endgültige Meinung fasst Augustin in seiner *De Civitate Dei* zusammen. Hier betont er die Autorität der zwei und siebzig Ältesten, die durch den Heiligen Geist getrennt arbeitend alle gleich übersetzten [87]. Wenn Unterschiede zwischen der Übersetzung und dem hebräischen Text bestehen, so sind sie von dem Heiligen Geist beabsichtigt worden [88]. Wenn Einzelheiten in der Übersetzung stehen, die auf geschichtlicher Ebene dem hebräischen Text zu widersprechen scheinen, so wird dadurch der Leser gemahnt, sich über diese Ebene hinweg zu erheben und die innere Bedeutung zu suchen [89]. Die Septuaginta wird von der Kirche benutzt und die Apostel zitieren nicht nur nach dem hebräischen Text sondern auch nach der Septuaginta [90]. So erkennt Augustin die Autorität von beiden an.

Der gelehrte Presbyter Hieronymus habe zwar eine Übersetzung aus dem Hebräischen angefertigt, welche die Juden als zuverlässig ansehen. Man könne aber nicht der Arbeit eines einzelnen Vorzug geben vor derjenigen der siebzig Ältesten [91]. Manche haben gemeint, man müsse die griechischen Handschriften anhand der hebräischen korrigieren. Sie haben aber die Zusätze der Septuaginta nicht entfernt, sondern nur die fehlenden Stellen ergänzt und diese und die Auslassungen durch kritische Zeichen notiert, welche sich auch in vielen lateinischen Handschriften finden [92].

Für Augustin ist also die Hexapla bzw. der hexaplarische Septuagintatext ein Hilfsmittel, durch das man gewisse Unterschiede zwischen der Septuaginta und dem hebräischen Text feststellen kann. Die Übersetzung des Hieronymus ist gefährlich, weil sie droht, die Autorität der Septuaginta zu ersetzen. Trotzdem ist Augustin bereit, sie manchmal als Zeugen des

---

[87] XVIII, 42-3, hg. E. Hoffmann, CSEL 40 (1900) 335ff. Zu der Geschichte der Simultanübersetzung vgl. auch *doctr. chr.* II, 15, 22, CCL 32 (1962) 47f.
[88] XV, 14,23; XVIII, 43, CSEL 40, 88.19-24, 113.5-9, 338.2-18; vgl. auch *cons. ev.* II, 66, 128, hg. F. Weihrich, CSEL 43 (1904) 230.
[89] XVIII, 44, CSEL 40, 339.8ff.
[90] XV, 14; XVIII, 43-4, CSEL 40, 88.24-6, 336.19ff., 340.7-11.
[91] XVIII, 43, CSEL 40, 336.24ff.
[92] XVIII, 43, CSEL 40, 337.20ff.

Hebräischen in seinen späteren Werken zu zitieren [93] und sogar zu einzelnen Stellen zuzugeben, dass ein Fehler oder sogar eine Fälschung im Text der Septuaginta stehen könnte [94]. Im Wechsel der Zeiten sind eine Fülle von Argumenten zu unserem Thema ersonnen worden, Argumente, die dann wie in einem Arsenal zur Verfügung standen. Daraus haben die einzelnen Verfasser jeweils eine Auswahl getroffen und mit eigener Betonung oder Umgestaltung oder neuen Zusätzen vorgetragen. In den verschiedenen Stimmen, die wir gehört haben, mischt sich Polemik und wissenschaftliches Interesse [95]. Hätten wir die Notizen über Hexaplalesarten in den verschiedenen griechischen und lateinischen exegetischen Werken untersucht, so hätten wir mehr von wissenschaftlichem Interesse und weniger Polemik bemerkt. Aber auch da, wo man es am wenigsten erwarten sollte, sogar in den Einzelheiten einer Übersetzung, können polemische Tendenzen im Hintergrund stehen [96].

---

[93] Vgl. Schmid, *op. cit.* (oben Anm. 82), S. 13.

[94] *Civ.* XV, 13, CSEL 40, 83.20ff.

[95] Die rabbinischen Urteile über die griechischen Übersetzungen sind hier nicht behandelt worden. Vgl. dazu Benoit, art. cit. (oben Anm. 15), H. L. Strack und P. Billerbeck, *Kommentar zum Neuen Testament aus Talmud und Midrasch* IV, 1, München 1928, S. 407f., 414, und III², München 1954, S. 486ff.; Barthélemy, *art. cit.* (oben Anm. 35), S. 188-191. Jüdische Kritik an der Septuaginta wird noch in mittelalterlichen islamischen Schriften widergespiegelt; vgl. E. Fritsch, *Islam und Christentum im Mittelalter*, Breslau 1930, S. 60-61.

[96] Dass Rufin und Hieronymus hinsichtlich der textkritischen Bemerkungen zum Alten Testament in ihren Origenesübersetzungen nicht unparteiisch verfahren, wird von Sgherri (*art. cit.* [oben Anm. 1], 3 Anm. 4; 6 Anm. 16; 12; 20 Anm. 57; 26 Anm. 84) and Barthélemy (*art. cit.* [oben Anm. 1], S. 203: «les traducteurs latins d'Origène, Jérôme et Rufin, tirent souvent la couverture chacun de son côté») in ihren Ausführungen berücksichtigt.

XI

LAW AND TEMPLE IN ORIGEN[1]

The question of the proper attitude to be taken to the Old Testament Law much occupied Christian writers of the second
century. Jews, Judaizing Christians and even pagans might
attack Christian failure to obey the law. Thus Justin in the
Dialogue with Trypho, which is addressed to a certain Marcus
Pompeius, perhaps a pagan enquirer (141; cf. 8), represents
Trypho and himself as in agreement that the chief Jewish
complaint against Christians was their failure to live according to the law (10), and he also describes Jewish Christians
who tell Gentile converts that they will not be saved unless
they observe the law (47). The Jew quoted by Celsus
reproaches those who after being deluded by Jesus have abandoned the law of their fathers,[2] and Celsus repeats this accusation.[3] The author of the *Epistle to Diognetus* replies to the
question why Christians do not worship in the same manner
as the Jews (3.1). On the other hand the views of Marcion and
the Gnostics, who relegated the Old Testament God who gave
the law to an inferior level, demanded a response from those
who maintained his identity with the Father of Christ. Marcion himself in his *Antitheses* used the contradictions between

---

1. I apologize for the shortcomings of this paper. Paradoxically they
must be taken as a tribute to the honorand of this volume. Preparing it
without his knowledge and hence without the benefits of direct consul-
tation, I have been doubly aware of the debt I owe to him on other occasions.
2. Origen, *Contra Celsum* 2.1ff. On Celsus's Jew, cf. E. Bammel,
'Der Jude des Celsus', *Judaica: Kleine Schriften,* I (Tübingen, 1986),
pp. 265-83, especially pp. 274-76 on this accusation.
3. Origen, *Contra Celsum* 5.25 and 33; cf. 3.5.

the law and the gospel to argue for two Gods,[4] and perhaps the most interesting discussion of Moses' law is the letter of the Valentinian Ptolemy to Flora, which is directed against two contrary sets of opponents, those who regard the law as ordained by God the Father and those who attribute it to the devil. Ptolemy himself ascribes it, or rather the part of it that is not of human origin, to the creator god, a god of justice who hates evil.[5] The extent of Christian embarrassment may be seen in concessions such as the theory of the Clementine *Homilies* that certain false chapters had been added to the written law subsequent to the time of Moses himself (2.38ff.; 3.3ff., 47ff.; cf. 16.10ff.) or the view favoured by the *Didascalia* and by Irenaeus that the legislation imposed after the worship of the golden calf was intended as heavy bonds or a yoke of bondage and was abolished by Jesus. They even apply Ezek. 20.25 'I gave them statutes which were not good' to this legislation.[6]

For those who continued to worship the Old Testament God the destruction of the Jerusalem temple too demanded an explanation.[7] The answers to the two problems were sometimes linked.[8] The desire to vindicate divine providence and to

---

4. According to Tertullian, *Adversus Marcionem* 1.19.

5. Epiphanius, *Panarion*, 33.3-7.

6. Irenaeus, *Adversus Haereses* 4.26 (Harvey); *Didascalia* (ed. H. Connolly; Oxford, 1929), pp. 12-15, 216-19, 222-30; cf. pp. lix-lx, lxiii-lxv for a comparison with Irenaeus.

7. Pagan critics attacked the Jewish God for his desertion of his worshippers (cf. e.g. Minucius Felix, *Octavius* 10.4; Celsus in Origen, *Contra Celsum* 8.69), and the failure of the Jewish revolts has been seen as a factor in the development of Gnostic dualism.

8. For Christian and Jewish reactions in general, cf. G.W.H. Lampe, AD 70 in Christian Reflection', in E. Bammel and C.F.D. Moule (eds.), *Jesus and the Politics of his Day* (Cambridge, 1984), pp. 153-71; H.J. Schoeps, 'Die Tempelzerstörung des Jahres 70 in der jüdischen Religionsgeschichte', *Aus frühchristlicher Zeit* (Tübingen, 1950), pp. 144-83, H. Windisch, 'Der Untergang Jerusalems (anno 70) im Urteil der Christen und Juden', *Theologisch Tijdschrift* 48 (1914), pp. 519-50, and C. Thoma, 'Auswirkungen des jüdischen Krieges gegen Rom (66–70/73 n. Chr.) auf das rabbinische Judentum', *Biblische Zeitschrift* ns 12 (1968), pp. 30-54, 186-210. The patristic view that the destruction of the temple was intended as a punishment will not be discussed here.

466

demonstrate the continuity of salvation history favoured a picture which gave positive but limited validity to those parts of the law which Christians no longer observed.[9] One of the most fruitful solutions[10] was the view that the ceremonial law[11] consisted of types and symbols intended only to be observed literally for a limited time until their fulfilment in Christ's incarnation.[12] To this was added the claim that the destruction of the Jerusalem temple brought the era of literal observance finally to a close.[13] The idea that the earthly temple and sacrifices had now been superseded was indeed developed prior to the destruction of the temple[14] and the preference for spiritual worship has pre-Christian roots in both Jewish and pagan thought, as Christian apologists were well aware.[15] Second-century writers make use of the claim that since the

9. For this reason the educative role of the law is often stressed; cf. for example Irenaeus, *Adversus Haereses* 4.24.2 and 25.3; Clement of Alexandria, *Paedagogus* 1.7.59.1 and 1.11.96.3f. (citing Gal. 3.24).

10. On the various criticisms of the law and attempted solutions, cf. W. Horbury, 'Old Testament Interpretation in the Writings of the Church Fathers', in M.J. Mulder and H. Sysling (eds.), *Mikra* (Assen and Philadelphia, 1988), pp. 758-61; M. Simon, *Verus Israel* (Paris, 1948); Schoeps, *art. cit.*, pp. 159ff. M.F. Wiles, *The Divine Apostle* (Cambridge, 1967), pp. 49-72, discusses the attitudes to the law developed in patristic exegesis of the Pauline epistles. Cf. also R.E. Taylor, 'Attitudes of the Fathers towards Practices of Jewish Christians', *TU* 79 (1961), pp. 504-11.

11. The term is used here for convenience. Early Christian writers usually specify 'the law concerning sacrifices, etc.'

12. This view appears in the *Epistle of Barnabas* and the letter of Ptolemy to Flora and is taken up by many later Christian writers including Clement of Alexandria. It is interesting to find that Irenaeus, while accepting it, nonetheless attacks his Gnostic opponents for overworking their use of typology (*Adversus Haereses* 4.32 [Harvey]).

13. Cf. G.W.H. Lampe, *art. cit.*, pp. 170-71; H.J. Schoeps, *art. cit.*, pp. 153ff.

14. Cf. Lampe, *art. cit.*, pp. 157-58; O. Cullmann, 'L'opposition contre le Temple de Jerusalem, motif commun de la théologie johannique et du monde ambiant'.

15. Cf. for example R.A. Kraft, *The Apostolic Fathers. 3: Barnabas and the Didache*, pp. 84, 130. According to Justin, *Dialogue with Trypho*, 117, contemporary Jews themselves were using the argument that God preferred the sacrifices of prayer offered by diaspora Jews to the temple sacrifices at Jerusalem.

destruction of the temple literal observance of the law has been impossible. Because the period of validity of the law was intended to be limited, it was laid down that sacrifice could be offered only in one place and the destruction of that place foreordained.

Elements of this argument are present already in the *Epistle of Barnabas*—the Old Testament sacrifices are types of Christ (7–8), the destruction of the temple was prophesied (16), the Christians are the spiritual temple of God (4.11; 16.7-10)—but the exposition of the limited validity of temple worship is missing, being replaced by the more negative idea that the people had already lost the covenant when Moses broke the two tablets because of their worship of the golden calf (4.7-8; 14.1-3).

The view of a historical development is particularly clear in Peter's speech in the Clementine *Recognitions*. Subsequent to the worship of the golden calf, in order that the people might be prevented from sacrificing to idols, Moses allowed them to sacrifice to God alone and appointed that there would be one place only in which this would be lawful (1.36-37, referring to Deut. 12.11). This was done however with a view to the fact that at the appropriate time the true prophet would teach them to cease from sacrificing (instituting baptism instead) and give warning of the destruction of the temple (1.37-38; cf. 1.64). The idea of the ceremonial law as symbolic is absent here.

Similarly Justin in his *Dialogue with Trypho* states that it was because of the people's sins that God allowed the temple to be called his house (22 end); the observation of sabbath, sacrifices, offerings and feasts was enjoined because of the hardness of the people's hearts (43, 46). All these things were types and symbols intended to end with the coming of Christ (40–43). God ordained that the passover lamb should be sacrificed in only one place, knowing that the time would come when that place would be captured and all the offerings cease (40). Justin divides the law into what is naturally good, pious and righteous, and what was appointed because of the hardness of the people's hearts (45) and represents Trypho as admitting that, as regards the latter category, the offering of sacrifices is no longer possible (46).

468

The same general picture emerges in Irenaeus, *Adversus Haereses*, in the context of the refutation of Gnostic criticisms of the God who gave the law and of the fact that he allowed the destruction of Jerusalem,[16] and a similar one in Tertullian.[17] Irenaeus, who is not writing against Jews or Jewish Christians, omits the argument that obedience to the law is impossible because of the destruction of the temple, whereas Tertullian does emphasize the commandment that sacrifice should be offered to God in only one place (*Adversus Iudaeos* 5; cf. 8 end, on the cessation of sacrifice, and 13, on the destruction of Jerusalem and its consequences).

The *Didascalia* states that the Lord caused the destruction of the temple and altar by the Romans and the cessation of sacrifices and asserts that the 'second legislation' with regard especially to the punishment of the wicked and idolaters and the performance of sacrifices, libations and sprinklings of ashes cannot be performed by those in dispersion under Roman rule. To attempt to follow this legislation is to fall under a curse, as is shown by Deut. 27.26 (Gal. 3.10).[18]

The approach of Origen is characterized by the fact that he regards all the writings of the Old Testament, both law and prophets, as divinely inspired and uses the distinction between letter and spirit or literal and spiritual understanding to solve any difficulties.[19] The coming of Jesus has, in his view, re-

---

16. 4.5-6 (Harvey): the law ended with John (Lk. 16.16) and Jerusalem was abandoned once her function had been fulfilled; 4.26-32: the people were subjected to a yoke of bondage after the worship of the golden calf; pure sacrifice (like that of Abel) is now offered to God by the church throughout the world; the earthly offerings and sacrifices were the types of heavenly things.

17. Cf. *Adversus Marcionem* 18: sacrifice was allowed to prevent idolatry; *Adversus Iudaeos* 2: Moses' law was temporary; 5: earthly and spiritual sacrifice were symbolized by the offerings of Cain and Abel; earthly sacrifices were to be offered in one place only, spiritual sacrifices in every land; 8: after the Jewish defeat libations and sacrifices ceased; 13: the Spirit dwelt in the temple before the advent of Christ, who is the true temple of God.

18. *Didascalia* (ed. H. Connolly), pp. 238-40.

19. *De Principiis* Book 4 is devoted to this topic. On Origen's exegesis cf. H. de Lubac, *Histoire et Esprit: l'intelligence de l'Ecriture d'après Origène* (Paris, 1950). On his views concerning the observance of the

moved the veil which had concealed the spiritual nature of the law of Moses.[20] Unlike certain earlier writers he does not regard parts of the law in a negative light[21] or state that Jesus abrogated the old law by replacing it with a new one.[22] Thus when Celsus attacks the Christians on the grounds that Jesus gave laws in opposition to those of Moses, Origen refutes him at some length as having failed to go beyond the literal meaning of the Old Testament,[23] and uses the distinction between letter and spirit to explain the 'statutes which were not good' of Ezek. 20.25.[24]

Origen often expounds his own characteristic view with particular reference to the impossibility of literal obedience to the law since the destruction of the temple.[25] A good brief account of his approach is given at the beginning of his tenth *Homily on Leviticus*. Those of the church, he says, receive Moses as a divinely inspired prophet who wrote in symbols about future mysteries. The things written or done in the law and prophets as types of the future were like the clay model which a sculptor makes of a bronze, silver or gold statue, no longer any use after the statue is completed. Thus the former great royal city of Jerusalem and its celebrated temple were destroyed after the advent of the true temple of God, and the former high priest, altar and sacrifices had no place after the true high priest had come and the true lamb had offered himself. Those who think that they ought to obey the law with

law, cf. N.R.M. de Lange, *Origen and the Jews* (Cambridge, 1976), pp. 89-96.

20. *De Principiis* 4.1.6; cf. 2 Cor. 3.14

21. See above p. 465. This does not mean that he did not differentiate different parts of the law.

22. Cf. Justin, *Dialogue* 11 and 43, declaring that Christ himself is the eternal law; Tertullian, *Adversus Iudaeos* 3 and 6; also the rejection of the law in *Epistle of Barnabas* 3.6.

23. *Contra Celsum* 7.18ff. (ed. P. Koetschau; GCS *Origenes* 2 [1899], pp. 169.10ff.).

24. *Contra Celsum* 7.20 (ed. Koetschau, pp. 171.31–172.22); *Homilies on Exodus* 7.2 (ed. W.A. Baehrens; GCS *Origenes* 6 [1920], pp. 206.19–207.6).

25. Origen's attitude to the destruction of the temple and many related topics are discussed in the excellent book of G. Sgherri, *Chiesa e sinagoga nelle opere di Origene* (Milan, 1982); cf. in particular pp. 93-110 on the destruction of Jerusalem and the temple.

470

respect to the fasts of the Jews should take note of Paul's words in Gal. 5.3 and obey the whole law, go up to Jerusalem thrice a year and so on—but this is impossible, since there is no altar or priest.[26]

Particularly striking is the allegorical exposition of Moses' death at the beginning of the second *Homily on Joshua*.[27] Jerusalem is destroyed, the altar abandoned, there are no sacrifices, offerings or drink-offerings, no priests, high-priests, or services of Levites, no one appears before the Lord thrice a year or offers gifts in the temple or sacrifices the Paschal lamb or eats unleavened bread or offers first-fruits or consecrates firstlings, but these have all been replaced by the spiritual service of Christianity. Origen here refers to a lost apocryphal book for a description of two figures of Moses, the one alive in the spirit, the other dead in the body, and interprets these as referring to the spiritual law and the letter of the law.

According to *Homily on Joshua* 17 the 'shadow and example of heavenly things' (Heb. 8.5), which existed on earth as long as the temple cult was carried out at Jerusalem, has been brought to an end with the destruction of the temples at Jerusalem and on Mount Gerizim. Thus Jesus' prediction in Jn 4.21-24 has been fulfilled. Jesus himself is the true temple, the true high-priest, and the true lamb of God.[28]

Interpreting Rom. 7.1-4, Origen states that the letter of the law appeared to be alive as long as the type and image of heavenly worship was carried out at Jerusalem, but since Jesus' incarnation and the destruction of Jerusalem together with the temple and altar it has been dead. There are no sacrifices, no priesthood, no services carried out by Levites, nor can the law any longer punish murderers or adulteresses. It is no longer possible for every male to appear before the Lord three times a year, nor to sacrifice the Paschal lamb, no sheaves of first-fruits or offerings are presented, there is no purification

---

26. *Homilies on Leviticus* 10.1 (ed. Baehrens, pp. 440.18–442.22).
27. *Homily on Joshua* (ed. Baehrens; GCS *Origenes* 7 [1921], pp. 296.10–297.19).
28. *Homily on Joshua* (ed. Baehrens, pp. 400.15–401.10). Cf. also 26.3 (pp. 462.17–463.16), and *Commentary on Matthew* 12.20 and 16.3 (ed. E. Klostermann; GCS *Origenes* 10 [1935], pp. 113.24–114.29 and p. 468).

of leprosy or impurity.²⁹ A similar list appears in the exposition of Gal. 3.24ff. by Jerome, who is no doubt following Origen's lost exegesis here.³⁰ The phrase in Romans 8.3, τὸ ἀδύνατον τοῦ νόμου ἐν ᾧ ἠσθένει διὰ τῆς σαρκός, Origen explains as referring to the impossibility of literal obedience to the law. Before the fall of Jerusalem the law was weak according to the flesh. Now that there is no temple, altar or place to sacrifice it is altogether dead.³¹

Sometimes this picture is elaborated with special reference to contemporary Judaism. In his *Homilies on Numbers* Origen interprets Moses' marriage with the Ethiopian woman in Num. 12.1ff. as referring to the union between the spiritual law and the church. The synagogue, represented by Miriam, attacks Moses, because the spiritual law does not teach the church to observe the circumcision of the flesh, the sabbath, new moons or sacrifices.³² Like Miriam in Num. 12.12-15, the people of the Jews, who had previously enjoyed the honour of possessing the high priests, priests, Levites, the temple, prophets and even receiving divine visitations, has been temporarily repudiated, without any of these privileges, and scattered throughout the earth.³³ In the passage just quoted from *Homilies on Joshua* 17, Origen states that the cessation of the temple cult was divinely planned in order to remove an obstacle to conversion to Christianity. He appeals to the Jews visiting Jerusalem not to lament over its ashes, but to look up and seek the heavenly Jerusalem, the heavenly altar and the high priest after the order of Melchisedek (Heb. 5.10). It is by the mercy of God that their earthly inheritance has been removed, that they may seek an inheritance in heaven.³⁴ The same argument, but without the appeal to the Jews, appears in

29. *Commentary on Romans* 6.7 (ed. C.H.E. Lommatzsch; Berlin, 1836–37, II, pp. 34-35). A similar interpretation is given in *Homilies on Genesis* 6.3 (ed. Baehrens; GCS *Origenes* 6 [1920], p. 69), with a challenge to 'those friends and defenders of the letter' to keep the letter of the law if they can.
30. *Commentary on Galatians* 2 (*PL* 26 [1845], 368 B-C); cf. also 375C on Gal. 4.8-9.
31. *Commentary on Romans* 6.12 (ed. Lommatzsch, II, pp. 67-68).
32. 6.4 (ed. Baehrens; GCS *Origenes* VII, p. 36.5-16).
33. 7.4 (pp. 44.1-23); cf. 7.3 (pp. 41.25–42.1).
34. 17.1 (ed. Baehrens; GCS *Origenes* VII, pp. 401.13–402.6).

the tenth *Homily on Leviticus*. Divine providence allowed the destruction of the city and temple to prevent admiration for the cult and ministry impeding the realization that the truth has now replaced the type.[35] Origen's attitude to the temple cult therefore is positive.[36] In his *Homilies on Numbers* he again exclaims on the magnificence and propriety of the temple cult and the fact that if it had continued in existence it would have prevented faith in the gospel.[37] In the *Contra Celsum* he explains the superiority of the Jews to other races in having only one temple, one altar, one place for burning incense, and one high priest.[38]

Most often Origen treats the destruction of the temple as the confirmation of a new era of spiritual observance inaugurated by the incarnation. In considering the arguments of Judaizing Christians, however, who think that the law should still be followed literally, he distinguishes between the situation during and shortly after the lifetime of Jesus and the subsequent cessation of the temple cult. The most interesting discussion occurs in an excursus on circumcision in the *Commentary on Romans*. Reflecting on the clash between Rom. 2.25 and Gal. 5.2 on the question of circumcision he admits that Peter and Paul did observe the law in certain respects and that circumcision may have been helpful for Jewish converts reluctant to give it up.[39] He also repeats arguments which had persuaded some gentile Christians to accept circumcision.[40] In order to investigate the question whether circumcision is still useful, he sets about examining the Old Testament instructions in order to see whether proselytes or foreigners are included in them. If the contents of the law are divinely inspired, he argues, these details are significant, and indeed the instructions to refrain

35. 10.1 (ed. Baehrens, p. 442.2-9).
36. Cf. *Comm. ser. in Matt.* 29 (ed. E. Klostermann; GCS *Origenes* XI [1933], p. 55.5-7), on the divine presence in and protection of the temple prior to its destruction.
37. 23.1 (ed. Baehrens, p. 210.13-27).
38. 5.44 (ed. Koetschau, p. 47.13ff.).
39. 2.13 (ed. Lommatzsch, I, pp. 120-21). Brief extracts from this discussion are preserved in Greek in Catena 10.19ff. (ed. A. Ramsbotham; *JTS* 13 [1911], pp. 217-18).
40. *Loc. cit.*, p. 124.

from blood and things that have been strangled, which are repeated in the Apostolic Decree (Acts 15.29) and still observed by gentile Christians, do include foreigners (Lev. 17.10-12, 13-14).[41] As regards sacrifices, the law about these which mentions foreigners does not say that they have to perform them but only how to if they do. As long as the temple was still standing gentiles did offer sacrifice there and indeed Jesus instructed the ten lepers to show themselves to the priest and make an offering, although one of them was a foreigner (Lk. 17.11-18, contaminated with Mt. 8.4).[42] Since its destruction, however, this has not been possible even for Jews, because it is only permitted in the one place. The same applies to the commandment that a proselyte who celebrates the Passover must be circumcised. The law commands that the Passover sacrifice take place in the Jerusalem temple, but this is now impossible. There is therefore no point in arguing about circumcision.[43]

Origen makes a similar admission concerning the period of Jesus' lifetime and immediately after in the *Contra Celsum*.[44] In reply to the accusation of Celsus's Jew referred to above, that Christians have abandoned the law of their fathers, he expounds the view that it was only after the resurrection that Jesus instructed his disciples in the spiritual interpretation of the law. According to *Homilies on Jeremiah* the intermediate time between the crucifixion and the destruction of the temple was allowed for repentance in particular for those of the Jews who were going to believe as a result of the signs and wonders done by the apostles.[45]

The time of transition, however, could only be of limited duration. As is clear from the passages cited above Origen considered that in the long term the continuance of the temple cult would have been a hindrance to conversion for both Jews and Gentiles. He reflects further on the matter in the *Contra*

---

41. *Loc. cit.*, pp. 124-29.
42. *Loc. cit.*, pp. 129-30.
43. *Loc. cit.*, pp. 130-31.
44. 2.1-2 (ed. Koetschau, pp. 126.12–129.24).
45. 14.13 (ed. E. Klostermann; GCS *Origenes* III [1901], p. 118.19-22).

Celsum[46] in his reply to Celsus's attack on the contradiction between the legislation of Jesus and that of Moses. Acknowledging the difference between the former manner of life of the Jews following Moses and the present way of life of Christians following Jesus' teachings, he argues that it would not have been suitable for converted Gentiles to live according to the letter of the law of Moses, since they were under Roman rule, nor could the Jews retain the structure of their society intact if they were going to follow the way of life according to the gospel. The Christians could not have killed their enemies or law-breakers according to the law of Moses, since even the Jews who want to do so are unable to follow the law in this respect. The ancient Jews on the other hand, who had their own constitution and territory, would have been entirely destroyed if they had not been allowed to fight their enemies and punish wrongdoers. The same divine providence which formerly gave the law and now has given the gospel of Jesus Christ has destroyed the city, temple and temple cult, not wishing the Jewish customs to prevail any longer, and has granted increase to the Christians, so that the Gentiles might be aided by Christ's teaching.[47]

During his time at Caesarea Origen was in contact with Jews[48] and Judaizing Christians.[49] He knew of their views and provides some interesting information about them. His observations on the significance of the destruction of the temple in the context of the question of the proper attitude to be taken to the Mosaic law are not simply the repetition of the commonplaces of his predecessors but are developed in awareness of rival arguments within the framework of his own biblical and historical expertise and desire to vindicate the unity of the two

---

46. 7.26 (ed. Koetschau, pp. 176.30–178.2). The passage makes interesting use of the terms πολιτεία and πολιτεύεσθαι, which is lost in a translation or paraphrase.

47. Cf. also *Contra Celsum* 4.32 (ed. Koetschau, p. 302.8-13), and 4.22 (p. 292.9-16), where Origen does speak of new laws given to the Christians.

48. Cf. de Lange, *Origen and the Jews*; H. Bietenhard, *Caesarea, Origenes und die Juden* (Stuttgart, 1974).

49. Cf. de Lange, *op. cit.*, pp. 36, 86-87; A. von Harnack, *Der kirchengeschichtliche Ertrag der exegetischen Arbeiten des Origenes*, I = *TU* 42.3 (1918), pp. 49, 68.

testaments and the beneficence of divine providence. His advocacy of 'spiritual interpretation' as a solution to the problem of
Old Testament interpretation did not destroy his interest in
historical events and their significance.

The subject continued to be treated by later writers. Eusebius
in his *Proof of the Gospel* gives a long and detailed exposition of
the fact that the law of Moses could only be observed by Jews
living in their own land.[50] Moses gave it to heal the Israelites
from idolatry but enacted in his foresight that its ordinances be
celebrated only in the Jerusalem temple. When the temple
was destroyed it was abolished and those attempting to obey it
became subject to the curse of Deut. 27.26.[51] He quotes this
verse no less than four times.[52] The *Apostolic Constitutions*
(6.25) also refer to this curse in showing that the sacrifices
according to the law can no longer be performed and the death
penalty no longer be inflicted since the defeat by the Romans,
as does Epiphanius in repeating the same stock argument
against the Nazaraeans.[53] John Chrysostom in his *Homilies
against the Jews*, attacking the Judaizing practices of Christians at Antioch, maintains that God allowed sacrifice for a
time in Jerusalem only as a concession to weakness but led the
Jews away from this practice by means of the destruction of
the city.[54] Inveighing against Julian's claim of Jewish support
in favour of animal sacrifice and his attempt to rebuild the
Jerusalem temple he asserts that the Jews themselves had
admitted that sacrifice was only allowed at Jerusalem.[55] In
reply to the same claim by Julian in his work *Against the
Galilaeans* Cyril of Alexandria repeats yet again that sacrifice

50. *Dem. Ev.* 1.3ff., with a summary at the beginning of 1.5.1 (ed. A.
Heikel; GCS *Eusebius* VI [1913], pp. 10.27ff., 20.16-19).
51. 1.6.31-40 (ed. Heikel, pp. 27.19–29.8).
52. 1.3.2, 1.3.25, 1.3.39, 1.6.37 (pp. 11.11, 14.35-6, 17.1-2, 28.20-22).
53. *Panarion haer.* 29.8.1.
54. 4.6 (*PG* 48.879-881; ET by P.W. Harkins, *Discourses against Juda-
ising Christians* = FC 68 [Washington, DC, 1979], pp. 88-91); cf. also
3.3.6-7 and 4.4.3-8 (*PG* 48.865end-866, 876-77; ET pp. 57-58, with note 43,
and 81-84).
55. 5.11.4-10 (*PG* 48.900-901; ET pp. 137-40); cf. also *Adv. Judaeos et
Gentiles Demonstratio* 16ff. (*PG* 48.835ff.).

476

was allowed in only one place so that it might cease when the temple was destroyed.[56] The remarks of the early Christian writers who have been cited above differ in detail according to the context of their reflexions and to whether they have pagan, Jewish or Judaizing Christian opponents in mind, and some of the earlier ideas were later dropped as being too extreme, but gradually a main stream of argumentation was worked out which could be repeated whenever occasion arose. This has been illustrated almost entirely from Greek writers. Unfortunately it has not been possible to consider Jewish reactions.[57] In conclusion reference may be made to a Westerner, Augustine, whose development of his own characteristic view on the subject has been examined by the honorand of this volume.[58] In attempting to show the role of the Roman destruction of Jerusalem in the divine plan for human history Augustine expounds the theory that the Jews were excluded from their homeland and dispersed throughout the rest of the world in order that they might act as witnesses to Christianity by means of their independent preservation and custody of the Old Testament scriptures.[59]

56. *Contra Julianum* 9 (*PG* 76.981B) replying to Julian's claim cited at 970C-D.
57. On these cf. the works listed in note 8 above. For examples of Jewish accommodation to the destruction of the temple by means of the substitution of other values and actions for the temple and cult, cf. note 15 above, Thoma, *art. cit.*, p. 199, and Bietenhard, *Caesarea, Origenes und die Juden*, p. 50.
58. E. Bammel, 'Die Zeugen des Christentums', to appear in H. Frohnhofen (ed.), *Die Anfänge des theologischen Vorurteils. Judaistische, neutestamentliche und frühchristliche Forschungen* (Hamburg, 1990).
59. Cf. e.g. *City of God* 4.34; *Sermon* 5.5 (ed. C. Lambot, CCL 41 [1961], pp. 55-56).

XII

Adam in Origen

Western discussion of the fall has been dominated by the views expressed by Augustine during the course of the Pelagian controversy. Just over a decade before the outbreak of this controversy, with the condemnation of Caelestius at Carthage for denying that Adam's sin injured the rest of the human race, the late fourth-century Origenist disputes had been terminated by the pronouncements of Theophilus of Alexandria and Anastasius of Rome against the heretical teachings attributed to Origen. Up to this date the rival theories on the origin of the human soul (creationism, traducianism or pre-existence) had been a matter for open discussion. Augustine himself had aired all three in his *De libero arbitrio* and sometimes speaks in his earlier writings of sin and the fall in terms that can best be understood of an individual fall in a previous existence.[1] Meanwhile opponents of Origenism were rejecting not only the theory of the fall of the pre-existent soul but also the suggestion that Adam's fall implicated the subsequent human race[2] and were propounding what seemed a naively optimistic view of the human condition. Pelagius himself, although strongly influenced by Origen's anti-gnostic emphasis on human free will, came to adopt this anti-Origenist optimism with regard to the fall, whereas Augustine in attacking Pelagianism retained Origen's view of the human condition in this life as a fallen one but, because of his rejection of the theory of pre-existence, placed the whole burden of responsibility for this condition on Adam's sin and condemnation.

Despite the fact, therefore, that Origen's views on the fall were not themselves adopted *in toto* by subsequent orthodoxy, they did play a very significant role in the development of that orthodoxy. Consideration of them only in relation to later controversy, however, is likely to result in over-simplification. In Origen's own time questions concerning not only the origin of the soul but also the significance of Adam's fall were wide open. Origen was faced with a confusing variety of earlier Jewish, Christian and gnostic views and of relevant texts in the Bible itself and in apocryphal literature.[3] It is not least because of the way that he attempts to do justice to this variety that a study of his own pronouncements on the subject of Adam is of interest.

The student who first encounters Origen and learns that he allegorized the story of Adam's fall in Genesis and at the same time that he believed that every soul has fallen before its entry into the body can easily gain the impression that Origen denied the existence of Adam as an individual and interpreted the story of his fall only as symbolizing the fall of every man's soul. This assumption is incorrect.[4]

In this paper the view will be presented that Origen did regard Adam as a historical figure, as the first man and the ancestor of the human race. The story of the garden of Eden and the fall does include details which cannot be taken literally even on the narrative level, but it none the less really happened, while at the same time, like other Old Testament stories, pointing to hidden mysteries and containing deeper levels of meaning as well.

The subject under consideration would more appropriately be examined in a book than in a brief paper. It involves questions which have been frequently debated by scholars and on which much has been written in recent years. These associated questions can only be touched on here with the utmost brevity. In view of the loss of the main source for Origen's views on Adam, his *Commentary on Genesis*, it would have been desirable to describe the interpretation of Adam's story in earlier and later writers likely to have influenced or been influenced by Origen. Here there is only room for a brief comparison with the relevant parts of the *Commentary on Genesis* of Didymus the Blind. It is also necessary to bear in mind that to ask the question 'What was Origen's teaching about Adam and his fall?' may be misconceived. In the majority of his works, Origen's aim is to expound scripture and to reflect the complexity of scripture. He discusses the problems raised by the biblical text and searches for parallel passages that may provide illumination, airs rival views and arguments, but does not provide dogmatic answers. In addition, corresponding to his view of the different levels of meaning in scripture, he may himself in expounding a biblical passage use language which can be understood on more than one level. A further problem is that the possibility must be taken into account that Origen altered his views between the composition of his *Commentary on Genesis* and the *De principiis* and his later works (although the fact that he refers back to his

Commentary on Genesis for the exegesis there of the account of the creation of the world and of man and of the story of Adam and the garden of Eden when writing the *Contra Celsum* in about AD 248–9 makes a significant change of view unlikely).[5] Another difficulty is the fact that of the surviving works of Origen only a small proportion is preserved in the original Greek. It will be necessary to refer also to catena extracts and the Latin translations, both sources which may be biassed in their selectivity[6] and whose reliability is open to question. The statements of Origen's views by his opponents provide valuable information, since they possessed writings which are now lost, but such statements must be used with caution, since they are likely to be influenced by the systematization of later Origenists. Bearing these caveats in mind and aiming to give some impression of the complexity and variety of Origen's treatment of the figure of Adam we will look at the evidence of the *De principiis* and of the charges made against Origen by fourth-century opponents in connection with his exegesis of Adam's story, and then, after outlining a tentative solution to the question of the relation of Adam's fall to that of the pre-existent soul, consider firstly how Origen may have dealt with the figure of Adam in the lost *Commentary on Genesis* and secondly how he refers to Adam in his surviving works.

Origen's account of the creation and fall of rational beings in *De principiis* is given without any reference to the Genesis story and indeed it is difficult to imagine how this version of the fall, in which all rational beings are created equal and fall a greater or lesser distance through neglect of the good,[7] could be identified with the story of Adam and Eve, which takes place in an environment in which there is already a differentiation of roles. Adam appears in *De principiis* as an historical figure.[8] In *De principiis* v.2, on biblical interpretation, Origen states that the historical narrative of scripture, beneath which the Spirit has hidden the symbolical meaning, includes the account of the visible works of creation, and of the creation of man and the descendants of the first men (IV.2.8, p.320.1–7). He states that the story of paradise and the fall provides clear examples of details (God planting a garden, the trees, God walking there, Adam hiding beneath the tree) which cannot be taken literally and demand a symbolic interpretation (IV.3.1, p. 323.7–324.4), but does not here state what that symbolic interpretation is. In IV.3.7 (p. 333.20–28) he states that Adam is said by Paul to be Christ and Eve to refer to the church. Christ is father of every soul, as Adam is of all men.

XII

The accounts of Origen's false teaching given by late fourth-century opponents include both general accusations concerning the pre-existence and fall of the soul based primarily on *De principiis* and also, as a separate item, specific accusations concerning the allegorization of the story of Adam, based primarily on the lost *Commentary on Genesis*.[9] Jerome's summary lists Origen's interpretation of the coats of skin in Genesis 3:21 as human bodies;[10] his allegorization of paradise, understanding the trees as angels and the rivers as heavenly powers;[11] and his statement that the image and likeness of God, in which man was created, was lost by him.[12] Also derived from Origen's exegesis of Genesis is the accusation that he allegorized the waters above the firmament (Genesis 1:6ff.) as angelic powers and those below the firmament as hostile powers.[13] This last accusation is anticipated by Basil,[14] though without mentioning Origen's name, and the view that the coats of skin are bodies and that paradise is not on earth but in the third heaven is attacked by Methodius of Olympus,[15] who is quoted by Epiphanius.[16] A further accusation concerning Origen's treatment of the figure of Adam appears in the description by Photius of a lost anonymous *Apology for Origen* in five volumes,[17] namely that the soul of the saviour was that of Adam. According to Socrates (*Historia ecclesiastica* III.7) Pamphilus and Eusebius defended Origen on a charge of this kind on the grounds that he interpreted a mystical tradition of the church.[18]

The statements of Origen's critics are likely to be distorted by exaggeration, misrepresentation and the tendency to regard speculations aired or discussed by Origen as Origen's own viewpoint, or to attribute the views of later Origenists to Origen himself. It is clear, however, that their criticism of Origen's understanding of the story of Adam's fall concerns the allegorization of the various details of the story of Adam (whose individual existence is not denied), not any identification of Adam's fall with that of rational beings in general. How then, it may be asked, did Origen relate the fall of Adam to the fall of rational beings described in *De principiis*? The answer Jerome would give to this question is clear from the work just quoted. Before man was made in paradise, souls dwelt among rational creatures in the heavens.[19] According to Origen's teaching all rational creatures, being incorporeal and invisible, if they have become negligent, slip gradually downwards and take to themselves bodies according to the nature of the places to which they sink (16, 368A). Origen uses Jacob's ladder to expound this gradual descent, with as many changes of bodies as there are stopping places between heaven and earth, to the bottom rung, that is flesh and blood (19, 370B–C).[20] This gradual descent expounded by Jerome is able without difficulty to include the general fall of the rational creatures from the state in which they were created (as expounded in *De principiis*) as its first stage and the story of Adam as its second or last stage. Adam is clothed in a body already in paradise, but it is only after his fall there that he is clothed in mortal flesh and blood (thus in *Ancoratus* 62.1–2 Epiphanius identifies *to sarkōdes tou sōmatos* (*ē auto to sōma*) with the coats of skin).

A scheme of the kind that Jerome implies is attributed to 'the allegorists' by Procopius of Gaza, *Commentary on Genesis* (PG 87.221A), and related to the exposition of Genesis 1:27, 2:7, and 3:21. The view of these allegorists is 'that the man according to the image signifies the soul, the man moulded from the soil [*chous*] the body made of fine particles [*leptomeres*] worthy of life in paradise, which some have called luminous [*augoeides*], and the garments of skin [are referred to by] "you have clothed me in skin and flesh and entwined me with bones and sinews" (Job 10:11). They say the soul uses as a vehicle first the luminous [body] which later put on the garments of skin.'

The theory that Origen did indeed think in terms of a gradual descent of the rational creatures from their original condition involving the assumption of bodies of differing degrees of thickness can be supported from passages in Rufinus' translation of *De principiis*.[21]

In *Contra Celsum* v.29–32, Origen narrates a biblical story which fits the fall of pre-existent souls and the view that souls fall gradually and in differing degrees much better than does that of Adam. He emphasizes that this (the story of the tower of Babel) is a story which indicates a secret truth and that the account of how souls become bound to bodies should not be revealed indiscriminately (v.31 and 29, pp. 32.20-1 and 31.6ff.). According to his paraphrase of the story (v.30), those on the earth remain without moving from the east as long as they pay attention to the light and the effulgence of the everlasting light. When they move from the east and pay attention to things alien to the east they lose their source of nourishment, and desire to collect material things and conspire by means of material things ('making bricks') against immaterial things. Corresponding to whether they have moved a greater or lesser distance from the east and to their brick-making activity, they are handed over for punishment to angels of varying character and led to different parts of the earth. Those who remain in the east (v.31) become the Lord's portion and their sins are at first tolerable, later increasing, despite the application of remedies, so that eventually they too are dispersed among the rulers of other nations.[22]

In the *Commentary on Matthew* xv.31ff., Origen gives an interpretation of the parable of the workers in the vineyard which makes clear the role of Adam as the first of those sent to labour in the present age. The 'day' of the parable is the whole of the present age; the master went out early and hired Adam and Eve to work the vineyard of religion. Thus the first rank is that according to Adam contemporaneous with the creation of the world, the second rank that according to Noah and the covenant with him, and so on (p. 442.22ff., p. 446.23ff.).

Procopius' statement on the interpretation by the allegorists of Genesis 1:27, 2:7 and 3:21 must be taken with caution, since his allegorists may be later Origenists, rather than Origen himself.[23] Origen certainly distinguished between the body of this life, which Paul calls the body of humiliation (Philippians 3:21), and the resurrection body, which is like the bodies of angels 'ethereal and luminous light' (*hopoia esti ta tōn aggelōn sōmata, aitheria kai augoeides phōs*).[24] How exactly this picture is to be related to Genesis 1:27, 2:7 and 3:21 is not entirely clear, because Origen is far more concerned with man's present condition and future hope than with the stages by which he reached his present condition. His references to the verses from Genesis are often associated with Pauline quotations. Thus he frequently distinguishes between the inner and outer man (2 Corinthians 4:16), identifying the inner man with the man made according to the image of God in Genesis 1:26 and the outer man with the man which God moulded taking soil from the earth in Genesis 2:7.[25] According to the *Commentary on John* II.23 (p. 79.3ff.), it is possible to understand the term 'man' (*anthrōpos*) in Genesis 1.26 of everything that has come to be in the image and likeness of God and thus as equally applicable to angels, since the rational beings are given their various names (men, angels, thrones, etc.) according to differences in rank, not in nature.

Commenting on Jeremiah 1:5 ('before I moulded you in the womb I know you') Origen states that the making (*poiēsis*) of Genesis 1:26 and the moulding (*plasis*) of Genesis 2:7 are to be distinguished. *Before* their *plasis* God knows those who are worthy of this knowledge.[26] The origin of this *plasis* or moulding is (according to Job 40:19) the serpent, who was the first of those who came to be in a body. When the saints were leading an immaterial and incorporeal life in blessedness, the so-called serpent fell from the pure life and deserved before all others to be bound in matter and a body.[27] He thus became the first 'choic'.[28] It is this 'choic', namely the devil, whose image we carry if we do his desires.[29] Being in heaven or on earth is not a matter of place but of disposition (*proairesis*). He who while still on the earth has his citizenship in heaven and lays up treasure in heaven, and has his heart in heaven, and bears the image of the heavenly, is no longer of the earth nor of the world below but of heaven and of the heavenly world, which is better than this one. The spiritual powers of wickedness (Ephesians 6:12) while in the heavens have their citizenship on earth and lay up treasure on earth, bearing the image of the choic.[30] It is noteworthy that Origen understands the 'choic' of 1 Corinthians 15:49 not of Adam but of the devil. Adam carried the image of the choic on account of his sin (*dia tēn hamartian*); both in Adam himself and in all men that which is according to the image of God is prior to the image of the evil one.[31] It is if one carries the image of the choic that the words addressed to Adam in Genesis 3:19, 'you are earth and unto earth you shall return', are rightly said to one.[32] If one carries the image of the heavenly, putting off the image of the choic, one is not earth.[33]

The evidence so far quoted is compatible with the view that Origen thought in terms of a first general fall of the rational beings as having preceded the moulding of man's bodily nature as described in Genesis 2:7 and a second fall of the protoplasts Adam and Eve, which resulted for them and their descendants in the conditions of life here on this earth. Scholars have tended, however, to be reluctant to think in this way in terms of 'two falls'. They have preferred either to think of Genesis 1:27 and 2:7 as referring to a double creation which happened simultaneously (therefore no fall before Genesis 2:7), or in terms of a fall before Genesis 2:7 which is symbolized by the story of Adam's fall (so that Adam's sin is identified with that of the pre-existent souls and there is no distinction between the bodily nature of Genesis 2:7 and human nature subsequent to Adam's fall).[34] A reason for the aversion to the theory of 'two falls' is no doubt the fear that, if combined with Procopius' suggestion of two stages of corporeality, it involves the implication that the first creation of Genesis 1:27 was incorporeal. Whether Origen thought it possible for rational creatures to exist in an incorporeal state is keenly disputed.[35] It may well, however, be an oversimplification to assume that Origen thought that there are only two possible kinds of corporeality (ethereal bodies and the gross material bodies of this life) and hence only two possible levels of corporeal existence. If one wishes to combine the theory of 'two falls' with the view that rational creatures cannot exist incorporeally, it may be necessary to think in terms of at least three levels of corporeality.[36]

The *Commentary on Genesis*, which would have made clear if not what view Origen held, then at least what views he aired and discussed and what speculations he put forward, is unfortunately lost. It was a lengthy and detailed work, consisting of thirteen volumes on Genesis 1–4, of which the first eight volumes were composed at Alexandria concurrently with *De principiis* (Origen refers back to the exposition of Genesis 1:1 in *De principiis* II.3.6, but had not yet expounded Genesis 1:26 when he wrote *De principiis* I.2.6). Only fragments survive and in speculating on the contents we depend on criticisms such as those listed above and on comparison with earlier and later writers on the same subjects. These include Philo, Basil of Caesarea, Gregory of Nyssa, Theodoret and Ambrose, as well as Procopius of Gaza's collection of extracts (preserved only in his own summarizing paraphrase). Particularly heavily indebted to Origen (but far briefer than Origen's lost Commentary) is Didymus' *Commentary on Genesis*, discovered at Tura in 1941 (the exposition of Genesis 1:1–6 survives only in a fragmentary state, that of 2.4–25 is lost).[37] The first of Origen's *Homilies on Genesis* translated by Rufinus gives a brief exposition of Genesis 1:1–30, concentrating chiefly on the 'moral' application. The commentary itself dealt with the early chapters of Genesis in great detail and it may be assumed that Origen discussed a variety of different possible interpretations of the verses concerned, without necessarily stating his own solutions. Furthermore it cannot be supposed that Origen saw the opening chapters of Genesis simply in terms of a chronological succession of events. Quite apart from the fact that 'before the world existed, time did not yet exist',[38] the narrative of the beginning of Genesis must be understood on more than one level, since it gives an account of the creation of the visible world beneath which deeper mysteries lie hidden. This means that to ask the question at what point or points in the Genesis account Origen would have located a fall or falls prior to that of Adam may well be to take an over-naive approach. None the less it is very probable that he did discuss the first general fall of the rational creatures at an early stage in his commentary. Light is thrown on this, as well as on the way in which the different levels of exegesis are related, by a comparison of Didymus' exposition of the waters above and below the firmament in Genesis 1.6–10 with that in the first *Homily on Genesis*.

Didymus supplements his literal interpretation of Genesis 1.6–10 with an allegorical interpretation clearly following the exegesis of Origen attacked by Basil, Epiphanius and Jerome (see above p. 65) and also linked to the 'Origenist' doctrine of the fall of rational creatures. After quoting biblical verses on good and bad spiritual waters (*SC* 233, 19.1–20.7), Didymus states that the rational creatures (*ta logika zō(i)a*) are indicated by the water (20.7–8) and that, whereas rational being, like water, is one in its substance (cf. 21.18–20), they have come to be in a state of either vice or virtue by means of their own impulse and will (20.8ff.; cf. also 28.14–16). In explaining what is meant by the firmament, Didymus speaks in terms of the individual soul. The firmament is the capacity of reason (*logos*) distinguishing good and evil placed in the commanding part of the soul (*hēgemonikon*) by God.[39] The waters beneath the firmament, or rational creatures which remained in a worse condition, are in different assemblies because evil is divisive, whereas virtue unifies, since he who has one virtue has all the virtues (26.11ff.). God wishes to benefit these scattered waters and orders that they be gathered together so that they may become like the water above the heavens, one not in number but in harmony. God's command in Genesis 1:9a, using the phrase *eis sunagōgēn mian*, refers to the final result aimed at; the statement of what happened in 1:9b, using the plural *eis tas sunagōgas autōn*, refers to progress on the way to this (28.11–29.22). The allegorical interpretation of Genesis 1:10 is applied to the individual soul. The soul, remaining the same in its substance, is freed from the waters covering it related to the abyss, and is called earth, receiving divine seed and bringing forth fruit (30.6ff.).

In Rufinus' translation of the first *Homily on Genesis* these verses are applied to the individual (pp.3–5). The first heaven (Genesis 1:1) is spiritual substance or our mind or spiritual man, who sees God. The firmament or corporeal heaven is our external man (later, however, p.10.10–11, 'nostrum firmamentum coeli' is explained as 'mentis nostrae uel cordis soliditas'). If man, when placed in the body, can distinguish the waters above and below the firmament, he will be called 'heaven' or 'heavenly man'. If he understands and shares in spiritual water, rivers of living water will flow from his belly (John 7:38, quoted also by Didymus, 19.4), and he will be separated from the water of the abyss below, where the prince of this world and his angels dwell. If we collect and disperse from ourselves the water beneath the heaven, that is, the sins and vices of our body, our 'dry land', our works done in the flesh, will appear, and our bodies will not remain 'dry' but be called 'earth', because they will be able to bear fruit to God.

The various levels of exegesis, literal (not included in the above summaries), allegorical and 'moral', are linked by the fact that the various levels of reality itself mirror one another, as also the microcosm man represents a reflection of the constitution of the macrocosm or universe. This latter point is stated explicitly in the first *Homily on Genesis*.[10] In the narrative of Genesis, the description of the creation of the visible world, referring allegorically to the microcosm man, is followed by the account of the creation of man (Genesis 1:26ff.), which may to some extent therefore be regarded as a doublet of what comes before.[11]

The exposition of Genesis 1:27 in the first *Homily on Genesis* utilizes the contrast between the inner incorporeal man made according to the image of God in this verse and the outer or corporeal man moulded from the earth in Genesis 2:7. It is in such qualities as his invisibility, incorporeality, incorruptibility, and immortality that the inner man is understood to be according to the image of God (p.15.7–14). 'Male and female' is specified already in Genesis 1:27, either in anticipation of the subsequent creation of woman, or because everything made by God is linked together, as heaven and earth, or as sun and moon, or (according to the allegorical interpretation) because our inner man consists of spirit (male) and soul (female), whose union produces good and useful attitudes and thoughts, which enable them to dominate the earth, that is, the flesh (pp. 18–19). There also survives an extract from the *Commentary on Genesis* on Genesis 1:26–7,[12] attacking the view that *to kat' eikona* is located in the body and arguing that the view that it is in the rational soul may be supported by a consideration of the capacities (*dunameis*) of the soul. That which in man is according to the image is characterized not by the form of the body but by actions, as is shown by St Paul's words in 1 Corinthians 15:49 and Colossians 3:10.

For the story of Adam, a number of extracts and quotations are preserved which may come from the lost commentary, perhaps in part also from the *Scholia on Genesis*.[43] Two sentences quoted with disapprobation by Eustathius of Antioch apparently introduce an allegorical interpretation of the trees in paradise (p. 56). Catena fragments include (pp. 56–7) an interpretation of *Edem* as *hēdu* together with the mention of a Hebrew tradition that Eden, where God planted paradise or the garden, is the centre of the world like the pupil of an eye, and that the river Phison is accordingly interpreted as *stoma korēs*; also a brief interpretation of Genesis 2:12 apparently on a 'moral' level (*chrusion kalon* refers to *kala dogmata*), and on 2:13 the information that the Hebrew for Ethiopia means *skotōsis*. A paragraph on Genesis 2:15

(pp. 57–8) refers God's placing Adam in paradise to the placing of those reborn in baptism in the church to work spiritual works. They receive a command to love all the brethren (Genesis 2:16). He who follows the arguments of the serpent and loves some and hates others disobeys the command. The resulting death is caused not by God but by the man who has hated his neighbour. These extracts give some idea of the variety of Origen's exegesis but are not informative on the relation of Adam's fall to the prehistory of the individual soul. More obviously relevant is the extract on the garments of skin in Genesis 3:21.[44] In this passage Origen rejects a literal interpretation as foolish and describes the interpretation of the garments as bodies as plausible but not clearly true, since Genesis 2:23, mentioning Adam's bones and flesh, then presents a problem. The view that they represent mortality (*nekrōsis*) is rejected on the grounds that in this case God and not sin would be the author of *nekrōsis* and flesh and bones would not on their own account be perishable. 'Moreover, if paradise is a divine place, let them say how each of the limbs performed its proper function there and was not created in vain.' With regard to the mention of a nostril (Aquila and Symmachus) or face (LXX) in Genesis 2:7, it must be said that one ought not to cling to the letter of scripture as being true but to seek the treasure hidden in the letter.

Origen does not here state his view explicitly, but his argument appears to deny that Adam and Eve had bodies of flesh and bones in paradise and hence to tend in the direction of the interpretation of which Epiphanius and Jerome accuse him (see above, p. 65). The problem is not just one of specifying the change undergone by Adam and Eve as a result of the fall but rather of identifying what exactly it is that is referred to in Genesis 3:21. Origen agrees with the view that mortality was a result of the fall (thus in the *Commentary on John* I.20 and XIII.34, pp. 25.2ff. and 259.34ff. he states that, but for the fall, man, 'having been made for incorruptibility', would have 'gained possession of incorruptibility', or 'would have remained immortal'), but he regards sin and not God as its author, and therefore rejects the identification of the garments with mortality. Two references in other works are equally non-committal, but not incompatible with an interpretation of the garments as the fleshly body of this life. In the *Contra Celsum* IV.40 (p. 313–25ff.), Origen states that the man thrown out with the woman from paradise, clothed in skin garments, which, because of human transgression, God made for those who had sinned, has a certain secret and mysterious meaning, superior to that of the descent of the soul in

XII

Plato, when it loses its wings and is carried here until it finds some firm resting place. In *Homily on Leviticus* VI.2 (p. 362.11–22) he states that Adam after his sin was clothed in animal skins, to be a sign of the mortality which he had received for his sin and of that weakness which came from the corruption of the flesh.[45]

The question of the kind of body Adam had in paradise is related to that of the kind of place paradise is. In the extract on Genesis 3:21 Origen allows for the view that paradise is a 'divine place' (*theion ti chōrion*), hence a place superior to this earth but none the less a place and not simply a spiritual condition. To examine all Origen's references to paradise would be a major task, which cannot be undertaken here.[46] The question of its location is complicated by the fact that terms like world (*kosmos*), heaven, earth and dry land are used of more than one level of existence;[47] also that Origen sometimes distinguishes between 'paradise' and 'paradise of God' or 'paradise of luxury'[48] (the former is where the robber went with Jesus at the first hour (Luke 23:43), the latter is where he will have been if he received and ate from the tree of life and of all the trees which God did not prohibit; it is also where the devil fell from;[49] it is the destination of martyrs after death).[50] In *Homily on Numbers* XXVI.5 Origen distinguishes various meanings of the word 'earth' (p. 251.27ff.). The earth on which we live was originally called 'dry land' and received the name 'earth' afterwards. Adam was driven out into the place called 'dry land' from paradise, which is not on the 'dry land' but on the 'earth'. Similarly it is the 'earth' which is promised to the meek in Matthew 5:5. Very frequently Origen uses language of paradise that can be understood on a moral or spiritual level. The paradise of God may be planted in our hearts.[51] If we mortify our limbs on earth and bear fruits of the spirit, the Lord may walk in us as in a spiritual paradise.[52] It is this level of understanding which provides a solution to the problematic verse, Genesis 3:8, where God is described as walking in paradise and Adam and Eve as hiding. God walks in paradise as he does in the saints, whereas the sinner hides himself from God.[53] In the beginning God planted a paradise of luxury, that we might enjoy spiritual luxuries.[54] The transplanted tree of Psalm 1:3 may be understood as the soul of the Saviour, transplanted into paradise, so that those worthy to be with Christ may be enlightened by him by the illumination of knowledge.[55] It may be noted that whereas conditions in the paradise of luxury may be understood to represent the life enjoyed by the rational creatures before the first fall and that to be attained by

73

XII

the saints after the resurrection, Adam himself in Genesis 2 to 3 does not exist in these conditions, since he does not partake of the tree of life and the other trees which God did not prohibit.

Further evidence for Origen's treatment of the figure of Adam in his *Commentary on Genesis* is provided by ten fragments from a papyrus codex of the fourth or fifth century, containing parts of the exegesis of Genesis 3:11ff.[56] Most of the fragments consist of only a few letters from each line, allowing the identification of the biblical verses discussed or quoted and some individual words, but not much more. Fragment III^v contains references to the versions of Theodotion and (probably) Symmachus, and the better preserved fragment VI a discussion of Genesis 3:15 (the enmity between the seed of the serpent and the seed of the woman on VI^v, with a reference to Stoic theories of heredity on VI^r). The passage from Procopius (*PG* 87.1, 205Cf.) which Sanz (p. 99) quotes as providing a parallel to fragment VI^v turns out to be taken from Didymus, *Commentary on Genesis* 98.31ff. Other parallels provided by Didymus concern the greater strength of the man over against the woman as an adversary of the serpent,[57] and the kindness with which God questions the protoplasts in Genesis 3:9ff.[58] More importantly, a comparison with Didymus may be able to throw light on features which Sanz found obscure. The most interesting of these is the quotation of a number of verses concerning Christ's incarnation and sinlessness.[59] The most likely context for these quotations is a comparison of Adam and Eve with Christ and the church, such as recurs a number of times in Didymus' *Commentary* attributed at first to certain persons (83.25ff., 93.23ff.) and later repeated without qualification (100.4ff., 101.27ff., 105.7ff.). According to this exegesis, which utilizes Ephesians 5:32 and 1 Timothy 2:14, Adam followed Eve not in transgression but to help her, while Christ, himself without sin, emptied himself and took on the form of a servant to help the fallen human race of which the church consists (there is an allusion to Philippians 2:7 in 105.9 and a quotation in 105.15). In 101.24ff., Didymus contrasts the cursing of the serpent in Genesis 3:14 with the milder words spoken to Adam in Genesis 3:17. It may be that the same point is being made in fragment IIa^r 2–4. The references to the bridegroom and bride in fragment VI^{r}9–10 and IIb^r 1–2 (as restored by Sanz) may belong to the context of Christ as bridegroom of the church,[60] in which case the seed of the woman and that of the serpent in fragment VI is probably to be understood allegorically (as in Didymus 99.1ff., of teachings). That Origen did indeed interpret Adam as Christ and Eve as the church is confirmed by

74

Socrates, who states that he established this fully in volume 9 of the *Commentary on Genesis*, also that Origen there illuminated the mystery concerning Christ's human soul (*empsuchon ton enanthrōpēsanta*).[61]

In view of Didymus' dependence on Origen it is worth listing a few points from his treatment of the paradise story as an indication of the kind of themes Origen may have discussed in his commentary. Didymus' exegesis of Genesis 2:4–25 is lost, but there are some references back to it in that of Genesis 3. Paradise is a divine place, the dwelling place of blessed powers (102.9–10). Those who think it even now exists on earth can be refuted from Genesis 3:24 (114.21ff.). It is a transcendent place, where thick bodies cannot be worn (107.20–22, 108.5–15). The robber of Luke 23:43 entered paradise in his naked soul (ibid.). Didymus seems to envisage the body worn in paradise as an intermediate stage between the incorporeal creation according to the image of Genesis 1:27 and the dense mortal body of the present life (107.4–20). This intermediate body is referred to as *to geōdes skēnos* in Wisdom of Solomon 9:15 (ibid.) and as *chous* in Genesis 2:7, which indicates the corporeal substance of the body appropriate for life in paradise (118.13–16). The garments of skin are the bodies referred to as skin and flesh in Job 10:11 (106.8ff.). As a result of his faults, man received dry land instead of the earth of the meek, to which he will return in a spiritual body after the resurrection (104.17ff. on Genesis 3:19).

A different view of man's condition in paradise seems to be envisaged in the speculations expressed in connection with God's words 'Where are you?' in Genesis 3:9 (90.9–91.11). Here Didymus considers what is meant by place in this context. Is it the task to which Adam has been assigned and which he has deserted? Some exegetes think of incorporeal substance as the first substrate of the soul and therefore reckon that the soul should be outside all place but that, when it has of itself made trial of a body, it is admonished with the words 'Where are you?' Moreover he who has his heart in heaven is not in a place, being above the world.

The nature of the fall is such that it can be applied to sin in general, both that of the pre-existent soul and also to human sin in this world. The command given to Adam indicated that he should eat of the tree of the knowledge of good and evil together with all the other trees and not alone, since human aptitude without the practice of virtue is very harmful (92.26ff.). The serpent wished Adam and Eve to become wise for evil and their eyes inclining towards evil to be opened, eyes which are not opened when virtue is active (81.19–21; cf. 83.7–25). After the fall Adam is addressed with the words of Genesis 3:22, because he has become like the devil, who fell from heaven, knowing what is good and what is evil, but not distinguishing so as to choose the good and shun the evil (109.2ff.). 'Naked' in Genesis 3:7 is explained as stripped of their previous virtue (83.1–7, 84.20–28, 92.10–12), the girdles of fig-leaves as excuses (85.5–86.7). Before their transgression, God was with Adam and Eve and did not walk outside them, but after they abandoned God by turning away from virtue, he distanced himself from them but still made them aware of their sin by means of the universal notions[62] which he implanted in them (85.2–5, 87.1–21).

Interwoven with the above exegesis is an allegorical interpretation derived from Philo[63] according to which Adam represents the mind (*nous*), Eve sensation (*aisthēsis*) and the serpent pleasure (*hēdonē*, 95.18–21, 82.29–83.1). The allegorical interpretation according to which Adam represents Christ and Eve the church has already been mentioned (above, p. 74). Didymus emphasizes, however, that not everything said of Adam applies to Christ (104.28ff.).

So far we have considered the attacks on Origen's treatment of Adam and speculated on the themes included in his *Commentary on Genesis*. A fairer picture may, however, be obtained if we examine Origen's references to Adam in his other surviving works and fragments. Such an examination may show which features Origen himself considered of particular significance and worthy of frequent repetition. We shall look first at the references to the story of Adam, then at the interpretation of Adam as Christ and Eve as the church, and finally at the question of the connection between Adam's fall and the fallen state of every man in this life.

There are a number of references to the story of Adam and his fall, some of which appear to be more or less straightforward, while others are open also to interpretation either on a higher level of the first fall, or on a moral level of every man. These references will be listed or summarized here in the order of the events of the story.[64]

God placed the man he moulded in paradise to work it and guard it.[65] If the woman had not been deceived and Adam had not fallen and man made for incorruption had obtained incorruption, Christ would not have descended.[66] In Genesis God places man in the paradise of luxury, giving him laws about eating and not eating such and such things and man would have remained immortal if he had eaten from every tree in paradise and refrained from eating from the tree of the knowledge of good and evil.[67]

In the *Commentary on John* XIII.37, p. 262.5ff., Origen considers the question whether the rational creature created by God was incomplete (*ateles*) when placed in paradise. It would not, however, be reasonable to call him who was able to work the tree of life and everything which God planted and caused to spring up 'incomplete'. So perhaps he was complete in some way (*pōs*) and became incomplete through the transgression. Origen seems here to be thinking on more than one level, since his use of *to logikon* (p. 262.9ff.) suggests that he is talking of rational creatures in general, yet he goes on to state that not only man fell from completeness to being incomplete but also the 'sons of God seeing the daughters of men' (Genesis 6:2) and all those who 'leave their own habitation' and 'kept not their first estate' (*archē*, Jude 6), explaining that the *archē* of existence for man was in paradise and that each of those who have fallen have their own *archē*.

Adam is counted as a prophet, since he prophesied in Genesis 2:24.[68] The devil envied Adam and deceived him by means of food (and tried to do the same to Christ).[69] When God saw the devil reflecting 'if a serpent could speak, I would have approached by means of it for the deception of the protoplasts', he allowed this.[70] Eve's gullibility and the unsoundness of her reasoning did not arise when she disobeyed God and listened to the serpent, but existed previously and were shown up, since the serpent approached her for this reason and seized on her weakness with his own shrewdness.[71]

Before his transgression, man is described as able to see with one kind of eyes (in Genesis 3:6 'the woman saw') and unable to see with another (Genesis 3:5,7 'your eyes will be opened', 'their eyes were opened'). The eyes which were opened were the eyes of sense perception. Previously they had rightly shut these, so as not to be distracted or hindered from seeing with the eye of the soul. On account of their sin, however, they shut the eyes of the soul with which they previously saw and which rejoiced in God and his paradise[72] (a similar distinction is made in *Homily on Numbers* XVII.3, p. 157.6ff. between the 'eyes of the earth' or 'sense of the flesh' opened in Genesis 3:7 and the 'better eyes' referred to in Genesis 3:6).

In *Homily on Jeremiah* XVI. 3 (p. 136.15ff.) Origen explains Genesis 3:8. Even though Adam sinned, his sin was not excessively bad. Therefore he hid from the face of God (thus showing a sense of shame), whereas Cain, being a greater sinner, went out from the face of God (a similar distinction is made in *Homily on Exodus* XI.5, p. 258.4ff.).[73]

In *Homily on Genesis* XV.2 (p. 128.24ff.) the death referred to in God's words to the first man in Genesis 2:17 is stated to be sin. He died as soon as he transgressed the commandment. The soul which has sinned is dead, and the serpent, who said 'You will not die', is proved to have lied. Comparing the deceit from the serpent with deceit from God, Origen states in *Homily on Jeremiah* XX.3 (p. 182.4ff.) that deceit from the serpent drove Adam and his wife out of the paradise of God. In the *Commentary on John* XX.25 (p. 360.18ff.), Origen summarizes the narrative of the fall before going on to explain the meaning of true life and death and its application to all men: Adam and Eve were not killed so far as they had not sinned, but on the day they ate from the forbidden tree they immediately died, killed by none other than the murderous devil, when he deceived Eve through the serpent and Eve gave to the man from the tree and the man ate.

Adam and Eve were the parents of all men.[74] In the *Commentary on John* XX.3ff. (p. 329.7ff.), Origen discusses spiritual and physical descent from Adam and other ancestors of the human race. According to the *Commentary on Matthew*,[75] there is a tradition that the body of Adam, the first man, is buried at Calvary, so that the head of the human race and father of all men may receive the benefit of resurrection together with his descendants.[76]

The interpretation of Adam as Christ and of Adam and Eve as Christ and the church is inspired by 1 Corinthians 15:45 and Ephesians 5:30–2. In expounding Romans 5:14,[77] Origen explains Adam as a type of Christ 'by opposites',[78] but elsewhere a positive parallelism appears. Often this applies to Christ incarnate and the church on earth.[79] In *Homily on Numbers* XXVIII.4 (p. 284.16ff.) the dispersion of the sons of Adam at the beginning of the world is compared with the distribution of the sons of the last Adam at the end of the world (here the element of contrast predominates, with a quotation of 1 Corinthians 15:22).

There are also hints of (and references which can be read in the light of) the exegesis according to which Adam symbolizes the unfallen soul of Christ and Eve the pre-existent church, whom he followed in his descent to this earth. Indeed it is possible that it was initially in this context that Origen regarded the story of Adam and Eve as symbolizing the first fall of the rational creatures. In the *Commentary on Matthew* XIV.17 (p. 325.27ff.) the word 'female' in Genesis 1:27 is applied to the church and Adam's words in Genesis 2:24 to the Lord's leaving the heavenly Jerusalem and cleaving to his fallen wife, the church which is his body.[80] In the *Commentary on John* XIX.4 (p. 302.17ff.), Origen explains that with respect to the knowledge of God the word 'knowing' in biblical usage implies 'being united with' and illustrates this point by the example of Adam and Eve, referring for its interpretation to Ephesians 5:32 and 1 Corinthians 6:16f.: Adam (= Christ) did not 'know' his wife when he made the statement of Genesis 2:23 but only when he clove to her (Genesis 4:1). In the *Commentary on the Song of Songs* II (p. 132.28ff.), Origen applies 1 Timothy 2:14–15 to the parallel of Adam and Eve with Christ and the church, prepared as his bride from the dispersion among the gentiles, a bride who was deceived and in transgression when he gave himself for her. Later in the same work (III, p.213.25ff.) it is stated that the serpent deceived Eve and infected all her descendants with the contagion of transgression.[81] In *Homily on Genesis* XV.5 (p. 133.23ff.) Adam's descent from paradise to the labours and troubles of this world to contend with the serpent is seen as parallel to that of the Lord, who descended to this world and became a great race (i.e. the church of the gentiles), in that both may be symbolized by Jacob's descent to Egypt. In the *Commentary on John* II.29ff. (pp. 86.1ff.), Adam's being sent from paradise to work the earth is compared with the sending of John the Baptist 'from heaven or from paradise or from wherever else' to this place on earth, and the guess is hazarded (p. 88.6ff.) that the Baptist may be one of the holy angels following the example of Christ's incarnation. In Book I of the *Commentary on John* Origen applies 1 Corinthians 15:45b to Christ as Adam, without making any contrast with the first Adam.[82] In *De principiis* IV.3.7 (p. 333.20–8) Christ as father of all souls is paralleled by Adam as father of all men, while Eve, interpreted as the church, includes fallen members among her offspring. The story of the woman being taken from Adam's rib while he slept and being 'built' by God is said to be an allegory in *Contra Celsum* IV.38 (p. 308.20ff.), but without further explanation. In a fragment on Proverbs 31:16 (*PG* 17.252A), however, it is stated that the church came forth from the side (*pleura*, rib) of Christ[83] (the preceding sentence seems to take not Eve but the garden of Eden as symbolizing 'the soul of the virtuous', which is identified with 'the church having the tree of knowledge and the tree of life; of knowledge as of the law, and of life as of the Logos').[84]

A different approach to the figure of Adam from that so far considered is taken in those passages where Adam is associated with the fallen condition of human life in this world. The reason for this association is that (whether or not a general fall of rational creatures symbolized by or previous to Adam's fall is envisaged) the terms under which man lives in his present life are those resulting from the expulsion of the protoplasts from paradise, as described in Genesis 3. In this connection, 'Adam' may be generalized to refer to fallen man or the bodily life of man. Origen frequently quotes in this context 1 Corinthians 15:22 ('in Adam all die') together with verses like Psalm 43:20 (LXX) and 26, Psalm 21:16 (LXX), Romans 7:24 and Philippians 3:21 (for example, *Commentary on John* XX.25, p. 361.7ff., on the devil as man's murderer and the subjection to him of this earthly region). These and other verses are cited in *Contra Celsum* VII.50 (p. 201.28ff.) together with the explanation that the 'place of affliction' referred to in Psalm 43:20 is the earthly region, to which Adam, which means 'man', came after being cast out of paradise for his sin (*dia tēn kakian*). In *Contra Celsum* IV.40 (p. 311.16ff.) Origen explains that, since Adam means 'man', the biblical texts stating that in Adam all die and are condemned in the likeness of Adam's transgression (an allusion to Romans 5:14, which Origen reads without the negative) are spoken of the whole race, also that the curses spoken against Adam and Eve apply to all men and women. Thus the words spoken in Genesis 3:17–19 mean that the whole earth is cursed; every man who has 'died in Adam' eats of it in grief all the days of his life, and it will bring forth thorns and thistles all the days of the life of the man who, in Adam, was cast out of paradise.[85] The sinner is called 'earth', since Adam is told 'You are earth and to earth you will go.'[86] We need the strength of God to apply to our own 'earth' (for Adam is told 'You are earth'), and without God's power we are unable to fulfil what is not according to the will of the flesh.[87]

The question how it can come about that all men 'die in Adam' and share the results of his transgression is considered by Origen in his exegesis of Romans 5:12ff., which survives only in the abbreviating paraphrase of Rufinus.[88] A number of solutions are aired, which need not be regarded as mutually exclusive. The simplest is that the devil gained power over men by means of the disobedience of the first man,[89] and it was because of Adam's sin that all men were condemned to mortality and that he was thrown out of paradise to this place of humiliation and vale of tears.[90]

In expounding Romans 5:12, Origen raises the question why sin entered 'through one man', when the woman sinned before Adam and the serpent before the woman.[91] The answer he suggests is that the

XII

succession of human descent which became subject to the death coming from sin is ascribed not to the woman but to the man. He compares the case of Levi, who was already present in the loins of Abraham when Melchizedek met him (Hebrews 7:9–10), and draws the conclusion that all men who are born or have been born in this world were in the loins of Adam when he was still in paradise, and thus that all men were driven out with him from paradise.[92] The idea of succession reappears, combined with that of inheritance of sin by the teaching of one's parents in the exegesis of Romans 5:14.[93] This succession from Adam is mentioned already in the exegesis of Romans 3:12, together with the idea of Adam as an example of decline from the right path.[94]

Outside the *Commentary on Romans* the most interesting discussion of the question of succession from Adam occurs in fragment 11 from the *Commentary on Matthew* (pp. 19–20, on Matthew 1:18, reading *gennēsis* ('birth') and contrasting this with *genesis* ('generation') in 1:1). According to this fragment, *genesis* is the first moulding by God and possesses incorruptibility and sinlessness, *gennēsis* is the succession from each other from the condemnation of death on account of transgression and possesses passibility and the tendency to sin. The Lord took the sinlessness but not the incorruptibility of *genesis*, and the passibility but not the tendency to sin of *gennēsis*, 'bearing the first Adam undiminished in his elements according to both'. In the case of Christ *genesis* is the path from being in the form of God to taking the form of a slave. His *gennēsis* was like ours, in that he was born from a woman, but superior to ours, in that it was not from the will of the flesh or of a man but from the Holy Spirit.

The idea of a sinful tendency inherited from Adam is not intended by Origen to replace the concept of a previous fall of the individual soul but is considered alongside it. The latter concept (and perhaps also the idea that subsequent to the first fall of rational creatures individual men may have suffered a further fall similar to that of Adam) is hinted at in the *Commentary on Romans*, at first cryptically (it is probably intended in the discussion of Romans 5:14, p. 342.11ff.: 'perhaps there were some who did something like what Adam is described as having done in paradise'; cf. 343.10ff., 352.6–8), then more obviously (p.355.1ff.: Paul says that each individual has sinned in the likeness of Adam's transgression, although he does not consider it safe to say openly where or when or how).[95] Since a choice is not made between these two explanations, it remains an open question whether it is because of its own previous fall or because of the taint of birth in succession from Adam (or rather it is

81

probably for both these reasons)[96] that the soul is already polluted on arrival in this life and requires purification. In expounding Romans 6:6,[97] Origen quotes Pauline and Old Testament verses to show that the body of this life is the 'body of sin', 'body of death' and 'body of humiliation', and refers to the Old Testament sin offering for newly born babies and the Christian practice of infant baptism as evidence that all have the pollution of sin at birth. That succession from Adam plays a role in this pollution is suggested in this passage by the observations that it was only after his sin that Adam knew his wife and begat Cain and that it was because of the virgin birth that Christ only had the likeness of the flesh of sin and not the flesh of sin itself.[98]

Perhaps the most interesting exegesis of the death of all men in Adam or the entry of sin through one man (1 Corinthians 15:22, Romans 5:12) is that which interprets 'Adam' as the unregenerate individual in this life. Such an exposition, combined with a different use of 1 Corinthians 15:45ff. from that described above, appears immediately after the discussion of succession from Adam in the *Commentary on Romans* v.1 (p. 327.3ff.): if a man is not yet renewed in the inner man according to the image of God but is still in this world and is 'choic' and bears the image of the 'choic', it is of him that the words 'sin entered this world and through sin death' are said. Every man is first 'from the earth, choic', when he walks in the image of the 'choic' and thinks according to the flesh, and only with difficulty does he eventually turn to the Lord, accept the guidance of the Spirit of God and being made spiritual become 'the last Adam as a life-giving spirit' (1 Corinthians 15:47). In the *Commentary on Romans* v.9 (p. 394.1ff.), the 'old man' of Romans 6:6, Ephesians 4:22 and Colossians 3:9 is explained as the man who lives according to Adam, subject to transgression and death.[99]

In the context of the interpretation of 'Adam' as the individual it is possible to draw a parallel between St Paul's description of the human condition in Romans 7:7ff. and the story of Adam, by assimilating the law forbidding desire with the tree of the knowledge of good and evil or the command not to eat from it. Hints of such an interpretation appear in the *Commentary on Romans*. At VI.11 (pp. 65.15–66.1) it is suggested that the tree of the knowledge of good and evil symbolizes the law, because the law contains both the letter that kills and the life-giving spirit. At VI.8 (pp. 48.16–49.1), on the words 'sin deceived me by means of the commandment' (Romans 7:11), the suggestion is made that 'sin' refers to the author of sin, of whom the words 'the serpent deceived me' (Genesis 3:13) are written. The words 'I once lived without the law' in

Romans 7:9 are explained as referring to the fact that every man lives without the natural law until he reaches the age of reason. During this time sin is dormant, but when he reaches the age to be able to distinguish right and wrong sin revives.[100] The parallel is limited, however, because the condition of man before he reaches the age of reason is not seen as equivalent to that of Adam before the fall.[101] On the contrary, because of the fall death reigns in man from his birth until the age of reason and it is only then that he becomes capable of receiving the grace of Christ (v.2, p. 353.13ff.). Thus the situation of man in this life is seen not so much in parallel to Adam's fall as in terms of the exhortation to reverse the results of the fall by turning to Christ.

There is no need to suppose that the theory of a succession of sin handed down from Adam to his descendants is incompatible with that of the fall of the individual soul before entering the body, or that Origen 'changed his mind' on this subject.[102] A particular situation (in this case the human condition) can have more than one cause. The individual soul may enter human life as the result of its own previous fall and here be subjected to conditions which are the result of Adam's condemnation. If we wish to systematize Origen's scattered hints and tentative suggestions, we must think in terms of the story of Adam (the first event in human history) as having taken place subsequent to and at a lower level than the fall of rational creatures from their original state of contemplation, also of individual souls having descended through more than one level before their entry into human life.[103] It is not without significance, however, that Origen himself nowhere spells out such a scheme in his surviving works.[104] His aim was not to dogmatize or to force his biblical material into a straitjacket, but rather to do justice to the multiplicity, complexity and variety of the biblical pronouncements concerning Adam, human nature and the fall. Some of this variety and also the difficulty of gauging the 'level' at which Origen's language is to be understood has been illustrated in the above study. In particular, more emphasis than usual has been put on the interpretation of Adam as symbolizing Christ, who followed his bride in her descent to this world. It may well be that there were changes of emphasis in Origen's writings over the years and that his treatment of the figure of Adam varied according to the particular biblical text or book he was interpreting.[105] If his works had been preserved entire, we might hope to map such variations. A survey of what survives makes one aware of the tantalizing gaps but also of that richness of his exegesis which made it a quarry for subsequent generations.

NOTES

1 The possibility of the pre-existence of the soul is aired in *De libero arbitrio* 1.24 and III.57–9. For an illuminating comparison of Origen and Augustine cf. H. Chadwick, 'Christian Platonism in Origen and in Augustine', in R. Hanson and H. Crouzel (ed.), *Origeniana Tertia*, Rome 1985, pp. 217–30, especially pp. 228–9 on the parallel between Origen and Augustine in their hierarchical view of the cosmos and their explanations of evil. At the time of his conversion, any influence of Origen on Augustine is likely to have come via Ambrose (later also via Hilary and the Latin translations of Origen's works, as these became available). Augustine's reflection of ideas on an individual fall of the soul however is primarily derived from Neoplatonism; cf. R. J. O'Connell, 'The Plotinian Fall of the Soul in St Augustine', *Traditio*, 19 (1963), 1–35.

2 Rufinus the Syrian, *De fide*, fiercely opposed to Origen, attacked the view that souls were made before bodies, that the garments of skin of Genesis 3:21 signify the human body, and that the transgression of Adam and Eve results in the punishment of their offspring or the subjection of the whole world to sin (ed. M. W. Miller, *Rufini Presbyteri Liber De Fide* (Catholic University of America Patristic Studies 96, Washington 1964), §§27, 36, 37–41, pp. 88, 108, 110–18). On this Rufinus cf. O. Wermelinger, *Rom und Pelagius*, Stuttgart 1975, pp. 11–15; also *JThS*, n.s. 28 (1977), 425–6

3 Cf. F. R. Tennant, *The Sources of the Doctrines of the Fall and Original Sin*, Cambridge 1903; N. P. Williams, *The Ideas of the Fall and of Original Sin*, London 1927. D. G. Bostock, 'The Sources of Origen's Doctrine of Pre-existence', in L. Lies (ed.), *Origeniana Quarta*, Innsbruck 1987, pp. 259–64, demonstrates the roots of Origen's doctrine of pre-existence in Jewish thought as found in the Bible, apocryphal writings and in Philo. For an excellent brief account of Philo, cf. H. Chadwick, 'Philo' in A. H. Armstrong (ed.), *The Cambridge History of Later Greek and Early Medieval Philosophy*, Cambridge 1967, pp. 137–57, especially p. 145 (fall of souls) and p. 146 (Adam and Eve and the 'coats of skins').

4 The distinguished scholar to whom this volume is dedicated would be the last to foster such a misconception and I hope that he will forgive my refuting it under his auspices (in his account of Origen in *Early Christian Thought and the Classical Tradition*, Oxford 1966, the discussion of the fall of rational beings (pp. 84–5, p. 115) is rightly kept separate from that of Adam's fall (pp. 90–1), as also, more recently, in 'Origenes' in M. Greschat (ed.), *Gestalten der Kirchengeschichte: Alte Kirche I*, Stuttgart 1984, pp. 136 and 143).

5 IV.37 (p. 308.7), 39 (p. 313.5–7), VI.49 (p. 120.18–27), 51 (p. 122.15–20), 60 (pp. 130.26–131.4). References to works of Origen are to the editions in the Berlin Corpus, where not otherwise specified. I have also used

H. Chadwick, *Origen*: *Contra Celsum*, Cambridge 1953. Old Testament references are to the Septuagint.

6 It is striking that the catena extracts on 1 Corinthians and Romans include nothing on the key passages 1 Corinthians 15:45–9 or Romans 5:12–21. The catena extracts on Ephesians make a much less 'Origenist' impression that Jerome's commentary on the same epistle.

7 II.9.2 and 6, pp. 165–6 and 169–70. On the nature of the first fall cf. H. Chadwick, *Early Christian Thought*, pp. 84–5, and 'Origen' in Armstrong (ed.), *The Cambridge History of Later Greek and Early Medieval Philosophy*, pp. 190–1; also M. Harl, 'Recherches sur l'origénisme d'Origène: la "satiété" (*koros*) de la contemplation comme motif de la chute des âmes', *TU*, 93 (1966), 373–405.

8 He is one of the just, along with Abel, Seth, etc., 1 *Praef.* 4, p. 9.15–16; he begat Seth according to his own image, 1.2.6, p. 34.21–3; he prophesied, 1.3.6, p. 58.5; if all worlds were the same, the story of Adam and Eve would be repeated, II.3.4, p. 119.6–7; the serpent described in Genesis as having misled Eve is said in the *Ascension of Moses* to have been inspired by the devil to cause the disobedience of Adam and Eve, III.2.1, p. 244.16–20.

9 Details of the specific accusations are given by Epiphanius in his *Ancoratus* (*GCS* 25 (1915)), *Panarion* (*GCS* 31 (1922)) and his letter against John of Jerusalem, which survives in Jerome's translation (Jerome, *Epistle* LI, *CSEL* 54 (1910), pp. 395ff.), and summarized by Jerome in his own work *Against John of Jerusalem* (7, *PL* 23.360B-D). Epiphanius' charges against Origen are discussed rather fully by J. F. Dechow, 'The Heresy Charges Against Origen', in Lies (ed.), *Origeniana Quarta*, pp. 112–22.

10 Cf. *Ancoratus* 62.1–2, p. 74, *Panarion* 64.4.9, p. 412, *Epistle* LI.5.2, p. 403.

11 Cf. *Ancoratus* 54.2ff., pp. 63f., attacking Origen for locating paradise not on earth but in the third heaven, *Panarion* 64.4.11, p. 413, *Epistle* LI.5.4f., p.404.

12 Cf. *Ancoratus* 55f., pp. 64ff. and *Epistle* LI.7, p. 409, attacking Origen and his followers for asking superfluous questions about the image of God in man, and *Panarion* 64.4.9, p. 412, and Epistle LI 6.5, p. 407.

13 Jerome, ibid., *Panarion* 64.4.11, p. 413, and *Epistle* LI.5.7, p. 405.

14 *Hexaemeron* Homily 3.9, *SC* 26, pp. 234–5.

15 *De resurrectione* I. 29 and 55, *GCS* 27 (1917), pp. 258 and 313–14.

16 *Panarion* 64.21 and 47, pp. 433 and 472–3.

17 *Bibliotheca* 117, ed. R. Henry, Paris 1960, vol. 2 pp. 88ff.

18 P. Nautin, *Origène*. *Sa vie et son oeuvre*, Paris 1977, p. 111 identifies the lost apology with that of Pamphilus; W. A. Bienert disagrees: 'Die älteste Apologie für Origenes?' in Lies (ed.), *Origeniana Quarta*, pp. 123–7.

19 *Against John of Jerusalem*, 7, 18, and 21, *PL* 23.360B, 369Cf., and 372A.

20 An interpretation of Jacob's dream along these lines is given by Philo, *De*

somniis I.134ff. (cf. U. Früchtel, *Die kosmologischen Vorstellungen bei Philo von Alexandrien*, Leiden 1968, p. 63). Philo's interpretation is commended by Origen in *Contra Celsum* VI.21, p. 91.21–8.

21 1.3.8, p. 63.1ff., 'non arbitror quod ad subitum quis evacuetur ac decidat, sed paulatim et per partes defluere eum necesse est'; II.2.2, p. 112.22ff., 'materialis ista substantia ... cum ad inferiores quosque trahitur, in crassiorem corporis statum solidioremque formatur ... ; cum uero perfectioribus ministrat et beatioribus, in fulgore caelestium corporum micat et spiritalis corporis indumentis vel angelos dei vel filios resurrectionis exornat'; see also *On Martyrdom* 45, p. 41.17ff., on the need of demons for suitable food to enable them to stay in this thick earthly atmosphere; *Contra Celsum* III.41–2, p. 237.15–16 and 24ff., Jesus' body changed to an ethereal and divine quality such as would be necessary for living in the aether and the regions above it, and VII.5, p. 156.22ff., contrasting the regions of the purer and ethereal bodies with the gross bodies here.

22 Another biblical verse applied to the descent of souls to bodies is Genesis 6:2; cf. Origen's references to such an interpretation in *Commentary on John* VI.42, p. 151.10ff., *Contra Celsum* V.55, p. 58.20–7.

23 In particular Didymus; cf. A. Henrichs, *Didymus der Blinde: Kommentar zu Hiob* I, Bonn 1968, pp. 313–14 n. 7.

24 *Commentary on Matthew* XVII.30, p. 671.10–21; cf. *Contra Celsum* V.19, p.20.27ff., where Origen, referring to 2 Corinthians 5:1–4, interprets the 'earthly house' as the body of this life, destroyed at death, and the 'tabernacle' (*skēnos*) as the corporeal nature which, though corruptible, is needed by the soul in order to pass from place to place, and which, in the resurrection, is not stripped off but clothed with a garment of incorruptibility on top. Cf. also *Contra Celsum* VII.32, p. 182.20ff., and H. Chadwick, 'Origen, Celsus, and the Resurrection of the Body', *HThR*, 41 (1948), 83–102.

25 Cf. *Dialogue with Heracleides* 11f., 15f., *SC* 67 (1960), pp. 78.16ff. and 88.28ff.; *Commentary on the Song of Songs* prol., p. 63.31ff. and p. liii; *Commentary on Romans* I.19 (ed. Lommatzsch, VI. pp. 66.12–67.21) and II.13 (p. 142.1ff.). On the 'double creation' and the inner and outer man, cf. G. Sfameni Gasparro, *Origene: Studi di antropologia e di storia della tradizione*, Rome 1984, chapters 2–3, pp. 101–55.

26 *Homily on Jeremiah* I.10, p. 8.28ff.

27 *Commentary on John* I.17, p. 21.4ff.

28 *choikos*, *Commentary on John* XX.22, p. 355ff.

29 *Commentary on John* XX.22, p. 354.33ff.

30 *On Prayer* 26.5, p. 362.7ff.

31 *Homily on Jeremiah* II.1, p. 17.7–16; cf. *Homily on Luke* 39, p. 219.22ff.

32 *Fragment on Jeremiah* 22, *GCS* Origenes III, p. 208.11ff., *Homily on Jeremiah* II.9 and III.1, *GCS* Origenes VIII, pp. 298.4–9, 26–9, 306.16–25.

33 *Homily on Jeremiah* XIV.8, p. 113.21–4; VIII.2, p. 57.30ff.

34 The latter view is taken by G. Bürke, 'Des Origenes Lehre vom Urstand des Menschen', *ZKTh* 72 (1950), 1–39, the former view by M. Simonetti, 'Alcune Osservazioni sull' Interpretazione Origeniana di Genesi 2, 7 e 3, 21', *Aevum*, 36 (1962), 370–81, and 'Didymiana', *VetChr*, 21 (1984), 129ff., followed by H. Crouzel in U. Bianchi and H. Crouzel (eds.), *Arché e Telos*, Milan 1981, pp. 42–5 and in *BLE*, 86 (1985), 137 (where he corrects his earlier view expressed in his *Théologie de l'image de Dieu chez Origène* (Paris 1956)). The treatment given to this question by these scholars, however, shows clearly that its solution is highly problematic. The possibility of two falls is raised briefly by H. Cornélis, 'Les Fondements cosmologiques de l'eschatologie d'Origène', *RSPhTh*, 43 (1959), 222 note 213; cf. also 217 note 193. A considerable advance is made in two contributions published in the proceedings of the fourth International Origen Congress, ed. L. Lies, *Origeniana Quarta* (Innsbruck 1987), of which I only received a copy after writing this paper: Paola Pisi, 'Peccato di Adamo e caduta dei NOES nell' esegesi origeniana', pp. 322–35, and M. Harl, 'La préexistence des âmes dans l'oeuvre d'Origène', pp. 238–58. (I was unfortunately unaware of the paper of P. Pisi until I received the proceedings and was unable to be present at the paper of M. Harl. I was, however, able to consult a summary provided by M. Harl for participants at the conference.) P. Pisi considers first the allegorical exegesis of Adam's fall in relation to the fall of the 'noes' and secondly the 'historical' reading and asks the question (pp. 326–7): 'Dobbiamo forse pensare ad una "protologia graduata", secondo cui la storia umana sarebbe segnata da due distinti e successivi momenti di caduta, rispettivamente la colpa precosmica dei *noes*, che porta all'assunzione di corpi pesanti, e posteriormente l'espulsione dei protoplasti dall'Eden, che inaugura il processo generativo, apportatore di una propria, e peculiarmente specifica, impurità?' – concluding, however, that there is a tension between the two fall accounts (that of the rational beings and that of the protoplasts) which remains fundamentally unresolved in Origen's thought. M. Harl devotes one section to the story of Adam (pp. 245–7), which she reads primarily on a historical level. She does not, however, place the account of the fall of rational beings and Adam's story in clear chronological succession, preferring to distinguish between different 'registers' of exegesis (p. 250).

35 Cf. *De principiis* I.6.4, II.2.2, pp. 85.14ff. and 112.15ff., and *Commentary on John* I.17, p. 21.12ff. The question has been discussed most often in connection with the resurrection and final restoration; an excellent brief summary of the debate is provided by G. Dorival, 'Origène et la résurrection de la chair', in Lies (ed), *Origeniana Quarta*, pp. 312–15. Origen himself does not commit himself to a decision in his surviving writings; cf. H. Chadwick, *Early Christian Thought*, pp. 86–7.

36 If one takes the view that the first creation was corporeal, one does not necessarily have to think in terms of the body of Genesis 2:7 (or alternatively one might wish to understand this verse on more than one level), and again it may seem most probable that the body of Adam in paradise was identical neither with the resurrection body nor with the body of this life. In *Contra Celsum* v.19 (see above, p. 86, n. 24) Origen distinguishes on the basis of 2 Corinthians 5:1–4 the *epigeios oikia* of this life, the *skēnos* and the garment of immortality put on top of the *skēnos* in the resurrection. Didymus (see below, p. 75) regards the *chous* of Genesis 2:7 as being the same as the *skēnos*. In some passages, Origen seems to think of the body as able to occupy various positions on a scale of increasing grossness or subtlety. Cf. above, p. 86, n. 21 and D. G. Bostock, 'Quality and Corporeity in Origen' in H. Crouzel and A. Quacquarelli (eds.), *Origeniana Secunda = Quaderni di 'Vetera Christianorum'*, 15 (1980), 323–37, especially 334. On the philosophical background to such a view, cf. U. Bianchi, 'Origen's Treatment of the Soul and the Debate over Metensomatosis', in Lies (ed.), *Origeniana Quarta*, p. 279, and Bostock, 'Quality and Corporeity', following H. Chadwick, 'Origen, Celsus and the Resurrection of the Body', pp. 101–2, and *Early Christian Thought*, pp. 86–8. According to P. Pisi (p. 326) the difference between Adam's body and that of postlapsarian humanity is not that between a luminous body and a heavy body but between purity and impurity. M. Harl (p. 247) writes in terms of 'un corps de terre permettant d'abord une croissance facile, devenant ensuite, après la désobéissance, plus lourd, corruptible (les tuniques de peaux), entraînant les "peines" d'une éducation plus dure'. See also above, pp. 72–4 and 75.

37 P. Nautin and L. Doutreleau, *SC* 233 (Paris 1976).

38 *Homily on Genesis* 1.1, p. 2.17–18.

39 20.18ff., 21.2ff.; compare Origen on the *logos* in *On Martyrdom* 37, p. 34.22ff.

40 P. 13.18–23; cf. also *Homily on Leviticus* v.2, p. 336.22–24, and, most illuminatingly, *Fragment on Jeremiah* 22, p. 208.11–18, which summarizes an exposition similar to that just described.

41 The very detailed discussion of the allegorical interpretation of the waters above the firmament in Origen's first *Homily on Genesis* and in other sources by J. Pépin, *Théologie Cosmique et Théologie Chrétienne*, Paris 1964, pp. 390–417, was written before the publication of Didymus' *Commentary on Genesis*. Particularly illuminating for the interconnection between the interpretation applied to spiritual powers and that applied to the individual are his remarks about the triple meaning of the word *dunameis* (virtues of the human soul, attributes of the divine essence, or spirits distinct from God and man, pp. 374ff. and p. 391).

42 Ed. Lommatzsch, VIII, pp. 49–52 = Theodoret, *Quaestiones in Genesim* 20, *PG* 80.113A–117A.

43 Cf. Lommatzsch, VIII, pp. 48ff., *PG* 12.91ff. There also survive three brief extracts in Latin on Genesis 2:25, 3:2–3 and 3:12, taken from an otherwise unknown 'Epistula Origenis ad Gobarum'. These are quoted in the catena of Johannes Diaconus on the Heptateuch as coming from Victor of Capua. They discuss the verses on a historical level. It is suggested by Nautin that the extracts were quoted in Pamphilus' *Apology for Origen* as evidence that Origen did not reject a literal interpretation of Adam's story; cf. J. B. Pitra, *Spicilegium Solesmense* I (Paris 1852), p. 267; P. Nautin, *Lettres et écrivains chrétiens* (Paris 1961), pp. 248–9; Nautin, *Origène*, pp. 175–6.

44 P. 58 = Theodoret, *Quaestiones in Genesim* 39, *PG* 80.140C–141B.

45 All three passages are well discussed by Simonetti, 'Alcune Osservazioni', *Aevum*, 36, 377. Cf. also H. Chadwick, *Origen: Contra Celsum*, p. 216 note 5 and *Early Christian Thought*, p. 90. G. Dorival, 'Origène et la résurrection de la chair', in Lies (ed.), *Origeniana Quarta*, pp. 291–321, shows Origen's caution in distinguishing the different biblical meanings of the word 'flesh'.

46 The ambiguity of Origen's references to paradise is reflected in the fact that Bürke, 'Des Origenes Lehre', p. 27, is able to understand them solely on a spiritual level as referring to 'der verklärte Urzustand der Schöpfung überhaupt', whereas M. Rauer, 'Origenes über das Paradies', *TU*, 77 (1961), 253–9, argues that Origen thought of paradise as a 'real place'. It should be noted that the catena fragment quoted by Rauer as evidence for paradise as a place with real trees (pp. 258–9) is wrongly attributed to Origen and is in fact part of Epiphanius' attack in *Ancoratus* 58.6–8, *GCS* 25, pp. 68.13–69.2. Although it is true that many of Origen's mentions of paradise as a place can simultaneously be understood as referring also symbolically to a condition of the soul, it can none the less be argued against Bürke (who tends to quote brief extracts of Origen out of context in a manner which is sometimes misleading) that he regarded paradise as an intermediate level where souls are trained in preparation for further ascent.

47 Cf. *De principiis* II.3.6, pp. 121.22–123.18; *Contra Celsum* VII.28–9, pp. 179.12–181.2. On the question of the number of heavens, cf. *Contra Celsum* VI.21, p. 91.15–28; Cornélis, 'Les Fondements cosmologiques', p. 224; Pépin, *Théologie cosmique*, pp. 390ff.; P. Nautin, 'Genèse 1, 1–2, de Justin à Origène', in *In Principio, Interprétations des premiers versets de la Genèse, Etudes Augustiniennes*, Paris 1973, pp. 90–1.

48 Cf. Harl, 'La préexistence des âmes', pp. 245–6. This distinction needs to be borne in mind if one attempts to apply the report of Procopius on the views of the allegorists to Origen's thought.

49 *Homily on Ezechiel* XIII.2, pp. 447.23–448.10, *Contra Celsum* VI.44, p. 115.13–20.

50 *On Martyrdom* 36 and 50, pp. 33.20ff. and 46.14–15; for the different orders or levels of existence in the afterlife cf. *De principiis* II.11.6, p. 190.1ff., III.

6.8–9, pp. 289.23ff., *Homily on Numbers* III. 3, p. 17.11ff. and XXVIII.2, p. 281.34ff.

51 *Homily on Jeremiah* 1.16, p. 16.10, *Homily on Joshua* XIII.4, p. 374.6ff.

52 *On Prayer* 25.3, p. 359.2–3.

53 *On Prayer* 23.3–4, pp. 351.14–352.14, referring to the fuller treatment in the *Commentary on Genesis*.

54 *Homily on Psalm 36*, I, PG 12.1326, *Excerpta in Ps.* 36.4, PG 17.121A; cf. *Commentary on the Song of Songs* I, p. 104.17ff.

55 *Selecta in Psalm.* 1, PG 12.1088–9; cf. *Commentary on John* XX.36, p. 375.14ff., *On Prayer* 27.10, p. 369.23ff.

56 Papyrus Graecus Vindobonensis 29829, 29883, edited, discussed and assigned to Origen by P. Sanz, *Griechische literarische Papyri christlichen Inhaltes* I (Vienna 1946), pp. 87–104. The ascription to Origen is questioned by H. Crouzel, *Bibliographie critique d'Origène*, Steenbrugge 1971, p. 408, but he does not give detailed reasons or suggest a different author.

57 Fragment VI^v 7–9 on Genesis 3:15a; Didymus 99.31ff. on Genesis 3:15b.

58 Fragment I^r 3ff. on Genesis 3:11, Didymus 90.9ff.

59 Hebrews 2:2 and Philippians 2:7–8 in fragment I, John 14:30 in fragment IV, Hebrews 4:15 in fragment IIb.

60 Cf. Didymus 102.12ff., 106.1ff.; also 63.9ff., where the Logos is bridegroom of the rational nature.

61 *HE* III.7; see also above, p. 65.

62 The *koinai ennoiai*, a Stoic doctrine utilized also by Origen; cf. Nautin's notes SC 233 *ad loc.* and H. Chadwick's note on *Contra Celsum* 1.4.

63 *Legum allegoriae* II.xviii.73. It also appears in Ambrose, *De paradiso* 2.11 (*CSEL*, 32 (1896), p. 271).

64 The references in *De principiis* have already been listed above, pp. 64 and 85, n. 8.

65 *Homily on Jeremiah* 1.10, p. 9.2–5.

66 *Commentary on John* 1.20, p. 25.2ff.

67 *Commentary on John* XIII.32, p. 259.34ff.; this reference occurs in the context of a discussion of spiritual nourishment.

68 *Commentary on the Song of Songs* II, p. 157.23ff.

69 Fragment 62 on Matthew 4:3–10 (p. 40.1ff.), fragments 95–6 on Luke 4:1ff. and 4:4 (pp. 264.3 and 265.8ff.)

70 Fragment 95 on Luke 4:1ff., p. 264.6ff.; cf. fragment 62 on Matthew 4:3–10, p. 40.14–22.

71 *On Prayer* 29.18, p. 392.9ff.

72 *Contra Celsum* VII.39, p. 189.23ff.; cf. Philo, *Quaestiones in Genesim* I.39 (quoted by H. Chadwick, *Origen: Contra Celsum*, pp. 426–7 note 8).

73 Cf. also *On Prayer* 23.3–4, quoted above, p. 73, and Philo, *Leg. all.* III.1.1.

74 Fragments 45 and 140 on John 3:29 and 17:11, pp. 520.20 and 574.7ff.

75 *Comm. Ser.* 126, p. 265.1ff.
76 Cf. fragment on Matthew 27:32–4, 551 III, p. 226.10ff., and *Commentary on Romans* v.2, ed. Lommatzsch, p. 352.8ff., where a quotation of Wisdom of Solomon 10:1 is used to show that Christ has saved Adam himself, together with the others to whom Adam was the cause of death.
77 *Commentary on Romans*, vol. 5, ed. Lommatzsch, pp. 322.9–14, 345.19ff., 349.13ff., 368.5ff.
78 Cf. also *Contra Celsum*, VI.36, p. 105.32ff.: 'through a tree came death and through a tree came life, death in Adam and life in Christ'; catena LXXXIV.82ff. on 1 Cor 15:20–23 (*JThS*, 3 (1902), 48): Christ is the first fruits for life of those who will live, Adam became the first fruits of the death of men.
79 *Homily on Genesis* IX.2, p. 90.1–6: Genesis 1:28 is said of Christ and the church; fragment 45 on John 3:29, p. 520.13–22: Christ and the church are the parents of all good works, thoughts and words; *Commentary on Romans* v.1, ed. Lommatzsch, pp. 345.7–19: Christ came to unite the church with himself; and, without reference to Eve and the church, fragment 140 on John 17:11, p. 574.7–14: we have Adam as beginning and head of our birth and Christ of our rebirth; *Commentary on Romans* I.13, ed. Lommatzsch p. 44.2ff.: both the first Adam, as vine and root of the human race, and Christ, the last Adam, bear both fruitful and unfruitful branches.
80 For this exegesis of Genesis 1:27 compare Didymus, *Commentary on Genesis* 62.21ff., especially 63.10–18, 'every rational nature occupies the position of female in relation to the Logos'.
81 Cf. also on the deception of Eve *Homily on Jeremiah* XX.3 and 8, pp. 182.5–8, 188.10–15, *On Prayer* 29.18, p. 392.9–13, *Contra Celsum* VI.43, p. 113.17–21: 'the serpent deceived the female race, which the man is said to have followed'.
82 1.18, p. 23.2–8: in that he became flesh he is Adam, which is interpreted 'man'; 1.31, p. 39.33ff.: Christ may be said to be beginning and end of the whole body of those who are saved, as for example 'beginning' in the man he assumed and 'end' in the last of the saints, or 'beginning' in Adam and 'end' in his sojourn on earth.
83 This parallel is elaborated by Methodius, *Symposium* III.8 (*GCS* 27 (1917), p. 35.9ff.).
84 Origen's understanding of Adam and Eve as Christ and the church needs to be seen in the whole context of his understanding of the church; cf. H. J. Vogt, *Das Kirchenverständnis des Origenes*, Cologne 1974, especially pp. 205ff.
85 *Contra Celsum* VII.28, p. 179.22ff.
86 *Homily on Ezechiel* IV.1, p. 359.23ff.
87 *Homily on Jeremiah* VIII.1, p. 55.10ff.; cf. also the passages referred to above, p. 68, on the image of the 'choic'.

88 Rufinus abbreviates the exposition of Romans 5:12ff. particularly heavily, partly no doubt because Origen's exegesis was very full here (cf. C. P. Bammel, *Der Römerbrieftext des Rufin und seine Origenes-Übersetzung*, Freiburg 1985, pp. 52 and 58–60), perhaps because he found some of the material unsuited to his intended readers. His selective approach may have resulted in some bias or distortion, but I see no reason to doubt that what he includes is derived from Origen.

89 Cf. *Commentary on Romans* v.1, Lommatzsch (ed.), pp. 339.5–340.6, and, for the word 'devil' as equivalent to sin and death, v.6, p. 373.10ff.; also *contra Celsum* 1.31, p. 83.3–5, on the devil's power over all human souls on earth.

90 *Commentary on Romans* v.4, pp. 363.15–364.5.

91 *Commentary on Romans* v.1, p. 324.17ff.

92 Ibid. p. 326.2–21, quoting 1 Corinthians 15:22; cf. also v.4, p. 364.5–7.

93 *Commentary on Romans* v.1, pp. 342.17ff.; cf. also v.2, p. 353.2ff., arguing that it is possible, when one reaches the age of reason, to turn away from the teaching of one's parents and to leave 'Adam', who engendered or taught one to death, and to follow Christ.

94 *Commentary on Romans* III.3, p. 181.5–15.

95 Cf. 356.9–13, 358.6ff.: the soul, created free by God, reduces itself to slavery by sin and, as it were, hands over to death the bond of its immortality, which it had received from its creator; p. 364.4–9: all are in this place of humiliation and vale of tears, whether because all born from Adam were in his loins and cast out with him, or that each individual is thought to have been driven out of paradise and received the condemnation in some other indescribable way that is known only to God.

96 I find unconvincing the suggestion tentatively put forward by C. Bigg, *The Christian Platonists of Alexandria*, Oxford 1886, pp. 202–3, and taken up by A. Harnack, *History of Dogma*, vol. 2, London 1896, p. 365 note 5, F. R. Tennant, *The Sources of the Doctrines of the Fall and Original Sin*, Cambridge 1903, pp. 298–9, and N. P. Williams, *The Ideas of the Fall and of Original Sin*, London 1927, pp. 223–4, that Origen first encountered the practice of infant baptism after his move to Caesarea and for this reason developed a doctrine of original sin.

97 *Commentary on Romans* v.9, p. 396.5ff.

98 Ibid. p. 397.5–7, p. 396.12–19; on the pollution of birth cf. also *Contra Celsum* VII.50, p. 200.21ff., *Homily on Leviticus* VIII.3, pp. 396.7–399.8, and *Homily on Luke XIV*, pp. 85.1ff., where it is argued that in putting on an earthly body, described as 'dirty garments' in Zechariah 3:3, Jesus put on pollution (*rhupos*) but not sin. On the pollution of life in the body cf. the full discussion by G. Sfameni Gasparro, *Origene*, pp. 193–252.

99 Cf. also, on the 'old' or 'choic' man, but without mention of Adam, *Commentary on Romans* IV.7, p. 281.15ff., *Homily on Genesis* IX.2, p. 89, *Homily on Judges* v.5, p. 495.9ff.

100 Cf. v.1, pp. 334.7–336.16; VI.8, p. 43.12ff. The parallel between Adam and a child not yet able to distinguish between good and evil is drawn in Ambrose, *De paradiso*, 6.31 (*CSEL* 32 (1896), 287.23ff.), where criticisms of the Genesis story made by the Marcionite Apelles and others are quoted (if ignorant of good and evil, Adam was no different from a child and ought not to have been blamed for his transgression). It is not possible here to examine Ambrose's use of Origen in this work; cf. A. Harnack, *Sieben neue Bruchstücke der Syllogismen des Apelles*, TU, 6.3 (1890), pp. 111ff.

101 In the *Commentary on John* XIII.37 (p. 261.32ff.) Origen discusses whether the rational creature was incomplete when placed in paradise and suggests rather that it became so through transgression. None the less his quotation of Hebrews 5:14 (p. 262.25ff.) suggests that the condition of the *teteleiōmenos* is different from that in paradise before the fall. (On this passage see above, p. 77, and the discussion by M. Harl, 'La préexistence des âmes', in Lies (ed.), *Origeniana Quarta*, p. 246.) In describing the final restoration (which will be similar to the beginning), Origen states that, when God is 'all in all', there will be no *mali bonique discretio*, since the mind will be aware of nothing except God (*De principiis* III.6.3, pp. 283.14–284.10).

102 The hypothesis of a 'change of mind' is implausible not least because the 'earlier' theory (re-)appears both in the *Commentary on Romans* itself and in the *Contra Celsum*; see above and Tennant, *The Sources of the Doctrines*, p. 302, Williams, *The Ideas of the Fall*, pp. 228–9. It may be noted that Didymus appears to have found no difficulty in accepting both the concept of the fall of the pre-existent soul and that of the succession (*diadochē*) of sin from Adam; cf. A. Henrichs, *Didymus der Blinde: Kommentar zu Hiob*, vol. 1, Bonn 1968, pp. 311–14.

103 If one does not think in terms of more than one stage in the descent, the uniqueness of the soul of Christ (as the only soul to have remained in union with God, *De principiis* II.6.3, p. 142) is jeopardized by the hypothesis, mentioned by Origen a number of times, that some souls have descended to this world, not because they deserved this as a result of their own fall, but in order to serve others (e.g. *De principiis* III.5.4, p. 275; *Commentary on John* II.31, p. 88). The problem of the apparent contradiction in *De principiis* on this question cannot be discussed here. Cf. Pisi, 'Peccato di Adamo', in Lies (ed.), *Origeniana Quarta*, p. 331, note 11.

104 Cf. the avoidance of so literal-minded an approach by M. Harl, 'La préexistence des âmes', in Lies (ed.), *Origeniana Quarta*, p. 250.

105 Thus we might surmise that he speculated more widely on the story of Adam in his *Commentary on Genesis* than in his later works, perhaps also that he moved in the direction of a more negative view of the figure of Adam himself (cf. *Commentary on John* XX.3, p. 329.25: it is still under investigation whether Adam is to be counted among the just or not).

XIII

Die Juden im Römerbriefkommentar des Origenes

Der Römerbriefkommentar des Origenes gehört zu seinen späteren Werken, wurde aber vor dem Matthäuskommentar und *Contra Celsum* verfaßt. Das Schicksal der Juden wird vor allem in der Exegese der Römerbriefkapitel 2 bis 4 und 9 bis 11 behandelt. Wir besitzen das Werk, als den einzigen einigermaßen vollständig erhaltenen Kommentar des Origenes in der lateinischen Übersetzung Rufins[1]. Dazu kommen kurze Papyrusauszüge aus der Erklärung der Kapitel 3 und 4[2] und Katenenauszüge zu den ersten acht Kapiteln des Römerbriefs[3]. Bei seiner Übersetzung hat Rufin es sich vorgenommen, das Werk auf die Hälfte zu kürzen[4]. Dabei hat er eine Auswahl aus der sehr ausführlichen Exegese des Origenes getroffen und in seinen eigenen Worten wiedergegeben. Es fehlten ihm einige Bände des griechischen Textes, wahrscheinlich der elfte und der vierzehnte Band mit der Exegese von 9,1-19 und 12,16-14,10a[5]. Im folgenden werde ich mich hauptsächlich auf Rufin stützen, weil die kurzen Papyrusauszüge zu den Kapiteln 3 und 4 sich nur in dem von Rufin gegebenen Zusammenhang verstehen lassen und weil zu den wichtigen Kapiteln 9-11 überhaupt keine griechischen Fragmente erhalten sind. Daß Rufin bei seinen Übersetzungen gelegentlich tendenziös verfährt, ist nicht zu verneinen. Was unser Thema angeht, so zeigt sich Rufin in manchen seiner selbständigen Äußerungen den Juden gegenüber feindlich gesonnen[6]. Solche Neigungen sind aber nicht charak-

---

[1] C.H.E.LOMMATZSCH (Hg.), Bd I-II (= Origenis opera omnia, Bd. VI-VII), Berlin 1836-7.

[2] J.SCHERER, (Hg.), Le Commentaire d'Origène sur Rom. III 5-V 7 d'après les extraits du Papyrus No 88748 du Musée du Caire, Kairo 1957.

[3] A.RAMSBOTHAM (Hg.), in: JThS 13-14, 1912/13, und K. STAAB, in: BZ 18, 1929.

[4] So bestätigt er selbst im Vorwort, LOMMATZSCH II, vif.

[5] Vgl. C.P.BAMMEL, Der Römerbrieftext des Rufin und seine Origenes-Übersetzung, Freiburg 1985, 43-104.

[6] Z.B. in seiner Streitschrift gegen Hieronymus II, 41, wo er behauptet, daß die Juden Hieronymus zu seinen Missetaten angespornt haben.

XIII

146

teristisch für den Römerbriefkommentar des Origenes, auch nicht in der Rufinschen Übersetzung.

Ich werde versuchen, das, was Origenes im Anschluß an Paulus über die zeitgenössischen Juden und über das Schicksal der Juden im Heilsplan Gottes sagt, zusammenzufassen. An vielen Stellen seines Kommentars erinnert Origenes den Leser daran, daß Paulus im Römerbrief wie ein Schiedsrichter zwischen Juden und Heiden steht. Er fordere beide Gruppen zum Glauben an Christus auf, heißt es zu Röm 3, 1-4, ohne daß er die Juden durch eine völlige Zerstörung der jüdischen Riten abstoße oder die Heiden durch eine Befürwortung der Gesetzesbeobachtung in Verzweiflung bringe. Ganz gleich, ob er über Verheißungen oder Strafen rede, teile er seine Worte zwischen den beiden Völkern[1]. In einer Bemerkung zu Röm 3, 5-8, die fragmentarisch auch auf griechisch erhalten ist, schreibt Origenes, daß Paulus durch den ganzen Text der Epistel zeigen will, welches Heil es vor Christus für diejenigen, die nach dem Gesetz lebten, gab, auf welche Weise durch die Menschwerdung Christi aus dem Unglauben Israels das Heil an die Heiden geschenkt wird, und wiederum daß nicht alle Heiden, sondern nur diejenigen, die glauben, zum Heil kommen und nicht ganz Israel verworfen, sondern daß der Rest gerettet werde (Röm 9,27)[2]. Mehrere Male im Laufe des Kommentars[3] betont Origenes, daß Paulus abwechselnd die Juden und die Heiden der Sünde überführt, sie aufmuntert und wieder zur Demut bringt.

Origenes entschärft gewissermaßen die Kritik, die Paulus gegen die Juden bringt, weil er jedesmal den Leser fragt, ob nicht dieselbe Kritik für die zeitgenössische Kirche gelte[4]. Daß Paulus selbst und die anderen Apostel Juden waren, wird öfters betont. Wenn Paulus in Röm 11,5 sagt, daß es auch zu dieser Zeit einen Überrest nach der Wahl der Gnade gebe, so meint er damit diejenigen, die, aus der Beschneidung kommend, an Christus geglaubt haben, das heißt, sowohl die Apostel

---

[1] LOMMATZSCH I, 144.

[2] LOMMATZSCH I, 160f; SCHERER, 124.

[3] Z.B. LOMMATZSCH I, 171f; II 191f. 244f. 251f. 266. 400.

[4] Z.B. LOMMATZSCH I, 72. 114-9; II 180. 194f.243f.

wie auch die anderen, die mit ihnen zum Glauben fanden[1]. Paulus selbst ist auf dem Weg nach Damaskus ein Beispiel dafür, daß Christus den Juden, welche falsche Wege gingen, zu einem Stein des Anstoßes wurde[2]. Weder alle Heiden noch alle Israeliten haben dem Evangelium geglaubt[3]. Zwischen den Juden und den Heiden, die an Christus glauben, ist kein Unterschied[4]. Sowohl die Juden wie auch die Heiden werden in jeweils zwei Teile geteilt, die Glaubenden und die Nichtglaubenden, diejenigen Juden, die die Kreuzigung Christi verlangten, und den Rest, der dem Glauben ihrer Väter folgend sich zu Christus bekannte[5]. Die alttestamentlichen Prophezeiungen über Israel und die Heiden können dementsprechend aufgeteilt werden, je nachdem, ob sie Verheißungen oder Drohungen enthalten. Diejenigen, die aus Israel und aus den Heiden zum Glauben kommen, werden in der Zeit dieser Welt durch das Wort der Lehre des Evangeliums gereinigt, diejenigen aber, die das Evangelium ablehnen, werden später durchs Feuer gereinigt werden[6]. 2,10f. versteht Origenes dahingehend, daß die nicht glaubenden Juden und Heiden, welche tugendhaft leben, für ihre Tugenden belohnt werden, auch wenn sie nicht zum ewigen Leben gelangen[7].

Die Frage, ob Beschneidung und Beobachtung des Zeremonialgesetzes noch nach der Zeit Christi von Nutzen seien, nimmt Origenes völlig ernst. Er widmet diesen Problemen einen sehr langen Exkurs am Ende der Exegese von Röm 2[8]. Manche Heidenchristen haben sich beschneiden lassen, aber die Befehle darüber im Alten Testament sind nur für die Nachkommen Abrahams und deren Sklaven gültig. In den Anfangszeiten war die Beschneidung für diejenigen Juden nützlich, die zum Christentum nicht kommen wollten, wenn sie diese Sitte aufgeben mußten. Paulus selbst wurde den Juden wie ein Jude und beschnitt den

---

1   LOMMATZSCH II, 231; vgl. II, 228.

2   LOMMATZSCH II, 189f.

3   LOMMATZSCH II, 217.

4   Röm 3,22; LOMMATZSCH I, 196. 202f.

5   LOMMATZSCH II, 270. 273f.

6   LOMMATZSCH II, 271.

7   LOMMATZSCH I, 98.

8   LOMMATZSCH I, 120ff.

148

Timotheus. Das Gesetz wurde am Anfang auch von den Glaubenden beobachtet, wie Petrus dies bezüglich der Speisevorschriften und Paulus bezüglich der Reinigungsopfer tat[1]. Zu Röm 7, 1-6 schreibt Origenes, daß die Menschwerdung Christi den Tod des Buchstabens des Gesetzes bewirkt habe. Die Apostel haben die Gesetzesbeobachtung nur wegen der Volksmenge praktiziert, lehrten aber, daß man dem Gesetz in der Neuheit des Geistes dienen muß. Dasselbe wußten die Propheten und Weisen im alten Volk Israel, welche schon die Herrlichkeit Christi sahen. Vor Christi Geburt wurde der Kult des Gesetzes in Jerusalem als Schatten und Vorbild ausgeführt. Nach Christi Menschwerdung aber ist das irdische Jerusalem zusammen mit seinem Tempel und Altar zerstört worden, so daß die Opfer und andere Gesetzesbestimmungen nicht mehr durchgeführt werden können[2]. Auch unter denjenigen, die das Gesetz beobachten wollten, lebe es nicht mehr[3].

Den Römerbriefvers 11, 11 erklärt Origenes dahingehend, daß die Juden in ihrer Ablehnung Christi nicht so gefallen sind, daß sie nicht wieder aufstehen und bekehrt werden können. Trotz ihrer Feindschaft der christlichen Mission gegenüber haben sie immer noch einige Vorzüge. Sie studieren das Gesetz, obwohl sie es nicht verstehen, weil sie ungläubig sind. Sie haben den Eifer nach Gott, wenn auch nicht mit Erkenntnis gepaart[4]. Zu Röm 10,20f. sagt Origenes, daß Christus von den Heiden, die ihn nicht suchten, gefunden wurde, weil er sie zuerst suchte. Die Juden aber befragen immer noch die Schriften über Christus und finden ihn nicht, weil das Kreuz ihnen ein Skandal ist[5]. Die Schriften sind ihnen zu einer Falle geworden, weil die Prophezeiungen über Christus nicht wörtlich erfüllt worden sind[6].

Der Leser des Römerbriefs mag vielleicht manchmal fragen, wer mit der Bezeichnung Juden gemeint sei - das alte Volk Israel, die nicht glauben-

---

[1] LOMMATZSCH I, 120; RAMSBOTHAM, Katenenauszug X.22, 217.

[2] LOMMATZSCH II, 34f.

[3] RAMSBOTHAM, Katenenauszug XXXV, 10.

[4] LOMMATZSCH II, 245-8.

[5] LOMMATZSCH II, 225f.

[6] Röm 11,9; LOMMATZSCH II, 241ff.

den Juden oder das wahre Israel. In einem auf Griechisch erhaltenen Fragment[1] erklärt Origenes, daß "*Jude*" nicht der Name eines Volkes, sondern die Bezeichnung einer Lebensweise sei. Dies zeige sich daran, daß man sich vom Judentum zum Heidentum bekehren kann und umgekehrt. Wenn man sich vornehme, nach dem Buchstaben des Gesetzes zu leben, ist man ein offensichtlicher Jude, wenn aber nach dem geistigen Gesetz, dann sei man ein Jude im Verborgenen (Röm 2, 28f.). Zu Röm 1,16 bemerkt Origenes, daß Paulus eine Dreiteilung der Menschheit vornimmt. Zu der üblichen griechischen Zweiteilung in Griechen und Barbaren setze er die Juden als erste Gruppe hinzu. Die Griechen werden vor den Barbaren eingestuft, weil sie nach Gesetzen leben, die Juden aber vor den Griechen, weil sie ihre Gesetze von Gott erhalten haben[2]. Bei dem Namen "*Israel*" unterscheidet Origenes zwischen dem leiblichen Nachkommen Israels und dem wahren Israeliten, der mit reinem Herzen Gott schaut. Er bezieht sich auf eine bekannte Etymologie des Namens[3].

Über das Schicksal der Juden spricht Origenes am deutlichsten in der Exegese des elften Kapitels. Er beruft sich auf die Stelle Deuteronomium 32,8f. Als Gott die Völker zerteilte und die Söhne Adams zerstreute, setzte er die Grenzen der Heiden entsprechend der Zahl der Engel Gottes. Israel wurde dann das Erbteil des Herrn und erhielt die Verheißungen, die Bundschließungen und die Gesetzgebung. Die Engel aber, denen die Heiden zugeteilt wurden, verführten Einzelne aus dem Erbteil des Herrn. Gott hätte dies verhindern können, aber er ließ es zu, daß einzelne Israeliten verblendet wurden, damit er an deren Stelle, die Erbteile der Engel zu sich nehmen konnte. So ist es dahin gekommen, daß wegen der Blindheit der Israeliten die Heiden in deren Erbschaft eingetreten sind und deren Reichtümer übernommen haben, und daß nicht nur ein Volk sondern die ganze Welt Gottes Teil geworden ist. Wenn aber die Fülle der Heiden eingegangen ist, dann wird Israel angespornt werden, sein verlorenes Heil wieder zu suchen, und wird sagen: "*Ich werde zu meinem ersten Mann zurückkehren*". Auf diese

---

[1]   SCHERER, 134.

[2]   LOMMATZSCH I, 47.

[3]   LOMMATZSCH II, 232; vgl. N.DE LANGE, Origen and the Jews, Cambridge 1976, 32 mit Anmerkung 28.

XIII

150

Weise werden die Ersten die Letzten, weil in der letzen Zeit das Volk Israel, welches das erste war, als letztes durch Glauben zum Heil kommen und die Fülle des Heils Gottes vervollständigen wird[1].

Zum Gleichnis des Ölbaums in Röm 11,16-24 schreibt Origenes, daß die Menschen nicht von der Natur her verschieden sind, sondern daß man durch die eigenen Willensentscheidungen zu einem guten oder bösen Baum, einem guten Ölbaum oder einem wilden Ölbaum, des Volkes Israel oder eines anderen, tadelnswerten Volkes wird. Weil aber die Willensfreiheit immer bleibt, kann ein Israelit, der ein Ast des guten Ölbaums war, zum Unglauben abfallen und ausgebrochen werden, und einer, der die Mitgliedschaft eines sündigen Volkes gewählt hatte, kann sich zum Glauben bekehren und in den guten Ölbaum eingepfropft werden[2]. Die Wurzel des guten Ölbaums ist nicht etwa einer der Patriarchen, sondern Christus selbst. Schon immer wurden diejenigen, die von auswärts zum Glauben und zur Lebensweise Israels kamen, in Christus, der der wahre Israel ist, eingepfropft. Seit seiner Menschwerdung aber wird sehr viel von dem wilden Ölbaum in diese Wurzel oder ihre Äste, die Apostel und Propheten Gottes, eingepfropft. Wenn aber die Heidenchristen übermütig werden und die ausgebrochenen Äste verspotten, dann werden sie wegen ihrer Sünden ausgeschnitten. Origenes betont, daß es eine härtere Strafe ist, ausgeschnitten als ausgebrochen zu werden. Die ausgebrochenen Äste aber können, wenn sie von ihrem Unglauben sich bekehren, von Gott wieder eingepfropft werden[3].

Der Kommentar des Origenes war der erste kirchliche Kommentar zum Römerbrief und wurde darum viel gelesen. Sich gegen Markion und andere Häretiker wendend, bemühte sich Origenes, die Rolle des Gesetzes und die Einheit der beiden Testamente zu verteidigen. Die Exegese des Origenes wird oft von modernen Kritikern wegen übertriebener Allegorese angegriffen. In seinem Paulusverständnis zeigt er aber trotz mancher typischer Origenismen einen verhältnismäßig gesunden historischen Sinn. Wegen der Ausführlichkeit seiner Exegese kann er der großen Fülle der biblischen Aussagen gerecht werden. Besonders wichtig

---

[1] LOMMATZSCH II, 248ff. 266ff; vgl. auch I, 247f und SCHERER, 190.

[2] LOMMATZSCH II, 258ff.

[3] LOMMATZSCH II, 262-5.

ist es, daß er sich nicht auf eine einfache Zweiteilung zwischen Juden und Kirche oder altem und neuem Israel beschränkt, sondern immer wieder betont, daß es auch im alten Volke Israel wahre Israeliten, die Christus voraussahen, gab, und daß die Kirche selbst aus glaubenden Juden und Heiden entstanden ist.

XIV

DIE PROPHETIE IN DER PATRISTISCHEN EXEGESE
ZUM ERSTEN KORINTHERBRIEF

Die Worte des Paulus in *1 Kor* 14,1 stellen den Leser vor das Problem der christlichen Prophetie. Was ist unter dem Begriff Prophetie zu verstehen? Ist die christliche Prophetie derjenigen der alttestamentlichen Propheten gleichartig? Ist die Aufforderung des Paulus, die Gabe der Prophetie anzustreben, auch für die spätere Kirche gültig?

Von der früheren patristischen Exegese zu *1 Kor* besitzen wir die Homilien des Chrysostomus [1] und kurze Kommentare von Theodoret [2], Ambrosiaster [3] und Pelagius [4]. Nur in Katenenauszügen erhalten sind die Kommentare von Origenes [5], Theodor von Mopsuestia, Severian von Gabala [6] und Cyrill von Alexandrien [7]. Ausserdem haben wir Auszüge aus einem anonymen lateinischen Kommentar des späten vierten oder frühen fünften Jahrhunderts, die vor etwa anderthalb Jahrzehnten in der Handschrift Budapest I von H. J. Frede entdeckt und veröffentlicht wurden [8]. Aus dem verlorenen Kommentar von Didymus dem Blinden sind Katenenauszüge nur zu den Kapiteln 15 und 16 erhalten [9]. Als Ersatz dafür werde ich ein

---

[1] PG 61, 9-381.
[2] PG 82, 225-376.
[3] Hg. H. J. Vogels, CSEL 81, 2 (1968).
[4] Hg. A. Souter, *Texts and Studies* IX, 2 (Cambridge 1926).
[5] Hg. C. Jenkins, *Journal of Theological Studies* [= JThS] 9-10 (1908-9).
[6] Hg. K. Staab, *Pauluskommentare aus der griechischen Kirche* (Münster 1933).
[7] PG 74, 856-916.
[8] H. J. Frede, *Ein neuer Paulustext und Kommentar* [Vetus Latina: Aus der Geschichte der lateinischen Bibel 7-8], Freiburg 1973-4.
[9] Staab, *op. cit.*, S. 6-14. Andere Erklärungen zu *1 Kor* sind völlig verlorengegangen. Hieronymus erwähnt diejenigen von Origenes, Dionysius, Pierius, Euseb von Cäsarea, Didymus und Apollinaris in seiner *Ep.* 49, 3 und zitiert die Ansichten von Theodor von Heraclea, Diodor

158

anderes Werk heranziehen, den anonymen Dialog zwischen
einem Montanisten und einem orthodoxen Gegner, der enge
Beziehungen zu Didymus zeigt und teilweise aus Exegesen der
Aussagen über die Prophetie im *1 Kor* besteht [10]. Derselbe Stoff
findet sich auch in der Schrift *De Trinitate* des Didymus [11].
Einen tiefen Einschnitt im altkirchlichen Verständnis der
Prophetie brachte die montanistische Krise mit sich. Der
Nachklang dieser Auseinandersetzungen hallt lange in der
Korintherbriefexegese nach. Man hat den Eindruck, dass Verse
aus diesem Paulusbrief eine wichtige Rolle im Selbstverständ-
nis der beiden Seiten spielten.

Nach den Berichten seiner Gegner hatte Montanus in
einem Zustand der Ekstase, wie er der überlieferten Sitte der
Kirche widersprach, seine Prophezeiungen geäussert [12]. Mehrere

---

von Tarsus, Apollinaris, Didymus und Acacius von Cäsarea in seiner
Ep. 119, 2-6 (hg. I. Hilberg, CSEL 54 (1910) S. 348 und 55 (1912) S. 447-54);
vgl. C. H. Turner, *Greek Patristic Commentaries on the Pauline Epistles*,
in J. Hastings, *A Dictionary of the Bible*: Extra Volume (Edinburgh
1904) S. 484.

[10] Der Text wurde von G. Ficker, in *Zeitschrift für Kirchengeschichte*
26 (1905), 446-463, veröffentlicht. Er wird zusammen mit anderen Quellen
zum Montanismus von P. de Labriolle, *Les sources de l'histoire du
Montanisme* (Paris 1913) S. 93-108, abgedruckt.

[11] PG 39, 269-992; Auszüge in de Labriolle, *op. cit.*, S. 152-60. Zur
Frage der Echtheit vgl. M. Geerard, *Clavis Patrum Graecorum* (Turn-
hout 1974), S. 111 (2570), A.I.C. Heron, *Some sources used in the De
Trinitate ascribed to Didymus the Blind*, in hg. R. D. Williams, *The
Evolution of Orthodoxy: Essays in Honour of Henry Chadwick* (Cam-
bridge 1989). Wie schon Ficker (a.a.O., S. 461; vgl. de Labriolle, op. cit.,
S. civ) bemerkte, gehören die Ausführungen über die montanistische
Prophetie nicht in den logischen Zusammenhang von *De Trinitate*.
Andererseits enthält die Argumentation über *1 Kor* 11, 5 bei Didymus
wichtige Glieder (Zitate von *1 Tim* 2, 12 und *1 Kor* 11, 3), welche im
Dialog fehlen (Labriolle, *op. cit.*, S. 159.24-160.25 und 105.11ff.). Man
möchte vermuten, dass wenigstens für die Exegesen der Stellen im 1
Korintherbrief weder Didymus von dem Dialog noch der Dialog von
Didymus abhängig ist, sondern dass beide aus derselben Quelle schöpf-
ten — auch wenn diese Quelle nur der verlorene Kommentar von Didymus selbst war. In diesem Kommentar hatte Didymus wiederum
die Korintherbriefexegese des Origenes benutzt. Das für Origenes charakteristische Mischzitat aus *1 Kor.* 12, 31 und *1 Kor.* 14, 1 (vgl. unten
S. 6 mit Anm. 52) sowie Lesarten in *1 Kor.* 6, 19 und *1 Kor.* 13, 11, die
mit Didymus gemeinsam sind, erscheinen auch im Dialog (vgl. Labriolle,
op. cit., S. cvi).

[12] Euseb, *Kirchengeschichte* V. xvi.7, xvii.2-3, Labriolle, *op. cit.*,
S. 71, 77.

Werke über die montanistische Prophetie sind uns verloren gegangen [13]. Der von Euseb zitierte anonyme Gegner des Montanismus erwähnt ein Werk des Miltiades, oder vielleicht eines unbekannten Alkibiades, darüber, dass ein Prophet nicht in Ekstase sprechen darf [14]. Nach Hieronymus hat Tertullian sechs Bücher über die Ekstase und ein siebtes Buch gegen den Antimontanisten Apollonius geschrieben [15]. Klemens von Alexandrien erwähnt in seinen *Stromateis* seine Absicht, ein Werk über die Prophetie zu schreiben, in welchem er vorhat, sich mit den Phrygiern auseinanderzusetzen [16].

In den erhaltenen Katenenauszügen des Origenes zu *1 Kor* 14 gibt es einen ausdrücklichen Angriff gegen die Montanisten und eine Stelle, die sich gegen die ekstatische Prophetie wendet. Zu Vers 30: «Wenn eine Offenbarung einem andern geschieht, ... so schweige der erste», findet sich folgender Auszug: «Sicherlich waren die Propheten also nicht in einem Zustand der Ekstase, denn sie hatten die Fähigkeit, zu schweigen und den Geist, der über ihnen war, aufzuhalten» [17].

In ähnlicher Weise zitiert Origenes in seinen anderen Schriften Verse aus demselben Kapitel zum selben Behufe. In der Ezechielhomilie VI, 1 wird der Vers 30 wieder als Beweis dafür gebracht, dass die Propheten nicht in Ekstase sondern im natürlichen Zustand, freiwillig und wissend, dem Wort, das zu ihnen kam, dienten [18]. Dass der Apostel uns auffordert, nach der Gabe der Prophetie zu streben, zeige, dass dies in

---

[13] Argumente aus solchen früheren Werken sind aber im Kapitel über die Montanisten im *Panarion* des Epiphanius erhalten. Epiphanius zeigt anhand biblischer Beispiele, dass der wahre Prophet nicht in Ekstase redet (*Panarion* 48.3ff., hg. K. Holl, S. 223ff. mit vielen Angaben von Parallelstellen im Apparat; Labriolle, *op. cit.*, S. xlix-lviii und 118ff.).
[14] Euseb, *Kirchengeschichte* V, xvii. 1, Labriolle, *op. cit.*, S. 76-7. Dagegen kann noch der Apologet Athenagoras die alttestamentliche Prophetie als ekstatisch beschreiben (*Legatio* 9.1).
[15] Hieronymus, *De Viris illustribus* 53, Labriolle, *op. cit.*, S. 174; vgl. Tertullian, *adv. Marcionem* IV.22, Labriolle, *op. cit.*, S. 20.
[16] Klemens, *Stromateis* IV.xiii.93.1, hg. O. Stählin, S. 289.12-15 (Labriolle, *op. cit.*, S. 50); vgl. I.xvii.85.3, hg. Stählin, S. 55.10-12.
[17] LXIX, vgl. LXX, hg. Jenkins, JThS 10, S. 40. Ganz anders Philo, vgl. R. Meyer, art. προφήτης, in G. Kittel, *Theologisches Wörterbuch zum Neuen Testament*, 6 (Stuttgart 1959) S. 822-3.
[18] Hg. W. A. Baehrens, GCS *Origenes VIII*, S. 378.6ff., 25ff.

unserer Macht stehe, schreibt er in der Exodushomilie IV.5[19].
Im Römerbriefkommentar Buch VII zitiert er Vers 32: « Die
Geister der Propheten sind den Propheten untertan », und
erklärt dazu, dass der Prophet nicht gegen seinen Willen zur
Weissagung gezwungen werde, wie diejenigen mit einem un-
reinen Geist, sondern dass er spreche, wenn er will und
Grund dazu hat[20].

Ganz in Übereinstimmung mit Origenes schreibt noch
Severian von Gabala in einem Auszug zu *1 Kor* 14, 28, dass
derjenige, der im Heiligen Geist redet, nach dem eigenen
Willen spricht und schweigt, wie die Propheten dies tun; nicht
aber diejenigen, die von einem unreinen Geist besessen werden[21]. Sowohl Severian[22] wie auch Chrysostomus[23] unterscheiden zwischen dem Prophet und dem Wahrsager (μάντις),
der nicht weiss, was er sagt. Nach Chrysostomus ist die Ekstase
für den letzteren charakteristisch, während der Prophet mit
nüchternem Verstand redet[24].

Bei dem ausdrücklichen Angriff des Origenes gegen die
Montanisten in den Katenenauszügen zu *1 Kor* 14 geht es um
die Prophetinnen. In den Versen 34-5 gebietet Paulus, dass die
Frauen in der Kirche schweigen sollen[25]. Origenes[26] wendet
sich gegen die Schüler von Priscilla und Maximilla, die diesem
Gebot nicht folgten. Man könne zwar als Prophetinnen die
Töchter von Philipp dem Evangelisten, sowie im Alten Testa-

---

[19] Hg. Baehrens, GCS *Origenes* VI, S. 176.26ff.; vgl. Origenes, Römerbriefkommentar, hg. C. H. E. Lommatzsch (Berlin 1836-7) ii, S. 307.4.
    [20] Hg. Lommatzsch, ii, S. 107.2ff.; ähnlich Hieronymus, *Comm.
in Eph.* 11.3, PL 26, 479BC, Labriolle, *op. cit.*, S. 171. Es war natürlich
auch wichtig, die christliche Prophetie gegenüber derjenigen der Heiden
und der Pseudopropheten im allgemeinen abzugrenzen; vgl. z.B. Origenes, *contra Celsum* VII.2-10, hg. P. Koetschau, GCS *Origenes* II, S.
153-162.
    [21] Hg. Staab, S. 270.
    [22] Hg. Staab, S. 270.13-14.
    [23] PG 61.241.
    [24] Vgl. auch PG 61.311 (zu *1 Kor.* 14, 28-9): Der Prophet braucht
keinen Dolmetscher, sondern er ist selbst Dolmetscher Gottes. Die
Prophetie muss man aber prüfen, damit nicht etwas Diabolisches
hereinschleiche.
    [25] Die Exegese dieses Verses wird von P. de Labriolle, « *Mulieres
in ecclesia taceant* », in *Bulletin d'ancienne littérature et d'archéologie
chrétiennes* 1 (1911) 3-24, 103-122, besprochen.
    [26] Katenenauszug lxxiv, hg. Jenkins, S. 41f.

ment Debora, Miriam die Schwester Aarons, und Hulda, und im Evangelium Anna aufführen, aber von keiner derselben wird berichtet, dass sie in der Kirche sprach. Er beruft sich auf den ersten Timotheusbrief 2, 12 und den Titusbrief 2, 3-4, um zu zeigen, dass Frauen über Männer keine Macht haben dürfen, und dass, wenn sie Unterricht erteilen, sie nur andere Frauen unterrichten dürfen.

Das Gegenteil von dem, was Origenes sagt, hatte Irenäus behauptet. Der Apostel Paulus, schreibt Irenäus in seinem *Adversus Haereses III.xi* [27], spricht eingehend über die prophetischen Gaben und weiss von Männern und Frauen, welche in der Kirche prophezeien. Diejenigen, welche die prophetische Gnade aus der Kirche verweisen, versündigen sich am Heiligen Geist und verfallen in eine unvergebbare Sünde. Irenäus versteht wahrscheinlich *1 Kor* 11, 2-16 dahin, dass Paulus von Frauen, die in der Kirche prophezeien, redet.

Zum elften Kapitel sind keine Katenenauszüge des Origenes erhalten, aber im anonymen *Dialogus Montanisti et Orthodoxi* beruft sich der Montanist auf *1 Kor* 11, 5 als Beweis dafür, dass die Frauen prophezeien dürfen, worauf sein Gegner antwortet, dass die Orthodoxen die weibliche Prophetie zwar nicht abweisen, dass es aber den Frauen nicht erlaubt sei, in der Kirche zu reden, oder über Männer Macht auszuüben [28]. Spuren dieser Fragestellung zeigen sich noch in den Auszügen aus dem Kommentar von Theodor von Mopsuestia. Zu Kapitel 11, 4-5 schreibt er, dass damals nicht nur Männer sondern auch Frauen prophezeiten [29], und zu Kapitel 14, 34-36, dass die Frauen vielleicht zu Hause prophezeiten, oder dass Paulus mit dem Befehl, dass die Frauen in der Kirche schweigen sollen, meine, dass sie nicht lehren dürfen [30]. Pelagius kommentiert die Erwähnung von Frauen, die prophezeien, in Kapitel 11, 5 mit der Bemerkung 'unter dem eigenen Geschlecht und zu Hause', und schreibt zu Kapitel 14, 34, dass

[27] Hg. W. W. Harvey, Cambridge 1857, II, S. 51.
[28] Hg. Labriolle, S. 105-6.
[29] Hg. Staab, S. 187. Vgl. Severian zu *1 Kor.* 11, 10, hg. Staab, S. 261-2. Der anonyme Kommentar in Budapest 1 führt zu *1 Kor.* 11, 5 eine Liste der biblischen Prophetinnen auf, hg. Frede, S. 141.
[30] Hg. Staab, S. 193.

Paulus anderswo sagt, dass Frauen unterrichten sollen, aber nur dem eigenen Geschlecht gegenüber[31].

Eine merkwürdige allegorische Auslegung der Vorschrift des Paulus, dass eine Frau, die prophezeit oder betet, ein Kopftuch tragen muss, findet sich bei Didymus und in dem *Dialogus Montanisti et Orthodoxi*. Diese Vorschrift könne man nicht wörtlich verstehen, weil man ununterbrochen beten muss[32], eine Frau aber bei der Taufe kein Kopftuch trägt. Was damit also gemeint sei, ist, dass eine Frau im eigenen Namen keine Bücher schreiben darf, sondern nur im Namen eines Mannes, der ihr im übertragenen Sinne zum Kopftuch dient. So habe die Jungfrau Maria im eigenen Namen kein Evangelium geschrieben, sondern den Evangelisten Lukas gleichsam als Kopftuch gehabt[33].

Die Frage, ob die Prophetie in verschiedenen Stadien der Heilsgeschichte verschiedene Rollen gespielt hat, wurde in den Auseinandersetzungen über den Montanismus viel erörtert. Nach einer Aussage Tertullians in seiner Schrift *De virginibus velandis*[34] gibt es vier solcher Stadien: erstens vor dem Gesetz, zweitens zur Zeit des Gesetzes und der Propheten, drittens zur Zeit des Evangeliums, und viertens die erst durch den Paraklet gebrachte volle Reife. In dem anonymen *Dialogus Montanisti et Orthodoxi* stützt sich der Montanist auf *1 Kor* 13, 9-10, 'unser Wissen ist Stückwerk und unsere Prophetie ist Stückwerk, wenn aber das Vollkommene kommt, so wird das Stückwerk aufgehoben werden', um damit zu zeigen, dass erst Montanus das Vollkommene des Heiligen Geistes, d.h. den Paraklet, erhielt, dass aber die Gegner des Montanus die Worte des Paulus aufheben, indem sie behaupten, es gebe keine Propheten nach Christus[35].

---

[31] Hg. Souter, S. 188.6-7, 211.20-2.
[32] *1 Thess* 5, 17.
[33] *Dialogus*, hg. Labriolle, *op. cit.*, S. 105-7; vgl. Didymus, *De Trinitate*, III.xli.3, Labriolle, *op. cit.*, S. 159.24-160.19.
[34] *De virginibus velandis* I, Labriolle, *op. cit.*, S. 14.
[35] Vgl. Hieronymus, *Ep.* 41.4 (Labriolle, *op. cit.*, S. 169): nach den Montanisten habe Gott, weil er weder durch Moses und die Propheten noch durch Christus die Welt hatte retten können, *ad extremum per Spiritum Sanctum in Montanum, Priscam, et Maximillam ... descendisse et plenitudinem, quam Paulus non habuerit dicens: 'Ex parte cognoscimus, et ex parte prophetamus' ... habuisse Montanum.*

Die Antwort des orthodoxen Gegners entspricht der Ko-
rintherbriefauslegung der meisten Exegeten von Origenes an,
nämlich dass alles in diesem Leben nur Stückwerk ist, das
Vollkommene aber erst im zukünftigen kommen wird[36]. Überraschend ist es, dass die Erklärung von Theodor dem von den
Montanisten ihren Gegnern zugeschriebenen Verständnis dieser
Verse darin ähnlich ist, dass er die Aufhebung der Prophetie
als ein Phänomen des gegenwärtigen Zeitalters ansieht. Zu
Kapitel 11, 4-5 schreibt Theodor, dass zur Zeit des Paulus die
Geistesgaben denjenigen, die die Taufe erhielten, augenfälliger
gegeben wurden, und dass die Prophetie häufig und vielfältig
war[37]. Der Katenenauszug zu Kap. 13, 8-13 lautet aber:
« Nachdem der Glaube über die ganze Erde ausgebreitet
worden ist, hören die Prophetie und das Zungenreden und das
stückweise Wissen als überflüssig auf und es bleiben diese
drei als notwendig» (nämlich Glaube, Hoffnung und Liebe)[38].
Ähnlich heisst es in dem anonymen lateinischen Kommentar
der Handschrift Budapest 1, dass die Prophetie, das Zungenreden und die anderen Wunder der Heilungen und Zeichen
am Anfang notwendig waren, um den Glauben der Ungläubigen zu bewirken, dass sie aber, nachdem die Heiden zum
Glauben gekommen waren, aufgehoben worden sind. Im nächsten Auszug wird die montanistische Benutzung des Verses
erwähnt[39]. In der Nachfolge Theodors steht auch die Erklärung
des Chrysostomus. Wenn die Prophetie und das Zungenreden
zum Zweck des Glaubens eingeführt wurden, schreibt er, so
sind sie überflüssig, wenn der Glaube überall ausgebreitet
worden ist[40]. Er zögert nicht, die zeitgenössische Kirche als
verarmt und der Geistesgaben ledig zu beschreiben[41]. Das,
was zur Zeit des Paulus geschah, das Zungenreden, die Prophetie, die augenscheinlichen Zeichen der Geistesgabe, ereignet

---

[36] Hg. Labriolle, *op. cit.*, S. 93f.; vgl. Didymus, *De Trinitate*, III.
xli.2, Labriolle, *op. cit.*, S. 156f.
[37] Hg. Staab, S. 187; vgl. Origenes, Katenenauszug LXXIII.20-1 zu
1 Kor. 14, 31, hg. Jenkins, JThS 10, S. 41.
[38] Hg. Staab, S. 191-2.
[39] Hg. Frede, S. 154, 62D und 62E.
[40] PG 61.287 oben.
[41] PG 61.312 unten.

164

sich nicht mehr[42]. Zur Zeit des Paulus gab es viel mehr Propheten als zur Zeit des Alten Testaments[43]. Die Kirchenleiter sprachen damals unter der Eingebung des Heiligen Geistes, jetzt aber nicht mehr, so gesteht Chrysostomus: Ἀλλ' οὐχὶ νῦν· τὸ ἐμαυτοῦ λέγω τέως[44].

Das Zugeständnis, dass die Wirkungen des Heiligen Geistes in der Kirche nicht mehr erkennbar sind, scheint das montanistische Bild der Katholiken zu bekräftigen. Chrysostomus zeigt damit, dass er dieser Kontroverse schon fern gerückt ist. Epiphanius dagegen wendet sich, in dem Abschnitt über die Montanisten in seinem *Panarion*, gegen die Möglichkeit, dass die Gnade in der Kirche aufgehört hat, mit den Worten: μὴ γένοιτο[45]. Der von Euseb zitierte anonyme antimontanistische Verfasser, dessen Argumente Epiphanius hier aufnimmt, behauptet, dass der Apostel es für richtig ansieht, dass die prophetische Gabe bis zur endzeitlichen Parusie in der ganzen Kirche sein solle, während die Montanisten noch im vierzehnten Jahr nach dem Tod von Maximilla keine Nachfolger in dieser Gabe aufzeigen können[46]. Seine weiteren Ausführungen zu diesem Thema zitiert Euseb nicht mehr. Bei den meisten Auslegern des *1 Kor* aber findet man eine Neigung, die Bedeutung des Wortes Prophetie in einer Weise auszuweiten, dass sie immer noch behaupten können, es gebe Propheten in der zeitgenössischen Kirche. Diese kirchliche Prophetie wird durch Heranziehung von Versen aus *1 Kor* 14, insb. 4-5 und 24-5, geschildert[47].

Origenes nimmt die beiden Listen der Geistesgaben in *1 Kor* 12 zum Anlass, um zwischen zwei verschiedenen Arten der Prophetie zu unterscheiden. Die erste, göttlichere und grössere Art, die es verdient, in 12,28 gleich hinter den

---

[42] PG 61.239 zu *1 Kor* 12, 1-2.
[43] PG 61.265.
[44] PG 61.312.
[45] *Panarion* 48.2, hg. Holl, S. 221.14-5, Labriolle, *op. cit.*, S. 116.
[46] Euseb, *Kirchengeschichte* V.xvii.4, Labriolle, *op. cit.*, S. 77-8.
[47] Tertullian, *Adv. Marcionem* V.8.12 und V.15.5, hatte mit einer Anspielung an *1 Kor.* 14,24 Propheten und Prophetie beschrieben als *qui de Dei spiritu sint locuti, qui et futura praenuntiarint et cordis occulta traduxerint* und als das, was *futura praenuntiet et occulta cordis reuelet et sacramenta edisserat*.

XIV

Aposteln als zweite Gabe aufgeführt zu werden, ist der Prophetie von Jesaia und Jeremia ähnlich. Die zweite Art wird in *1 Kor* 14, 24-5 beschrieben und wird gegen Ende der Liste in 12, 10 aufgeführt. Sie besteht darin, dass der Prophet sagt, 'Dies hast Du in deinem Herzen' oder 'Von dieser Sünde bist Du in die Kirche gekommen', und ist eine Gabe, deren alle Christen teilhaftig werden können[48]. Ganz ähnlich beschreibt Origenes in einem Katenenauszug zum Epheserbrief 4, 11-12 den Propheten des Neuen Testaments durch eine Anspielung auf *1 Kor* 14, 24 als denjenigen, der die Ungläubigen prüft und überführt. Solche Propheten können immer in der Kirche sein und sind nötig, um den Leib Christi zu erbauen (ὅπως οἰκοδομῆται; vgl. *1 Kor* 14, 3-4)[49]. Im Römerbriefkommentar zu *Rm* 12, 7[50] unterscheidet Origenes wieder zwischen der Prophetie des Alten Testaments, die nur bis zu Johannes dem Täufer Bestand hatte[51], und derjenigen, über die der Apostel im *1 Kor* redet. Er bringt ein Mischzitat aus *1 Kor* 12, 31 und 14, 1[52], um zu zeigen, dass diese Art der Prophetie von jedem angestrebt werden kann, und charakterisiert sie durch ein Zitat aus *1 Kor* 14, 3. Bei Paulus werde von Prophetie gesprochen, wenn jemand zur Erbauung und zur Ermahnung und zur Tröstung der Menschen redet. Danach zitiert er *1 Kor* 14, 24-25 als Beschreibung einer anderen Art der Prophetie. Er erklärt, dass der einzelne seine eigenen Sünden erkennt, wenn ethische Texte in der Kirche behandelt werden. Auch

---

[48] Katenenauszug XL-XLVIII, hg. Jenkins, JThS 10, S. 31-2. Vgl. Theodoret, der zu *1 Kor.* 14,24-5 das Beispiel von Ananias und Saphira anführt und zu *1 Kor.* 14,4 die Prophetie als τὴν λογισμῶν ἀποκάλυψιν καὶ τὴν τῶν κρύβδην γινομένων φανέρωσιν beschreibt, PG 82, 344C und 340A.
[49] Katenenauszug XVII.36-43, hg. J. A. F. Gregg, JThs 3 (1902) 414; ähnlich Hieronymus, *Comm. in Eph.*, II.iv, PL 26.500A; *Prophetas: non illos qui futura uaticinentur, quales in ueteri legimus Testamento; sed qui infideles et imperitos arguant atque diiudicent.*
[50] Hg. Lommatzsch, ii, S. 306-8.
[51] *Lk.* 16,16. Er charakterisiert sie als diejenige, durch die gesagt wird: «Dies sagt der Herr». Vgl. Chrysostomus, PG 61.265: Εἰ δέ φησιν ὁ Χριστὸς, ὅτι Ὁ νόμος καὶ οἱ προφῆται ἕως Ἰωάννου, περὶ ἐκείνων φησὶ τῶν προφητῶν τῶν τὴν παρουσίαν αὐτοῦ προαναφωνησάντων.
[52] S. 306: *aemulamini autem dona maiora magis autem ut profetetis.*

XIV

das anhand des Gesichts, der Sitten oder der Gebärden der Menschen gebildete Urteil der Weisen erscheine als Prophetie. Ein anderes Bild der kirchlichen Prophetie bringt Origenes in der Exodushomilie IV.5 [53]. Hier beschreibt er denjenigen als Prophet, der die Aussagen und Taten der Propheten in der Predigt erklärt. Er zitiert *1 Kor* 14, 32 als Beleg dafür und das Mischzitat aus *1 Kor* 12, 31 und 14, 1 als Beweis, dass man das Seinige tun soll, um diese prophetische Gabe anzustreben [54].

Von den späteren Auslegern des *1 Kor* machen Cyrill und Severian einen ausdrücklichen Unterschied zwischen den Propheten des Alten und denjenigen des Neuen Testaments [55]. In einem Auszug zu Kap. 14, 2 behauptet Cyrill [56], dass nach der Menschwerdung Christi und seiner Auferstehung die Prophetie im Sinne der Voraussage der Zukunft nicht mehr passe, dass also jetzt unter Prophetie die Erklärung der Worte der Propheten zu verstehen sei. Severian [57] bringt dieselbe Auslegung wie Cyrill aber auch noch eine zweite, dass nämlich die alten Propheten über das Volk prophezeiten bezüglich des Abfalls der Juden und der Berufung der Heiden und der Fleischwerdung Christi, die neuen aber über Einzelne, wie im Falle von Petrus und Ananias.

Der Beispiel von Petrus und Ananias zeigt, dass die Prophetie im Sinne der Voraussage nicht mit Johannes dem Täufer aufhörte. Paulus selbst wird von Origenes als Prophet durch Voraussagen der Zukunft aufgewiesen [58]. Daher schrei-

---

[53] Hg. Baehrens, GCS *Origenes* VI, S. 176.19-177.5.

[54] In der Psalmenhomilie 3, 10 (PG 12, 1345B) werden die Propheten, die in der Kirche reden, mit den das Gotteswort regnenden Wolken gleichgesetzt und als *operarii inconfusibiles recte tractantes uerbum ueritatis* beschrieben. Origenes wendet den Vers *1 Kor.* 14, 29 hier auf diese Prediger und in der Josuahomilie 21, 2 auf die eigene Predigt an: *me ergo dicente, quod sentio, uos discernite et examinate* (hg. Baehrens, GCS *Origenes* VII, S. 431.1-3).

[55] Vgl. auch Chrysostomus, oben Anm. 51.

[56] PG 74, 889C.

[57] Katenenauszug zu *1 Kor.* 11, 4, hg. Staab S. 261; vgl. zu 12, 28, S. 264.5-6.

[58] Katenenauszug XXIV.28-37 zu *1 Kor.* 5,3-5, hg. Jenkins, JThS 9, S. 364-5. Eine Beschreibung der Prophetie als πρόρρησις μελλόντων findet sich im Katenenauszug 21 zu *Mt* 1, 22, hg. E. Klostermann, GCS *Origenes* XII, S. 24.

ben manche Exegeten, dass die Prophetie entweder Voraussage oder Schrifterklärung sein kann, und tun es, ohne zwischen alten und neuen Propheten zu unterscheiden. So verfahren Ambrosiaster in der Erklärung von *1 Kor* 12, 28 [59] und der Kommentar von Budapest 1 zu *1 Kor* 11, 4 [60]. In *1 Kor* 11, 4 versteht Ambrosiaster die christliche Prophetie im ersten Sinne. Prophezeien, schreibt er, bedeutet die Voraussage der Ankunft des Herren in den Worten des Glaubensbekenntnisses. In *1 Kor* 14, 4 und 12 [61] spreche Paulus aber von Bibelexegeten als Propheten [62].

Eine Bestimmung der Prophetie als 'Unterrichten', die sich in manchen Exegeten findet, scheint von *1 Kor* 14, 3-4 herzurühren. So steht in dem anonymen Kommentar von Budapest 1 zu *1 Kor* 14, 3. *Notandum quoniam 'prophetiam' doctrinam dicit* [63]. Chrysostomus unterscheidet zwar zu *1 Kor* 12, 28 zwischen Propheten, die vom Heiligen Geist reden, und Lehrern, die manchmal auch aus dem eigenen Vernunft sprechen. Er schreibt aber (mit einem Hinweis auf den weiteren Verlauf der Epistel), dass Paulus mit Propheten diejenigen meint, welche durch ihre Prophetie unterrichten und alles zum allgemeinen Nutzen sagen [64].

Alle drei der eben angeführten Arten der Prophetie werden im Kommentar des Pelagius erwähnt. Prophezeien bedeutet entweder unterrichten oder die Zukunft voraussagen, schreibt er zu *1 Kor* 11, 4 [65]. In *1 Kor* 12, 10 und 13, 2 werde die Voraussage gemeint [66]. Zu *1 Kor* 12, 28 versteht er Propheten

---

[59] Hg. Vogels, S. 141.10f. (mit Agabus als Beispiel).
[60] Hg. Frede, S. 141, 51A; die Prophetie wird auf zweierlei Weise verstanden; sie ist einmal die Voraussage der Zukunft, sodann aber, wenn man die rätselhaften Worte der Propheten durch denselben Geist erklärt.
[61] Ambrosiaster liest *ut profetetis* am Ende dieses Verses.
[62] Hg. Vogels, S. 121.6-7, S. 150.22-3, S. 152.20.
[63] Hg. Frede, S. 155,064.
[64] PG 61, 265-6; vgl. die Auslegung von *1 Kor.* 14,22-5, PG 61,307-10. Vgl. Theodor zu *1 Kor.* 14,34-6 (Prophetie und Unterricht sind verschieden) und zu *1 Kor.* 11,4-5 (damals war die Prophetie vielfältig, entsprechend den Bedürfnissen, insbesondere aber pflegten die Propheten die Heuchler, die, um die Kirche in Versuchung zu führen, hereinkamen, zu überführen); hg. Staab, S. 193.8-9, S. 187.19-20.
[65] Hg. Souter, S. 187.17.
[66] Hg. Souter, S. 196.20, S. 201.18.

als diejenigen, welche die dunklen Worte der Propheten erklären, und als diejenigen, welche die Menschen ermahnen[67].
Die letztere Bedeutung belegt er mit einem Zitat aus Kap.
14, 3; und zu 14, 3 selbst behauptet er, dass derjenige, der dies
alles besitze, nämlich die Fähigkeit, den Menschen zur Erbauung, Ermahnung und Tröstung zu dienen, als Prophet
anzusehen sei[68].
   Wenn es so viele verschiedene Erscheinungsformen der
Prophetie gibt, so liegt es nahe zu fragen, wie es möglich ist,
alle unter dem einen Begriff Prophetie zu verstehen. Ambrosiaster erklärt, dass der Bibelexeget, ähnlich demjenigen, der
die Zukunft voraussagt, Prophet genannt wird, weil beide
Dinge, die unbekannt bzw. dunkel sind, ans Licht bringen[69].
Theodor bietet eine etwas umständliche Begriffsbestimmung der
Prophetie im Katenenauszug zu *1 Kor* 12, 10. Danach gehört
es nicht nur zur Prophetie, dass man die Zukunft voraussagt,
sondern auch dass man das, was in Taten oder Absichten undeutlich (ἄδηλα) ist, den vielen sagt, oder auch dass man die
Vergangenheit und das Unbekannte allen Menschen sagen kann,
wie Moses das schon tat[70]. Eine elegantere Definition des
Wortes wird von Origenes im Katenenauszug zu *1 Kor* 14, 6
angeboten. Hier heisst es: 'Die Prophetie ist die Kunst der
Deutung der Dinge, die dunkel sind, durch das Wort' (Προφητ-
εία ἐστὶν ἡ διὰ λόγου τῶν ἀφανῶν σημαντική).[71]. Am Ende des
Auszugs heisst es, man könne die Begriffe auch im uneigent-

---

[67] Hg. Souter, S. 200.17-20.
[68] Hg. Souter, S. 206.9-11.
[69] Hg. Vogels, S. 150.22-5.
[70] Hg. Staab, S. 190.9-12. Vgl. die in G.W.H. Lampe, *A Patristic
Greek Lexicon* (Oxford 1961), zitierten ähnlichen Definitionen (s.v. IIA
und C) von Diodor und Chrysostomus.
[71] Hg. Jenkins, JThS 10, S. 36. Der Text von Jenkins ist falsch
interpungiert. Mit dem nächsten Wort (γνῶσις) fäng eine Definition der
γνῶσις an. Falls nichts ausgefallen ist, muss man zu dem Adjektiv
σημαντική das Hauptwort τέχνη hinzudenken (wie dies z.b. im Falle von
μουσική, κυβερνητική, ῥητορική, ποιητική geschieht). Vgl. C.P. Bammel,
Origen's Definitions of Prophecy and Gnosis, JThS, NS 40 (1989) S. 490.
[72] So kann in einem Ausnahmefall διὰ λόγου durch δι' ἔργων
ersetzt werden; vgl. Katenenauszug 61 in Jer., Katenenauszug 10 in
Reg., hg. Klostermann, GCS *Origenes* 3, S. 228.19-21; S. 298.24-5.

DIE PROPHETIE IN 1 KOR.   169

lichen Sinne gebrauchen, wenn man die eigentliche Bedeutung
verstehe[72]. Unter ἀφανῆ können die Zukunft, die rätselhaften
Worte der Heiligen Schrift und die Geheimnisse der Mensch-
enherzen alle miteinbegriffen werden. Dies ist also als eine
Bestimmung der Prophetie gemeint, von der man die verschiedenen einzelnen Bedeutungen des Wortes ableiten kann[73].

---

[73] Über diese Definition vgl. C. P. Bammel, *Origen's Definitions
of Prophecy and Gnosis*, JThS, NS 40 (1989) S. 489-93.

XV

DIE PAULUSKOMMENTARE DES HIERONYMUS: DIE ERSTEN WISSENSCHAFTLICHEN LATEINISCHEN BIBELKOMMENTARE?

Hieronymus ist von der Nachwelt als Bibelwissenschaftler bewundert worden. Seine Pauluskommentare [1] sind seine ersten erhaltenen Kommentare.[2] Er schrieb sie zu Bethlehem, wahrscheinlich im Sommer 386,[3] als er schon die Grundlagen seiner Gelehrsamkeit durch das Studium der biblischen Sprachen und der griechischen Exegeten gelegt hatte. Er hatte bereits mit der Neubearbeitung der lateinischen Bibel begonnen, zahlreiche Homilien des Origenes zum Alten Testament übersetzt und einige exegetische Probleme in Briefen an Damasus und Marcella [4] behandelt. Im Vorwort zu seiner Übersetzung der Lukashomilien des Origenes erwähnt er einen Plan, auch dessen Matthäus-, Lukas- und Johanneskommentare zu übertragen.[5] Dies führte er nicht aus, sondern er zog es vor, seinen eigenen Ruf als Exegeten dadurch aufzubauen, dass er im eigenen Namen Kommentare verfasste. Dies bot ihm verschiedene Vorteile, vor allem denjenigen, dass er schneller und unabhängiger arbeiten konnte. Die Kommentare des Origenes waren ausserordentlich umfangreich. Es war also eine viel leichtere und lohnenswertere Arbeit, daraus den wich-

---

[1] Es gibt keine kritische Ausgabe dieser Kommentare. Sie werden hier nach PL 26 (1845) zitiert. A. Souter, *The Earliest Latin Commentaries on the Epistles of St. Paul*, Oxford 1927, 101-4, bringt eine Handschriftenliste.

[2] Eine schon vor dem Aufenthalt in der syrischen Wüste geschriebene allegorische Auslegung des Propheten Obadja ist nicht erhalten. Vgl. *Comm. in Abd.*, Prol., CCL 76 (1969) 349-351. Der Predigerbuchkommentar, den Hieronymus schon früher angefangen hatte, wurde wahrscheinlich erst nach den Pauluskommentaren fertiggestellt; zur Datierung vgl. S. Leanza, *Sul Commentario all' Ecclesiaste di Girolamo*, in hg. Y.-M. Duval, *Jérôme entre l'Occident et l'Orient*, Paris 1988, 267ff.

[3] Vgl. P. Nautin, *La date des commentaires de Jérôme sur les épîtres pauliniennes*, in *Revue d'histoire ecclésiastique* 74 (1979) 5-12; Pierre Jay, *L'exégèse de saint Jérôme d'après son "Commentaire sur Isaïe"*, Paris 1985, 407-9.

[4] *Ep.* 18, 20-21, 25-6, 28-9, 34, 36.

[5] Origenes, *Hom. Lc.*, hg. Max Rauer, GCS *Origenes* IX (1959) 1-2.

XV

tigsten Stoff zusammenzufassen und ein paar Bemerkungen aus anderen
Quellen oder aus eigener Erfindung einzumischen als eine vollständige
Übersetzung zu unternehmen.[6]

Es ist allgemein bekannt, dass Hieronymus in einem viel grösseren
Ausmass als seine Vorgänger die Methoden der griechischen Bibelwissen-
schaft an den lateinischen Westen vermittelte.[7] So ist es vielleicht interessant, seine Arbeitsmethoden und Ziele und die Art der Benutzung seiner
Quellen in diesen ersten Kommentaren zu untersuchen.

Zu diesem Zweck können wir erstens seine Aussagen in den Kommentaren selbst und seine späteren Äusserungen in der Streitschrift gegen
Rufin und in seinem Briefwechsel mit Augustin prüfen und zweitens die
erhaltenen Reste seiner Quellen heranziehen. Im Folgenden werde ich
zuerst über die Aussagen des Hieronymus in seinen Vorworten berichten,
und dann die Quellen für die einzelnen Kommentare untersuchen.

Wie aus seinen Vorworten hervorgeht, schrieb Hieronymus seine
Pauluskommentare in der Reihenfolge Philemon, Galater, Epheser, Titus.
In den Einleitungen zu den beiden kurzen Kommentaren, Philemon und
Titus, steht nichts über seine Quellen und Methoden, aber in denjenigen
zum Galater- und Epheserbrief berichtet er ausführlich darüber. Hier
spricht er auch über den Mangel an würdigen Vorgängern, über seine
eigene Vorbereitung für die Arbeit, und allgemein über die Aufgabe eines
Kommentators.

---

[6] Zu den Methoden des Hieronymus vgl. z.B. die Bemerkungen Doutreleaus über
seine Benutzung des Zachariaskommentars von Didymus - hg. L. Doutreleau, *Di-
dyme l'Aveugle sur Zacharie 1, Sources Chrétiennes* 83 (Paris 1962) 129-135.

[7] In der Aneignung der Exegese des Origenes sind Hilarius (den Hieronymus
schätzte; vgl. *Ep.* 5.2, *De Viris Illustribus* 100, *Comm. in Mi.* 2, Prol., CCL 76,473)
und Ambrosius (den er angriff; vgl. *De Viris Illustribus* 124, Origenes, *Hom Lc.*,
Praef., hg. Rauer, 1-2, J. N. D. Kelly, *Jerome. His Life, Writings, and Controversies*,
London 1975, 143-4) die wichtigsten Vorgänger des Hieronymus; vgl. auch *Apol.*
1.2.5-10, 2.14.12-13 und 3.14.6-8 (hg. Pierre Lardet, *Sources Chrétiennes* 303 (Paris
1983) 10, 134, 250). Zur Exegese des Hieronymus vgl. Angelo Penna, *Principi e
carattere dell'esegesi di S. Gerolamo*, Rom 1950; Louis N. Hartmann, *St. Jerome as
an Exegete*, in hg. F. X. Murphy, *A Monument to Saint Jerome*, New York 1952, S.
35-81; P. Jay, *op. cit.* (oben Anm. 3) mit einer nützlichen Bibliographie, 435-445; zu
seinen Vorgängern unter den lateinischen Exegeten vgl. Manlio Simonetti, *Profilo
storico dell'esegesi patristica*, Rom 1981, Cap. IV, 81ff.; zu seiner Bekanntschaft mit
der griechischen christlichen Literatur vgl. Pierre Courcelle, *Les lettres grecques en
Occident*, Paris 1948, 78-115; G. Bardy, *St. Jerome and Greek Thought*, in Murphy,
op. cit., 83-112. Vgl. auch die beispielhafte Arbeit von Yves-Marie Duval, *Le Livre
de Jonas dans la littérature chrétienne grecque et latine. Sources et influence du
Commentaire sur Jonas de saint Jérôme*, Paris 1973.

Im Vorwort zum Galaterbriefkommentar beschreibt er sein Werk als eine Arbeit, die von lateinischen Schriftstellern noch nicht in Angriff genommen sei. Marius Victorinus habe zwar Pauluskommentare veröffentlicht, als heidnisch ausgebildeter Rhetoriker aber habe er keine Bibelkenntnisse besessen.[8] Er selbst könne deswegen das Nötige leisten, weil er Origenes gefolgt sei.[9] Origenes habe in einem fünfbändigen Kommentar, im zehnten Buch seiner *Stromata*, und auch in verschiedenen Homilien und Exzerpten den Galaterbrief behandelt. Auch gäbe es kurze Kommentare [10] von Didymus dem Blinden, Apollinaris von Laodicea, Eusebius von Emesa, Theodor von Heraclea, und einem sonst unbekannten alten Häretiker namens Alexander. Er behauptet, dies alles gelesen und danach seinem Sekretär aus dem Gedächtnis eine Mischung von Fremdgut und Eigengut in hoher Geschwindigkeit[11] diktiert zu haben.[12] Auch im Vorwort zum Epheserbriefkommentar nennt Hieronymus Origenes als seine erste Quelle - diesmal mit einem dreibändigen Kommentar. Dazu habe er noch einige, aber nur wenige Lesefrüchte aus den kurzen Kommentaren von Apollinaris und Didymus gesammelt und manche eigene Gedanken beigetragen. So könne das Werk entweder als ein fremdes oder als ein eigenes angesehen werden.[13] Er erwähnt im selben Vorwort, dass er sich selbst seit seiner Jugend immer durch Lektüre und durch Befragung von gelehrten Männern um die Erklärung der Heiligen Schrift bemüht und auch Didymus in Alexandrien zu diesem Zweck besucht habe.[14] Später im Verlauf des Kommentars nennt er Gregor von Nazianz als einen dieser gelehrten Gesprächspartner.[15]

---

8 Es scheint, dass Hieronymus Ambrosiaster als Vorgänger nicht erwähnen wollte; vgl. Kelly, *Jerome*, 148-9.

9 PL 26, 308A-B.

10 *Commentarioli* (309A; vgl. 442C).

11 Über das rapide Arbeitstempo vgl. *Comm. Gal. Lib.* 3 Praef. (*statim dicto quodcumque in buccam uenerit*) und *Comm Eph. Lib.* 2 Praef. (*sciatis me ... interdum per singulos dies usque ad numerum mille uersuum peruenire*) PL 26, 400B und 477A.

12 PL 26, 308B-309A.

13 PL 26, 442C-D: *sciatis Origenem tria uolumina in hanc epistulam conscripsisse, quem et nos ex parte secuti sumus. Apollinarium etiam et Didymum quosdam commentariolos edidisse, e quibus licet pauca decerpsimus, et nonnulla quae nobis uidebantur adiecimus siue subtraximus, ut studiosus statim in principio lector agnoscat hoc opus uel alienum esse uel nostrum.*

14 PL 26, 440A-B.

15 Zu Eph 5,32, PL 26, 535Dff. Über den Einfluss Gregors auf Hieronymus vgl. Jean-Marie Matthieu, *Grégoire de Naziance et Jérôme* und Claudio Moreschini,

190

Die Aufgabe des Exegeten beschreibt Hieronymus im Vorwort zum dritten Buch des Galaterbriefkommentars als die Erklärung der Worte des Apostels, als *obscura disserere, manifesta perstringere, in dubiis immorari*.[16] Im Vorwort zum Epheserbriefkommentar schreibt er, der Exeget müsse sich in die Gedanken des Apostels versetzen, müsse verstehen, warum er schrieb, durch welche Methode er seine Meinung stütze, und welches die Besonderheiten seiner Adressaten waren, weil ja die Paulusbriefe entsprechend der Zeit und dem Ort der Abfassung und der Empfänger verschiedene Gründe und Themen haben.[17] Dies alles macht den Eindruck, dass Hieronymus auf die philologische und historische Erklärung des Textes Gewicht legt und dass er im Stande ist, die gelehrte griechische exegetische Tradition vor allem in der Nachfolge des Origenes den Lateinern zugänglich zu machen.

Von den Quellen des Hieronymus in seinen Pauluskommentaren besitzen wir noch zahlreiche Katenenauszüge aus dem Epheserbriefkommentar des Origenes,[18] einige kurze Katenenauszüge aus dem Galaterbriefkommentar des Eusebius von Emesa,[19] und ausserdem ein paar weitere Auszüge aus den Pauluskommentaren des Origenes, die in der Apologie des Pamphilus enthalten sind.[20] Von den anderen von Hieronymus erwähnten Kommentaren ist nichts mehr erhalten.[21] Nach seinen eigenen

---

Praeceptor meus. Tracce dell'insegnamento di Gregorio Nazianzeno in Gerolamo, in hg. Yves-Marie Duval, *Jérôme entre l'occident et l'orient*, Paris 1988, 115-127 und 129-138.

[16] PL 26, 400C.

[17] PL 26, 440B-C.

[18] Hg. J. A. F. Gregg, in *Journal of Theological Studies* 3 (1902) 233-244, 398-420, 554-576.

[19] Hg. Karl Staab, *Pauluskommentare aus der griechischen Kirche*, Münster 1933, 46-52.

[20] PG 17, 541-616.

[21] Zu den Pauluskommentaren dieser anderen Exegeten vgl. C. H. Turner, art. *Greek Patristic Commentaries on the Pauline Epistles*, in hg. James Hastings, *Dictionary of the Bible, Extra Volume*, Edinburgh 1904, 489 (der 'alte Häretiker' Alexander vielleicht ein von Tertullian, *De carne Christi* 16-17, erwähnter Valentinianer) und 497-50. Von Didymus und Apollinaris sind Katenenauszüge zu anderen Paulusbriefen, von Theodor von Heraclea verschiedene Auszüge, von denen die wichtigsten solche zum Matthäusevangelium und zum Johannesevangelium sind, erhalten. Vgl. Staab, *op. cit.*, xix-xxv, und zu Theodor hg. M. Geerard, *Clavis Patrum Graecorum* II (Turnhout 1974) 284-5, und Joseph Reuss, *Matthäus-Kommentare aus der griechischen Kirche* [Texte und Untersuchungen 61], Berlin 1957, xxvi-xxix, und *Johannes-Kommentare aus der griechischen Kirche* [Texte und Untersuchungen 89], Berlin 1966, xx-xxiii.

Aussagen aber hat Hieronymus Origenes als Hauptquelle benutzt.[22] Dass
dies tatsächlich der Fall war, wird sowohl durch den Vergleich mit den
erhaltenen Origenes-Auszügen, wie auch durch die zahlreichen Parallelen
zu den aus seinen anderen Schriften bekannten Methoden und Ansichten
des Origenes deutlich gemacht. Der Grund, warum Hieronymus seine
Quellen für die Philemon- und Titusbriefkommentare nicht erwähnt, ist
wahrscheinlich, dass er hier nur Origenes benutzte.[23] Nach der von
Hieronymus gegebenen Liste der Werke des Origenes in seinem Brief
33,[24] hat Origenes nämlich einbändige Kommentare zu Titus und Philemon und eine Homilie zu Titus geschrieben.

Aus dem Philemonbriefkommentar des Origenes ist ein Auszug von
ungefähr einer Spalte Länge in der Apologie des Pamphilus erhalten,[25] an
dessen Text sich Hieronymus verhältnismässig eng anschliesst.[26] Die
Auszüge aus dem Titusbriefkommentar sind Teile eines langen Exkurses
über Häretiker zu Titus 3,10-11.[27] Hieronymus hat nur den ersten Teil in
seinen Kommentar zu diesem Vers aufgenommen, den Rest hat er als
überflüssig beiseite gelassen.[28]

---

[22] In seinem Vorwort zur *De Principiis*-Übersetzung beschreibt Rufin die
Pauluskommentare des Hieronymus als Übersetzungen aus Origenes (*Tyrannii Rufini
Opera*, hg. M. Simonetti, CCL 20, Turnhout 1961, 245.31-2). Hieronymus zitiert
diese Stelle in seiner Apologie gegen Rufin 1.8 (hg. Lardet, 24), ohne zu verneinen,
dass er *multa de tomis (Origenis)* übersetzt habe.

[23] Wenn dies stimmt, müsste Hieronymus die Hauptargumente sowohl gegen, wie
auch für die Kanonizität des Philemonbriefs, welche er im Vorwort (PL 26, 559D-
602C) bringt, bei Origenes schon vorgefunden haben (anders Theodor Zahn, *Geschichte des Neutestamentlichen Kanons* I.1 (Erlangen 1888) 268ff. und II.1
(Erlangen 1892) 997ff.; vgl. auch Adolf von Harnack, *Der kirchengeschichtliche Ertrag der exegetischen Arbeiten des Origenes*, Teil 2 [Texte und Untersuchungen
42.4], Leipzig 1919, Anhang, S.141-168: *Origenistisches Gut von kirchengeschichtli-
cher Bedeutung in den Kommentaren des Hieronymus zum Philemon-, Galater-,
Epheser- und Titusbrief*, insbesondere S.141-143.

[24] Vgl. P. Nautin, *Origène, sa vie et son oeuvre*, Paris 1977, 228-9, 245 und 254.

[25] PG 17, 591C-593C.

[26] Zu Philemon 4ff., PL 26, 609A-C. Die Texte werden von Nautin, *art. cit.*
(oben Anm. 3), 349-351, in parallelen Spalten gedruckt. Der Vergleich dieser beiden
Fassungen macht den Eindruck, dass Hieronymus mit einer gewissen Selbständigkeit
den von Origenes gebotenen Stoff umformt und zusammenfasst.

[27] PG 17, 553-556 und 604.

[28] PL 26, 596C-597A entspricht PG 17,553B-C. Auch die ersten Namen in der
Häretikerliste des Hieronymus (597B) stammen aus Origenes (PG 17, 554A-B, 556C).
Die Bemerkung *Superfluum est ire per singula* bezieht sich wohl auf die unnötig lan-
gen Ausführungen des Origenes.

XV

Aus dem Galaterbriefkommentar bringt die Apologie des Pamphilus vier Auszüge. Von drei kurzen Abschnitten erscheinen zwei[29] in zusammengefasster und einer[30] in umgestalteter Form bei Hieronymus. Der vierte Auszug stammt aus einem Exkurs, von dem nur der letzte Teil, der sich auf Gal 4,4 bezieht, bei Hieronymus wiederkehrt.[31]

Die Auszüge in der Apologie des Pamphilus erlauben uns also, durch Stichproben zu bestätigen, dass Origenes die Hauptquelle der Pauluskommentare des Hieronymus war.[32] Ebenso wichtig ist das einstimmige Urteil über den Charakter dieser Kommentare bei allen Wissenschaftlern, die sie studiert haben, dass sie hauptsächlich aus einer Zusammenfassung der Kommentare des Origenes bestehen. Es seien z. B. Zahn,[33] Turner,[34] Harnack,[35] Souter,[36] Nautin,[37] sowie zum Epheserbriefkommentar Frede,[38] und Deniau[39] genannt. Harnack[40] und Souter[41] haben 'Orige-

---

[29] PG 17, 584A-B und 584C - 585A entsprechen PL 26, 312C-D zu Gal 1,1 und 322A zu Gal 1,11-12. Interessant ist auch, dass Hieronymus die hier widerlegten häretischen Ansichten mit Namen (Ebion und Photinus) versehen hat.

[30] PG 17, 589B - 590A entspricht PL 26, 366B zu Gal 3,19-20. Turner, *art. cit.* 493, hat darauf hingewiesen, dass im Titel dieses Auszugs möglicherweise Gal statt Col zu lesen ist. Diese Vermutung wird durch den Vergleich mit Hieronymus als richtig erwiesen.

[31] PG 17, 585B-588A. Die letzten Sätze, 588A, entsprechen PL 26, 372A.

[32] Eine weitere Quelle für die Pauluskommentare des Origenes sind die (meist textkritischen) Randnotizen in der Handschrift Athos Lawra 184.B.64, dem sogenannten Codex von der Goltz; vgl. Ed. Freiherr von der Goltz, *Eine textkritische Arbeit des zehnten bezw. sechsten Jahrhunderts* [Texte und Untersuchungen 17.3b], Leipzig 1899, und Kirsopp Lake und Silva New, *Six Collations of New Testament Manuscripts*, in *Harvard Theological Studies* 17 (Cambridge Mass. 1932) 141-219. Hieraus erfahren wir z.B., mit welchen Versen die fünf Bände des Galaterbriefkommentars anfingen. Eine Notiz über die Quellen des Paulus zu Tit 1,12 (von der Goltz, *op. cit.*, 89, Nummer 215) entspricht dem, was Hieronymus darüber berichtet: 571C (*Dicitur autem iste uersiculus in Epimenidis Cretensis poetae oraculis reperiri*) und 573B (*Callimachus in suo poemate est usus exordio*); vgl. 573A (*in laudibus Jovis*).

[33] *Op. cit.* II.2, 426ff. (zu Gal und Eph).

[34] *Art. cit.*, 493-6.

[35] *Op. cit.*, 141ff. (Phlm), 146ff. (Gal), 154ff. (Eph), 165ff. (Titus).

[36] A. Souter, *The Earliest Latin Commentaries on the Epistles of St. Paul*, Oxford 1927, 108-123.

[37] Nautin, *art. cit.*,11, nimmt an, dass die Benutzung des Origenes in allen vier Kommentaren ähnlich stark war. Vgl. auch Jay, *op. cit.* (oben Anm.3), 335 Anm.4 und 408.

[38] H. J. Frede (hg.), *Epistula ad Ephesios* [Vetus Latina 24/1], Freiburg 1962-4, 28*.

nistisches Gut' in den Kommentaren des Hieronymus gesammelt, und Deniau[42] hat verschiedene Kriterien vorgeschlagen, um die Benutzung des Origenes festzustellen. Hinzuzufügen ist, dass es sich bei der Arbeit an der Vorbereitung einer neuen Ausgabe des Römerbriefkommentars des Origenes herausgestellt hat, dass es sehr viele inhaltliche und methodische Parallelen zwischen den Kommentaren des Hieronymus und diesem Kommentar gibt.[43] Vor allem ist dies der Fall beim Galaterbriefkommentar, der oft einen ähnlichen Stoff behandelt.

Zum Galaterbriefkommentar haben wir weiteres Material in den Aussagen des Hieronymus selbst. Erstens wird seine Benutzung der Auslegung des Origenes in den *Stromata* dadurch bestätigt, dass er zu Gal 5,13 einen längeren Abschnitt daraus wörtlich zitiert,[44] und danach einige Male auf Origenes verweist,[45] zweitens wiederholt er seine Aussage über seine eigenen Quellen in seinem Briefwechsel mit Augustin. Augustin hatte die Exegese des Hieronymus zu Gal 2,11ff.[46] angegriffen, wonach Paulus die Verstellung des Petrus nicht wegen eines wirklichen Gegensatzes, sondern um den Anstoss für die Heidenchristen wegzuräumen, getadelt hatte.[47] In seiner Antwort zitiert Hieronymus die Liste seiner

[39] Francis Deniau, *Le Commentaire de Jérôme sur Ephésiens nous permet-il de connaître celui d'Origène?* in H. Crouzel, G. Lomiento und J. Rius-Camps (hg.), Origeniana I [Quaderni di "Vetera Christianorum" 12], Bari 1975, 163-179. Zum Galaterbriefkommentar vgl. auch M. A. Schatkin, *The Influence of Origen upon St. Jerome's Commentary on Galatians,* in *Vigiliae Christianae* 24 (1970) 49-58.

[40] *Op. cit.,* 141-168.

[41] *Op. cit.,* 115-123.

[42] *Art. cit.,* 174f.

[43] Diese werden im zweiten Apparat der Ausgabe, C. P. Hammond Bammel, *Der Römerbriefkommentar des Origenes* angegeben. Bis jetzt ist nur der erste Band mit Buch 1-3 erschienen [Vetus Latina. Aus der Geschichte der lateinischen Bibel 16], Freiburg 1990.

[44] PL 26, 406B - 408A (*Hunc locum quia ualde obscurus est, de decimo Stromatum libro transferri placuit ad uerbum*). Der übersetzte Abschnitt behandelt Gal 5,13-23.

[45] PL 26, 408A (*Hucusque Origenes*), 414D zu Gal 5,19-21 (*in eo loco, ubi supra de decimo Origenis Stromate uerbum transtulimus ad uerbum*), 421C zu Gal 5,24 (*Origenes hunc locum superioribus nectens, ita legit*). Vgl. auch 348B zu Gal 3,1 (*Hoc quia in exemplaribus Adamantii non habetur, omisimus*), 392A zu Gal 4,28 (*Origenes hunc locum edisserens ...*).

[46] PL 26, 338Cff.

[47] Augustin, *Ep.* 28.3ff. und 40.3ff. (hg. A. Goldbacher, CSEL 34 (Wien 1895ff.) 107ff. und 71ff. Über diese Auseinandersetzung vgl. P. Auvray, *Saint Jérôme et saint Augustin. La Controverse au sujet de l'incident d'Antioch,* in *Recherches de science religieuse* 29 (1939) 594-610.

griechischen Quellen aus seinem eigenen Vorwort und behauptet, Augustin könne nur das, was nicht in diesen Quellen sich finde, als seine eigene Meinung verurteilen. Vor allem habe er offen zugestanden, dass er dem Kommentar des Origenes gefolgt sei. Die von Augustin angegriffene Auslegung habe Origenes im zehnten Buch seiner *Stromata* zuerst gebracht, und die anderen Exegeten, einschliesslich Johannes von Konstantinopel, seien ihm darin gefolgt.[48] Hieronymus bringt auch hier eine interessante Mitteilung über seine Methode in seinen Kommentaren, nämlich die Aussage, dass er die Schriften seiner Vorgänger liest und verschiedene Erklärungen bringt, damit der Leser wähle, was er bevorzuge. Dies sei die gewöhnliche Sitte sowohl bei heidnischer Literatur wie auch bei der Heiligen Schrift.[49]

Nur bei dem Galaterbriefkommentar haben wir die Möglichkeit, mit erhaltenen Resten einer anderen Quelle als Origenes einen Vergleich durchzuführen. Aus dem Kommentar in zehn Büchern von Eusebius von Emesa sind 22 meist kurze Auszüge erhalten.[50] Die Beziehungen zu Hieronymus sind keineswegs eng. In ungefähr 8 Auszügen zeigen sich mögliche Berührungen mit Hieronymus.[51] Nur in einem Fall scheint Hieronymus Teile einer Exegese des Eusebius zu übersetzen.[52] Manche

---

[48] Hieronymus, *Ep.* 112 .4 und 6 (hg. I. Hilberg, CSEL 55 (Wien 1912) 370-2 und 372-3).

[49] *Ep.* 112.5 (hg. Hilberg, 372.21-4): *me maiorum scripta legere et in commentariis secundum omnium consuetudinem uarias ponere explanationes, ut e multis sequatur unusquisque quod uelit. quod quidem puto te et in saeculari litteratura et in diuinis libris legisse et probasse.*

[50] Staab, *op. cit.,* 46-52. É. M. Buytaert, *L'héritage littéraire d'Eusèbe d'Émèse,* Louvain 1949, 145*-152* (nach seiner Numerierung sind es nur 20 Auszüge); auf S.175-7 bespricht Buytaert die Auszüge und ihre Beziehung zu Hieronymus. Eusebius war ein führender Arianer bzw. "Halbarianer", der Alexandrien und Antiochien besuchte, zum Bischof von Emesa wahrscheinlich im Jahre 341 erhoben wurde, Constantius nach Persien begleitete, und vor dem Jahre 361 starb. Zur Exegese des Eusebius von Emesa vgl. auch Y.-M. Duval, *op. cit.* (oben Anm.7), 256-7 mit Anm. 81.

[51] Buytaert, *op. cit.,* 176-177, führt sieben solcher Stellen auf. Er weist auch auf die Möglichkeit hin, dass die Lesart *per Christum* im Lemma des Hieronymus zu Gal 4,7 (374C) aus Eusebius übernommen sei.

[52] Im Auszug zu Gal 1,11-14 (Staab, 47-8) entsprechen folgende Sätze dem Text des Hieronymus (324B-C): S.48 Zeilen 1-2 ἐν τῷ Ἰουδαισμῷ (Gal 1,14). Καὶ οὐκ εἶπεν ἐν τῷ νόμῳ / *in Judaismo, non in lege Dei.* Zeilen 12-13 πολλοὺς καὶ οὐ πάντας διὰ τὸ σύμμετρον, συνηλικιώτας δὲ διὰ τὸ μὴ κατὰ τῶν πρεσβυτέρων δοκεῖν ἐπαίρεσθαι ... πατρικῶν δὲ παραδόσεων εἶπεν καὶ οὐ νομίμων / *Nec supra omnes sed supra plurimos, nec supra senes sed supra coaetaneos, ut et studium suum*

Ähnlichkeiten könnten einfach daher rühren, dass beide denselben Vers umschreibend erklären.[53] In mehreren Fällen hat man bei der Lektüre des Hieronymus den Eindruck, dass Eusebius eher von der Quelle des Hieronymus abhängt als Hieronymus von Eusebius, dass also beide in derselben auf Origenes zurückgehenden Tradition stehen.[54]

Was die allgemeine Richtung der Auszüge des Eusebius angeht, so scheint er den Gegensatz zwischen Gesetz und Gnade [55] stärker zu betonen als Hieronymus, der es, Origenes folgend, vorzieht das Gesetz positiv

---

referret in lege, et iactantiam declinaret. Paternas autem traditiones, non Domini mandata commemorans ... Die Zeilen 12-13 zeigen auch Beziehungen zu Hieronymus 324C.1-4.

[53] Zu Gal 2,9 (Staab, 48.21, Hieronymus 336C), zu Gal 2,21 (Staab, 49.4-6, Hieronymus 346B-C), zu Gal 3,23 (Staab, 49.18-19 τοῦ νόμου παρεντεθέντος μεταξὺ τῆς ἐπαγγελίας καὶ αὐτῆς τῆς παρουσίας τῆς πίστεως, Hieronymus 367B lex ... inter repromissionem et completionem eius media subrepsit), und zu Gal 6,12-13 (Staab, 51.20-52.4, Hieronymus 435C).

[54] Zu Gal 1,4 schreibt Hieronymus (314B), dass die Häretiker diesen Vers zum Anlass nehmen, um zu behaupten, es gebe zwei verschiedene Schöpfer von dem gegenwärtigen und dem zukünftigen Aeon, es sei aber nicht der Aeon böse, sondern das, was in dem Aeon geschieht. Eusebius (Staab, 47.5-6) schreibt, dass Paulus in diesem Vers zeige, dass das Böse nicht ἀγέννητον sondern πρόσκαιρον sei. Zu Gal 1,10 scheinen sowohl Hieronymus (321D) wie auch Eusebius anzunehmen, dass ein Gerücht im Umlauf war, dass Paulus in Judaea das Gesetz heimlich beobachtete; vgl. dazu auch Eusebius zu Gal 1,11-14 (Staab 47.28-9) und zu Gal 4,20 und Hieronymus zu Gal 5,11 (404B-D). Die Frage, warum Petrus manchmal Kephas genannt wird, erwähnt Eusebius schon zu Gal 2,9 (Staab 48.22-5), Hieronymus aber erst zu Gal 2,11ff. und in einem anderen Zusammenhang (340Cff., wo er die von Clemens Alexandrinus vertretene Meinung, dieser Kephas sei nicht der Apostel Petrus, widerlegt). Zu Gal 4,14 bespricht Hieronymus mehrere Möglichkeiten, den von Paulus erwähnten πειρασμός zu erklären, von denen die letzte (381B persecutiones et plagas corporis) im Fragment von Eusebius anscheinend vorausgesetzt wird (Staab, 51.5-9 διωγμοί). Zu Gal 4,20 erwägt Hieronymus verschiedene Erklärungen des Ausdrucks ἀλλάξαι τὴν φωνήν μου, darunter diejenige, dass Paulus, wie ein Schauspieler seine Stimme oder wie ein Arzt seine Behandlungsmethode den Empfängern anpasst (387A-C). Eusebius (Staab 51.10-17) lässt Paulus selbst (anscheinend ironisch) fragen, ob die Galater seine Worte für ein Schauspiel halten würden, wenn er seine Stimme geändert hätte (aber der Zusammenhang hier ist ein ganz anderer). Zu Gal 6,15 bringt Hieronymus (436B-437A) eine origenistische Erklärung, welche die neue Kreatur auf den Auferstehungsleib bezieht, der weder die Beschneidung des Juden, noch das Unbeschnittensein des Heiden besitzt (noua conditio sine his partibus corporum, quae possunt secari). Eusebius schreibt, dass der Christ weder die Beschneidung des Juden noch das Unbeschnittensein des Heiden besitzt, weil er eine eigene schönere Beschneidung hat.

[55] Bzw. zwischen Gesetz und Kreuz Christi, Gottessohnschaft, oder Geist, vgl. die Auszüge zu Gal 1,1; 1,4; 2,18; 2,20; 2,21; 3,23; 5,16.

XV

zu bewerten und einen Unterschied zwischen dem tötenden Buchstaben des Gesetzes und dem lebendigmachenden Geist[56] zu machen.[57] Der Kommentar, für den wir die beste Möglichkeit haben, die Verfahrensweise des Hieronymus zu prüfen, ist derjenige zum Epheserbrief. Von den kurzen Kommentaren des Apollinaris und Didymus ist nichts erhalten, dagegen 37 teilweise umfangreiche Katenenauszüge aus dem Kommentar des Origenes, welche eine erstaunlich enge Übereinstimmung mit Hieronymus aufweisen. Nach der eigenen Beschreibung des Hieronymus könnte man schon den Eindruck haben, dass sein eigener Kommentar hauptsächlich aus einer Zusammenfassung desjenigen des Origenes besteht,[58] und dieser Eindruck wird durch den Vergleich mit den Katenenauszügen bestätigt.[59] Es ist auch bezeichnend, dass bei dem Versuch des Hieronymus in seinen Streitschriften gegen Rufin, sich vor dem

---

[56] 2 Kor 3,6.

[57] Möglicherweise reagiert Eusebius, ähnlich wie Augustin, gegen Origenes, wenn er betont, dass Paulus sich nicht verstellte, aber die kurzen Auszüge erlauben hier keine sicheren Schlüsse; vgl. Eusebius zu Gal 1,10; 1,11-14; 4,20 und oben Anm. 54.

[58] Vgl. oben S. 189 mit Anm. 13. Später in seiner Streitschrift gegen Rufin (1 Ap. 21) hat er seine Angaben über seine Quellen wiederholt und die Werke von Didymus und Apollinaris als *opuscula* und seine eigene Methode als *uel transferens uel imitans* bezeichnet. Ähnlich wie in seinem Briefwechsel mit Augustin (vgl. oben S. 194 mit Anm. 48) erklärt er dort, dass er nur für das, was in seinen griechischen Quellen nicht steht, Verantwortung übernimmt (*Quidquid ergo in explanatione huius epistulae uitii potuerit demonstrari, si ego illud in graecis uoluminibus, unde in latinum uertisse me dixi, ostendere non potuero, crimen agnoscam, et meum erit quod alienum non fuerit*). Also ist er keineswegs bestrebt, seinen eigenen Anteil überzubewerten.

[59] Vgl. Gregg, *art. cit.* (oben Anm. 18), Harnack, *op. cit.* (oben Anm. 23) 155ff., Frede, *op. cit.* (oben Anm. 38), Deniau, *art. cit.* (oben Anm. 39). Harnack urteilt zusammenfassend: "die fast vollständige Übereinstimmung wäre noch deutlicher, hätte nicht Hieron. frei, öfters willkürlich und verkürzt übersetzt bzw. erweitert, umgegossen oder paraphrasiert, und hätte nicht der Katenenschreiber ebenfalls öfters den Text verkürzt." Frede (S. 28*) schliesst (nach einer Prüfung und Verbesserung des Textes von Vallarsi anhand der Handschrift Karlsruhe Aug. lxxxi und einem Vergleich mit den Katenenauszügen des Origenes): "Dadurch wird augenfällig, dass der gedankliche Anteil des Hieronymus an seinem Kommentar ungemein dürftig ist und seine Leistung im wesentlichen darin besteht, dass er das Werk des Origenes (und in weit geringerem Masse Exzerpte anderer griechischer Autoren: siehe seine Praefatio) übersetzt und so erhalten hat. Auch die Verteilung von Lemma und Kommentar wie die Einteilung in drei Bücher entspricht Origenes". Nach Deniau (S. 166) haben mehr als vier Fünftel des Textes der Katenenauszüge ihre Entsprechung (als Übersetzung oder Paraphrase) bei Hieronymus. Er charakterisiert den Vorgang des Hieronymus (S. 175) als "paraphraser, abréger ou modifier".

Vorwurf der origenistischen Aussagen in diesem Kommentar zu verteidigen, er nur zwei ganz kurze Entlehnungen aus Apollinaris und gar keine aus Didymus anführt.[60] Abgesehen von diesen beiden Hinweisen haben wir kaum die Möglichkeit, die Benutzung von Apollinaris oder Didymus in den Pauluskommentaren zu identifizieren. Es liegt aber nahe, Erwähnungen von Häretikern des späteren dritten oder vierten Jahrhunderts entweder einer dieser Quellen oder Hieronymus selbst zuzuschreiben,[61] während die gelegentliche Polemik gegen Porphyrius[62] vielleicht auf Apollinaris, der ja ein Werk von 33 Bänden gegen Porphyrius verfasst hatte, zurückgeht. Zitate aus der lateinischen Literatur und manche persönliche Reminiszenzen sind eigene Beiträge des Hieronymus.[63]

Der Vergleich mit den Katenenauszügen ist besonders interessant für die Methode des Hieronymus. Hieronymus scheint sich nicht nur sehr eng, sondern fast ausschliesslich an Origenes gehalten zu haben.[64] Während aber der Katenist nur einzelne Sätze auswählt, wechselt Hieronymus zwischen Übersetzung und Zusammenfassung, sodass er oft den ganzen Gedankengang deutlich macht, aus dem der Katenist nur Bruchstücke zitiert hat. Was die Methode der Exegese angeht, so ist die Tatsache für das Verständnis des Vorgehens des Hieronymus besonders wichtig, dass Origenes regelmässig verschiedene Ansichten und Argumente zur Erklärung des Paulustextes erörtert. Er führt diese meist durch Ausdrücke

---

[60] Die Stellen, die Hieronymus (1 *Ap.* 24-5) Apollinaris zuschreibt, sind 469D.2-470A.7 (*Alius uero ... potest*) zu Eph 2,7 und 478A.1-5 (*Licet quidam ... acceperit*) zu Eph 3,1. Seine Behauptung (1 *Ap.* 25), dass Apollinaris an letzterer Stelle *contra Origenis uadens dogma* sei, stimmt nicht. Sowohl diese, wie auch die vorangehende Origenes zugeschriebene Exegese, beziehen das Wort δέσμιος auf die *uincula carnis*.

[61] Vgl. die Liste bei Souter, *op. cit.*, 124-125. Möglicherweise gehen christologische Aussagen wie 446A.11-B.2 (zu Eph 1,3), 506D.8-10 (zu Eph 4,21) auf Didymus zurück. Die Polemik aber gegen Sabellius zu Eph 4,5-6 (496A.4-6) entspricht Origenes, Katenenauszug (hg. Gregg, *art. cit.*, oben Anm. 18) XVII.1-2, Hieronymus hat nur den Namen des Sabellius hinzugefügt. Auf ähnliche Weise hat Hieronymus zu Gal 1,1 und Gal 1,11-12 die Polemik, die er bei Origenes vorfand, selbst mit den Häretikernamen von Ebion und Photinus versehen; vgl. oben Anm. 29.

[62] Vgl. Souter, *op. cit.*, 123, Hieronymus, *Ep.*112.6 (hg. Hilberg, 372-3) und *De Viris Illustribus* 104.

[63] Vgl. Souter, *op. cit.*, 125ff., Deniau, *art. cit.*, 174, sowie unten Anm. 86 und 87.

[64] Wo ein längerer Katenenauszug erhalten ist, bleibt in dem Kommentar des Hieronymus zum selben Vers kaum Platz für die Benutzung anderer Quellen oder eigener Beiträge; vgl. z.B. Katenenauszug XXII und PL 26, 516B-517C zu Eph 4,31; XXXIV.17 - XXXV.12 zu Eph 6,14b-6,16 und 550D-552A.

XV

198

wie: "der eine wird sagen, der andere wird sagen" ein.[65] Oft stellt er eine Frage und erwägt dann mehrere Antworten dazu.[66] Manchmal bezeichnet er eine Ansicht als die einfachere,[67] als heterodox,[68] als die eigene Meinung,[69] oder bringt sie als Alternative zu einer schon berichteten eigenen Meinung.[70] Nur selten schreibt er solche Ansichten bestimmten Vorgängern ausdrücklich zu.[71] Diese Arbeitsweise des Origenes bietet Hieronymus die Möglichkeit, den Eindruck zu verschaffen, dass er über die Ansichten von mehreren verschiedenen Paulusexegeten berichtet, während er tatsächlich alles nur aus Origenes schöpft.[72] Die Meinungen

[65] Beispiele werden in den folgenden Anmerkungen gegeben. Zu Eph 2,14bff. hat Origenes offensichtlich zwei verschiedene ausführlichere Auslegungen geboten; die Auslegung auf Israel und die Heiden wird vom Katenisten nicht wiedergegeben, aber durch seine Worte XII.12-13 und 36-38 vorausgesetzt.

[66] I.1-9, IX.103-110, IX.168ff., XIV.15ff., XVII.71ff., XXVI.7-11, XXXI.19ff.

[67] IX.169-170, X.1ff., XIX.56, XXIV.6, XXIV.15, XXVIII.1.

[68] II.15-20.

[69] II.21, XIX.57.

[70] VIII.29, VIII.63ff., XXIII.15ff., XXXIII.43ff., XXXIV.1-10.

[71] VIII.7 (τις τῶν πρὸ ἡμῶν, eine Bemerkung über die Sprache des Paulus), XXII.40ff. (τινες, welche den Text von Mt 5,22 interpoliert haben), XXXI.21 (τινες, eine Erklärung von Eph 6,2), XXXII.11 (οἱ περὶ ταῦτα δεινοί, eine Definition von ἰσχύς), XXXVII.13-18 (τινες, eine enkratistische Auslegung von Eph 6,24).

[72] So gibt er zu Eph 1,1 sowohl seine eigene Ansicht wie auch diejenigen von zwei anderen Gruppen von Kommentatoren an (443A-B *uidetur mihi, alii uero ... intelligunt, nonnulli ... existimant*). Es stehen aber sowohl die Fragestellung, wie auch zwei der drei zitierten Lösungen im Katenenauszug des Origenes (I.1, I.12ff., I.6-7). Zu Eph 2,6 führt Hieronymus eine einfachere und eine "geistige" Erklärung vor (468C-D *qui simplicius est responsurus, hoc asserit ... Alius uero qui resurrectionem, et regnum Christi spiritualiter intelligit, non deliberauit dicere ...*), welche beide sich im Katenenauszug X befinden; und ähnlich zu Eph 5,14 (525B *qui simplici responsione contentus est, dicet ... Alius uero ... memorabit*; vgl. XXVI.8-11). Zu Eph 2,14bff. sind anscheinend sowohl die Auslegung, die Hieronymus (474B) als *iuxta uulgatam interpretationem* bezeichnet, wie auch die auf Col 1,20 fussende aus Origenes geschöpft; vgl. oben Anm. 65. Zu Eph 4,32 stehen sowohl die durch *Alius uero ... simpliciter accipiet* eingeführte Erklärung (518A = XXIII.15), wie auch die vorangehenden Exegesen, zu Eph 5,5 sowohl der durch *Respondeat quis* eingeführte Einwand (521B, XXIV.46-54), wie auch die durch den Einwand infragestellte Erklärung (521A, XXIV.37-45) bei Origenes. Auch zu Eph 1,9 (453A-B), zu Eph 4,14 (501C-D), zu Eph 5,1 (517C-518A) und zu Eph 5,18 (527D-528A) entsprechen Alternativerklärungen bei Hieronymus denselben Alternativerklärungen bei Origenes (V.9-37, XVII.71-80, XXIII.1-22, XXVIII.1-6). Zu Eph 6,13 wird eine dritte Erklärung von Origenes durch die Worte τρίτος δὲ παρὰ τὰς δύο ἐκδοχὰς ἔσται τις λόγος λέγων und von Hieronymus durch *Tertia quoque a quibusdam interpretatio subinducitur dicentibus* (550A). Zu Eph 6,1ff. wird eine ganze Auseinander-

von Origenes selbst nimmt Hieronymus manchmal in den eigenen Mund,[73] manchmal schreibt er sie *quibusdam* zu,[74] manchmal, aber selten, kritisiert er sie.[75] Man kann also Quellenwechsel bei Hieronymus weder durch die Art der Anführung, noch durch einen Widerspruch oder einen plötzlichen Übergang zu einer neuen Bemerkung feststellen.[76] Was den Inhalt des Kommentars angeht, so ist das Hauptinteresse der Katenenauszüge aus Origenes erstens die genaue philologische Erklärung des Paulustextes[77] und zweitens die Erläuterung seines Gedankenganges, vor allem bezüglich der christlichen Spiritualität und der Ethik. Hieronymus übernimmt beides. Dadurch, dass er die sprachlichen Beobachtungen und Erklärungen des Origenes wiedergibt, bietet er seinen lateinischen Lesern Einblick in die Methoden eines griechischen wissenschaftlichen Kommentars. Die Terminologie des Paulus wird anhand von philosophischen Definitionen,[78] von biblischen Parallelen,[79] vom hebräischen

---

setzung mit Argumenten auf beiden Seiten (XXXI.19-46) von Hieronymus wiedergegeben (537C-538C).
[73] Vgl. 478A (*Puto autem ...*), XIII.11 (νομίζω); 501A (*Videtur autem mihi*), XVII.51 (δόξει δέ); 510C (*Arbitror itaque*), XIX.73. Ähnlich verfährt er mit den Beobachtungen des Origenes; vgl. 528B (*Frequenter annotauimus*) und XXVIII.9 (πολλάκις δὲ τετηρήκαμεν). Wenn Origenes auf eine eigene frühere Erklärung verweist, so schreibt dies Hieronymus einfach ab: 521C *in superioribus ... dixeramus auaritiam pro adulterio positam* entspricht XXIV.55-6 ἐν τοῖς ἀνωτέρω ὑπενοήσαμεν τὴν πλεονεξίαν τετάχθαι ἐπὶ τῆς μοιχείας, aber Origenes hatte an den beiden früheren Stellen dies auch ausdrücklich geschrieben (XXIV.6-8 und XVIII.36-46), Hieronymus aber nicht (519B und 505B-C). Zu Eph 5,7 schreibt Origenes, ohne an Eph 3,6 zu denken, οὐ μέμνημαι δὲ ἀλλαχοῦ παρὰ τὴν ἐνεστηκυῖαν λέξιν τὸν συμμέτοχον εἰρῆσθαι (XXV.15-16), und ebenso Hieronymus, *non memini alibi me legisse, excepto praesenti loco, comparticipem* (523A). So müsste man annehmen, dass auch Stellen wie 525B (*Ego certe secundum paupertatulam meam, omnes editiones ueterum Scripturarum, ipsaque Hebraeorum uolumina diligenter euentilans, numquam hoc scriptum reperi*) aus Origenes übernommen sind.
[74] So zu 1,7, 450C (*quidam dicunt*, vgl. IV.12ff.), zu 1,15ff., 459A-B (*quidam sic intelligunt*, vgl. IX.25-9); auch zu 2,4, wo die durch *sunt qui ... putent* bezeichnete Erklärung einer Beobachtung des Origenes im Römerbriefkommentar (hg. Bammel, Lib.I.19.30-33) entspricht.
[75] So zu Eph 1,1b (wo er einen anderen Text als Origenes liest), *Quidam curiosius quam necesse est, putant ...* (443B); vgl. II.1-12.
[76] Letzteres Phänomen findet sich auch in den Katenenauszügen aus Origenes; vgl. z. B. II.47-8, Hieronymus 446A.3-5 entsprechend.
[77] Zu den Methoden des Origenes vgl. Bernhard Neuschäfer, *Origenes als Philologe*, Basel 1987.
[78] z. B. 452A zu Eph 1,9, eine stoische Definition von *sapientia* und *prudentia* (der Text des Origenes ist nicht erhalten, V.1-8 setzt aber eine solche Definition vor-

200

Sprachgebrauch[80] oder vom Zusammenhang[81] her erläutert. Der syntakti-
sche Aufbau seiner Sätze[82] wird erklärt und Probleme der Interpunk-
tion,[83] der Textkritik,[84] Sprachfehler und Soloecismen[85] werden besprochen. Man muss allerdings zugeben, dass manche dieser Erörterungen
etwas flüchtig übersetzt worden sind und nur dann richtig verständlich
werden, wenn man den griechischen Text des Apostelbriefs vor sich hat.
Auf der anderen Seite hat Hieronymus manchmal eigene Bemerkungen

---

aus); vgl. Origenes, *Hom. in Jer.* 8.2, hg. E. Klostermann, GCS *Origenes* 3 (Leipzig
1901) 57.11f. und 15f., und E. Klostermann, *Überkommene Definitionen im Werke
des Origenes*, ZNTW 37 (1938) 60-61 zu σοφία und φρόνησις. 510BC zu Eph 4,26
über die zwei Bedeutungen von *ira* entspricht XIX.68-73, aber der technischer
Wortschatz des Origenes fehlt bei Hieronymus. 516B-C zu Eph 4,31 über *amaritudo*,
furor und *ira* bringt eine Zusammenfassung in einer anderen Reihenfolge von
XXII.1-21, wo Origenes die Bedeutung dieser Worte anhand philosophischer Definitionen, sowie des biblischen und alltäglichen Sprachgebrauchs erörtert. Zu der Definition von *ira* bei Origenes, vgl. Neuschäfer, *op. cit.*, 147 und 405 Anm. 69 und 73.

[79] z.B. 465B-C zu Eph 2,1 über παράπτωμα als biblisches Wort (entspricht
IX.158-166), 521D zu Eph 5,5 über *idololatria* als *fornicatio* (aus XXIV.57-60); vgl.
auch 528B-C zu Eph 5,19 mit XXIX.1-10.

[80] 449A zu Eph 1,5 über das Wort εὐδοκία als eine Erfindung der Übersetzer des
Alten Testaments (vgl. III.29-35), 520C-521A zu Eph 3,4 über εὐχαριστία, die Bedeutung des entsprechenden hebräischen Worts und die Hexaplalesarten zu Prov
11,16 (aus XXIV.22-33 übernommen).

[81] 503B-D zu Eph 4,19 wird *auaritia* etwas umständlich durch den Zusammenhang in 1 Thess 4,3ff. erklärt, XVIII.36-47 entsprechend; vgl. auch 517C zu Eph
4,32 über *benigni* (aus XXIII.1-5), 520A zu Eph 5,3-4 über *stultiloquium* (entspricht
XXIV.19-20), 521B-C zu Eph 5,5 über *turpitudo* (aus XXIV.46-54).

[82] 456A zu Eph 1,13 (VIII.1), 466B-C zu Eph 2,1ff. (IX.203-207), und 485C zu
Eph 3,13 (XIV.15ff.) wird das Problem, worauf die Relativpronomina sich beziehen,
behandelt. Vgl. auch 465A-B zu Eph 2,1ff. (IX.146ff.), 477Bff. zu Eph 3,1ff. (XIII.
1ff.).

[83] Vgl. 448B-C zu Eph 1,5 (III.14-16), 453A-B zu Eph 1,9 (V.16ff.), 537B zu Eph
6,1ff. (XXXI.1-7).

[84] 465B zu Eph 2,1ff. (IX.155), *coniunctionem ... ab indoctis scriptoribus additam*;
516C über *sine causa* in Mt 5,22 (XXII.40-44); 520D-521A über die Hexaplalesarten in Prov 11,16 (XXIV.30-33). Für einige andere Hinweise auf Hexaplalesarten
in den Pauluskommentaren vgl. Souter, *op. cit.*, 115-6.

[85] 456A-B zu Eph 1,13 (VIII.5ff.) das zweite *in quo* ist überflüssig; 458A-C zu
Eph 1,15ff. (IX.1-10) ein *Hyperbaton*; 478A zu Eph 3,1ff. (XIII.11) *uitiosa elocutio*;
485C zu Eph 3,13 (XIV.18-19) vielleicht ein *Hyperbaton*; 524B zu Eph 5,10
(XXV.49-53) *contextus eloquii turbatus*; 524D zu Eph 5,12 (XXV.67-70) vielleicht
ein *Hyperbaton*.

über die Probleme der Übersetzung ins Lateinische[86] oder die lateinischen Handschriften[87] hinzugefügt.

Bei dem Vergleich der Katenenauszüge mit dem Kommentar des Hieronymus merkt man sehr bald den Unterschied, dass Hieronymus sehr häufig charakteristische 'origenistische' Ansichten äussert, während solche in den Auszügen des offensichtlich sehr vorsichtigen Katenisten nur sehr selten angedeutet werden. Dass die Erörterung dunkler Geheimnisse und der Lehren des Apostels über himmlische Mächte und Dämonen besonders wichtig für die Themenführung des Epheserbriefs sei, wird schon von Hieronymus im Vorwort sowohl zum ersten wie auch zum dritten Buch vorausgesagt.[88] Man hat den Eindruck, dass dies für ihn ein besonderer Anziehungspunkt bei der Kommentierung dieses Briefs war. Solche Themen ziehen sich manchmal durch mehrere Abschnitte hindurch. Hieronymus bringt in diesem Zusammenhang 'origenistisches' Gut manchmal als Eigenes,[89] manchmal Abstand nehmend,[90] manchmal einem *alius* oder *quidam*[91] zuschreibend. Es ist wichtig, die wenigen Parallelstellen, die in den Katenenauszügen erhalten sind, zu überprüfen, um ein Urteil über die diesbezüglichen Methoden des Hieronymus unabhängig von seinem späteren Streit mit Rufin fällen zu können.

Zu Eph 1,17 macht Origenes einen Unterschied zwischen γνῶσις und ἐπίγνωσις. Wenn ἐπίγνωσις die Wiedererkennung dessen, was man früher wusste, aber vergessen hatte, bedeutet, so haben diejenigen, die ἐν ἐπιγνώσει Gottes kommen, ihn schon früher gekannt.[92] Hieronymus

---

86 Vgl. 453Df. zu Eph 1,10, 457B zu Eph 1,14, 485Aff. zu Eph 3,13 (vgl. XIV.22ff.), 504Df. zu Eph 4,19 (vgl. XVIII.18ff.), 505C-D zu 1 Thess 4,6, 522C zu Eph 5,6, 540A zu Eph 6,4, 542C zu Eph 6,6, 542D zu Eph 6,10.

87 487C-D zu Eph 3,14, 513B zu Eph 4,29, 530C zu Eph 5,22.

88 441A-442C, insbesondere 442A, und 513Cff. Deniau, *art cit.*,164 mit Anm. 3, zeigt, dass dieses Verständnis des Epheserbriefs besonders charakteristisch für Origenes war. Er weist u.a. auf VIII.11-21, XXXIII.31ff., Cat. in 1 Cor. XVIII.1-16 (hg. C. Jenkins, JTS 9 (1908) 354) und *De Princ.* III.2.4 hin.

89 z. B. 455B-C zu Eph 1,12 (zu *ante sperauimus*); 495B-C zu Eph 4,4 (*Aut certe - reformabimur*).

90 z. B. 493A zu Eph 4,1 (*Est et alia expositio, quae recipienda sit, necne, erit in potestate lectoris*); vgl. 478A zu Eph 3,1 (*licet quidam ...*).

91 539A zu Eph 6,1ff. (*iuxta quosdam, qui antequam in corpora ista descendant, animas degere in caelestibus arbitrantur ...*); 548B zu Eph 6,12 (*Aiunt quidam ...*; vielleicht sind diese aber die eben erwähnten Philosophen).

92 IX.25-29 εἰ γὰρ μὴ ταὐτόν ἐστι γνῶσις θεοῦ καὶ ἐπίγνωσις θεοῦ ἀλλ' ὁ ἐπιγινώσκων οἱονεὶ ἀναγνωρίζει ὃ πάλαι εἰδὼς ἐπελέλητο, ὅσοι ἐν ἐπιγνώσει γίνονται θεοῦ πάλαι ἤδεσαν αὐτόν.

erweitert diese Beobachtung mit der Erklärung, dass diejenigen, die dies so verstehen, an ein früheres Leben im Himmel denken, aus dem sie in die Körper dieses Lebens gefallen sind.[93] Es fragt sich, ob Hieronymus diese Erklärung auf eigene Initiative zur Verdeutlichung des Hintergrunds des Gedankens hinzugesetzt hat, oder einen Anlass dazu irgendwo im nicht mehr erhaltenen Text des Origenes gefunden hatte. Zu Eph 2,4 ("wir waren Kinder des Zornes von Natur") wird dagegen eine Erklärung, welche denselben Gedankenkomplex voraussetzt, nicht nur von Hieronymus ohne Kritik oder Erläuterung übersetzt, sondern ohne Bedenken in den eigenen Mund genommen.[94] Ähnlich übernimmt er zu Eph 4,13 eine Exegese des Origenes, welche allem Anschein nach den Universalismus impliziert.[95] Ein anderes Beispiel zeigt, wie falsch es wäre, sogenannte 'origenistische' Ansichten, die Hieronymus kritisiert, einfach Origenes zuzuschreiben. Zu Eph 5,6 wendet sich Hieronymus gegen diejenigen, die behaupten, es werde keine Strafen für die Sünden geben. Der Katenenauszug zeigt, dass er dies schon bei Origenes vorfand.[96]

---

[93] 459A-B *quidam sic intelligunt, ut inter* γνῶσιν *et* ἐπίγνωσιν, *hoc est inter notionem et agnitionem, illud intersit: quod notio eorum sit quae ante non sciuimus, et ea postea scire coepimus. Agnitio uero eorum quae prius scientes deinceps scire desiuimus, eorumque postea recordamur, et priorem quandam uitam in caelestibus suspicantur, post quam in corpora ista deiecti et obliti Dei patris, nunc eum per reuelationem cognouimus.*

[94] IX.221-4 ἡμεῖς δὲ οἰόμεθα διὰ τὸ σῶμα τῆς ταπεινώσεως γεγονέναι τέκνα φύσει ὀργῆς. 467B *Nos uero dicimus secundum primum omnes homines natura filii irae, uel propter corpus humilitatis corpusque mortis* ...

[95] XVII.50ff. τίνες πάντες καταντήσομεν εἰς τὴν ἑνότητα τῆς πίστεως ζητητέον, πότερον πάντες ἀπαξαπλῶς ἄνθρωποι, ἢ ἡμεῖς οἱ κληρωθέντες ἐν Χριστῷ. δόξει δὲ πρὸς τὸ πρότερον ἀποδεδόσθαι ... 501A *Quaerendum quos omnes dixerit occurrere in unitate fidei: Utrumnam omnes homines, an omnes sanctos, an certe omnes qui rationis capaces sunt? Uidetur autem mihi de omnibus hominibus dicere* ... Interessanterweise fehlen die Worte *an certe omnes qui rationis capaces sunt* im Katenenauszug - wohl aus Vorsicht, wegen der damit verbundenen Frage der Rettung des Teufels.

[96] 522B-C *Quia igitur sunt plerique qui dicunt, non futura esse supplicia* (und dass die Sünde selbst und das schlechte Gewissen an die Stelle einer Strafe trete) *Has itaque persuasiones et decipulas fraudulentas uerba inania appellauit.* XXV.2-4 κενοὺς ἔοικε φάσκειν λόγους τοὺς διά τινος πιθανότητος ἀνατρέπειν θέλοντας τὸν περὶ τῶν προσαγομένων τοῖς κακῶς βεβιωκόσι κολάσεων λόγον· ἀπάτης γ' οὖν φησιν εἶναι τοὺς τοιούτους λόγους καὶ κενούς. Wahrscheinlich hat der Katenist nach λόγον einige Sätze ausgelassen.

Hieronymus hatte seine Pauluskommentare geschrieben, als seine Begeisterung für Origenes noch unvermindert anhielt.[97] Später während der origenistischen Streitigkeiten wurde diese frühere Begeisterung ihm zum Vorwurf gemacht. In einem Brief, in dem er seine Empörung über die Verfahrensweise Rufins in der *De Principiis*-Übersetzung ausdrückt, ruft er seine Gegner auf, seinen Epheserbriefkommentar durchzublättern - dann werden sie merken, dass er sich immer gegen die Lehren des Origenes gestellt habe.[98] Rufin (im ersten Buch seiner *Apologia contra Hieronymum*) hat ihn beim Wort genommen. Er wählte sechzehn Stellen aus, in denen Hieronymus in diesem Kommentar origenistische Lehren entweder aus eigenem Mund oder durch einen *quidam* oder *alius* vorträgt.[99] In seiner Antwort, die angeblich nur auf mündliche Berichte über den Inhalt der Rufin'schen Schrift basierte, verteidigte Hieronymus sechs dieser Stellen.[100] Es ist wichtig, sich klar zu machen, dass weder Rufin noch Hieronymus über die Art der Quellenbenutzung in diesem Kommentar informieren will. Die Absicht Rufins ist es zu zeigen, dass Hieronymus dieselben Lehren vorträgt, deretwegen er Origenes verurteilt, während Hieronymus dagegen beweisen will, dass er von solchen Lehren immer

---

[97] Vgl. Ferd. Cavallera, *Saint Jérôme, sa vie et son oeuvre* I.2, Louvain 1922, 115ff. (über 'Saint Jérôme et Origène'). Zu der Stellung des Hieronymus noch im Jahre 393 vgl. den wichtigen Aufsatz von Yves-Marie Duval, *Jérôme et Origène avant la querelle origéniste. La cure et la guérison ultime du monde et du diable dans l'In Nahum*, in *Augustinianum* 24 (1984) 471-494, insbesondere 471-3 und 492-4 (mit dem Schluss: "Même s'il en atténue les affirmations ou les hypothèses les plus audacieuses, Jérôme est loin encore de les condamner").

[98] *Ep.* 84.2 (an Pammachius und Oceanus), hg. I. Hilberg, CSEL 55 (Wien 1912) 122.6-9, *quodsi uolunt super Origene meum scire iudicium ... replicent in epistulam ad Ephesios tria uolumina, et intellegent me semper eius dogmatibus contra isse*; so auch schon in seinem früheren Brief an Vigilantius (*Ep.* 61.2).

[99] *Ap. contra Hieronymum* I.22-45 (zitiert nach der Ausgabe von M. Simonetti, CCL 20 (Turnhout 1961) 37-123. Er weist auch auf eine solche Stelle im Philemonbriefkommentar hin (*Ap. contra Hieronymum* I.42.23-28).

[100] *Ap. contra Rufinum* I.21-29 (zitiert nach der Ausgabe von Pierre Lardet, *Sources Chrétiennes* 303 (Paris 1983)).Vgl. zu dieser Auseinandersetzung Deniau, art. cit., 168-172, Kazimierz Romaniuk, *Une controverse entre saint Jérôme et Rufin d'Aquilée à propos de saint Paul aux Ephésiens*, in *Aegyptus* 43 (1963) 84-106, und E. A. Clark, *The Place of Jerome's Commentary on Ephesians in the Origenist Controversy: the Apokatastasis and Ascetic Ideals*, in *Vigiliae Christianae* 41 (1987) 154-171. Romaniuk stellt die Frage, ob Hieronymus wirklich zu jener Zeit 'Origenist' war. Clark richtet ihr Interesse auch hauptsächlich auf die theologische Entwicklung des Hieronymus.

Abstand nahm.[101] Es ist unwahrscheinlich, dass Rufin oder Hieronymus bei der Abfassung ihrer Streitschriften Einblick in die griechischen Quellen des Kommentars nahmen. Das einzige angebliche Origeneszitat, das Hieronymus bringt, hat er nicht frisch übersetzt, sondern wörtlich aus seinem eigenen Kommentar abgeschrieben.[102] Er bezeichnet einige origenistische Stellen aus seinem Kommentar als die Meinung des Origenes und andere harmlose Stellen als seine eigene Meinung; es lässt sich aber zeigen, dass er aller Wahrscheinlichkeit nach auch die harmlosen Stellen aus Origenes übernommen hatte.[103] Was in diesem Zusammenhang sehr interessant ist, ist die Weise, in der die beiden Gegner sich über die Methoden eines biblischen Kommentars äussern. Beide setzen sich mit der Gewohnheit, verschiedene Exegesen unter den Bezeichnungen *alius, qui-*

---

[101] Hinsichtlich der sechs behandelten Stellen versucht Hieronymus in fünf Fällen zu zeigen, dass er selbst Abstand genommen hatte (*Ap.* I.22.13-15, 60-62; 24.4-5; 25.18ff.; 27.1-6, 13ff.; 28.11-15, 29.1ff.). In drei Fällen meint er, dass die von Rufin angegriffene Äusserung sowieso harmlos sei (*Ap.* I.23.1-3,25ff.; 25.28ff.; 29.12ff.).

[102] *Ap.* I.28.16-32 (= 534A.2-B.4).

[103] (1) Zu Eph 1,4:- 446C.9-D.2, wird von Hieronymus als seine eigene Meinung und derjenigen des Origenes entgegengesetzt bezeichnet (*Ap.* I.22.1-15). Die Herkunft aus Origenes wird aber durch die Parallele zur Exegese von Rm 1,1 in *Philokalie* XXV (hg. J. Armitage Robinson, *The Philocalia of Origen*, Cambridge 1893, 226) bestätigt. Auch sonst im Epheserbriefkommentar erwähnt Origenes die πρόγνωσις θεοῦ; vgl. VIII.48-9, X.1-2, XI.11-12. Was 448A.6 - B.5 (*Ap.* I.22.45ff.) angeht, so bringt III.1-12 ähnlichen Stoff offensichtlich aus demselben Zusammenhang. Es fehlen aber im Katenenauszug alle Hinweise auf die Präexistenz einschliesslich des Satzes, in dem auf ein Argument gegen die vorangehende diesbezügliche Erklärung hingewiesen wird. Man möchte annehmen, dass der Katenist dies deswegen ausgelassen hat, weil auch die vorangehende Erklärung bei ihm fehlt.
(2) Zu Eph 2,7:- 469A.11-C.1 (*Ap.* I 24.1-5 *nos triplicem expositionem posuimus: in prima quid nobis uideretur, in secunda quid Origenes opponeret ...*). Der zweite Teil (469C.1ff.) ist nicht dem ersten entgegengesetzt, sondern setzt den ersten voraus. Es haben also beide dieselbe Quelle.
(3) Zu Eph 3,1ff.:- 477C.11-D.1 (*Ap.* I 25.6-23). Hieronymus nimmt hier die Beziehung auf die geschichtliche Lage des Paulus, über die er schon vorher im Philemonbriefkommentar geschrieben hatte, als seine eigene Meinung in Anspruch. Aller Wahrscheinlichkeit nach stammt beides aus Origenes.
(4) Zu Eph 5,29:- 533C.10-14 (*Ap.* I.28.6, 29.1ff.). Hieronymus beschreibt die in seinem Kommentar als *simplex intelligentia* bezeichnete Erklärung als seine eigene und behauptet, er habe in den Worten, *Magis itaque ad tropicam intelligentiam sermo referatur* (*Ap.* I.28.11-15) seine Ablehnung des folgenden gezeigt (!). Die Katenenauszüge zeigen, dass Origenes selbst oft auf diese Weise erst eine einfachere, und dann eine 'geistige' oder weniger einfache Erklärung bringt; vgl. oben Anm. 67 und 72. Wahrscheinlich gehen also auch in diesem Fall beide auf ihn zurück.
Deniau, *art. cit.* 171, urteilt im allgemeinen ähnlich.

XV

dam usw. einzuführen, auseinander. Nach Rufin ist dies als eine *rhetorica figura* anzusehen, die bei Rednern gewöhnlich ist, wenn sie, um Anstoss zu vermeiden, in der Person eines anderen die eigene Meinung äussern. Wenn der in einem Kommentar als *quidam* oder *alius* bezeichnete fingierte Sprecher nicht widerlegt oder als Häretiker angegriffen wird, sondern seine Meinung durch Bibelstellen belegt wird, so ist er als ein zweites "ich" zu betrachten. Origenes habe auch selbst diese Gewohnheit gehabt und könne ebensogut wie Hieronymus dadurch entschuldigt werden. Er sei aber viel vorsichtiger als Hieronymus gewesen.[104] Während Origenes über solche Fragen sich immer behutsam und vorsichtig durch den Mund eines fingierten Sprechers geäussert habe, habe Hieronymus sich nicht gescheut, verborgene Geheimnisse zu verkünden, alsob ein Engel aus dem Himmel oder Christus selbst durch ihn spräche.[105]

Was die Wiederholung der gefährlichen Theorien des Origenes angeht, so gibt Hieronymus zu, dass er bei seiner Zusammenfassung der Worte des Origenes ihren Sinn offengelegt habe, d. h. er hat, wie man bei der Lektüre des Kommentars bald bemerkt, die gefährlichen Vermutungen des Origenes manchmal offener und drastischer wiedergegeben als er sie bei Origenes selbst vorfand.[106] Zu der Frage der Aufgabe des Exegeten behauptet Hieronymus, dass der Exeget die Meinungen vieler Vorgänger zusammen mit den Begründungen dafür wiederholen sollte, damit der Leser selbst ein eigenes Urteil fassen könne. Rufin müsste diese Methode aus der Schulzeit bekannt sein - er habe sicher damals die Kommentare der verschiedenen Grammatiker über die lateinischen Klassiker gelesen.[107]

[104] *Ap. contra Hieronymum* I.30.8-31. Vgl. Duval, *art. cit.*, 493: 'On n'oubliera cependant qu'Origène lui-même est rarement catégorique et qu'il enveloppe souvent ses hypothèses dans de prudentes atténuations'.

[105] Vgl. *Ap. contra Hieronymum* I.45.14ff.

[106] *Ap.* I.22.35-45, insbesondere 37-8, *lectori sensum eius aperuerim*. Die Stelle, worauf dies sich bezieht, ist 447B1ff.: *Itaque priusquam animae, inquiunt, praecipitarentur in mundum ... .* Vgl. auch *Ap.* I.26.6-9, und oben S. 201f. mit Anm. 91 und 93.

[107] *Ap.* I.16.15ff.; vgl. auch oben Anm. 49. Er wiederholt dieselbe Behauptung im Vorwort zum Jeremiaskommentar (CCL 74 (1960) 1-2). Zu dieser Auffassung eines Kommentars vgl. Neuschäfer, *op. cit.*, 351 Anm. 277. Für weitere Aussagen des Hieronymus über die Aufgabe und Methoden eines Kommentars vgl. Jay, *op. cit.* (oben Anm. 3), 69ff.

In ihren eben zitierten Urteilen verfahren weder Rufin noch
Hieronymus unvoreingenommen.[108] Rufin schreibt, alsob Hieronymus für
das in seinem Kommentar Geschriebene allein verantwortlich wäre,
obwohl Hieronymus doch manchmal etwas mehr Abstand von den Aussagen des Origenes genommen hatte als Rufin zugibt. Hieronymus dagegen möchte den Eindruck geben, dass er auch dort, wo er verschiedene
Vorschläge des Origenes übersetzte, die Meinungen mehrerer Exegeten
zitierte, dass also nur die 'origenistischen' Äusserungen aus Origenes selbst
stammten und dass er sich selbst immer dagegen gesetzt hatte. In Wirk-
lichkeit aber scheint Hieronymus den grössten Teil seines Kommentars
fast ausschliesslich aus Origenes geschöpft zu haben und die 'origenistischen' Irrtümer, die er darin angedeutet vorfand, manchmal bedenkenlos
selbst übernommen, manchmal einem *quidam* zugeschrieben in ver-
gröberter und übertriebener Form summarisch wiedergegeben zu haben.

Was das Zitieren der Ansichten verschiedener Sprecher angeht, so hat
Rufin wohl recht, dass im Falle des Origenes dies ein rhetorisches Mittel
ist, um eigene Vorschläge und Vermutungen einzuführen. Bei seiner
Übersetzung des Kommentars des Origenes hat Hieronymus dieses Mittel
übernommen. Nichtdestoweniger ist es nicht unwichtig, dass er dadurch
den Eindruck erwecken will, dass er mehrere frühere Exegeten zitiert.
Dadurch gibt er ein methodisches Vorbild für spätere lateinische Exegeten.

Zusammenfassend können wir also schliessen, dass die wissenschaftliche
Leistung des Hieronymus in diesen Kommentaren eine zweifache ist.
Erstens macht er durch seine philologische Erläuterung der Sprache des
Paulus seine lateinischen Leser mit den Methoden eines wissenschaftlichen
griechischen Bibelkommentars bekannt und zweitens lehrt er sie, sowohl
durch sein Beispiel wie auch durch seine Aussagen über seine Methode,
dass es die Aufgabe des Exegeten ist, über die Meinungen verschiedener
Vorgänger zu berichten.

Es seien zum Abschluss die Urteile von Souter und Harnack über diese
Kommentare zitiert. Nach Souter: "The commentaries hold their commanding position, because their author approached his task with a well-
furnished mind and a perfectly trained pen, with a knowledge of Greek
and Hebrew as well as Latin, with a determination to use the very best

---

[108] Vgl. aber den Urteil von Cavallera, *op. cit.*, 99, "Les textes cités par Rufin
sont exacts et les laborieuses explications de Jérôme ... ne donnent pas pleine
satisfaction".

authorities at his command, with a fine care for the diction of Scripture in the three languages, and for the true text ... and above all, with a live intellect and a real Christian faith. Our investigation has indeed shown ... that his work is compilation, but the whole has passed through his mind and bears the stamp of his peculiar genius".[109] Harnack druckt sich weniger positiv aus, schätzt den Wert der Kommentare aber ähnlich hoch ein. Zum Galaterbriefkommentar schreibt er: "Wer sich gründlich mit den Kommentaren und Homilien des Orig. beschäftigt hat, den mutet dieser Kommentar des Hieron. inhaltlich wie ein kastriertes und um seinen wissenschaftlichen und christlichen Ernst gebrachtes, stark, aber flüchtig aufgeputztes Werk des Origenes an"; und zu allen vier: "Die vier grossen Kommentare des Hieron. zu vier Paulusbriefen gehören als Leistungen des Hieron. zu den unerfreulichsten Früchten seiner Schriftstellerei; aber sie sind mit Recht vom Abendland als unschätzbar beurteilt worden; denn es empfing in ihnen einen Reichtum wissenschaftlicher und erbaulicher Bibelerkenntnis, mit dem sich nichts vergleichen lässt, was es selbst aufzubringen vermochte. Dieser Reichtum ... gebührt in der Hauptsache ausschliesslich dem Origenes."[110]

Sind diese Kommentare auch ein unverschämtes Plagiat, [111] so müssen wir doch für jedes Bruchstück des grossen Meisters, den Hieronymus so hoch lobte und so scharf tadelte, auf welche Weise es auch immer auf uns gekommen ist, überaus dankbar sein.

---

[109] Souter, op. cit. 137-8.

[110] Harnack, op. cit., 147 und 168.

[111] Vgl. dazu auch Rufin, De adulteratione librorum Origenis 14 (hg. Simonetti, 16.10-16): Sed quod auctores obtrectatorum eius hi sunt qui uel in ecclesia disputare latius solent, uel etiam libros scribere, qui totum de Origene, uel loquuntur uel scribunt, ne ergo plures ipsorum furta cognoscant, quae utique, si ingrati in magistrum non essent, nequaquam criminosa uiderentur, simpliciores quosque ab eius lectione deterrent.

XVI

PAULINE EXEGESIS, MANICHAEISM AND PHILOSOPHY IN THE EARLY AUGUSTINE

Augustine tells us that after the 'conversion' effected in him by the perusal of Platonist books he turned to the writings of the apostle Paul and found confirmation there of the truth he had perceived. This information is given not only in the *Confessions* (7.21 *auidissime arripui ... prae ceteris apostolum Paulum ... et inueni quidquid illac uerum legeram, hac cum conmendatione gratiae tuae dici*), but also in the earlier *Contra Academicos* (2.2.5 *titubans properans haesitans arripio apostolum Paulum ... perlegi totum intentissime atque castissime. tunc uero quantulocumque iam lumine adsperso tanta se mihi philosophiae facies aperuit ...*).[1] Paul however was also the apostle of the Manichees. Augustine was not merely combining Platonist insights with a return to his childhood religion,[2] he was also replacing his earlier Manichaean reading of Paul with a new 'Platonising' understanding.[3]

The aim of this paper[4] is to examine firstly the Manichaean use of Paul which is likely to have been familiar to Augustine during his Manichaean period and secondly the new understanding apparent in his ear-

---

[1] Cf. also *De Beata Vita* 1.4, where he speaks of the Christian scriptures in general: lectis autem Plotini paucissimis libris ... conlataque cum eis, quantum potui, etiam illorum auctoritate, qui diuina mysteria tradiderunt, sic exarsi ... On these passages cf. John J. O'Meara, "Arripui, aperui, et legi", *Augustinus Magister. Congrès International Augustinien*, Paris, 21-24 Septembre 1954, 59-65.

[2] Cf. *Contra Academicos* 2.2.5: *respexi tamen, confitebor, quasi de itinere in illam religionem, quae pueris nobis insita est et medullitus inplicata; uerum autem ipsa ad se nescientem rapiebat.*

[3] Cf. *Contra Academicos* 1.1.3: *ipsa (philosophia) me penitus ab illa superstitione ... liberauit; Contra Academicos* 3.20.43: *apud Platonicos me interim, quod sacris nostris non repugnet, reperturum esse confido.* In *Confessions* 7.21 Augustine states that on his rereading of Paul the supposed internal contradictions and disagreements with the law and prophets disappeared.

[4] It supplements a paper on 'Augustine, Origen and the Exegesis of St. Paul' (now published in *Augustinianum* 32 (1992), 341-368) which I delivered at the Oxford Patristic Conference in 1991 and also at the Patristic Seminar in Cambridge, where Christopher Stead kindly commented on it.

2

liest writings after his conversion and to relate this to the change in the structure of his philosophical approach. The writings considered will be those up to and including the *De Moribus Ecclesiae Catholicae et de Moribus Manichaeorum,* which is the first explicitly anti-Manichaean treatise and also the first to make extensive use of Pauline quotations.[5] Since we have no Manichaean writings composed by Augustine I will use his anti-Manichaean writings as evidence for the kinds of views he was familiar with as a Manichee himself.[6]

The Use of Paul in African Manichaeism as known to Augustine

Augustine[7] has preserved a considerable amount of Manichaean material in his anti-Manichaean writings, in particular the *Contra Faustum,* where he quotes Faustus' book against the Catholic Christians in full,[8] the *Contra Adimantum,* in which he summarises Adimantus' attack on the law and the prophets point by point, and the records of his debates at Hippo with Fortunatus and Felix.[9] In addition Augustine's *Opus Imperfectum* reproduces part of the *Epistle to Menoch* suposedly by Mani, which had been quoted by Julian.[10]

---

[5] Maria Grazia Mara bases her article 'Agostino e la polemica antimanichea: il ruolo di Paolo e del suo epistolario', *Augustinianum* 32 (1992), 119-143, on later writings of Augustine than those considered here.

[6] On Augustine's Manichaeism cf. e.g. Henry Chadwick, 'The attractions of Mani', in *Compostellanum* 34.1-2 (1989), 203-222, reprinted in *Heresy and Orthodoxy in the Early Church* (Aldershot 1991), Erich Feldmann, 'Christus-Frömmigkeit der Mani-Jünger', in ed. Ernst Dassmann and K. Suso Frank, *Pietas. Festschrift für Bernhard Kötting* (Münster 1980), 198-216. On Augustine's early acquaintance with the bible cf. A.-M. la Bonnardière, 'L'initiation biblique d'Augustin', in *Saint Augustin et la Bible* (Paris 1986), 27-47.

[7] F. Decret gives a table of Pauline references by Fortunatus, Faustus and Felix in his *Aspects du Manichéisme dans l'Afrique romaine* (Paris 1970), 171-2, and gives a fuller discussion than is possible here of the use of Paul by Manichaeans in Africa in 'L'utilisation des Épîtres de Paul chez les Manichéens d'Afrique' in J. Ries etc., *Le Epistole Paoline nei manichei, i donatisti e il primo Agostino* (Rome 1989), 29-83.

[8] Faustus, who provides the fullest account of African Manichaean teachings, was much admired by the Manichees with whom Augustine had associated (according to *Confessions* 5.6.10).

[9] The following references to these writings are to the edition by J. Zycha (Vienna 1891).

[10] On this epistle cf. G. J. D. Aalders, 'L'Épître à Menoch, attribuée à Mani', *Vigiliae Christianae* 14 (1960), 245-9.

XVI

PAULINE EXEGESIS, MANICHAEISM AND PHILOSOPHY   3

Adimantus and Faustus make clear the scriptural basis on which the Manichees relied in attacking the 'Jewish superstition' and 'Semi-Christianity'[11] of their Catholic opponents. The Old Testament is the property of the Jews, the repository of alien promises (*Contra Faustum* 10.1, p.310.10 ff., 18), its prophecies did not refer to Jesus (*Contra Faustum* 12.1, p.329.1 ff.). Adimantus' list of its contradictions with the New Testament make clear the gulf between its teachings and the Christian Gospel. To accept the Gospel however means not a literal belief in all that is written in it but obedience to its precepts (*Contra Faustum* 5.1-2, p. 271.13-15, 272.8-11). The Gospel accounts were written not by Jesus himself or his apostles, but long after by certain unknown 'semi-Jews', who attached the names of apostles or followers of apostles to their own compositions (*Contra Faustum* 32.2, p.761.17-22, 33.3, p.788.16-23). This critical view of the Gospels must give greater weight to Paul. Mani's own letters imitate the style of Paul, and the use of the Acts of Paul contributes to his favourable image.[12] On the other hand both Gospels and Pauline Epistles have been interpolated (*Contra Faustum* 18.3, p.491.27 ff.)[13] and Paul himself wrote as one with imperfect knowledge. Faustus quotes *2 Corinthians* 5.16-17 and *1 Corinthians* 13.11 to show Paul's progress from an old and inferior confession to a new and better one (*Contra Faustum* 11.1, pp.313-4). Manichees are taught by the Paraclete which parts of the New Testament are to be accepted and which rejected (*Contra Faustum* 32.6). Thus Felix argues in his debate with Augustine that the promised Paraclete only came in the person of Mani and was not yet present in Paul, who claims only to know in part (*1 Corinthians* 13.9; *Contra Felicem* 1.2, p.802, 1.9, p.811).

Adimantus' proof of the incompatibility of Old and New Testaments is based primarily on Gospel verses, but Paul also plays an important role. *1 Timothy* 6.16 and 1.17 are of central importance[14] as showing that God dwells in unapproachable light and is invisible, unlike the Old

---

[11] Faustus in *Contra Faustum* 1.2, p.251.23.

[12] On Mani's own attitude to Paul cf. J. Ries, 'Saint Paul dans la formation de Mani', in J. Ries etc. (*op. cit. n.7*), 7-27, and F. Decret, *ibid*, 29-40, Hans Dieter Betz, 'Paul in the Mani Biography', in ed. Luigi Cirillo, *Codex Manichaicus Coloniensis* (Marra editore Cosenza 1986), 215-234.

[13] Faustus gives alternative explanations of Pauline verses he dislikes (*Romans* 1.3, *1 Timothy* 4.14 ff., *Titus* 1.15), suggesting that they are either spurious or represent an earlier incorrect view or must be explained differently (*Contra Faustum* 11.1, pp.313-4, 30.1, p.748, 31.1, p.756).

[14] Faustus also appeals to *1 Timothy* 6.16 at *Contra Faustum* 20.2, p.536.12-13.

XVI

4

Testament 'demon of the Jews'[15] (*Contra Adimantum* 10, p.134.19-20 and 28, p.187.21-2), and *1 Corinthians* 14.33 as showing that he is a peace-loving God, not one who delights in battles (*Contra Adimantum* 20, p.179.9-11). *Colossians* 1.15-16 is used to contrast the creation through Christ with that described in *Genesis* 1 (*Contra Adimantum* 1, p.116.9-15). The Manichaean dualist anthropology, according to which God is author only of the good soul, not of the body and the 'fleshly' soul,[16] can be supported by *1 Corinthians* 15.50 ('flesh and blood will not inherit the kingdom of God'),[17] and Adimantus sets this verse against the Old Testament understanding that 'the soul of flesh is blood' (*Deuteronomy* 12.23, *Contra Adimantum* 12, p.138.8-23). The rejection of the Old Testament law with its prescription of circumcision and observance of days, years and seasons is confirmed by Paul in *1 Corinthians* 7.18-19, *Galatians* 5.12, and *Galatians* 4.10-11 (*Contra Adimantum* 16, p.161.10-17, 162.4-6, 13-15). For the Manichaean vegetarianism and refusal to drink wine, so contrary to the spirit of *Deuteronomy* 12.15 ff., Adimantus can appeal to *Romans* 14.21 and *1 Corinthians* 10.21 (*Contra Adimantum* 14, p.148.1-11).

In rejecting the Old Testament Faustus appeals to the example of the apostles and in particular to Paul's rebuke of the Galatians for their reversion to circumcision and to servitude to the 'weak and beggarly elements' (*Galatians* 4.9). To accept the Old Testament would be to abandon Christ's gift of liberty and to put on the yoke of bondage from which he freed us (*Galatians* 5.1, *Contra Faustum* 8.1, pp.305-6). Even the Catholics ignore most parts of the Old Testament, regarding them, in Paul's words of *Philippians* 3.8, as dung, claims Faustus (*Contra Faustum* 32.1, p.761.3). The contents of the Old Testament are alien and both Old and New Testaments forbid the coveting of alien goods (*Exodus* 20.17, *Romans* 7.7, *Contra Faustum* 10.1, p.310). Moses is to be rejected because he cursed 'everyone who hangs on a tree' (*Deuteronomy* 21.13); and that this really does refer to the crucifixion of Christ and subsequent Christian martyrs is shown by Paul in *Galatians* 3.13 (*Contra Faustum* 14.1, p.404.2-7). Christians should serve Christ alone,

---

[15] This designation is used by Faustus, *Contra Faustum* 18.2, p.491.6; cf. also 25.1, p.726.6-9 (the god of Abraham, Isaac and Jacob just one among many gods).

[16] Cf. the *Epistle to Menoch* quoted by Julian in Augustine, *Opus Imperfectum* 3.174-6, ed. M. Zelzer (Vienna 1974), 475f., and Augustine, *De Duabus Animabus* 1 and *Retractationes* 15 on the *De Duabus Animabus*.

[17] Quoted also by Fortunatus in Augustine, *Contra Fortunatum* 19, p.97.6-7.

following Paul, who said 'Our sufficiency is of God, who has made us suitable ministers of the New Testament' (2 *Corinthians* 3.5-6, *Contra Faustum* 15.1, p.417.5-9).

Faustus' view of the relationship between Judaism and Christianity is expressed most forcefully in his exposition of *Romans* 7.2-3. These verses show that those who unite themselves to Christ without previously repudiating the author of the law commit spiritual adultery. This applies particularly to Jews, who should regard their god as dead when converted to belief in Christ. A gentile who gives up his idolatry and then worships both the god of the Hebrews and Christ is no different from a woman who after the death of one husband marries two others (*Contra Faustum* 15.1, p.417.12-418.5).

Faustus' negative attitude to the Old Testament is apparent in his explanation of Paul's statements about the law in the Epistle to the Romans. He distinguishes three kinds of laws, firstly the law of the Hebrews referred to as the 'law of sin and death' in *Romans* 8.2, secondly the law of the gentiles, referred to as the 'natural law' in *Romans* 2.14-15, and thirdly the 'law of the spirit of truth in Christ Jesus' of *Romans* 8.2 (*Contra Faustum* 19.2, p.497.17-25). The law which Jesus came to fulfil was not the Jewish law, but more ancient precepts ('thou shalt not kill, thou shalt not commit adultery, thou shalt not bear false witness'), which had been promulgated in early times among the nations by Enoch, Seth and other righteous men (*Contra Faustum* 19.3, pp.498-9). This ancient law was corrupted by the Hebrew writers who infected it with their disgusting precepts about circumcision and sacrifices (*Contra Faustum* 22.2, pp.591.15-592.3).

Similarly, in Faustus' view, there are three kinds of prophets, the prophets of the Jews, the prophets of the gentiles, referred to by Paul in *Titus* 1.12, and the prophets of the truth, referred to in *1 Corinthians* 12.28 (cf. also *Ephesians* 4.11; *Contra Faustum* 19.2, pp.497-8). Faustus does not think that the Hebrew prophets prophesied Christ, but if they did know and foretell Christ the criminal nature of their lives would mean that Paul's words in *Romans* 1.21 about the wise men of the gentiles would apply to them (12.1, pp.329-30).

Faustus supports the Manichaean belief in two principles, God and 'Hyle' or the devil, by a reference to *2 Corinthians* 4.4, explaining that Paul calls the hostile substance 'the god of this age', because its worshippers call it 'god' (*Contra Faustum* 21.1, p.569.11-18). He applies *1 Timothy* 6.16 to God the Father, as dwelling in unapproachable light and *1 Corinthians* 1.24 to the Son, asserting that, since the Son is

6

twofold, as God's power and God's wisdom, his power dwells in the sun and his wisdom in the moon (*Contra Faustum* 20.2, p.536.11-17). Faustus' understanding of anthropology and of conversion is illuminated by Pauline verses which contrast the old man and the new man. Paul makes clear that there are two men (in each person) which he calls outer and inner (*2 Corinthians* 4.16, *Romans* 7.22, *Ephesians* 3.16), earthly and heavenly (*1 Corinthians* 15.47-9) and old and new (*Romans* 6.6, *Ephesians* 2.15, *Ephesians* 4.22-4, *Colossians* 3.9-10) (*Contra Faustum* 24.1, pp.717-21). It is not the outer, earthly or old man, but the inner, heavenly and new man that is formed by God according to his own image, and it is not at our first carnal birth that God thus creates us but at our conversion and rebirth in the spirit (*Ephesians* 4.22-24 and *Colossians* 3.9-10). At the time of this new birth we put off differences of sex, race and status, and are made one in the likeness of Christ (*Colossians* 3.11; *Galatians* 3.27-8). Paul refers to this second birth in *Galatians* 4.19, *1 Corinthians* 4.15, and, speaking of himself, in *Galatians* 1.15-16 (*Contra Faustum* 24.1, pp.717-721). In describing Manichaean spiritual worship Faustus states that he regards himself as the rational temple of God, alluding to Paul's words in *1 Corinthians* 3.16, *2 Corinthians* 6.16 and *Romans* 12.1 (*Contra Faustum* 20.3, p.537.17-18). Also Pauline is Faustus' view of the Manichaean church as the bride of Christ (*Contra Faustum* 15.1, p.416.8, cf. *Ephesians* 5.25-7, *2 Corinthians* 11.2, *Romans* 7.4).[18]

In his debates with Fortunatus and Felix Augustine attempts to press home his argument against the Manichaean position, that, if God is incorruptible, there can have been no reason for him to have sent souls, which consisted of part of his own substance, to be corrupted by evil. Against this Fortunatus and Felix assert Manichaean dualism and attempt to explain Manichaean anthropology, appealing not infrequently to Pauline verses for proof or illustration. Felix, in arguing that there is a power independent of God, which wars against God, quotes *Romans* 8.7 concerning the *prudentia carnis, 2 Corinthians* 4.4 on the *deus saeculi huius,* and *2 Corinthians* 12.7-9 on the *angelus satanae* (*Contra Felicem* 2.2, p.830). The power which holds us in captivity and

---

[18] An example of Manichaean misuse of Paul is the adaptation of *Galatians* 3.13b at *Contra Faustum* 20.2, p.336.21, to apply to the Manichaean teaching of the *Jesus patibilis* (*omni suspensus ex ligno*). Cf. on this Ludwig Koenen, 'Augustine and Manichaeism in Light of the Cologne Mani Codex', in *Illinois Classical Studies* 3 (1978), 178-9, and, for another example of Manichaean adaptation of Paul, 179 n. 101 (*Galatians* 3.13a).

from which Christ came to save us is not a power of God, since the
curse uttered against everyone who hangs on a tree, from which Christ
freed us, as described by Paul in *Galatians* 3.13, is surely not spoken by
a power of God (2.10, p.839).[19] Fortunatus makes fuller use of Pauline
quotations. When challenged by Augustine as to why God sent us here,
he quotes *Philippians* 2.5-8 and states that he understands this not only
of Christ, but also of the descent of human souls and their liberation
from 'this death, which is alien to God' (7, p.87.20-88.10). Maintaining
that there are two opposed substances in this world (14, p.91.5-18), he
quotes *Ephesians* 2.1-18 to support his view of the soul's captivity in
the evil substance and reconciliation to God through Christ (16, p.92.17-
93.13). *Ephesians* 2.3 ('we were by nature children of wrath') is therefore said of the body. The word 'enmity' in *Ephesians* 2.16 shows that
there is indeed a substance opposed to God, which 'enmity' Christ
'killed' when he freed our souls from it (16, p.95.9-21). Thus, whereas
Augustine, quoting *1 Timothy* 6.10,[20] claims that the root and source of
all evils is in human sinful desire (*Contra Fortunatum* 21, pp.100-101),
Fortunatus maintains that human sinful desire is only a small portion of
the evil present in the whole world (*Contra Fortunatum* 21, p.102). That
the human soul sins not by its own will but under compulsion from the
substance opposed to God is shown by Pauline verses describing the
hostility of the flesh to God, its lusting against the spirit, and the law in
our members which leads us captive to the law of sin and death (he
quotes *Romans* 8.7, *Galatians* 5.17, and *Romans* 7.23-25 combined with
Galatians 6.14b, *Contra Fortunatum* 21, p.103).[21] Souls were sent forth
against the hostile substance in order to subject it by their sufferings.
That evils are present not just in human bodies but in the whole world is
shown by Paul's words in *Ephesians* 6.12[22] about our struggle not only

---

[19] Other Pauline verses quoted by Felix are *Romans* 3.4 (*omnis homo mendax,
solus deus uerax*) used as an argument for relying on his scriptures (*Contra Felicem*
I.6, p.808.9) and *1 Corinthians* 13.9, as showing that the Paraclete was not in Paul
(*Contra Felicem* I.9, p.811.5-8).
[20] In the Latin version of this verse used by Augustine and Fortunatus (*radix omnium malorum est cupiditas*) the special reference of the Greek to the desire for
money has disappeared.
[21] Cf. also Augustine's own description in *Confessions* 5.10.18 of his earlier Manichaean view that *non esse nos qui peccamus sed nescio quam aliam in nobis peccare
naturam* (reminscent of *Romans* 7.17 and 20).
[22] Fortunatus' quotation alters the word order and omits *in caelestibus* .

8

against flesh and blood, but against the powers of darkness (*Contra Fortunatum* 22, p.107).[23]

During his period as a Manichaean hearer Augustine will have become familiar with Manichaean psalms similar to those preserved in the Coptic Manichaean Psalm-book from Egypt.[24] The Pauline allusions in these Psalms[25] include references to the 'old man' (3.31, 167.23-4) and the 'new man' (46.18, 88.2, 150.29), to the impediments against doing good caused by the flesh (135.11-12, cf. *Romans* 7.18),[26] to the god of this Aeon (56.31, 172.26-7; cf. *2 Corinthians* 4.4) and the rulers (?) of this Aeon (4.17; cf. *1 Corinthians* 2.8; cf. also the probable reference to *Ephesians* 6.16, 'the darts of the [evil one]', at 64.4-5). At 194.3 Christ's putting on the likeness of man is described with an allusion to *Philippians* 2.7. Pauline themes concerning law, commandments and judgement recur in these Psalms and the Pauline picture of the Christian life as a race is frequent.[27]

African Manichaeism and Philosophy

In the time of Augustine's youth Manichaeism was better equipped to answer philosophical objections to Christianity than was African Catholic Christianity. This aspect of Manichaeism can be illustrated from the work of Faustus. Although Faustus' *capitula* are written in answer to Catholic questions directed against Manichaeism they in fact present a religious system which meets and disarms many of the pagan criticisms of Christianity. This is not necessarily to claim that Faustus himself had elaborated his arguments in response to Platonist attacks. It may rather be the case that he inherited a tradition of argumentation which had been developed earlier by Manichees, Marcionites and Gnostics aware of

---

[23] As well as the Pauline verses mentioned above, Fortunatus also quotes *Romans* 9.20 as a response to Augustine's question why God sent us here (*Contra Fortunatum* 26, p.109.8-9). At *Contra Fortunatum* 16, p.95.13-14, he refers to Paul's description of his own ancestry in *Romans* 11.1.

[24] Cf. Feldmann (*op. cit. n. 6*), 207 ff.

[25] The following examples refer to the page and line numbers in *A Manichaean Psalm-Book,* Part II, ed. C. R. C. Allberry (Stuttgart 1938). A number of other Pauline verses are listed in Allberry's index, p.48*.

[26] Cf. also on the flesh the reference to *1 Corinthians* 15.50 at 121.9, and on the body that to *2 Corinthians* 5.6 at 135.21.

[27] Cf. Allberry's index (*op.cit. n. 25*) p.48* under *1 Timothy* 4.7; also pp.3* and 5* under ἐντολή and νόμος.

XVI

pagan philosophical objections to Christianity.[28] Since Porphyry's more detailed attack against the Christians does not survive, our fullest information about the features which Platonist philosophers found objectionable in Christianity comes from Celsus. In what follows therefore Faustus' position will be compared chiefly with Celsus' criticisms.[29]

An obvious point for attack on the Christians was their reliance on their own and the Jewish scriptures, and it was here that Porphyry went much further than Celsus. In this respect Faustus simply accepts and takes over the pagan criticisms. Thus he takes a negative view of Moses and the patriarchs and prophets (12.1, p.330.11-18, 14.1, pp.401-4, 22.1-5, pp.591-5, where however he suggests that the Old Testament stories may be slanders), he rejects the Old Testament (4.1, p.268, 15.1, pp.415-8), and its prophecies of Christ (12.1, pp.328-30, also 13.1, p.378.8, referring to pagan reactions to circular arguments about the witness of the prophets to Christ and vice versa), he attacks the genealogies of Jesus in Matthew and Luke (3.1, pp.261-2, 7.1, pp.302-3), and he asserts the unreliability of the Gospels (32.1-2, pp.760-2).

The particularity of the Christian view of salvation history, which Celsus found offensive,[30] is largely done away with by the rejection of any special role for Judaism (*Christianam nouitatem Hebraicae uetustati non misceo*—8.1; 9.1; 10.1, pp.305-6, 307 and 310; the god of Abraham the god only of the circumcised—25.1, pp.725-6; gentile prophets are more relevant to gentile converts—13.1-2, pp.377.20-2, 378.25-379.6; cf. also the more positive view of the *lex gentium* in 19.2, pp.497f.),[31] also by the Manichaean doctrine of the 'cosmic Jesus' (20.2, p.536.19-23), as well as by the fact (not mentioned by Faustus) that reincarnation gives repeated chances of salvation for the individual soul.

The Catholic attachment to the body, shown in the doctrines of incarnation and resurrection, is found particularly disgusting by Celsus.[32] This however is abandoned by the Manichees, since they view the fleshly nature as evil, and adopt a docetic Christology (29.1, p. 744.1-5).

---

[28] Cf. W. H. C. Frend, 'The Gnostic-Manichaean Tradition in Roman North Africa', *Journal of Ecclesiastical History* 4 (1953), 13-26, especially 20-22.

[29] As quoted in Origen, *Contra Celsum*, ed. P. Koetschau (Leipzig 1899).

[30] Cf. e.g. 5.41 (no special divine favour towards the Jews), 4.2-3, 6-7 and 6.78 (objections to the particularity of the incarnation), 3.71 and 6.53 (the Christian view implies unjust favouritism and incompetence in God's dealings with the human race), 4.23 (the arrogance of Jews and Christians).

[31] On Manichaean universalism cf. Decret (*op cit. n.7*), 39-40.

[32] Cf. 3.41-2, 7.13, 5.14, 8.49.

10

Another feature of Christian teaching which Celsus dislikes is the way it deals with the problem of evil—he states that 'In the existing world there is no decrease or increase of evils either in the past or in the present or in the future' (4.62), and rejects the idea of the devil (6.42) or that God 'inflicts correction on the world' (4.69), though he allows that the question is a difficult one (4.65) and that pagan myths 'hint at a sort of divine war' (6.42) and suggests that evils inhere in matter (4.66) and that the body is not made by God (4.52). It is here that Faustus claims complete originality for the Manichees, since the Manichaean belief in two principles, God as the origin of all good things, and 'hyle' as the origin of evil, separates them fundamentally both from pagans, who believe in a single principle as the source of all things, and from the Catholic Christians, who are merely a schism of paganism in this respect (20.3-4, pp.537-8). All these features together with the Manichaean spiritual worship (20.3-4, pp. 537.15-538.18), Christ-centered piety, and radical obedience to the Gospel precepts (5.13, pp.271-4) must have given Manichaeism considerable appeal.

In those of Augustine's early writings which are considered in the next section he not only gave evidence of his own philosophical dedication and developed a non-dualist explanation of the problem of evil on the basis of Christian Platonism, he also attempted to demonstrate the providential role of the Christian church and its teachings, showing that Catholic understanding of the Old Testament was far different from what the Manichees supposed and that even the doctrines of incarnation and resurrection could be accepted.

Augustine's earliest writings after his conversion

Augustine's *Confessions* tell us of his realisation at Milan, aided by Ambrose's sermons and the Platonist books, that God is incorporeal, unchangeable and the source of all existence, that his creation is good, and that evil is not a contrary substance but a turning away of the will from God.[33] His reading of Paul, according to *Confessions* 7.21.27, made him realise the need for divine grace to bring freedom from the power of sin[34] and healing that he might see and hold on to the divine vision. The *Confessions* were written from a position of hindsight in which later in-

---

[33] *Confessions* 7.16.22.
[34] He quotes *Romans* 7.22-5 and alludes also to other Pauline verses.

sights are not always clearly separated from the account of Augustine's spiritual and intellectual development before and after his conversion.[35] Augustine's earliest extant works, which were composed after his conversion during his retreat with his friends at Cassiciacum before his return to Milan for his baptism,[36] show him less immediately concerned with the exposition of new anti-Manichaean insights than with the refutation of the Academic position that truth is unattainable and the demonstration that his own search for truth is in accordance with the highest philosophy, that of Plato himself and Plotinus.[37] It is only in the more personal or biographical passages that hints of his newly found Christian faith are given.[38] In addition to his general assertions that all is governed by divine providence[39] he shows awareness of divine gui-

---

[35] The difference between the picture given by the *Confessions* and that of the dialogues written at Cassiciacum is caused not only by the changes in Augustine's perception between 386 and 397, but also by his different position and expectations about his readers (recently retired professor of rhetoric, or Christian bishop). There has been much debate about how great this difference is; earlier contributions to the question are conveniently described by John. J. O'Meara, 'Augustine and Neo-platonism', *Recherches Augustiniennes* 1 (1958), 91 ff., and by Eckard König, *Augustinus Philosophus. Christlicher Glaube und philosophisches Denken in den Frühschriften Augustins* (Munich 1970), 9 ff., who warns against false assumptions that Augustine must have been *either* a Christian *or* a Platonist during this period. For a well balanced account of Augustine's development cf. Henry Chadwick, *Augustine* (Oxford 1986),15 ff.

[36] The order of Augustine's works is more or less apparent from his *Retractationes*. Those looked at here are the *Contra Academicos, De Beata Vita, De Ordine, Soliloquia* (all written at Cassiciacum), *De Immortalitate Animae* (written at Milan), and *De Quantitate Animae* and *De Moribus Ecclesiae Catholicae et de Moribus Manichaeorum* (written, or at least started, at Rome). The exact dating of the *De Moribus Ecclesiae Catholicae et de Moribus Manichaeorum* is controversial and it may be that Augustine made some later additions to Book 1 and only wrote Book 2 after his return to Africa; cf. John Kevin Coyle, *Augustine's "De Moribus Ecclesiae Catholicae"* (Fribourg 1978), 66-98. In what follows the first three of these works are quoted from the edition by Pius Knöll (Vienna 1922), the following three from that by Wolfgang Hörmann (Vienna 1986). There is no modern critical edition of *De Moribus Ecclesiae Catholicae et de Moribus Manichaeorum*. It is quoted here from the Maurist edition, Volume 1 (Paris 1836), which is reprinted in PL 32. Coyle, *op. cit.,* 277 ff., reprints the Maurist text of Book 1 from PL and supplies a commentary.

[37] *Contra Academicos* 3.17.37 ff. and especially 3.18.41 ff.; cf. *Solil.* 1.4.9. In *De Ordine* 2.20.53 however Alypius praises Augustine's teaching as agreeing with that of Pythagoras. In the *Confessions* Augustine mentions his inclination towards the Academic philosophers at 5.10.19 (during the account of his stay at Rome) and 5.14.25.

[38] In his *Confessions* 9.4.7 Augustine states that Alypius was unwilling that the name of Christ should be included in the writings composed at Cassiciacum.

[39] Cf. *Contra Academicos* 1.1.1, *De Ordine* 1.1.1-2, 1.5.14, 2.1.2 etc.

12

dance in his own spiritual journey and those of his friends.[40] Divine revelation is necessary in the search for truth[41] and the acceptance of authority must supplement reason[42] not only for the uneducated but also as an entrance door or cradle for those intending later to proceed by the aid of reason.[43] He alludes to Christian truths in philosophical language and refers to Christian teachings, scriptures and sacraments as *mysteria* [44] and *sacra.* [45] In the *Contra Academicos* Augustine writes of himself at the beginning of Book 2 and the end of Book 3. He is seeking truth with the greatest concentration and is confident of reaching his destination. His perception of divine guidance behind Romanianus' assistance in this quest is more a matter of faith than of reason.[46] In his return to his childhood religion and perusal of Paul it was that religion which was drawing him to itself.[47] He accepts the authority of Christ but desires to grasp truth by the power of reason as well as that of belief.[48]

At the beginning of the *De Beata Vita* (1.4-5) Augustine again gives a brief account of his spiritual history, making special mention of his debts to Ambrose and to his addressee Theodorus.[49] The dialogue itself is given an overtly Christian ingredient by the participation of Augustine's mother Monica. His conclusion to the work (4.34-5) on the happiness to be sought in the knowledge of God contains Christian overtones (allusion to *1 Corinthians* 1.24, quotation of *John* 14.8, Trinitarian lan-

---

[40] Cf. *Contra Academicos* 1.1.3 (especially his prayers on behalf of Romanianus), *De Beata Vita* 1.1 (end) and 1.4, *De Ordine* 1.4.10 (using a line from the *Aeneid*), 1.8.22-3, 1.11.33.

[41] Cf. *Contra Academicos* 3.5.11 and 6.13 (in non-Christian language: *numen aliquod ... solum posse ostendere homini, quid sit uerum*).

[42] *Contra Academicos* 3.20.43, cf. *De Beata Vita* 1.4 (quoted below n.44), *De Ordine* 2.5.16. In so far as it is applied to the uneducated masses Augustine's use of this theme agrees with what he himself reports about Porphyry; cf. O'Meara (*op. cit. n. 35*), 102 ff.

[43] *De Ordine* 2.9.26.

[44] *Contra Academicos* 2.1.1 (end), *De Ordine* 2.5.15-16, 2.9.27, 2.16.46; cf. *De Beata Vita* 1.4 (*illorum auctoritas qui diuina mysteria tradiderunt*).

[45] *Contra Academicos* 3.19.42, 3.20.43 (end), *De Ordine* 2.9.27.

[46] *Contra Academicos* 2.2.4: *... quod quaero intentissimus ueritatem ... tu animasti ... cuius autem minister fueris, plus adhuc fide concepi, quam ratione conprehendi.*

[47] *Contra Academicos* 2.2.5: *ipsa ad se nescientem rapiebat.*

[48] *Contra Academicos* 3.20.43: *non credendo solum sed etiam intellegendo.* On the relation between the two in the early Augustine cf. König (*op. cit.* n.35), 131 ff.

[49] For Ambrose cf. also 4.35, where Monica quotes an invocation of the Trinity from one of his hymns.

guage), which are greeted by Monica with an invocation of the Trinity and an appeal to faith, hope and love (cf. *1 Corinthians* 13.13) as the path to this knowledge.

In the *De Ordine* the partners in the dialogue maintain that God rules all things in order despite the problem of apparent evil. Various approaches to this problem are suggested—the partial nature of the human viewpoint (1.1.2, like looking at one stone only in a mosaic pavement, 2.4.11 ff., 2.7.24, 2.19.51), the need for the contrast of opposites within the order of the universe (1.7.18), the justice of God distinguishing between the virtuous and the wicked and giving to each their due (1.7.19 and 2.7.22)—and the idea of evil as a negation seems perhaps to be hinted at in what is said about darkness and stupidity (2.3.10)—but the reader is left feeling that there are still many questions to be answered about the origin of evil (cf. especially 2.17.46). While insisting on the great value of a training in the liberal arts for those seeking divine truth, Augustine also asserts the compatibility of true philosophy with Christian teaching on the Trinity and Incarnation (2.5.16), and praises the divine authority which reveals itself in the Christian religion (2.9.27). The piety of the participants in the dialogue, represented most strikingly by Licentius, whose conversion from poetics to philosophy it celebrates, is shown in their prayers and psalm-singing (1.8.21-3, 2.20,52); at 1.10.29 Augustine describes his own almost daily weeping and prayers to God for his wounds to be healed.

The *Soliloquies,* in which Augustine expresses his longing for knowledge of God and the soul and seeks a definition of truth and an answer to the question whether the soul is immortal, is given a religious direction by the prayers which introduce its various sections and which show Augustine's sense of complete dependence on God (1.1.1 ff., 2.1.1, 2.6.9). The long and beautiful prayer which opens the work, much of it biblically inspired, is however confessed by Augustine to be put together not from what he already knows but from material collected and memorised from various sources, in which he has put his faith as far as he could (1.4.9, cf. 1.2.7). Here, as elsewhere, Augustine shows a strong awareness of the need for cleansing, healing and trust in divine mercy if the eyes of the soul are to seek the vision of God (1.6.12, 1.9.16 ff., 1.15.30).

The Pauline quotations and allusions in the dialogues written at Cassiciacum are not at all plentiful, but they are linked to some of the most important themes of Augustine's thought of this period, his attitude to philosophy and the capacity of human reason to approach divine

14

truth, the preference for a philosophy compatible with Christianity rather than one linked with loose moral teachings or paganism, the divine
providential care shown in the recall of human souls by means of the incarnation of God's son, who is his power and wisdom, the soul's exile
from God and path back to the divine vision through faith, hope and
love.[50] Augustine refers to *1 Corinthians* 1.24 for its description of
God's son as *ipsa summi dei uirtus atque sapientia* in *Contra Academicos* 2.1.1, and there is an allusion to the same verse (a favourite one with
the Manichees) in *De Beata Vita* 4.34.[51] In addition he alludes to *Colossians* 2.8 in *Contra Academicos* 3.19.42 as well as in *De Ordine* 1.11.32
(the rejection by *sacra nostra* or the divine scriptures of the philosophy
of this world, but not of true philosophy).[52] Augustine's reading of Paul,
in particular the well-known passage in *Philippians* 2.5 ff., surely lies
behind his philosophically couched references to the incarnation at *Contra Academicos* 3.19.42[53] and *De Ordine* 2.9.27.[54] In the optimistic view
which he takes in the *De Ordine* of the progress attainable by reason he
may have the beginning of the Epistle to the Romans in mind (*Romans*
1.20, 2.14-15)—this is confirmed by what seems to be an allusion to *Romans* 2.15 in *De Ordine* 2.8.25 (*ipsa dei lex ... in sapientes animas
quasi transcribitur*), and by his quotation of *Romans* 1.20 in *Confessions* 7.17.23.[55] In the opening prayer at the beginning of the *Soliloquies* a number of Pauline allusions refer to the divine victory over contrary forces. Augustine may have been thinking of *Romans* 8.37 and its

---

[50] On these themes and their relationship to the Platonism of Porphyry as later described by Augustine cf. O'Meara (*op. cit. n.35*), 104-111.

[51] *accepimus autem etiam auctoritate diuina dei filium nihil esse aliud quam dei
sapientiam.* Cf. also *De Quantitate Animae* 33.76: *uirtutem dei atque sapientiam.*

[52] Cf. also the fuller quotation of this verse at *De Moribus Ecclesiae Catholicae*
21.38 and at *Confessions* 8.2.3 and the discussion by Coyle (*op. cit. n. 36*), 113 ff.

[53] *animas ... numquam ista ratio subtilissima reuocaret,* nisi summus deus popu-
lari quadam clementia diuini intellectus auctoritatem usque ad ipsum corpus huma-
num declinaret atque summitteret, *cuius non solum praeceptis sed etiam factis excita-
tae animae redire in semet ipsas et resipiscere patriam ... potuissent.*

[54] *auctoritas diuina* ipsum hominem agens ostendit ei, quo usque se propter ipsum
depresserit ... *doceat enim oportet et factis potentiam suam et* humilitate clementiam
*et praeceptione naturam, quae omnia sacris, quibus initiamur, secretius firmiusque
traduntur.* Cf. also *De Ordine* 2.5.16: *quantum autem illud sit, quod hoc etiam nostri
generis corpus tantus propter nos deus adsumere atque agere dignatus est, quanto
uidetur uilius, tanto est clementia plenius ...*

[55] Cf. Pierre Courcelle, *Recherches sur les Confessions de saint Augustin* (Paris
1950), 175-7, also below p.17 on the quotation of *Romans* 1.25 in *De Quantitate Animae* 34.77.

XVI

context when he wrote *Deus, per quem uincimus inimicum* (1.3).[56] The words *Deus, per quem mors absorbetur in uictoriam* (1.3) are clearly derived from *1 Corinthians* 15.54,[57] and the proximity of this allusion makes it likely that a reminiscence of *1 Corinthians* 15.53 lies behind the following words *Deus qui nos ... eo, quod est, induis.* Later in the same section there is an unmistakable allusion to *Galatians* 4.9 (*Deus, per quem non seruimus infirmis et egenis elementis*).[58]

The triad of *1 Corinthians* 13.13, faith, hope and love,[59] is appealed to as the necessary foundation in the search for God at the conclusion of *De Beata Vita* (4.35, in the mouth of Monica, following an invocation of the Trinity) and *De Ordine* 2.8.25. The same triad plays a more important role in Book 1 of the *Soliloquies.* It appears twice in Augustine's opening prayer, once in an invocation (1.1.3, *Deus, cui nos fides excitat, spes erigit, caritas iungit*) and once in a prayer for the increase of these virtues that he may return to God (1.1.5), and then again later in 1.13.23, characterising the path of those who are able to approach wisdom without detours (*His credere, sperare, amare satis est*). In the central section, 6.12-7.14, faith, hope and love are explained as necessary for the healing of the eyes of the soul, that it may look towards God and may desire this vision. Faith and hope however are no longer necessary when the vision has been attained, whereas love is thereby increased, although it is only after the impediments of the mortal body have been laid aside that security of possession renders hope and faith superfluous. Augustine does not quote Paul explicitly in this passage, but he clearly has in mind *1 Corinthians* 13.8-13. In addition *Romans* 8.24 lies behind his words in 1.7.14: *Fides quare sit necessaria, cum iam uideat? Spes nihilominus, quia iam tenet.* 2 *Corinthians* 5.6-8 confirms not only the idea that faith is necessary as long as we are in the mortal body, but also the view of this mortal life as a journey in a foreign country separated from our true home (*quamdiu sumus in corpore peregrinamur a Domino*),[60] something central to Augustine's religious attitude not only in his later

---

[56] He quotes this verse elsewhere with the rendering *superuincimus*, rather than the Vulgate *superamus;* cf. the apparatus criticus to *Romans* 8.37 in J. Wordsworth and H. J. White, *Nouum Testamentum Latine* 2.1 (Oxford 1913), 107.

[57] Augustine quotes this verse in *Confessions* 9.4.11 in his account of his stay at Cassiciacum.

[58] In his *Commentary on Galatians* Augustine understood this verse of pagan religion. It could also be that he has the Manichaean worship of the sun and the moon in mind here too.

[59] On this triad in Neoplatonism cf. König (*op. cit. n.35*), 59 ff.

[60] The verb *peregrinari* is used by Augustine in *De Beata Vita* 1.2 (*a sua patria*

works but already in the Cassiciacum dialogues. The *Contra Academicos*, the earliest of these dialogues, is permeated by the idea of the search for truth as a journey which cannot reach its final destination during this mortal life (cf. in particular Augustine's use of this metaphor at 1.1.1 (sea voyage), 1.4.11, 2.2.5 (of himself: *respexi tamen, confitebor, quasi de itinere in illam religionem ...*), 2.9.22, 3.2.3 (sea voyage), 3.14.30 and 3.15.34), and the same picture of the voyage to the harbour of philosophy, which here is shown to differ for different individuals, is fully developed and applied to Augustine's own wanderings in the opening sections of the *De Beata Vita* (1.1-5).[61] In the two passages of the *Soliloquies* already referred to Augustine depicts himself as a runaway slave who needs faith, hope and love as his journey money for his return journey to God (1.1.5), and takes up again (from the beginning of the *De Beata Vita*) the idea of differing paths towards wisdom, combining it with the view that faith, hope and love form the most direct path.

There are only indirect references to Manichaeism in Augustine's earliest works. Thus in *Contra Academicos* Augustine mentions his own liberation from superstition (1.1.3) and his hopes for Romanianus in this respect (2.3.8). In *De Beata Vita* (1.4) he alludes to his earlier adherence to persons who thought that physical light is to be worshipped and that God and the soul are corporeal. In *De Ordine* 2.17.46 he includes some arguments against characteristic Manichaean views in a passage raising questions about the origin of evil (*quid enim potuit deo nocere mali nescio qua illa natura? si enim dicunt non potuisse, fabricandi mundi causa non erit; si potuisse dicunt, inexpiabile nefas est deum uiolabilem credere, nec ita saltem, ut uel uirtute prouiderit, ne sua substantia uiolaretur; namque animam poenas hic pendere fatentur, cum inter eius et dei substantiam nihil uelint omnino distare*).[62] The opening prayer of the *Soliloquies* is generally anti-Manichaean and more particularly in the emphasis in 1.2 that evil does not exist and that the whole creation with its better and its lower parts is in harmony, and in the statement in 1.4 that nothing has true existence apart from God.

---

peregrinari); cf. also *De quantitate animae* 31.63: *illo secretissimo et tranquillissimo mentis habitaculo, a quo nunc, dum haec incolit, peregrina est.* For later quotations of this verse cf. for example the index of scriptural passages in the edition of the *Enarrationes in Psalmos* in CCL 40 (1956), 2251. *Hebrews* 11.13-16 may also lie behind the use of this imagery; cf. Robert J. O'Connell, *St. Augustine's Early Theory of Man* (Cambridge Mass. 1968), 75.

[61] Augustine of course also has the wanderings of Aeneas in mind in this passage.
[62] Cf. *Confessions* 7.2.3 (Nebridius' argument against the Manichees).

After his return from Cassiciacum to Milan but before his baptism Augustine composed the *De Immortalitate Animae*. Perhaps the most purely philosophical of his works and one which Augustine himself later found obscure, it shows clearly the new structure of his thought that was to be so important in his later anti-Manichaean argumentation. The power which creates and preserves the whole physical universe, itself incorporeal, is the source of existence in everything that exists (7.14). That Truth, which is supreme being and the source of truth and existence in individual true things, has no opposite, since the opposite of existence is non-existence, i.e. does not exist (12.19). The soul, itself incorporeal and occupying an intermediate position between the highest being and corporeal creation (15.24), has wisdom through conversion towards the source of its being and may lose wisdom through turning away from this source, in which case it tends towards nothingness, but does not perish (12.19 and 7.12). There are no clear biblical quotations in this work, but it is perhaps not too fanciful to see a reminiscence of *Romans* 8.35 ff. behind the passage in 5.11 where Augustine asks by what power the soul can be separated from that supreme Reason which gives it life and concludes that neither any bodily force nor any other soul can do this.

During his stay at Milan Augustine began a series of treatises on the liberal arts, of which only the *On Music* survives. Book 6 of this work contains interesting discussion of the habit-forming power of sin based on *2 Corinthians* 5.6-8 (6.5.14 and 6.11.33) and a passage on the joy of contemplation of God in the afterlife quoting *1 Corinthians* 15.53, *Romans* 8.11 and *Philippians* 1.23-4 (6.15.49). Since however Augustine only completed the work after his return to Africa, it will not be discussed here.

It was during his stop at Rome on the way back to Africa after his baptism that Augustine wrote (or started to write)[63] his first anti-Manichaean work, the *De Moribus Ecclesiae Catholicae et de Moribus Manichaeorum*. During the same stay at Rome he also wrote the *De Quantitate Animae* and began the *De Libero Arbitrio*, whose second and third books he completed later when he was a priest at Hippo. The *De Libero Arbitrio* will not be considered here.[64] The *De Quantitate Animae* continues the philosophical approach of the earlier dialogues and is mainly

---

[63] See above n.36.

[64] Pauline quotations are confined to the third book, which was written later; cf. the index in the edition by W. M. Green (Vienna 1956),155.

occupied by arguments against a corporeal view of the soul. This of
course can be seen as anti-Manichaean, since the Manichees thought of
the soul as consisting of a fine substance.[65] There are obvious pieces of
anti-Manichaean polemic at 33.71, where Augustine attacks the view
that plants have souls with the power of sensation and therefore feel
pain and see and hear, and 34.77, where he denies that the heavenly bodies are superior to the nature of the human soul.[66] The influence of
Augustine's recent baptism is apparent in a number of references to the
teachings and scriptures of the Catholic Church, some of which are accompanied by Pauline quotations. At 3.4 Augustine praises the fact that
the 'mysteries' teach that the soul which wishes to be restored to the
likeness of God should despise all bodily things and renounce this
material world, since there is no other means of salvation, renewal
(*renouatio*) or reconciliation to its creator. This renewal is described at
28.55 with an appeal to the divine scriptures and allusions to *Ephesians*
4.22,24, *Colossians* 3.9-10, and *2 Corinthians* 3.18 (putting off the old
man and becoming a new man, and being renewed according to the
image of God). It involves withdrawal from the body by means of reason and knowledge, since the more the soul descends to the level of the
senses the more it makes a man similar to a brute beast.[67] The last part
of the *De Quantitate Animae* (33.70 ff.) consists of an account of the
seven steps or levels of the soul's activity, ascending from its life-giving
function, shared even with plants, to its final destination in the vision
and contemplation of Truth. The fourth step is that of the moral purification of the soul, when it follows the authority and advice of wise men,
believing that God speaks through them, and entrusts itself to divine
assistance (33.73; cf. also 34.78 on the need for strength and piety at this
step in order to investigate and understand the contents of the many writings of the church). When we have ascended these levels we will recognise how true those things are which we are commanded to believe (including the resurrection of the body, the incarnation, virgin birth and
other miracles of the Gospel story) and how healthful the nourishment

---

[65] Cf. for example 30.61: the soul is not spread through the body like blood.
[66] The Manichees venerated the sun and moon according to Augustine, *Epistle*
236.2 (*solem etiam et lunam ... adorant et orant*).
[67] 18.54. I suspect that behind this passage lies an understanding of the fall based
on *Psalm* 48 (49).13 and 21 (*homo cum in honore esset non intellexit, comparatus est
iumentis insipientibus et similis factus est illis*), such as is found in Origen, *Commentary on Romans* 2.5 (ed. C. P. H. Bammel (Freiburg, 1990), 116, ll. 73-9, from which
the above quotation of the verse is taken).

XVI

given us by the Mother Church. Augustine here appeals explicitly to the metaphor used by Paul in *1 Corinthians* 3.2, the milk lovingly given to the infants in Christ who are not yet ready for solid food.[68] There are two Pauline allusions in the next section (34.77), where he states that the Catholic Church hands down that no creature is to be worshipped but only the creator (cf. *Romans* 1.25), from whom, through whom and in whom are all things (*Romans* 11.36). Augustine's concluding summary to the *De Quantitate Animae* (36.80-81) presents a picture of a divinely regulated universe in which the soul's endowment with free will does not allow it to disturb the divine order. The soul has indeed torn itself away from God by sin and has rightly been thrust into this mortal existence, but it has not been abandoned by God, it can exercise virtue even here, and every punishment and reward assigned to it contribute to the beauty and harmony of the whole.

The *De Moribus Ecclesiae Catholicae et de Moribus Manichaeorum* is strikingly different from Augustine's earlier treatises, firstly in the directness of its attack on the Manichees and secondly in its ample use of biblical quotations and proof-texts. In this work Augustine sets out to defend the Old Testament scriptures against the Manichees and to show the superiority of Christian continence based on love to Manichaean superstition (1.2). The central part of the work is a demonstration based on rational argumentation that true happiness is to be found in the love of God (3.4 ff.) and an explanation of the four cardinal virtues (15.25 ff. and 19.35 ff.). Though the Manichees agree on the prime importance of love of God and one's neighbour they do not accept that it is on these two commandments that all the Law and the Prophets hang (28.57, 29.59 ff.).

In reading the *De Moribus Ecclesiae Catholicae* one becomes aware how much the structure of Augustine's thought has changed since his own Manichaean period. The insights of the various writings he had composed since his conversion are now put together in an anti-Manichaean context. The Manichees had regarded God as spread through space and corruptible. Augustine emphasises God's incorporeality and incorruptibility. The Manichees had separated Old and New Testaments and had made a division in their perception of the material world between the realm of light and the realm of darkness. Augustine sees all being as God's creation and human history including both Testaments

---

[68] On this imagery in Augustine cf. also O'Connell (*op. cit. n.60*), 77-9, with references also to *1 Thessalonians* 2.7 and *Hebrews* 5.11-14.

20

and the world-wide expansion of the Christian church as part of one
divine providential plan for fallen humanity. Whereas the Manichees
had confused the creator and his creation in supposing the human soul to
be part of God, Augustine emphasises that the human soul or mind is
not of the same nature as God; though created in the divine image it is
able to fall and only becomes like God when subjected to him. Whereas
the Manichees based their claims on the supremacy of reason and expected conversion to result in instant perfection, Augustine now realised
that daily renewal of the inner man was necessary and that the ascent
from worldly desires to the purifying love of God was only possible for
those nourished at the breast of the universal church and accepting the
authority of the church's scriptures.[69]

Throughout the work Augustine makes abundant use of Paul. Pauline proof-texts are used along with texts from the Gospels and from the
Old Testament[70] to support the main contentions about the supremacy of
love of God[71] and neighbour,[72] to illustrate the exposition of the four
virtues, and to refute superstitious ideas about pollution caused by meat,
wine or marital relations. Thus in the section on temperance (19.35 ff.)
Augustine quotes *1 Timothy* 6.10 as showing that the root of all evils is
desire (for lower things), *2 Corinthians* 4.18 to show that we should set
our hearts not on visible, temporal things, but on what is unseen and
eternal, *Galatians* 1.10 as rejecting fame, *Colossians* 2.8 as rejecting the
desire for superfluous knowledge, and *Romans* 12.2 as rejecting the love
of things of this world in general and showing that one becomes like that
which one loves. This section also includes a digression on the fall and

---

[69] One can read Augustine's invocation of the Catholic Church at 30.62 as a summary of these anti-Manichaean insights: *merito, ecclesia catholica, mater Christianorum uerissima, non solum ipsum Deum, cuius adeptio uita est beatissima, purissime
atque castissime colendum praedicas; nullam nobis adorandam creaturam inducens
... et ab illa incorrupta et inuiolabili aeternitate ... excludens omne quod factum est ...
neque confundens quod aeternitas, quod ueritas, quod denique pax ipsa distinguit, nec
rursum separans quod maiestas una coniungit; sed etiam proximi dilectionem atque
caritatem ita complecteris, ut uariorum morborum, quibus pro peccatis suis animae
aegrotant, omnis apud te medicina praepolleat.*

[70] This use of parallel texts is his main defense against the Manichaean attacks on
the Old Testament; cf. 1.2; also 10.16-17 (the Catholic understanding of the law and
prophets is different from what the Manichees think), 29.59-61 (attack on the Manichaean claim that the New Testament is interpolated).

[71] Cf. 8.13 ff., 11.18 ff., where *Romans* 8.28, 35-6 and 38-9 are expounded in detail, also 16.26 quoting *Romans* 8.35 and 28,18.34 quoting *Ephesians* 3.17-18 and
26.50 quoting *Romans* 8.28.

[72] 26.50 quoting *Romans* 13.10.

on Christian renewal (see below). In the section on fortitude (22.40 ff.) Augustine quotes *Romans* 5.3-4, in that on justice (24.44) he alludes to *Romans* 1.25 (that one should worship the Creator only, and not the creation) and in that on prudence (24.45) he quotes *1 Corinthians* 5.6 as enjoining caution. In his description of Catholic ascetics[73] he states that they follow the authority of Paul in maintaining themselves by the work of their hands (33.70, cf. *1 Corinthians* 4.12, *Ephesians* 4.28, *1 Thessalonians* 4.11, *2 Thessalonians* 3.10). They do not reject particular types of food as polluted (33.71) remembering that to the clean all things are clean (*Titus* 1.15, to which Augustine adds *1 Corinthians* 6.13 and 8.8), and that love must be given priority (Augustine here quotes and expounds *Romans* 14.21, 2-4, 6 and 12-15, and *1 Corinthians* 6.12).[74] They allow the drinking of a little wine for the sake of one's health, following Paul's admonition to Timothy (*1 Timothy* 5.23), and they devote themselves more assiduously to piety than to physical exercise, following *1 Timothy* 4.8. In countering the Manichaean view that baptised persons should not marry or have possessions Augustine quotes at length from Paul as both demonstrating the ideal for the strong and allowing the lower level for the weaker members of the community (35.78-80, quoting *1 Corinthians* 6.11-7.7 and 7.14).

The various themes of the work are illustrated, argued or developed with reference to Pauline verses. Augustine quotes *Romans* 11.36 in support of the Catholic doctrine of the Trinity, that Father, Son and Holy Spirit are one God (14.24 and 16.29) and argues for the divinity of the Holy Spirit on the basis of *Romans* 5.5 and 8.20 (13.23; cf. 16.29). Christ is shown to be the power of God and the wisdom of God by *1 Corinthians* 1.24, a favourite verse both of the Manichees and the early Augustine (13.22 and 16.27).[75] That the human mind is created and not of the same nature as God is shown by Paul's use of the phrase *alia creatura* in *Romans* 8.39 (12.20). Augustine points to the danger that if the human mind does not recognise the gulf between itself as a creature and its Creator its pride and presumption may cause it to fall away, whereas if it desires lower things, it may become stupid and wretched

---

[73] According to Coyle (*op. cit. n.36*), 93-8, all this part of the work may be a later addition.

[74] Cf. John Burnaby, *Amor Dei* (London 1938), 91: 'perhaps nothing in the *De Moribus* is more noteworthy than the extent to which in its last chapters Augustine has for his portraying of the Christian life absorbed the spirit of St. Paul'.

[75] The sections on the Trinity in which these quotations occur may be later additions according to Coyle (*op. cit. n.36*), 241-259.

22

and be separated from the love of God by its affection for the material world (12.20-21)—he seems here to have *Romans* 1.21 ff. in mind as well as the passage in *Romans* 8 to which he refers directly. The dangers of desire for lower things are again emphasised in a later section (19.35-6) with a quotation of *1 Timothy* 6.10 and a reference to the story of Adam's disobedience in paradise as indicating that the sin of the soul is of this kind. This mystery is also hinted at by Paul's words in *1 Corinthians* 15.22 (loosely quoted as 'In Adam we all die and in Christ we shall all rise').[76] When Paul warns us to put off the old man and put on the new (cf. *Colossians* 3.9-10, *Ephesians* 4.22-4) he refers to Adam, who sinned, as the old man and the man whom the Son of God assumed in the incarnation as the new man. *1 Corinthians* 15.47-9 and *2 Corinthians* 4.16 show the same thing, that we should despise the snares of the body and turn all our love to the invisible realm, so as to be renewed in God. Augustine quotes *2 Corinthians* 4.16 again in the final section (35.80), where he attacks the Manichees for expecting immediate perfection of baptised Christians, whereas Paul speaks of a daily renewal and gradual progress. This renewal can also be seen in terms of becoming like God or being conformed to God rather than to this world (13.22)—Augustine here alludes to *Romans* 12.2 and quotes *Romans* 8.29 (cf. also 16.29, where he quotes the same verse again).

It represents a change over against Augustine's earlier philosophical dialogues that in the *De Moribus Ecclesiae Catholicae* he discusses the divine providential plan in the guidance of human history and the relationship of the Old Testament and New Testament dispensations. Here too Pauline verses play a role. When man had fallen from the divine laws through his desire for mortal things, says Augustine (7.12), divine providence did not desert him but showed both severity in punishment and mercy in salvation (surely an allusion to *Romans* 11.22) and provided a path by means of the separation of the patriarchs, the bond of the law, the predictions of the prophets, the mystery of the incarnation, the witness of the apostles, the blood of the martyrs, and the inclusion of the gentiles.[77] God himself in his mercy (27.54) sent medicine for the sins of the human race (28.55) and gave the two Testaments as a rule of discipline (28.56). The Old Testament is more characterised by coercion working through fear, the New Testament by instruction working

---

[76] On the fall cf. also 7.12 and 22.40 (*corpus homini grauissimum uinculum est, iustissimis Dei legibus, propter antiquum peccatum*).

[77] Even heresies have a role to play; cf. 17.30 quoting *1 Corinthians* 11.19.

through love—or in the words of the apostles bondage and liberty (cf. *Galatians* 4.24 ff., 5.1). Augustine takes up this distinction between fear and love (cf. *2 Timothy* 1.7, *Romans* 8.15, *1 John* 4.18) in a later section (30.64), in which a quotation of *1 Corinthians* 15.56 ('the sting of death is sin, but the strength of sin is the law') is followed by the kernel of Augustine's later exegesis of *Romans* 7.7 ff.—the awareness of the scorned precept slays the sinner; the attempted performance of works under the law is in vain, when lust lays waste the mind and is restrained by fear of punishment rather than being overwhelmed by love of virtue.

In the *De Moribus Ecclesiae Catholicae* Augustine develops his earlier emphasis on the role of the Church and on the need for the acceptance of authority as a step on the path to knowledge. Authority should precede reasoning, just as love precedes knowledge (2.3 and 25.47; cf. also 7.11 and 14.24). The Christian scriptures are validated by the testimony of churches spread throughout the whole world (29.61). The Catholic Church provides teaching adapted to the various levels of its recipients and regulates social relations (30.62-3, including an allusion to *Romans* 13.7), nourishing those who are still infants at the breast (10.17 and 30.64; cf. Augustine's use of this metaphor drawn from *1 Corinthians* 3.2 in the *De Quantitate Animae*) so that they may be led to perfect manhood (10.17 quoting *Ephesians* 4.13) and so that death may be swallowed up in victory (30.64 quoting *1 Corinthians* 15.54-5). In appealing to the Manichees to give a hearing to the teachers of the Catholic Church Augustine quotes *Ephesians* 3.14-19 as showing that this is where the Christian faith is to be found (18.33-4).

The *De Moribus Manichaeorum* uses fewer Pauline citations and is more limited in its subject matter. A discussion of the nature and source of evil (the corruption of created beings, which are good only by participation in supreme Goodness, their falling away from true existence and tending towards non-existence) is followed by an attack on Manichaean teachings and pseudo-asceticism. Augustine uses one Pauline quotation in arguing against the Manichaean view of the soul as part of God (11.22; in this case *Galatians* 5.13 would imply that part of God is in bondage), and a number of Pauline quotations in showing what Paul's purpose was in recommending abstention from meat and wine (14.31-35; *Romans* 14.21, *Romans* 13.14, *Romans* 14.1-15.3, *1 Corinthians* 8.4-13, *1 Corinthians* 10.19-25, *1 Corinthians* 10.28–11.1).

At a later date (by around 396) Augustine's understanding of Paul was to undergo certain striking developments, which might perhaps cause one to wonder whether he was reverting to a more pessimistic outlook owing something to his earlier Manichaeism.[78] In the period immediately after his conversion his reading of Paul supported a Christian Platonism which was derived not only from his own reading of Platonist books[79] but also from Christian teachers and laymen at Milan.[80] The most important Pauline contribution to this Christian Platonism is the emphasis on love (faith, hope and love characterising the soul's path to the divine vision, love of things that are unseen versus desire for wordly things, love of God and love of neighbour), and on the renewal of the inner man in becoming conformed to or like the creator. Pauline verses are used to support an 'other-worldly' religious attitude which a modern reader would be unlikely to regard as Paul's main message.[81] In addition Augustine's view of the church as a mother providing suitable sustenance to those of different levels is based on Paul.[82] Although he continues to quote or allude to individual Pauline verses favoured by the Manichees (for example *1 Corinthians* 1.24, *Philippians* 2.5-8, *Galatians* 4.9),[83] it seems that his Manichaean understanding of Paul has 'gone underground'. Only in the works composed at Rome after his baptism do major Manichaean Pauline themes begin to resurface and be reworked. The cluster of Pauline verses which refer to the two men (old/new, outer/inner, earthly/heavenly) in each individual and to the renewal of the inner man according to the image of God are central both

---

[78] Cf. pp.349 ff. and pp.352 ff. of the article cited above n. 4. On the general question cf. Alfred Adam, 'Das Fortwirken des Manichäismus bei Augustin', *Zeitschrift für Kirchengeschichte* 69 (1958), 1-25, reprinted in *Sprache und Dogma* (Gütersloh 1969), 141-166, Frend (*op. cit. n.28*), Johannes van Oort, 'Augustine and Mani on concupiscentia sexualis', in ed. J. den Boeft and J. van Oort, *Augustiniana Traiectina* (Paris 1987), 137-152.

[79] On some of the agreements and differences between Augustine and the Platonists he read cf. John J. O'Meara, *The Young Augustine* (London 1954), 143 ff. and (*op. cit. n.35*), 104-111 (comparing what Augustine later says about Porphyry with Augustine's own views), Chadwick (*op. cit. n.35*), 30 ff.

[80] Cf. in particular Pierre Courcelle, *Late Latin Writers and their Greek Sources* (Cambridge Mass. 1969), 131 ff. and 171-189, especially 181-2, and (*op. cit. n.55*) on the influence of Ambrose, Manlius Theodorus and Simplician on Augustine; also Prosper Alfaric, *L'Évolution intellectuelle de saint Augustin* (Paris 1918), 372 ff., and John J. O'Meara, *The Young Augustine,* 116 ff. On Augustine's Christian Platonism cf. also Henry Chadwick, 'Christian Platonism in Origen and Augustine', in *Origeniana Tertia* , ed. Richard Hanson and Henri Crouzel (Rome 1985), 228 ff., reprinted in *Heresy and Orthodoxy in the Early Church* (Aldershot 1991), item XII.

[81] See above, pp.14 ff.16-17,20.

[82] See above pp.17,21.

[83] See above pp.5, 13 and 20, 6, 7 and 13, 4 and 14.

for Manichaean anthropology and for Augustine's new and very different Platonising understanding of Christian progress.[84] Augustine's defense of the role of the Old Testament law contains a critical element based on Paul (the contrast between bondage and liberty of *Galatians* 5.1 etc.)[85] and shared with the Manichees, and he begins already at Rome to work out a new understanding of *Romans* 7.7 ff., a key passage both for the Manichaean dualist approach and for his own later Pauline exegesis.[86] It is perhaps characteristic of Augustine that an initial enthusiasm for and preoccupation with new insights and new influences is followed by a resurgence and attempted incorporation of earlier attitudes.[87] It has only been possible above to touch on the very beginning of this process.

---

[84] See above pp.7,16-17 and 20.
[85] See above pp.4 and 21.
[86] See above pp.7 and 21.
[87] I tried to show this with regard to one particular example on pp. 359 ff. of the article cited above n. 4.

XVII

AUGUSTINE, ORIGEN AND THE EXEGESIS OF ST. PAUL [1]

In this paper I shall be comparing Augustine's Pauline exegesis with that of Origen and considering the question of the influence of Origen on Augustine up to the beginning of the Pelagian controversy. The writings of Augustine which I will take into consideration fall into three groups: firstly the early writings prior to 394, many of them aimed against Manichaeism, secondly the expositions of Paul in the exegetical works on *Romans* and *Galatians* of 394-5 and in the *De diversis quaestionibus* and the *Ad Simplicianum de diversis quaestionibus* of 396, and thirdly the earliest anti-Pelagian treatises of 411-412.

Our own knowledge of Origen's Pauline exegesis comes chiefly from four sources. These are his surviving works in general, his *Commentary on Romans* translated by Rufinus together with various Greek extracts from that work, the *catena* extracts on *1 Corinthians* and *Ephesians*, and fourthly the commentaries by Jerome on *Galatians*, *Ephesians*, *Titus* and *Philemon*, which are largely based on Origen [2]. Augustine too had the opportunity for some general exposure to Origen's ideas on Paul through other writings of Origen and through those who had used Origen. More particularly the Pauline commentaries of Jerome are likely to have been available to him from about 393 and the *Commentary on Romans* translated by Rufinus could have reached him between about 407 and 411.

This paper is arranged in four parts, the first part concerning Augustine's knowledge of Origen in general and the remaining three parts divided according to the three groups of Augustine's works already

---

[1] This paper was delivered at the Eleventh International Conference on Patristic Studies in Oxford in August 1991. I am grateful to Professor Grossi for his offer to publish it in *Augustinianum*.

[2] I am preparing an article on Origen's Pauline exegesis for *Aufstieg und Niedergang der römischen Welt* II,27/4. In this paper therefore I will not go into the details of Origen's own views and their development or consider the question whether the impression given to Augustine about Origen's views by the various sources available to him was an accurate one.

mentioned. My main aim has been to show that Augustine did indeed read and react to Rufinus' translation of Origen's *Commentary on Romans* by about 411. The function of the first three sections therefore is primarily introductory.

Part I: AUGUSTINE AND ORIGEN

As I have already mentioned, Augustine was influenced by Origen both indirectly, through other writers who were dependent on him, and also directly by using Latin translations of his works [3]. The translations by Jerome and Rufinus however only became available to him after the composition of his own earliest writings, and perhaps paradoxically his own thought is closest to Origen in his earlier period. It is difficult to assign exact dates to the beginnings of his direct acquaintance with Origen and his works. The translations by Jerome of Old Testament homilies and homilies on Luke, made between about 381 and 390 [4], may have reached him some time after about 393, when direct contact was effected by means of a visit by Alypius to Bethlehem [5]. As I have already said, it likely that it was at this stage that he obtained copies of

[3] On this cf. Berthold Altaner, *Augustinus und Origenes. Eine quellenkritische Untersuchung*, in *Historisches Jahrbuch* 70 (1951) 15-41; Gerard Bartelink, *Die Beeinflussung Augustins durch die griechischen Patres*, in J. den Boeft and J. van Oort (ed.), *Augustiniana Traiectina*, Paris 1987, pp.14-18, making some important additions to Altaner's article as well as useful general comments; also Robert J. O'Connell, *Augustine's Rejection of the Fall of the Soul*, in *Augustinian Studies* 4 (1973) 10ff.; A.-M. La Bonnardière, *Jérôme "informateur" d'Augustin au sujet d'Origène*, in *Revue des Études Augustiniennes* 20 (1974) 42-52, together with other writings referred to there p.42 note 1. Agostino Trapè, *Nota sul giudizio di S. Agostino su Origene*, in *Augustinianum* 26 (1986) 223-237, considers Augustine's attitude to the controversy about Origen. Vittorino Grossi, *La presenza in filigrana di Origene nell' ultimo Agostino (426-430)*, in *Augustinianum* 30 (1990) 423-440, includes a section on the years before 426 too (pp.425-428). G. Sfameni Gasparro, *Agostino di fronte alla "eterodossia" di Origene*, in *Augustiniana (= Mélanges T. J. van Bavel)* 40 (1990) 219-243, only became available to me after I had completed this paper.
[4] Cf. ed. Angelo Di Berardino, *Patrology*, Vol. 4, Westminster, Maryland 1986, pp. 229f.
[5] Augustine, *ep.* 28.1 refers to this visit. An earlier date is not impossible however. Aurelius already had copies of the translations of Origen's *Homilies on Jeremiah* and the *Song of Songs* when he wrote to Jerome to announce that he had been made bishop of Carthage (in 391), *ep.* 27*, ed. J. Divjak, CSEL 88 (1981) 130-133. Jerome's reply enclosed further specimens of his own composition and suggested Aurelius send someone to Bethlehem to copy his works.

Jerome's own Pauline commentaries (which had been composed in about 387 [6]). Rufinus' more numerous translations of Origen were only completed between 398 and 410, so were not available until later. Possible intermediaries between Rufinus and Augustine are Paulinus of Nola, with whom Augustine was in correspondence from 395 onwards, the contact again having been effected by Alypius, and also Rufinus' friend Melania the elder, who visited Augustine in about 407 [7], and Melania the younger and Pinian, who travelled to Africa in 410 or 411 [8]. It could also be that there were other intermediaries of whom we are unaware. In any case Augustine sooner or later received copies of Rufinus' translations not only of various writings of Origen, but also of Eusebius, Basil, Gregory Nazianzen and the *Historia Monachorum* [9].

Prior to Augustine's receipt of the translations of Jerome and Rufinus the influence of Origen could have been mediated to him by Latin writers who used Origen, in particular by Ambrose, through the sermons which Augustine heard as well as by his writings [10], and by Hilary of Poitiers. Later on he would also have been able to use writings of Jerome which were based on Origen, not only Jerome's Pauline commentaries but a number of others too.

Augustine's attitude to the use of Origen will have been affected by the Origenist controversies of the 390's and the condemnation of Origen's errors by Theophilus of Alexandria and Anastasius of Rome in 400. It is likely that Augustine heard of the disputes involving Jerome and Rufinus from participants on both sides, although our evidence comes only from his correspondence with Jerome [11]. Augustine's friend Alypius will surely have used his visit to the Holy Land to make contact with the Latin monastery under Rufinus and Melania the elder at Jerusalem as well as with Jerome's monastery at Bethlehem. Augustine's

---

[6] Cf. Di Berardino, *op. cit.*, p.232.

[7] Cf. Paulinus of Nola, *ep.* 45; C. P. Hammond, *The Last Ten Years of Rufinus' Life*, in *Journal of Theological Studies* NS 28 (1977) 416-417.

[8] Cf. Gerontius, *Vita Melaniae* 19-20, ed. D. Gorce, SCh 90 (1962) 164-9; Augustine, *ep.* 124.

[9] Cf. Berthold Altaner, *Augustinus und die griechische Patristik*, in *Revue Bénédictine* 62 (1952) 201-215, together with the earlier articles referred to there. The articles of Altaner are conveniently reprinted in his *Kleine Patristische Schriften*, Berlin 1967.

[10] One should not forget also the influence during the earlier period of Augustine's discussion partners, some of whom, such as Alypius, had been with him already in Milan.

[11] Augustine's correspondence with Jerome is conveniently described by J. N. D. Kelly, *Jerome. His Life, Writings and Controversies*, London 1975, pp. 217-220, 263-272 and 317-318.

earliest letters to Jerome, *Epistles* 28 and 40, written in about 394-398, encourage Jerome in his translation of the Greek biblical commentators, referring indirectly to Origen [12], but show also that he is aware of current criticisms of Jerome, both for his Old Testament translation from the Hebrew [13] and also for his volte face in condemning as heretical a writer whom he had earlier loaded with extravagant praise [14]. These letters also attack a passage from Jerome's *Commentary on Galatians* on Paul's rebuke to Peter at Antioch which was based on Origen, though it is not clear whether Augustine was aware of this indebtedness at this stage [15]. In any case Augustine's letter 40 failed to arrive and instead circulated in Italy, giving rise to rumours that he had written a book against Jerome [16].

After an interruption in the correspondence the bad feeling generated was dispelled by means of conciliatory approaches from Augustine [17]. By this time the condemnation of Origenism had taken place with Jerome emerging from the controversy on the winning side. In Jerome's letter 102 to Augustine of 402 or 403 he refers to Rufinus' *Apology* against himself, stating that he hears that it has reached Africa, and he encloses a copy of his own 2nd *Apology* against Rufinus and promises to send the longer 1st *Apology* [18]. At least by this stage therefore, if not before, Augustine will have been informed about the controversy. Augustine's reply of about 404 professes ignorance of Rufinus' attack on Jerome and expresses his distress that the friendship between the two, who had been so intimately united in their biblical studies and ascetic devotions in the Holy Land, should have been replaced by such bitter enmity [19]. Subsequent to this Jerome eventually wrote to Augustine in defence of his own exegesis of *Gal.* 2,11ff., stating that he had followed Origen and later Greek commentators [20]. Augustine retorted that of

---

[12] *Ep.* 28.2.

[13] *Loc. cit.*

[14] *Ep.* 40.9; cf. *ep.* 28.2.

[15] *Ep.* 28.3ff., *ep.* 40.3ff.

[16] Cf. *ep.* 67.2 and *ep.* 72.4.

[17] *Ep.* 67 and 71.

[18] *Ep.* 68.3 in the collection of Augustine's letters. Eugene TeSelle, *Augustine the Theologian*, London 1970, pp.263-264, considers what Augustine would have learnt from Jerome's *Apologies* about Origen's objectionable teachings and the resulting changes in his own thought. It may be however that he dates these changes too early; see below note 61.

[19] *Ep.* 73.6-9.

[20] *Ep.* 75.4-6.

seven Greek commentators appealed to by Jerome, Jerome himself had condemned four as heretical, and that Jerome had recently shown as much extravagance in attacking Origen as he had previously in praising him [21].

Augustine's personal friendship with supporters of Rufinus, in particular the two Melanias and Pinian, as well as Paulinus of Nola, will have led him to take a cautious approach over the Origenist dispute [22], at least initially. There is a long period of reticence on the subject, before Augustine joins his voice to the chorus of polemic against Origenist errors. Although we do not have explicit information about his knowledge of the questions at issue (which could have come verbally as well as through relevant writings of Jerome, Rufinus and others), his silence should surely be attributed to deliberate restraint rather than naive ignorance [23]. The defenders of Origen, in particular Rufinus, argued that his disputed teachings were either matters for debate (such as the question of the origin of the soul), not of heresy versus orthodoxy, or not taught by him. Among the important aristocratic Christian refugees who arrived in Africa after the sack of Rome in 410 were Rufinus' friends Pinian (together with Melania and Albina) [24] and Anicia Faltonia Proba, with her granddaughter Demetrias [25]. Augustine was in contact with both families during their stay in Africa. It is not surprising therefore that it is only at a later stage after his encounter with Orosius that we find him writing against heretical errors of Origen, firstly in his work addressed to Orosius, *Contra Priscillianistas et Origenistas*, then also in his *Civitas Dei*, where he refers to Origen's *De principiis*, and in

---

[21] *Ep.* 82.23.

[22] Augustine's correspondence with Paulinus of Nola from 408 onwards on the nature of the resurrection body shows his cautious interest in a topic disputed in connexion with Origen; cf. Augustine, *ep.* 95 to Paulinus, especially 4, on the caution needed in expounding Scripture and the reasons for bitter quarrels arising, and 7-8 on the resurrection body; cf. Grossi, *art. cit.*, pp. 427-428.

[23] It may however show ignorance of one of the more obscure charges made against Origen that Augustine states in his *De Genesi ad litteram* 6.27.38 that Adam lost the divine image through his sin (as well as later awareness of it that he qualifies the statement in his *Retractationes*).

[24] Pinian was with Rufinus in Sicily in 410 shortly before his death, apparently encouraging him in his translation of Origen; cf. Rufinus' preface to his translation of Origen's *Homilies on Numbers*.

[25] Rufinus had addressed letters of exhortation to Proba, which were known to Gennadius (*De uiris inlustribus* 17). Jerome thought the family was inclined to Origenist views (cf. his *ep.* 130.16 to Demetrias).

his *De haeresibus*, chapter 43. In this last chapter he distinguishes between the accusations of Epiphanius, the assertions of Origen's defenders and of those well versed in his works, and the teachings where there is no doubt concerning his heresy [26]. Augustine's general attitude is marked by cautious restraint and avoidance of personal polemics; his interest is directed to the teachings in question rather than to the individual [27].

The use of works of Origen by Augustine was investigated by Berthold Altaner in an article published in 1950 [28], but without any reference to Pauline exegesis. Altaner provides evidence for the use of Jerome's translation of the *Homilies on Luke*, and perhaps those on the *Song of Songs*, of *De principiis*, which was translated by both Rufinus and Jerome, and of Rufinus' translations of the *Homilies on Genesis, Leviticus* and *Judges*. Some of the passages in question occur in later works of Augustine, such as the *Civitas Dei* and the *Quaestiones in Heptateuchum*, but in at least two cases a problem arises over the chronology. This is that Altaner cites evidence of dependence of passages in Augustine's *De Genesi contra Manichaeos* of 388-389 on Origen's *Homilies on Genesis* and *Leviticus* [29], which were translated by Rufinus more that a decade later [30]. The solution to this must be that Augustine's dependence on Origen comes via some other route here. Altaner himself suggests the lost translation of Origen's *Homilies on Job* by Hilary of Poitiers, Hilary's own *Commentary on the Psalms*, and the lost translation of Eusebius of Caesarea's *Commentary on the Psalms* by

---

[26] The teachings of Origen which Augustine denounces in his later works are in fact a travesty of Origen constructed by anti-Origenists. Augustine would not have found them in this form in the exegetical works available to him in Latin translation, nor even unambiguously expressed as "teachings" in Rufinus' translation of the *De principiis*. Such denunciations no doubt partly have the function of a safeguard enabling the denouncer to retain the useful insights of Origen and continue reading him without risking being accused as an Origenist.

[27] That Augustine continues to speak highly of Origen is shown by Grossi (*art. cit.*, p.427 note 10), who also illustrates Augustine's interest in particular teachings of which Origen was accused.

[28] See above note 3.

[29] Altaner, *art. cit.*, pp. 24-28. Cf. also the additional examples of influence without an obvious source in an available Latin translation given by Bertelink, *art cit.*, pp.15-18.

[30] For the date cf. C. P. Hammond, *art. cit.*, pp.393-4 and 403. It is very improbable that Rufinus translated these earlier than 388 and even more unlikely that such translations would have been obtained by Augustine by that date.

Eusebius of Vercelli [31]. When one remembers how often Origen repeats himself and how often he is plagiarised by later writers, the hypothesis of influence via some such source which is unknown to us or has not so far been noticed seems most plausible [32].

Altaner's investigations reveal interesting areas where Augustine's thought is influenced by Origen, including some of his ideas about angels and his concept of the five spiritual senses of the inner man, as well as a number of individual pieces of exegesis such as the allegorical interpretation of the coats of skin in *Genesis* 3,21 [33]. They also show up the difficulty of achieving certainty in identifying direct use by Augustine of a particular work, particularly since Augustine seldom names his sources and is too independent a thinker to follow them slavishly [34]. This is one of the reasons why I have taken a different and rather broader approach in this paper.

Part II: AUGUSTINE'S EARLY WRITINGS PRIOR TO 394 [35]

There are a number of reasons why the structure of Augustine's early thought is similar to that of Origen's. One must be the influence of Ambrose, who himself was strongly influenced by Origen [36]. Another is that both Origen and Augustine make use of a Platonist framework in providing a theodicy against heretical attacks, in the case of Origen against the attacks of Marcion and the Gnostics on the creator god of the Old Testament and his dispensation, in the case of Augustine against Manichaean dualism. For both Origen and Augustine the assertion of the value of the material order but also of its subordination to the spiritual

---

[31] Altaner, *art. cit.*, p.26. He also suggests that the Manichaeans opposed by Augustine in his *De Genesi contra Manichaeos* could have criticised views of Origen.

[32] Cf. the important article of B. Studer, *Zur Frage des westlichen Origenismus*, in *Studia Patristica* IX = TU 94 (1966) pp.270-287.

[33] *Art. cit.*, pp.26-28.

[34] On Augustine's methods in handling his sources, cf. Altaner, *Augustins Methode der Quellenbenützung*, in *Sacris Erudiri* 4 (1952) 5-17.

[35] It is not possible here to give references to the copious secondary literature on the development of Augustine's thought. Useful surveys are given by Alberto Pincherle, *La formazione teologica di Sant' Agostino*, Rome 1947, and Eugene TeSelle, *Augustine the Theologian*, London 1970.

[36] Giuseppe Ferretti, *L' influsso di S. Ambrogio in S. Agostino*, Faenza 1951, was unfortunately not available to me.

realm form part of their anti-heretical stance [37]. For both Origen and the early Augustine the endowment of the soul with free will, its fall from God and the divine provision for its return are central to their theodicy. In his early works Augustine writes of this fall in terms which can be understood as applying to every man. Like Origen, Augustine sees the return to God in terms of a progress, or more specifically a transfer of the affections, from earthly to heavenly things, something which is difficult so long as the soul is weighed down by the body [38]. Augustine supports this picture by reference to Pauline verses which are dear also to Origen. Thus in the *De vera religione* 48-49 and the *De moribus Ecclesiae Catholicae* 36-37 Augustine appeals to the Pauline distinction between the old, outer or earthly man and the new, heavenly or inner man, quoting *Col. 3, 1 Cor.* 15 and *2 Cor.* 4.

In defending the Old Testament against Manichaean attack in his early works Augustine quotes Paul to support the distinction between a literal and a spiritual interpretation in a manner reminiscent of Origen. Thus in *De utilitate credendi* 9 he quotes Pauline verses much favoured by Origen, *2 Cor.* 3,6 "The letter killeth, but the spirit giveth life", and *2 Cor.* 3,14-16 on the veil over the reading of the Old Testament, in order to show that the Old Testament contains mysteries which should not be taken literally but understood through Christ [39]. Like Origen he emphasises the need for teachers who will provide milky food for the weak but speak wisdom among the perfect [40].

Augustine's early commentary, the *De Genesi contra Manichaeos*, gives a figurative or spiritual explanation of the opening chapters of *Genesis*, very much in the manner of Origen. As I have already mentioned, the allegorical interpretation of the coats of skin in this work is noted by Altaner as being derived from Origen.

Augustine's first close acquaintance with the letters of Paul will have been during his period among the Manichaeans, who attributed central

---

[37] Like Origen Augustine turns to *1 Cor.* 15 in order to refute the heretical view that the resurrection is of the soul alone and to show that the body too will rise but that it will be changed to a heavenly body; cf. *Contra Adimantum Manichaeum* 4-5, written in about 394.

[38] Both Origen and Augustine like to quote *Sap.* 9,15 to show this; for Augustine cf. e.g. *De vera religione* 41, *Confessions* 7.17 etc.

[39] Cf. *Confessions* 6.4 on Ambrose's frequent references to *2 Cor.* 3,6 and the impression made on Augustine; also *Retractationes* on *De utilitate credendi* 9.

[40] *De vera religione* 51.

AUGUSTINE, ORIGEN AND THE EXEGESIS OF ST. PAUL   349

importance to Paul [41]. Later he refuted the Manichaean interpretations of certain passages but in some cases none the less retained a special preference for Pauline verses emphasised by the Manichaeans [42]. While correcting the Manichaean view of the Old Testament law, Augustine still retained their emphasis on it as a yoke of bondage from which Christ has brought freedom, following *Gal.* 5,1 [43].

In Augustine's debate with the Manichaean Fortunatus at Hippo in 392, the two opponents each put forward their rival views on the origin of evil and on human sin and conversion, quoting Pauline verses in support. Rival interpretations are claimed for *Eph.* 2,1-18 and in particular *Eph.* 2,3 "We were by nature children of wrath" (16-17). Against Fortunatus' Manichaean dualism Augustine argues that the source of evil is voluntary sin followed by the punishment for sin (14-15). Fortunatus rejects Augustine's assertion of free will, stating that men sin under compulsion from the hostile nature, until such time as the soul recognises its true origin and earns reconciliation to God (20). Augustine cites *1 Tim.* 6,10 to show that the root of all evils is desire (*cupiditas*), whereas Fortunatus claims that desire is only the door of sin but not its author (21). Fortunatus cites verses from *Rom.* 7-8 and *Gal.* 5,17 on the wisdom of the flesh and its hostility to God, the lusting of the flesh against the spirit, and the law in our members which wars against the law in our minds. Augustine here concedes a point to Fortunatus to the extent that he now gives a qualification of his previous (20) strong assertion of free will. The first man did have unimpeded free will, whereas his descendents have been cast into necessity by the force of habit. This fleshly habit is what is referred to by Paul as the wisdom of the flesh. As long as we live according to the flesh we are under compulsion, until such time as we are freed by the grace of God, inspiring us with divine love (22). The same distinction is made very

---

[41] Cf. F. Decret, *L'utilisation des Épîtres de Paul chez les Manichéens d'Afrique*, in J. Ries etc., *Le Epistole Paoline nei Manichei, i Donatisti e il primo Agostino*, Rome 1989, pp. 28-83.

[42] Thus *Phil.* 2,5-8 on Christ's self-humiliation was a favourite passage with Augustine and with the Manichaeans, being quoted by Fortunatus in his debate with Augustine at Hippo in 392 (cf. also *Confessions* 7.9). The Pauline verses already referred to on the old, outer or earthly man and the new, inward or heavenly man were used by the Manichaeans (*Contra Faustum* 24), but with an idiosyncratic interpretation, since they denied that the outer man was made by God.

[43] Cf. *De utilitate credendi* 9 and *Contra Faustum* 8; also *Contra Fortunatum* 2.22 correcting the Manichaean interpretation of the "law of sin and death" of *Rom.* 8,2, which they identified with the law of Moses (cf. Faustus in *Contra Faustum* 19).

much more forcefully and clearly in *De libero arbitrio* 3.48-54, where Augustine again relies on *Gal.* 5,17 and verses from *Rom.* 7 as well as *1 Tim.* 6,10 and *Eph.* 2,3 [44].

Augustine's earliest works after his conversion had taken a philosophical approach, making little reference to the bible. From about 388 onwards he included anti-Manichaean polemic and more frequent appeals to biblical texts and after his return to Africa he embarked on biblical exegesis with the *De Genesi contra Manichaeos* and the beginning of the *De diversis quaestionibus*. Already by 392 in the passage I have just quoted from the debate with Fortunatus a shift is becoming noticeable in Augustine's thought, which will gradually take him away from the emphasis on free will which is so dear to Origen. Origen would indeed agree with Augustine to the extent of maintaining that the conditions of this mortal life are an obstacle to the attainment of virtue and indeed that they make complete virtue impossible, and also that these conditions are the result of Adam's fall and the punishment imposed in *Gen.* 3,17-19, which affects all Adam's descendents. He does not however regard these conditions as completely preventing exercise of the will in choosing whether to do good or bad prior to conversion. Augustine's pessimistic view of human capabilities came to be combined with certain other features which contributed to a characteristic framework of ideas very different from that of Origen. One point may be mentioned now, others will arise shortly.

Seen from the viewpoint of Origen the fact that each individual soul has fallen before being assigned to life in the mortal body as a descendent of Adam means that there is no injustice involved in the soul being born into circumstances which impede the practice of virtue. If one rejects Origen's view, the question necessarily arises why we should be punished for the sin of Adam and Eve. Augustine explicitly faces this problem in his *De libero arbitrio* 3.53-59. For the moment he leaves open the question of whether or not the soul preexists the body [45]. He tries to show that its involvement in Adam's punishment is fair in any case and he emphasises the divine aid given in overcoming the obstacles of life in this world. This passage from *De libero arbitrio* 3 may have been written as late as or later than Augustine's Pauline commentaries,

[44] Cf. Malcolm E. Alflatt, *The Development of the Idea of Involuntary Sin in St. Augustine*, in *Revue des Études Augustiniennes* 20 (1974) 113-134.

[45] Augustine was later confronted more urgently with the same question in relation to the fate of unbaptised infants; cf. *ep.* 166 to Jerome.

so I will now go on the consideration of the latter in Part III of this paper.

Part III: AUGUSTINE'S PAULINE EXEGESIS IN 394-396

In 394-5 Augustine composed three works of Pauline exegesis, the *Expositio quarumdam propositionum ex Epistola ad Romanos*, the *Expositio Epistolae ad Galatas* and the *Epistolae ad Romanos inchoata expositio*, which he only continued as far as *Rom.* 1,7. In addition passages from the Pauline epistles are expounded in the *De diversis quaestionibus*, which was started after Augustine's return to Africa but only finally collected together after he became bishop, and in the *Ad Simplicianum de diversis quaestionibus* of the year 396 [46]. If one approaches Augustine's *Expositio quarumdam propositionum* after reading Origen one is immediately struck by the contrast. Here is a writer standing outside the main stream of Greek patristic exegesis, but with his own theological preoccupations which impose a forceful pattern on Paul's thought. Augustine expounds the epistle in the form of short statements of Paul's meaning, whereas Origen shares his own exploration with the reader, often leaving questions open or providing alternative interpretations. Origen writes commentaries of enormous length, bringing to bear all the techniques of pagan literary and textual scholarship and all the learning acquired during a lifetime of biblical studies. The detailed discussions of individual problems and the long excursuses mean that the reader may lose the thread of Paul's argument,

---

[46] Much has been written on Augustine's Pauline exegesis. Cf. in particular M. G. Mara, *L'influsso di Paolo in Agostino*, in J. Ries, *op. cit.*, pp.125-162, and the studies of Augustine on *Rom.* 7 and *Rom.* 9 referred to by Mara, p.152 note 183; also William S. Babcock, *Augustine's Interpretation of Romans (A.D. 394-6)*, in *Augustinian Studies* 10 (1979) 55-74. Babcock concentrates particularly on the exegesis of *Rom.* 7 and 9 and on the question whether Augustine was influenced by Tyconius. J. Patout Burns, *The Interpretation of Romans in the Pelagian Controversy*, in *Augustinian Studies* 10 (1979) 43-54, concentrates on *Rom* 7 and 9, and includes some comparison with Rufinus' translation of Origen's *Commentary on Romans*. P. Gorday, *Principles of Patristic Exegesis. Romans 9-11 in Origen, John Chrysostom and Augustine*, New York/Toronto 1983, deals briefly with the question of Augustine's sources for his exegesis of Romans (pp. 139ff.) and states the view that "Augustine does not show any sign of knowing Rufinus' version of Origen's Romans-commentary" (p.141). This would be true of Augustine's Pauline exegesis of the years 394-6. Marie-François Berrouard, *L'exégèse augustinienne de Rom. 7,7-25 entre 396 et 418*, in *Recherches Augustiniennes* 16 (1981) 101-196, gives a very detailed study for those verses only.

XVII

although it would not be fair to say that Origen himself is unable to see the wood for the trees. With Augustine on the other hand one immediately has the impression of someone who has read Paul's epistle as a whole and attempted to grasp its main message. This is conveyed in the opening words of the commentary already and the comments on individual verses reinforce the impression. The central message which Augustine identifies is that of the relationship between works of the law and grace.

Perhaps the most striking feature is Augustine's use of a fourfold scheme to describe the condition of human life: firstly before the law, when we do not resist our sinful desires, secondly under the law, when our attempts to resist them only make things worse, thirdly under grace, when we appeal for help, our past sins are forgiven and we receive divine aid, and fourthly in peace, after the resurrection, since it is only then that we are freed from fleshly desires. This scheme is elaborated with reference to verses from *Rom.* 3-8 and recurs throughout the commentary. It is also expounded in the *De diversis quaestionibus* 66. It is characterised by the complete break between stage 2 (law) and stage 3 (grace), something which I think may be influenced both by Augustine's own conversion experience and also by the Manichaean view of the complete disjunction between law and gospel [47].

If one looks for a central theme in Origen's *Commentary on Romans*, the relationship between Jews and Gentiles in the divine dispensation is perhaps the most prominent of the various recurrent themes [48].

There are two possible reactions to the contrast between Augustine and Origen. One is to conclude that Augustine has understood the central point of Paul's theology, whereas Origen has not. The other is to regard Augustine as having imposed his own theological preconceptions onto Paul without regard for the complexity of Paul's thought or the historical context in which he was writing. If I say a little in support of the second viewpoint this is not to deny that there is a certain validity in the first.

---

[47] On possible influence here from Tyconius, *Liber Regularum* 3 (ed. F. C. Burkitt, *Texts and Studies* 3, Cambridge 1894, pp.12ff., especially pp.15-16), cf. Babcock, *art. cit.*, pp.68-69.

[48] Cf. Theresia Heither, *Translatio Religionis. Die Paulusdeutung des Origenes*, Cologne 1990, pp. 57ff.; C. P. Bammel, *Die Juden im Römerbriefkommentar des Origenes*, in Herbert Frohnhofen (ed.), *Christlicher Antijudaismus und jüdischer Antipaganismus*, Hamburg 1990, pp. 145-151.

XVII

One of the problems in expounding the epistle to the *Romans*
concerns the interpretation of Paul's references to the law. What exactly
does he mean by the word *law*, and does he mean the same each time he
uses it? When is he speaking solely of the law of Moses applicable only
to Jews, and when of law in general, applicable to all men, and what is
meant by the latter? Whereas Origen provides detailed and frequent
discussions, together with suggested alternative explanations according
to the different meanings of the word law, Augustine does not tackle this
question. Whereas Origen distinguishes various different kinds of law,
including the law of Moses, which in its literal sense is superseded by
the Gospel, the written laws of other peoples, the natural law written in
men's hearts, and the law of sin described by Paul as dwelling in his
members [49], Augustine simply refers to the law without further
qualification both where the Mosaic law is clearly intended [50] and where
he is apparently speaking of law in general [51]. Coupled with this is the
fact that Augustine takes virtually no interest in the historical situation
in which Paul was writing, whereas Origen, being much closer in date to
Paul, has an unusually clear grasp of the problems Paul faced.

In turning to Augustine's *Commentary on Galatians* one finds a much
greater awareness of the historical context and far more readiness to
make distinctions when speaking about law. It may be that this should
be attributed at least in part to Augustine's reading of Jerome's
Commentary on Galatians, which is largely based on lost expositions of
Origen. In addition Augustine also had Marius Victorinus as a
predecessor for the exegesis of *Galatians*, as well as Ambrosiaster, who
had written on *Romans* too [52]. It is striking that Augustine now opens his
commentary with an outline of the historical situation and that in the
course of the work he makes it clear when he is speaking of the Old
Testament law and what aspects of it are referred to. He also now
introduces a division within the law between the ceremonial
observances, which were shadows of things to come but a yoke of

---

[49] Cf. Riemer Roukema, *The Diversity of Laws in Origen's Commentary on Romans*,
Amsterdam 1988.

[50] E.g. 7-8,20,27-28,48,52 (where there seems to be a transition from Mosaic to general
law).

[51] The reader may guess that Augustine identifies the law in general with the
commandment "Thou shalt not covet" of *Rom.* 7,7 (cf.37-38), but this is not made explicit.

[52] It is not possible here to compare these earlier commentaries with that of Augustine.
On Augustine's *Commentary on Galatians* cf. M. G. Mara, *Storia ed esegesi nella Expositio
epistulae ad Galatas di Agostino*, in *Annali di Storia dell' Esegesi* 2 (1988) 93-102.

servitude when observed literally, and secondly the moral precepts of the decalogue, which are fulfilled only through faith and love, since it is only thus that righteousness is carried out through love of righteousness (43-44) [53].

In 396 Augustine wrote his *Ad Simplicianum de diversis quaestionibus*, in the first book of which he discusses two passages from Romans at some length, *Rom.* 7,7-25 and *Rom.* 9,10-29. These discussions are generally regarded as marking an important transition in his thought. I will pick out one or two points from each part which are particularly relevant in the present context. The first concerns the question of the law. As in the *Expositio quarumdam propositionum* Augustine embarks on his exegesis of *Rom.* 7,7-25 without enquiring what law is meant and without asking historical questions. Differently from his approach in expounding *Galatians* he makes no reference to the Jewish ceremonial law or the need to understand this spiritually. It is only when he reaches section 16 that he raises the question what law the apostle is speaking of. It turns out that the reason the question arises is that the Manichaeans refer Paul's negative statements about the law to the law which was given to the Jews and his positive statements to the law of Christ. Against this Augustine argues forcefully that both negative and positive statements refer to the same law, and that this is the law which contains the commandment "Thou shalt not covet". The law is good and the commandment is good, but it came in that sin may abound, only increasing concupiscence by forbidding it. It can only be fulfilled by love, "in the newness of the spirit", as Paul puts it in *Rom.* 7,6. Augustine now introduces a new interpretation of *2 Cor.* 3,6, "The letter killeth, but the spirit giveth life". The law is only a "letter" to those who do not fulfil it in the New Testament spirit of love. Those who are renewed by the spirit are freed from the condemnation of the law. The spirit gives life, because the fulfilment of the law is the love shed abroad in our hearts by the Holy Spirit.

---

[53] This distinction owes something to Manichaean ideas, if we can take Faustus as representative. As quoted by Augustine in his *Contra Faustum* Faustus distinguishes between the Jewish observances from which Christ liberates us, and the moral precepts contained in the decalogue, which are fulfilled by Christ. Unlike Augustine on the other hand Faustus identifies the latter category with the natural law of *Rom.* 2,14-15, regarding it as having been handed over by angels to different races in ancient times (*Contra Faustum* 19, 22 and 32).

Another important new point made in the discussion of *Rom.* 7,7-25 concerns the limited free will of those under the law [54]. Quoting *Rom.* 7,18, "To will is present with me, but to do that which is good I find not", Augustine comments that this might seem to remove free will, but in fact to "will" is within our power, it is the carrying out of that which is good which is not in our power, and this inability is the penalty of original sin. In this mortal life one thing remains for free will [55], and that is to turn to God in supplication [56].

The second passage from *Romans* discussed in the *Ad Simplicianum de diversis quaestionibus* is *Rom.* 9,10-29 on the calling of Jacob and rejection of Esau. Augustine had already dealt with these verses in the *De diversis quaestionibus* 68, and it is instructive to compare the two. The earlier treatment contains much that is characteristic of Origen's approach to the problem, in particular the concern to affirm the justice of God's call and the suggestion that it may be preceded by hidden merits of souls (*animarum occultissima merita*) [57].

It also contains an important difference from Origen, which was to be significant for Augustine's later thought. This is the interpretation - surely mistaken - of the potter's clay of *Rom.* 9,21 not as something neutral, ready to be formed into either honourable or dishonourable vessels, but as already negative, as the *massa peccati* of humanity, condemned as a result of Adam's sin in Paradise (68.3) [58]. The consequences of this are not yet elaborated. In addition Augustine already anticipates his own later discussion in his emphasis in connexion with *Rom.* 9,16 that God's call precedes man's will, and thus that it is God who works that will in man.

The discussion in the *Ad Simplicianum de diversis quaestionibus* starts with an account of Paul's purpose in the epistle as being to prevent boasting and to show that the grace of the Gospel is not given in return for merits. Although in this introductory section and also in the *De*

---

[54] 11.

[55] "liberum arbitrium".

[56] 14.

[57] 68.3 and also 68.1 and 4.

[58] Cf. Ambrosiaster, *Commentary on Romans* 9,21 (we are all *ex una atque eadem massa* and are all sinners) and on *Romans* 5,12, second and third recensions only (all sinned in Adam *quasi in massa*). Later, in his *Contra duas epistulas Pelagianorum* 4.4.7, Augustine appealed to the latter passage to justify his incorrect interpretation of the words *in quo* in *Rom.* 5,12. On the limited extent of Ambrosiaster's influence on Augustine, cf. Pincherle, *op. cit.*, pp. 182-5.

diversis quaestionibus [59] Augustine shows some awareness that Paul is concerned with the calling of the Gentiles and rejection of the Jews, he does not apply this to the main part of his exegesis, which concentrates rather on God's calling and rejection of individuals [60]. Reporting on this chapter many years later in his *Retractationes* Augustine stated that he had struggled to maintain human free will, but that the grace of God had prevailed. The picture which results is a harsh one. God's calling is not according to merit, nor is it according to future merits foreseen by divine foreknowledge. God's grace precedes all merit and even the good will in us is a gift of God. Why then does he call some and reject others, and how is divine justice shown in this? Augustine's answer is that all men are a 'massa peccati', because of Adam's sin. All deserve to be punished. It is not unjust for God to exact that debt from some and not from others.

INTERLUDE

During the fifteen years or so until 411 Augustine's attention was much occupied by controversy with the Donatists. In the same period news will have reached him of the disputes about Origenism and the condemnation of Origen's teachings. It may be however that at this stage he kept an open mind on the subject, since it is only in his later writings that he expresses his rejection of 'Origenist' teachings [61].

Meanwhile in Italy ideas were being discussed which would lead to the outbreak of the Pelagian controversy [62]. Opposition to the disputed teachings of Origen played a major role. Several of the opinions for which Caelestius was later to be accused at Carthage were put forward

---

[59] 68.6.

[60] Cf. 1.2.19, where he states that God calls some Jews and some Gentiles. For a comparison with Tyconius cf. Babcock, *art. cit.*, pp.72-3.

[61] See above p. 345. The date of Augustine's rethinking his views on the preexistence of souls and the nature of man's body in paradise may be later than is suggested by TeSelle, *op. cit.*, pp.263-264, according to Robert J. O'Connell, *art. cit.*, pp.1-32, in particular p.26 note 88, and in his book, *The Origin of the Soul in St. Augustine's Later Works*, New York 1987. Cf. also Sfameni Gasparro, *art. cit.*, especially p.230 note 42.

[62] On the background to the Pelagian controversy cf. the excellent brief account by Vittorino Grossi in ed. Angelo di Berardino, *Patrology* 4, Westminster, Maryland 1988, pp. 463ff. On Pelagianism and the individual Pelagian authors and writings cf. Flavio G. Nuvolone, art. *Pélage et Pélagianisme*, in *Dictionnaire de Spiritualité* 12.2 (Paris 1986) col. 2889-2942.

by Rufinus the Syrian [63], a fervent opponent of Origenism, who was sent by Jerome to Rome and Milan in 399 and stirred up trouble for his namesake Rufinus of Aquileia [64]. His work *De fide* [65], written during the first decade of the fifth century, fiercely attacks Origen for his views of creation and the fall (17ff., cf. also 36 and 51), while retaining an emphasis on human free will and divine justice and benevolence which is reminiscent of Origen (cf. 19, 24, 33, 35-6, 39, 50). Origen however is not the only object of attack. Equally mistaken are the views of certain unnamed opponents, who teach a traducianist view of the human soul (28) and convict the whole world of iniquity because of one man Adam (39). Rufinus the Syrian himself rejects the idea of a "hard fall" and states that God forgave Adam and Eve and arranged the conditions of this life for their good, giving them death to free them from sin and misery, and a life of toil to assist them in virtue (32-36). Human nature, created good, was not made evil by the fall (as Old Testament examples show), and children are baptised not because of Adam's sin, but in order that they may share in the inheritance of the heavenly kingdom (39-41, 48).

It would be wrong simply to identify Rufinus the Syrian's unnamed opponents with Augustine, but their views are certainly related to those put forward by Augustine, especially in his *De diversis quaestionibus ad Simplicianum* [66]. Presumably this work had stimulated discussion. Concern about Augustine's ideas seems also to be reflected in the anonymous work *De induratione cordis Pharaonis* [67] and in the correspondence of Paulinus of Nola [68], as well as having affected

---

[63] On Rufinus the Syrian cf. H. I. Marrou, *Les attaches orientales du Pélagianisme*, in *Académie des Inscriptions et Belles Lettres, Comptes rendus des séances de l'année 1968*, pp. 461-472, who shows the relation of his statements to those condemned at Carthage in 411; also G. Bonner, *Rufinus of Syria and African Pelagianism*, in *Augustinian Studies* 1 (1970) 31-47; Eugene TeSelle, *Rufinus the Syrian, Caelestius, Pelagius*, in *Augustinian Studies* 3 (1972) 61-95; Otto Wermelinger, *Rom und Pelagius*, Stuttgart 1975, pp. 11ff.

[64] Cf. C. P. Hammond, *The Last Ten Years of Rufinus' Life*, in *Journal of Theological Studies*, NS 28 (1977) 425-6.

[65] Cf. the edition with translation, introduction and commentary by Mary W. Miller, *Rufini Presbyteri, Liber De Fide*, Washington 1964.

[66] Cf. Bonner, *art. cit.*, pp. 43ff.; TeSelle, *art. cit.*, pp. 72ff. and 80ff.

[67] Cf. Teselle, *art. cit.*, pp. 83ff., and Nuvolone, *art. cit.*, col.2919-2920, and *Problèmes d'une nouvelle édition du De Induratione Cordis Pharaonis attribué a Pélage*, in *Revue des Études Augustiniennes* 26 (1980) 115-6.

[68] Cf. the lost letter to which Jerome replied in his *ep.* 85, and Paulinus, *ep.* 23.44 and 30 to Severus.

XVII

358

Pelagius himself [69]. Rufinus of Aquileia will no doubt have been aware of the questions under discussion when he chose to translate Origen's *Commentary on the Epistle to the Romans* into Latin [70]. What was it, we may ask, that stimulated Paulinus of Milan to bring an accusation against Caelestius? Perhaps the opinions of Rufinus the Syrian had already been debated at Milan at the time of his visit there in 399. In addition the *De diversis quaestionibus* of Augustine addressed to Ambrose's successor, Simplician of Milan, will surely have been included in discussions taking place at Milan. It seems that the bishops of Milan, Simplician and Venerius, were not very impressed by the campaign against Origenism [71]. Rufinus the Syrian's rejection of the doctrine of a "hard fall" and resulting sinfulness of all mankind will not have found favour with Milanese Christians standing in the tradition of St. Ambrose. Paulinus himself was presumably sympathetic to Augustine's viewpoint.

Part IV: AUGUSTINE'S EARLIEST ANTI-PELAGIAN TREATISES OF 411-412

In the autumn or early winter of 411 Pelagius' pupil Caelestius was accused of heresy before a council at Carthage and a number of propositions supposedly maintained by him were condemned [72]. They included the statements that Adam's sin injured only himself and not the human race, and that new-born infants are in the same condition as Adam was before the fall, and also that the Law no less than the Gospel brings men to the kingdom of heaven, and that there were sinless men even before the coming of Christ [73]. Augustine's writings in opposition to these propositions contain a sudden upsurge of interest in the

---

[69] Cf. TeSelle, *art. cit.*, p. 82; Giovanni Martinetto, *Les premières réactions antiaugustiniennes de Pélage*, in *Revue des Études Augustiniennes* 17 (1971) 83-117.

[70] I have discussed the relation of this translation to the issues debated in a paper entitled *Traduzione di Rufino del Commento di Origene alla lettera ai Romani e la controversia pelagiana*, to be published in the proceedings of the *Convegno Internazionale di Studi: Esegesi e storia in Rufino di Concordia*, held at Concordia, Portogruaro and Sesto al Reghena, 18-20 May 1990.

[71] Cf. C. P. Hammond, *The Last Ten Years of Rufinus' Life*, in *Journal of Theological Studies* NS 28 (1977) 388-389.

[72] On the date cf. F. Refoulé, *La datation du premier concile de Carthage contre les Pélagiens*, in *Revue des Études Augustiniennes* 9 (1963) 41-49. On the general circumstances cf. Otto Wermelinger, *Rom und Pelagius*, Stuttgart 1975, pp. 4ff.

[73] It should be noted that the "Pelagian" failure to acknowledge divine grace because of an overemphasis on the capabilities of human free will was not yet a point at issue.

interpretation of the epistle to the Romans. My own impression is that one of the reasons for this concentration on Romans is the fact that he had recently obtained a copy of Rufinus' translation of Origen's commentary on that work [74]. A point of particular interest is that whereas Augustine's earliest anti-Pelagian treatise, the *De peccatorum meritis et remissione et de baptismo parvulorum*, shows a positive influence of Origen in the adoption of certain new ideas and taking over of individual comments, the following treatise, *De spiritu et littera*, gives evidence of a reaction against Origen's views.

In the *De peccatorum meritis et remissione* Augustine is able to support his own views on the transmission of sin, baptism and the possibility of sinlessness by means of arguments put forward by Origen. In Book 1.9 Augustine argues against his opponents' assertion that sin is transmitted from Adam merely by imitation and not by propagation. If this were correct, he claims, St Paul in *Romans* 5,12 would have ascribed the origin of sin not to Adam, from whom the human race is propagated, but to the devil, whom men imitate in sinning. The same argument occurs in Rufinus' translation of Origen's commentary on *Rom.* 5,12, where Origen gives the same reason for Paul's wording in this verse, namely the descent of the human race from Adam [75]. In addition Origen, in expounding the words "body of sin" in *Rom.* 6,6 and "flesh of sin" in *Rom.* 8,3, provided an idea about the mechanism whereby Adam's sin is propagated to his descendents. It is the impulse of concupiscence, which transmits the pollution of sin to those conceived by sexual intercourse. Christ was free from this pollution because of his virginal conception, so his flesh only had the likeness of sinful flesh, as Paul states in *Rom.* 8,3. It is because of this transmitted taint referred to by Paul as "body of sin" that the Church has received a tradition to baptise infants [76]. Augustine takes up these arguments in Book II,11,15 and 38, also referring to *Rom.* 8,3.

---

[74] It is not caused by Pelagius' commentary, since Augustine only read Pelagius' *'expositiones breuissimas'* after writing the *De peccatorum meritis et remissione* Books I-II; cf. Book III.1, ed. C. F. Urba and J. Zycha, CSEL 60 (1913), p. 129. Nor is there any particular emphasis on the exegesis of Romans in Rufinus the Syrian's *Liber de Fide* (cf. the index in ed. Miller, p.196), which Augustine did have before him according to Refoulé, *art. cit.*

[75] The more important texts from Augustine and Origen are quoted in the appendix, below pp. 365 ff.

[76] Cf. Appendix of Texts 1B. Cf. also Augustine, *De peccatorum meritis et remissione* 1.58, ed. Urba and Zycha , pp. 57-58, for the same understanding of *Rom.* 6,6. This is not to

On the question of the possibility of sinlessness Augustine could find much to agree with in Origen's *Commentary on Romans*. The same quotations (*Job* 14,4-5 and *Ps.* 51,5) are used by both authors to show that infants already have sin from the first day [77]. In expounding *Rom.* 3,10ff. Origen quotes *Ps.* 143,2 to show that no one except Christ is justified in the sight of God, and he goes on to argue for the impossibility of complete justice or understanding under the conditions of life in the body as described in *Sap.* 9,15 [78]. Augustine agrees and quotes the same verses [79]. Both Origen and Augustine give examples of holy men from the Old Testament who none the less were not without fault. The lists are not identical but both include Noah's getting drunk and Job's confession of his sins [80]. In the preface to his commentary [81] Origen points out that in *Phil.* 3,12-13 and 15 Paul uses the word "perfect" in two different senses, saying first that he is not perfect and then that he is perfect. This point is taken up by Augustine in II.20-22.

The impossibility of sinlessness in this life had already been repeatedly argued by Augustine in his anti-Donatist polemic [82]; it is more striking therefore to find that the influence of Origen on *Romans* has caused him to introduce a quite new aspect into his interpretation of what is meant by law in Paul's *Epistle to the Romans*, namely the inclusion of the law of nature. In Book 1.12, in speaking of the law of *Rom.* 5,13 and 20, he offers an alternative explanation in the style of Origen, suggesting an interpretation *either* in terms of the natural law, present in all those who have reached the age of discretion, *or* of the law

---

deny that there were other influences on Augustine as well; cf. Johannes van Oort, *Augustine and Mani on concupiscentia sexualis*, in J. den Boeft and J. van Oort (ed.), *Augustiniana Traiectina*, Paris 1987, pp. 137-152.

[77] Cf. Appendix of Texts 1C.

[78] Ed. C. H. E. Lommatzsch, Vol. 1, Berlin 1836, pp. 178-180; ed. C. P. Hammond Bammel, Freiburg 1990, pp. 210-212.

[79] II.8 and 12, ed. Urba and Zycha, pp. 78f. and 83.

[80] Augustine II.12 ff.; Origen, ed. Lommatzsch, Vol. 1, pp. 329-331 and p. 190. Origen's interpretation at Vol.2, pp. 60-61, that Daniel laments *our* sins, is however opposed by Augustine, II.13, ed. Urba and Zycha, pp. 84-85; cf. C. P. Hammond Bammel, *Philocalia IX, Jerome, Epistle 121, and Origen's Exposition of Romans VII*, in *Journal of Theological Studies* NS 32 (1981), p.69.

[81] Ed. Lommatzsch, Vol. 1, pp. 2-3; ed. Bammel, p. 38.

[82] He had quoted *Job* 14,4-5 and *Ps.* 51,5 for this purpose already in his *Contra litteras Petiliani* 2.232, and they had been used similarly by Jerome in a passage (no doubt dependent on Origen) in his *Adversus Iovinianum* quoted by Augustine in *De peccatorum meritis et remissione* III.13, ed. Urba and Zycha, p. 140.

XVII

of Moses. In Book 1.65-66 he argues that infants have no sin of their own, since they have no awareness of either the natural or the written law and no use of the faculty of reason [83], and he gives the example of an infant striking its parents in anger and the parents' amused reaction. The same example is used by Origen in his exposition of *Rom.* 5,13, and it seems clear that Augustine has copied him here [84].

As if anxious not to be associated in any way with Origenist views Augustine includes at Book 1.31-32 [85] a refutation of those who attempt to justify God's inscrutable judgements towards mankind by means of human conjectures and improbable fables about previous sins of souls in their heavenly habitation. If, as seems likely, he was using Rufinus the Syrian's *De fide* in his refutation of Caelestius' views [86], he will have been alerted to the danger that his own position might be associated with Origenism. Perhaps it is for the same reason that in Book III.13-14 [87] he argues that the doctrine of original sin is so much a part of the church's tradition that it was even held by the heretic Jovinian and assumed as a common basis by Jerome in arguing against him.

The reaction against Origen is more apparent in the *De spiritu et littera* of 412. In this work Augustine rejects Origen's methods of explaining Paul's use of the term "law" and reverts again to his earlier interpretation of Romans, presenting Paul's argument by means of verses drawn from throughout the epistle, and taking the passage in *Rom.* 7 about the commandment which was found to be unto death as central. This passage shows that Paul's words in *2 Cor.* 3,6, "The letter killeth, but the spirit giveth life", are to be understood not with reference to the literal and figurative senses of the Jewish law, a purpose for which

---

[83] A similar view of infants is implied in *ep.* 98 to Boniface (on baptism), dated after the *De peccatorum meritis et remissione* by Vittorino Grossi, *Il battesimo e la polemica pelagiana negli anni 411/413*, in *Augustinianum* 9 (1969) 54ff. Cf. 4, ed. Goldbacher, CSEL 34, p. 525.16-17 (*infantis animam ... ubi (ratio) adhuc sopita erat*), and 2, ed. Goldbacher, p. 523.2-4 (*aetatis accessu ... propria incipiet habere peccata*).
[84] Cf. Appendix of Texts ID. It is also likely that Augustine's comment on variants in *Rom.* 5,14 (I.13, ed. Urba and Zycha, p. 14) is indebted to Origen (the variants are also mention in *ep.* 157 to Hilary of Syracuse, and by Ambrosiaster; cf. C. P. Hammond Bammel, *Der Römerbrieftext des Rufin und seine Origenes-Übersetzung*, Freiburg 1985, pp. 219f.).
[85] Ed. Urba and Zycha, pp. 29ff. It is possible that this passage (together with Book II.59) is a later addition; cf. note 61 above.
[86] On this cf. Refoulé, *art. cit.* The parallels which Refoulé quotes (pp. 44-46) seem convincing, but in some respects the arguments of those whom Augustine opposes (usefully listed by Wermelinger, *op. cit.*, pp. 286-289) have developed further.
[87] Ed. Urba and Zycha, pp. 139-141.

XVII

Origen had repeatedly quoted them, but of the command to live rightly, which is itself the letter that killeth, unless the lifegiving Spirit is present to inspire good desire in our hearts [88]. This provides the key to the understanding of Romans, and Augustine rejects possible references to the Jewish ceremonial law and the law of nature. He provides a somewhat forced interpretation of Paul's clear mention of the law of nature in *Rom.* 2,14-15, arguing that the Gentiles who do the works of the law by nature are to be understood as Gentiles believing in the Gospel, whose nature has been restored by the Spirit of grace [89]. Origen's exposition of these verses must have been most objectionable to him, since it promises rewards for good works to unbelieving Jews and Gentiles [90].

Confirmation that Augustine's concentration on arguing for his own interpretation of *Romans* in this work is indeed connected at least in part with his reaction to reading Origen emerges in certain minor points where he clearly corrects Origen, for example his provision of a rival explanation of Paul's name, which emphasises his humility, introduced by the words "as it seems to me" [91], or his rejection of Origen's attempt to draw a distinction in *Rom.* 3,30 between the words "from faith" and "through faith" [92], an attempt which results in diminishing the distinction between law and grace.

It would be interesting to continue looking at further works of Augustine, for instance his *Epistle* 157 to Hilary of Syracuse, written in 414, which gives yet another discussion of *Romans*, showing more positive contacts with Origen, but time does not permit this. It has only been possible to look briefly at Augustine's first two major anti-Pelagian works. I have tried to convey to you my impression that Augustine is stimulated in these works, not only by the new questions being debated, but also by his recent reading of Origen on *Romans*. This impression is based on consideration of the development of Augustine's Pauline interpretation in general as well as on individual passages. If it is correct, it sheds interesting light on Augustine's methods. A powerful

---

[88] 5-8, ed. Urba and Zycha, pp. 157-160.

[89] 43-7, ed. Urba and Zycha, pp. 196-202.

[90] Cf. Appendix of Texts 2A.

[91] 12, ed. Urba and Zycha, pp. 163f. (*Paulus apostolus - qui cum Saulus prius uocaretur non ob aliud, quantum mihi uidetur, hoc nomen elegit, nisi ut se ostenderet paruum tamquam minimum apostolorum ...*); cf. Origen, ed. Lommatzsch, pp. 6-9; ed. Bammel, pp. 42-4.

[92] Cf. Appendix of Texts 2B.

and logical thinker himself, by 411 he had already formed his own view of what he saw as the core of Paul's message and was able to argue forcefully for it. Origen's *Commentary on Romans*, even in the drastically reduced version of Rufinus, was a work of Pauline exegesis greatly superior to anything Augustine had so far had at his disposal. His engagement with it shows his openness to stimulation and his acceptance of some new ideas, but equally his exceptional independence of thought, his readiness to disagree and to argue ruthlessly, even perversely, for his own views, and above all his concentration on those insights which he had come to regard as central to the Christian message.

Postscript: ORIGENISM AND THE BEGINNING OF THE PELAGIAN CONTROVERSY

Because Pelagius was attacked by Jerome as a disciple of Origen and is known to have been influenced by Origen in his Pauline commentary and in the development of some of his ideas [93] it may seem natural to assume that the Pelagians were closer to Origenism than their opponents. For the beginning of the controversy however, when Pelagius himself was not personally involved, the opposite was the case. As we have seen, Rufinus the Syrian, whose views seem to have been taken over by Caelestius, was motivated by opposition to Origen, whereas Augustine's assertion of original sin agreed with Origen. If O'Connell is correct in arguing that the passages in the *De peccatorum meritis et remissione* which oppose Origenist-type views were only added when Augustine revised the work considerably later [94], it may be that initially he was unaware that he might be laying himself open to a charge of championing doctrines which implied an Origenist view of the preexistence of the soul. His *ep.* 143 to Marcellinus however shows that

---

[93] Cf. R. F. Evans, *Pelagius: Inquiries and Reappraisals*, London 1968, pp. 6-25; A. J. Smith, *The Commentary of Pelagius on Romans compared with that of Origen-Rufinus*, in *Journal of Theological Studies* 20 (1918-19) 127ff.; Torgny Bohlin, *Die Theologie des Pelagius und ihre Genesis*, Uppsala 1957.

[94] See note 61 above. Robert J. O'Connell's stimulating book, *The Origin of the Soul in St. Augustine's Later Works*, New York 1987, in which he argues more fully for this dating, only became available to me after I had written this paper. In this *postscript* I follow the main lines of O'Connell's view on the development of Augustine's thought on the origin of the soul, but differ from him in supposing that Augustine's reticence about the Origenist controversy before his encounter with Orosius is caused by caution rather than ignorance.

certain critics had now accused him of teaching either traducianism or that the soul is imprisoned in the body as a punishment for previous sins (*ep.* 143.5). In his reply to this Augustine claims that the words from his *De libero arbitrio* quoted by the critics in fact left open the question of the origin of the soul. He continues to leave the question open and gives a summarising account of his views on original sin which leaves the impression that the matter is unproblematic (*ep.* 143.6). It seems that at this stage he still regarded the origin of the soul (including the option of preexistence) as a matter for debate [95]. In his *ep.* 164.20 (to Evodius) he has moved somewhat further, in that he now pronounces a firm rejection of the idea that souls are thrust into bodies as if into prisons because of their previous misdeeds. This however is a rejection of only one form of the doctrine of the preexistence of the soul. It seems likely that at this stage a three-cornered debate was taking place and that Origen's view still had its proponents, whereas Augustine's critics had been pressing him to make a choice between either traducianism or the Origenist teaching or rejecting the doctrine of original sin. Augustine himself refers to arguments used by those who favour the Origenist view as being easier to combine with the doctrine of original sin (*ep.* 166.27) [96], and Jerome gives warnings on the same subject in his *ep.* 130.16 to Demetrias. The dilemma into which Augustine was driven is expressed with as great an urgency and clarity as any of his opponents could wish for in his *ep.* 166 to Jerome, written after the arrival at Hippo of Orosius. If one rejects both traducianism and the "Origenist" teaching of the fall of the soul before its entry into the body, and adopts the option of creationism (as did Jerome), it becomes impossible to see how God can justly condemn to eternal punishment unbaptised infants who have died before committing sins. Moreover the argument that sin is transmitted to Adam's descendents as a result of the concupiscence by means of which they are conceived explains only why their flesh is tainted with original sin, but not why their souls should deserve punishment [97]. Jerome

---

[95] See above note 65.

[96] *Ep.* 166.27: *illi sibi uidentur de hac facilius exire quaestione, qui animas adseuerant pro meritis uitae prioris singulas singulis corporibus implicari.* Augustine goes on to express his fervent rejection of the idea of the body as a prison, and gives a number of reasons for his disagreement.

[97] Cf. *ep.* 166.10 and 22. This problem seems not yet to have struck Augustine in his *ep.* 143.6 to Marcellinus, but he shows awareness of it in his *ep.* 164.19 to Evodius. Cf. also *De peccatorum meritis et remissione* III.18 (quoting Pelagius on *Rom.* 5,15) and II.59 (which may be a later addition).

XVII

however had himself quite clearly expressed his support for the doctrine of original sin in his treatise against Jovinian and his *Commentary on Jonah* [98]. How is this dilemma to be solved? Augustine's own answer must surely be implied in the following statement which he includes in the preliminary list of his own most firm convictions concerning the soul: "Certus etiam sum *animam* nulla dei culpa, nulla dei necessitate uel sua, sed *propria uoluntate in peccatum esse conlapsam*" [99].

APPENDIX OF TEXTS:
AUGUSTINE [100] AND ORIGEN'S *COMMENTARY ON ROMANS* [101]

1. *De peccatorum meritis et remissione*

1A. Propagation of Sin from Adam - *Rom.* 5,12 speaks of Adam, not the devil

1.9, pp. 10-11: Sentiunt ... ipsum peccatum non propagatione in alios homines ex primo homine, sed imitatione transisse ... Sed si peccatum apostolus illud commemorare uoluisset, quod in hunc mundum non propagatione, sed imitatione intrauerit, eius principem non Adam sed diabolum diceret ... Proinde apostolus cum illud peccatum ac mortem commemoraret, quae ab uno in omnes propagatione transisset, eum principem posuit, a quo propagatio generis humani sumpsit exordium.
Origen on *Rom.* 5,12, L1, p.325: Quomodo per unum hominem ... uidebitur introisse peccatum? A muliere enim initium peccati et ante mulierem a serpente siue a diabolo ... Sed uide in his apostolum naturae ordinem tenuisse et ideo quoniam de peccato loquebatur ex quo mors in omnes homines pertransierat successionem posteritatis humanae quae huic morti subcubuit ex peccato uenienti non mulieri adscribit sed uiro.

---

[98] *Ep.* 166.6. The passages from these two works of Jerome referred to here by Augustine are quoted in full in the *De peccatorum meritis et remissione* III.12-13 (which might suggest that he had written these chapters only a short time before). Augustine may well have been aware that Jerome is dependent on Origen here. The dilemma therefore is how to retain the doctrine of original sin, so characteristic of Origen (though not only of Origen), but to combine it with a tenable view of the origin of the soul and the maintenance of divine justice.
[99] *Ep.*166.5. O'Connell in his book shows how vestiges of the doctrine of preexistence still remain in Augustine's later view of the origin of the soul.
[100] Ed. C.F. Urba and J. Zycha, CSEL 60 (1913).
[101] L1 and L2 = ed. C.H.E. Lommatzsch, Vol. 1 and Vol. 2, Berlin 1836-7; B1 = ed. C. P. Hammond Bammel, Freiburg 1990

1B. Sin propagated by concupiscence, so Christ only has *similitudo carnis peccati* (*Rom.* 8,3)

II.38, pp. 110-111: Tenuit quandam et in carnis natiuitate medietatem, ut nos quidem nati essemus in carne peccati, ille autem in similitudine carnis peccati, nos non solum ex carne et sanguine, uerum etiam ex uoluntate uiri et uoluntate carnis ... Ideo virginem matrem non lege carnis peccati, id est non concupiscentiae carnalis motu concipientem, sed pia fide sanctum germen in se fieri promerentem, quam eligeret creauit, de qua crearetur elegit.

II.11, p. 82: (Why does a just man not beget a just son?) Quasi ex hoc quisque carnaliter gignat quod iustus est et non ex hoc quod in membris eius concupiscentialiter mouetur, et ad usum propagandi lex peccati mentis lege conuertitur.

II.15, p. 87: Sunt omnes, sicut dicit apostolus, naturaliter, hoc est originaliter, irae filii, quoniam filii sunt concupiscentiae carnis et saeculi ... Quis enim erit mundus a sordibus? Nemo, nec si unius diei fuerit uita eius (*Job* 14,4-5).

Origen on *Rom.* 6,6, L1, pp. 396-7: De Saluatore quodam loco dicit: quia uenerit in similitudine carnis peccati (*Rom.* 8,3) ... In quo ostendit quod nostra quidem caro peccati sit caro Christi autem caro similis sit carni peccati. Non enim ex semine uiri concepta est ... Corpus ergo peccati est corpus nostrum quia nec Adam scribitur cognouisse Euam uxorem suam et genuisse Cain nisi post peccatum. Denique et in lege pro paruulo qui natus fuerit iubetur offerri hostia ... Pro quo peccato offertur unus hic pullus? Numquid nuper editus paruulus peccare potuit? Et tamen habet peccatum pro quo hostia iubetur offerri a quo mundus negatur quis esse nec si unius diei fuerit uita eius (*Job* 14,4-5). De hoc ergo etiam Dauid dixisse credendus est illud quod supra memorauimus: *quia in peccatis concepit me mater mea* (*Ps.* 51,5). Secundum historiam enim nullum matris eius declaratur peccatum. Pro hoc et ecclesia ab apostolis traditionem suscepit etiam paruulis baptismum dare.

Origen on *Rom.* 8,3, L2, p. 69: Omnes enim nos homines qui ex semine uiri cum muliere conuenientis concepti sumus illa necessario utimur uoce qua dicit Dauid: *quoniam in iniquitatibus conceptus sum et in peccatis concepit me mater mea* (*Ps.* 51,5). Uerum qui ex nulla uiri contagione sed solo Spiritu Sancto super uirginem ueniente et uirtute altissimi obumbrante uenit ad corpus immaculatum naturam quidem corporis nostri habuit pollutionem tamen peccati quae ex concupiscentiae motu conceptis traditur omnino non habuit.

1C. *Job* 14,4-5 and *Ps.* 51,5 prove human sinfulness from birth (David's birth not illegitimate)

1.34, p. 34: scriptum est neminem esse mundum, nec si unius diei fuerit uita eius. unde est et illud in Psalmis: ego enim in iniquitatibus conceptus sum et in

XVII

AUGUSTINE, ORIGEN AND THE EXEGESIS OF ST. PAUL   367

peccatis mater mea me in utero aluit; aut enim ex persona generali ipsius
hominis dicitur aut, si proprie Dauid hoc de se dicit, non utique de fornicatione,
sed de legitimo conubio natus fuit.
Origen, see above on *Rom.* 6,6, L1, p. 397.

1D. Infant hitting parent does not commit sin, as not yet subject to natural law

1.65-66, pp. 65-66: Doceamus quomodo per propriam uoluntatem ... nihil
mali commiserint infantes ... nulla omnino praecepti capacitas, nullus uel
naturalis uel conscriptae legis sensus aut motus, nullus in alterutram partem
rationis usus ... At hoc ignorantiae est, in qua profundissima iacet, qua etiam
matrem, cum post exiguum tempus ualuerit, percutiet iratus ... Haec non modo
feruntur, uerum etiam diliguntur in paruulis.
Origen on *Rom.* 5,13, L1, pp. 334-335: Puer ergo paruulus quattuor fere aut
quinque annorum si ut fieri solet indignatus uirga percutiat patrem aut matrem,
quantum ad praeceptum mandati spectat mortem debet. Sed quia lex in illo
nondum est naturalis quae eum doceat non debere iniuriam facere patri uel
matri nec scit in hoc crimen impietatis ammitti; et est quidem species peccati
quod facit; matrem enim percutit uel maledicit sed mortuum est in eo peccatum
quia per absentiam naturalis legis quae in eo nondum est peccatum ei non potest
reputari; nondum enim est intra eum ratio tanta quae eum doceat hoc quod facit
fieri non debere, et ideo etiam a parentibus non solum non reputatur ad culpam
sed ad gratiam iucunditatemque suscipitur.

2. *De spiritu et littera: Disagreement with Origen*

2A. *Rom.* 2,10. Will unbelievers receive a reward for good works?

44, p. 198: quibus autem gentibus bene operantibus gloriam, honorem
pacemque promitteret extra euangelii gratiam constitutis? quia enim
personarum acceptio non est apud deum ... ideo siue Iudaeus siue Graecus, hoc
est quilibet ex gentibus crediderit, salutem in euangelio pariter habebit.
Origen on *Rom.* 2,7-11, L1, pp. 97-99, B1, pp. 127-128: *gloria autem et
honor et pax omni operanti bonum, Iudaeo primum et Graeco.* Quod ut ego
capere possum de Iudaeis et gentibus dicit utrisque nondum credentibus ...
(unbelieving Jews and Greeks, though unable to receive eternal life, will not
lose *bonorum operum gloriam et honorem et pacem*) ... Dubitari igitur non puto
quod is qui pro malo opere condemnari meruisset idem si operatus esset opus
bonum remuneratione boni operis dignus haberetur ... Inde denique est quod et
in hoc loco subiungit: *non enim personarum acceptio est apud deum.*

XVII

2B. *Rom.* 3,30. Is there a distinction between *ex* and *per*?

50, p. 205: unus enim deus qui iustificat circumcisionem ex fide et praeputium per fidem; quod non ad aliquam differentiam dictum est, tamquam aliud sit *ex fide* et aliud *per fidem*, sed ad uarietatem locutionis ... (*Gal.* 3,8 and 2,15-16) ... ecce et praeputium dixit iustificari ex fide et circumcisionem per fidem.

Origen on *Rom.* 3,29-30, L1, pp. 223-225, B1, pp. 253-256: Non nos otiose praetereat quod dicit quia circumcisionem ex fide iustificet et non per fidem; praeputium uero per fidem et non ex fide. Non enim mihi uidetur superflua apud eum haberi ista praepositionum commutatio, quia inuenimus ab eo et in aliis locis non ut libet sed obseruanter haec posita et necessario differentiam distinctionis huius esse seruatam ... (*Rom.* 11,36; *1 Cor.* 11,12 and 12,8-9; *Jn.* 1,3-4). Quod si requirat aliqui curiosius hi qui ex fide iustificantur per quem iustificentur, et rursus hi qui per fidem iustificantur ex quo iustificentur ... dicere possumus quod qui ex fide iustificantur initio ex fide sumto per adimpletionem bonorum operum consummantur et qui per fidem iustificantur a bonis operibus exorsi per fidem summam perfectionis accipiunt.

XVIII

RUFINUS' TRANSLATION OF ORIGEN'S COMMENTARY ON ROMANS AND THE PELAGIAN CONTROVERSY

Rufinus did not die an untimely death. He was spared involvement in the Pelagian controversy, which broke out only a few months after his demise in 411 with the condemnation of Pelagius' disciple Caelestius by a council at Carthage for the denial of original sin. We may regard Rufinus as fortunate to have escaped the polemics of the following years. He shared the same friends with Pelagius: Paulinus of Nola, the ascetic couple Pinian and Melania, and the family of Anicia Proba ([1]). Pelagius had been influenced in the development of his ideas by Rufinus' translations of Greek works ([2]). In particular he had used Rufinus' translation of Origen's Commentary on Romans immediately it became available in about 406 in order to compose his own commentary on the Pauline Epistles ([3]). Since the extant manuscripts of the translation of Origen on Romans derive from a copy found by Rufinus' friends after his death which they describe as not yet published or revised it would seem that Pelagius was able to use this work in advance of its publication ([4]). Like Rufinus Pelagius and Caelestius left Rome as refugees from the Gothic invasion. Rufinus died on the island of Sicily, where Pelagian ideas were soon afterwards found to be flourishing. Pelagius and Caelestius travelled on to Africa and, while Caelestius was coming under attack at Carthage, Pelagius continued his journey to Palestine, where he came into conflict with Jerome. Pelagius revived ac-

---

([1]) Cf. PETER BROWN, *Religion and Society in the Age of Saint Augustine* (London 1972), pp. 183-226.

([2]) Cf. TORGNY BOHLIN, *Die Theologie des Pelagius und ihre Genesis* (Uppsala 1957).

([3]) Cf. BOHLIN, op. cit., pp. 87-103, and A.J. Smith, JThS 20 (1918-19), pp. 127ff.

([4]) Cf. C.P. HAMMOND, "A product of a fifth-century scriptorium", JThS, NS 29 (1978), p. 373.

cusations against Jerome originally made by Rufinus and Jerome responded by attacking Pelagius as a disciple of Rufinus (⁵).

It may therefore be interesting to ask whether Rufinus' translations did indeed support Pelagian views and where he would have stood in relation to the issues debated in the Pelagian controversy. The translation of Origen's Commentary on Romans is of particular interest because the exegesis of Romans played an important role in the controversy. Indeed the Pelagian ideas condemned at the Council of Carthage had been developed in reaction against the earlier exegesis of Romans published by St Augustine between 394 and 396.

The charges against Caelestius concerned Adam's sin and its results for the rest of the human race, and the possibility of leading a sinless life for those under the law before the coming of Christ. During the debate at the Council the practice of infant baptism was used as evidence for the view that newly born infants already have sin (⁶). It is not surprising that Caelestius' views were condemned at Carthage since they contradicted the views already expressed by Augustine. In his *De Diversis Quaestionibus ad Simplicianum* of 395-6 addressed to Simplician of Milan Augustine had taken Romans chapter 9 as a basis in developing his characteristic view of original sin, according to which as a result of Adam's sin all men are a lump of sin or "massa peccati" deserving punishment by divine justice (⁷). God's mercy is shown in his forgiving some men and calling them by his grace, his justice in his punishing others. This is combined with a view of law based on Romans chapter 7 according to which the function of the law is not to prevent sin but to give knowledge of sin and even to increase sinful concupiscence by its prohibition so that men may become aware of their need for grace. Already in his *Expositio quarundam propositionum epistulae ad Romanos* of 394-5 Augustine had depicted human development in four stages: firstly "before the law" when we follow the desires of the flesh in

---

(⁵) Cf. ROBERT F. EVANS, *Pelagius: Inquiries and Reappraisals* (London 1968), pp. 6ff.

(⁶) Cf. OTTO WERMELINGER, *Rom und Pelagius* (Stuttgart 1975), pp. 4ff; EUGENE TESELLE, "Rufinus the Syrian, Caelestius, Pelagius", *Augustinian Studies* 3 (1972), pp. 61ff.

(⁷) He had taken the potter's clay of Rom 9,20-21 as a "massa peccati" already in his *De Diversis Quaestionibus 83* chapter 68.3, but draws the consequences more forcefully in the *De Diversis Quaestionibus ad Simplicianum*.

ignorance; secondly "under the law" when we know that these desires are forbidden and struggle against them in vain; thirdly "under grace" when our past sins are forgiven and divine help enables us to refrain from following the desires of the flesh; and fourthly "in peace" after the resurrection, when we are no longer troubled by fleshly desires ([8]). Augustine's picture of a God who condemns men to punishment for a sin committed by their remote ancestor and who gave the law not to help men but merely to show up their sinfulness had provoked a reaction which led to the enunciation of the "Pelagian" views for which Caelestius was condemned.

I will return to this point later. At the moment I suggest that we turn to Rufinus' translation of Origen's Commentary on Romans in order to see what statements it makes on the disputed points. We shall not be the first to do so. In the earliest manuscript of this work, Lyons Bibliothèque de la Ville ms. 483, which was written in the fifth century and preserved until the ninth century at Verona ([9]), a contemporary reader has left marginal notes at four significant points. The most striking of these notes states "Against those who deny the propagation of sin" - "contra eos qui traducem negant peccati" - and directs attention to a passage which discusses the phrase "body of sin" in Rom 6,6 and does indeed give a striking affirmation of the hereditary transmission of sin. It is stated here that our flesh is the flesh of sin, but the flesh of Christ is only similar to the flesh of sin because of his virginal conception. It was only after the fall that Adam knew his wife Eve and begat Cain. Newborn infants are already unclean with sin at birth, and it is for this reason that the law prescribed a sacrifice for them and that the church baptises them ([10]).

([8]) Cf. WILLIAM S. BABCOCK, "Augustine's Interpretation of Romans (A.D. 394-396), *Augustinian Studies* 10 (1979), p. 59.

([9]) On this manuscript cf. CAROLINE P. HAMMOND BAMMEL, *Der Römerbrieftext des Rufin* (Freiburg 1985), pp. 110ff. and the articles referred to there.

([10]) De Saluatore quodam loco dicit: quia uenerit in similitudine carnis peccati (Rom 8,3)... In quo ostendit quod nostra quidem caro peccati sit caro Christi autem caro similis sit carni peccati. Non enim ex semine uiri concepta est... Corpus ergo peccati est corpus nostrum quia nec Adam scribitur cognouisse Euam uxorem suam et genuisse Cain nisi post peccatum. Denique et in lege pro paruulo qui natus fuerit iubetur offerri hostia... Pro quo peccato offertur unus hic pullus? Numquid nuper editus paruulus peccare potuit? Et tamen habet peccatum pro quo hostia iubetur offerri a quo mundus negatur quis esse nec si unius diei fuerit uita eius (Job 14,4-5)...

Another note, which is partly destroyed and no longer legible, draws attention to a comment on Rom 1,24 which gives a very strong assertion of the human soul's freedom of choice, without which reward or punishment would be unfair ([11]).

A second illegible and only partially preserved note marks a passage in Book I which discusses the impossibility of obedience to the Mosaic law according to the letter ([12]).

The fourth note reads "requirendum et animaduertendum diligenter" - "to be inquired into and noted carefully". It refers to a discussion of Rom 5,13 "sin is not imputed when there is no law". Origen states here that a four - or five - year old child who hits his father or mother in anger is not guilty of transgression of the commandment forbidding this, because he has not yet reached the age of reason and therefore is not yet subject to the natural law ([13]).

The questions therefore that interest this fifth-century annotator of Origen's Commentary on Romans concern original sin, the freedom of the will, the impossibility of obedience to the Mosaic law

---

Pro hoc et ecclesia ab apostolis traditionem suscepit etiam paruulis baptismum dare (Lommatzsch, p. 396-7). Quotations from the Commentary on Romans are according to the text of my forthcoming critical edition in the series Vetus Latina, *Aus der Geschichte der lateinischen Bibel*, 16ff. (Freiburg 1990ff.), but with the page numbers of the edition of C.H.E. Lommatzsch, Berlin 1836-7.

([11]) Non enim ui res agitur neque necessitate in alteram partem anima declinatur; alioquin nec culpa ei nec uirtus possit adscribi nec boni electio praemium nec declinatio mali supplicium mereretur; sed seruatur ei in omnibus libertas arbitrii ut in quod uoluerit ipsa declinet sicut scriptum est: "ecce posui ante faciem tuam uitam et mortem ignem et aquam" (cf. Dt 30,15, Sir 15,16-17) (Lommatzsch, p. 57).

([12]) Sed et cum dicit: "etenim in quo infirmabatur lex per carnem..." carnem legis sine dubio litteram legis dicit. Per litteram namque infirmatur lex ut non possit impleri. Quis enim impleret uel de sabbato... uel de legibus leprae in stamine...? (Lommatzsch, p. 37).

([13]) Legem naturalem, quae certo aetatis tempore ubi rationis capax esse quis coeperit et iusti iniustique aequi atque iniqui habere discrimen... Puer ergo paruulus quattuor fere aut quinque annorum si ut fieri solet indignatus uirga percutiat patrem aut matrem, quantum ad praeceptum mandati spectat mortem debet. Sed quia lex in illo nondum est naturalis quae eum doceat non debere iniuriam facere patri uel matri nec scit in hoc crimen impietatis ammitti; et est quidem species peccati quod facit; matrem enim percutit uel maledicit sed mortuum est in eo peccatum quia per absentiam naturalis legis quae in eo nondum est peccatum ei non potest reputari; nondum enim est intra eum ratio tanta quae eum doceat hoc quod facit fieri non debere, et ideo etiam a parentibus non solum non reputatur ad culpam sed ad gratiam iucunditatemque suscipitur (Lommatzsch, pp. 334-5).

and the question whether children can become guilty of sin before reaching the age of reason. We may note that he was interested in issues debated at an early stage of the Pelagian controversy and that he was not an adherent of Pelagianism himself.

It would be possible to find many other statements in the translation of Origen's Commentary on Romans relevant to the questions of original sin, the impossibility of leading a sinless life, the role of the law and the status of just men under the law ([14]). Instead of discussing these I shall take a second line of approach and look at Augustine's earliest anti-Pelagian writings in order to see whether he shows the influence of Rufinus' translation of Origen. As far as I know this question has not been examined. An article by Altaner on Augustine's use of Origen ([15]) does not include the Commentary on Romans, although it is not unlikely that copies would have been brought from Sicily to Africa after Rufinus' death or perhaps even earlier direct from Rome carried by Rufinus' friend Melania the elder when she visited Augustine in 407 ([16]).

If we turn to Augustine's first anti-Pelagian work, the *De peccatorum meritis ac remissione et de baptismo paruulorum* of 412, we are struck almost immediately by an argument for the propagation of sin derived from Origen's commentary. In Book I chapter 9 Augustine states that his opponents are said to believe that sin is transmitted from Adam not by propagation but merely by imitation. He argues that if this were correct, St Paul in Romans 5,12 would have ascribed the origin of sin not to Adam, from whom the human race is propagated, but to the devil whom men imitate in sinning ([17]). The same argument occurs in Rufinus' translation of Origen's

---

([14]) Rufinus' translation of the Commentary on Romans is looked at for points of relevance to the Pelagian controversy by Bohlin, op. cit., and J. Patout Burns, "The interpretation of Romans in the Pelagian Controversy", *Augustinian Studies* 10 (1979), pp. 43-54.

([15]) B. ALTANER, "Augustinus und Origenes: Eine quellenkritische Untersuchung", *Historisches Jahrbuch* 70 (1951), pp. 15-41.

([16]) Cf. C.P. HAMMOND, "The last ten years of Rufinus' Life", JThS, NS 28 (1977), p. 416-7.

([17]) Sentiunt... ipsum peccatum non propagatione in alios homines ex primo homine, sed imitatione transisse. ... Sed si peccatum apostolus illud commemorare uoluisset, quod in hunc mundum non propagatione, sed imitatione intrauerit, eius principem non Adam sed diabolum diceret... Proinde apostolus cum illud peccatum

commentary on Rom 5,12, where Origen gives the same reason for Paul's wording in this verse, namely the descent of the human race from Adam ([18]). In addition the passage on original sin marked by the fifth-century annotator of the manuscript Lyons 483 has also left traces in Augustine. At Book II chapter 38 Augustine states that Christ was only born in the likeness of the flesh of sin, not in the flesh of sin, because his conception was not by the impulse of carnal concupiscence ([19]). At Book II chapters 11 and 15 he states that the reason that all men are by nature children of wrath according to Ephesians 2,3 is that they are the offspring of carnal concupiscence ([20]). The view which Augustine came to adopt is stated more explicitly in the translation of Origen's commentary on Rom 8,3: Christ had the nature of our body, but not the pollution of sin, which is transmitted to those conceived by the impulse of concupiscence ([21]).

ac mortem commemoraret, quae ab uno in omnes propagatione transisset, eum principem posuit, a quo propagatio generis humani sumpsit exordium. Augustine, *De Peccatorum Meritis et Remissione*, I.9 (ed. C.F. Urba and J. Zycha, CSEL 60 (1913), pp. 10-11).

([18]) Quomodo per unum hominem... uidebitur introisse peccatum? A muliere enim initium peccati et ante mulierem a serpente siue a diabolo ... Sed uide in his apostolum naturae ordinem tenuisse et ideo quoniam de peccato loquebatur ex quo mors in omnes homines pertransierat successionem posteritatis humanae quae huic morti subcubuit ex peccato uenienti non mulieri adscribit sed uiro. Origen, Commentary on Romans 5, Lommatzsch, p. 325.

([19]) Tenuit quandam et in carnis natiuitate medietatem, ut nos quidem nati essemus in carne peccati, ille autem in similitudine carnis peccati ... Ideo virginem matrem non lege carnis peccati, id est non concupiscentiae carnalis motu concipientem, sed pia fide sanctum germen in se fieri promerentem, quam eligeret creauit, de qua crearetur elegit. AUGUSTINE, *De Peccatorum Meritis et Remissione*, II.38 (CSEL 60, pp. 110-111).

([20]) Quasi ex hoc quisque carnaliter gignat quod iustus est et non ex hoc quod in membris eius concupiscentialiter mouetur, et ad usum propagandi lex peccati mentis lege conuertitur (op. cit. II.11). Sunt omnes, sicut dicit apostolus, naturaliter, hoc est originaliter, irae filii. quoniam filii sunt concupiscentiae carnis et saeculi ... Quis enim erit mundus a sordibus? Nemo, nec si unius diei fuerit uita eius (Job 14,4-5) (op. cit. II.15).

([21]) Omnes enim nos homines qui ex semine uiri cum muliere conuenientis concepti sumus illa necessario utimur uoce qua dicit David: "quoniam in iniquitatibus conceptus sum et in peccatis concepit me mater mea". Uerum qui ex nulla uiri contagione sed solo Spiritu Sancto super uirginem ueniente et uirtute altissimi obumbrante uenit ad corpus immaculatum naturam quidem corporis nostri habuit pollutionem tamen peccati quae ex concupiscentiae motu conceptis traditur omnino non habuit. Origen, Commentary on Romans 5,6, Lommatzsch, p. 69. On

It is even more interesting to find that Augustine has been influenced by the passage marked by the early annotator on the freedom from sin of the child who hits its parents. In Book I chapters 65-66, in arguing that in the baptism of infants it is original sin not individual sin that is remitted, since infants do not commit sins, he uses Origen's illustration, adapting it to fit a yet younger child, and states that such a child cannot have committed sin, since it lacks the capacity of reason and is not subject to either the natural or the written law (22). This passage is all the more striking, since it contradicts Augustine's earlier exegesis of Romans, which had made no mention of the natural law and depicted the stage of life before the law as one of sinful ignorance. He now appears to take awareness of sin as a precondition of committing sin, whereas previously he had not done so (23).

How are we to explain these parallels between Augustine's first anti-Pelagian treatise and Rufinus' translation of Origen's Commentary on Romans? At the one extreme we might put forward the theory that Augustine himself is the annotator of the surviving fifth-century manuscript, at the other we might ascribe the parallels to chance and to indirect influence on Augustine through other writers who had used the works of Origen. The possibility that Augustine himself annotated our manuscript cannot, I think, be totally excluded, but I regard it as more likely that the annotator was some other early reader familiar with the issues discussed by Augustine and his opponents (24). On the other hand I am convinced that Augustine read Rufinus' translation of Origen's Commentary on Romans during the period when he was producing his earliest anti-Pelagian works.

Origen's views on the subject of original sin and the succession from Adam, cf. C.P. BAMMEL, "Adam in Origen", in ed. Rowan Williams, *The Making of Orthodoxy: Essays in Honour of Henry Chadwick* (Cambridge 1989), pp. 79ff.

(22) Doceamus quomodo per propriam uoluntatem ... nihil mali commiserint infantes ... nulla omnino praecepti capacitas, nullus uel naturalis uel conscriptae legis sensus aut motus, nullus in alterutram partem rationis usus ... At hoc ignorantiae est, in qua profundissima iacet, qua etiam matrem, cum post exiguum tempus ualuerit, percutiet iratus ... Haec non modo feruntur, uerum etiam diliguntur in paruulis. AUGUSTINE, *De Peccatorum Meritis et Remissione*, I.65-6 (CSEL 60, pp. 65-6).

(23) See above p. 132-133.

(24) A similar problem arises in connexion with a marginal note in Vat. Reg. 141 of Rufinus' translation of Gregory Nazianzen; cf. C.P. HAMMOND BAMMEL, "Products of fifth-century Scriptoria", JThS, NS 35 (1984), pp. 375-6.

There is further evidence in these works of Augustine's reactions to Origen's exegesis both in certain ideas which he adopts and in those which he opposes ([25]). To examine this however would take us away from our initial question, namely: Did Rufinus' translations support Pelagian views and where would Rufinus have stood in relation to the issues debated in the Pelagian controversy?

We have just seen that with regard to the doctrine of original sin Rufinus' translation of Origen on Romans was clearly opposed to Pelagian views. The same work makes very clear statements about free will, which are known to have influenced Pelagius ([26]), but on the other hand the opponents of Pelagianism never claimed to deny free will. It is possible for example to cite a parallel from Jerome to the passage on free will marked by our fifth-century annotator ([27]). Should we then regard Rufinus not as a proto-Pelagian but as a proto-Augustinian? The answer to this question must surely be a firm "no". The characteristic views of *both* Augustine *and* his Pelagian opponents were formed as a result of the rejection of ideas of Origen, in particular of Origen's belief in the pre-existence of the soul. Rufinus however refused to condemn this doctrine and maintained that the question of the origin of the soul was as yet undecided ([28]). In translating works of Origen he was making available ideas which were different from those of both Augustine and the Pelagians. It is probable that he was doing this deliberately and that he was aware of the points under discussion. To make this clear it is necessary to look at the background to the Pelagian controversy.

Augustine had started to form his ideas about free will and original sin before the controversy about Origen arose. These ideas are expressed in his early anti-Manichaean works and his *De Libero Arbitrio*. At this period he was strongly influenced by Neoplatonism and also by the attitudes of Origen as mediated through Ambrose. He states that the rival theories on the origin of the soul, namely creationism, traducianism or pre-existence, are open to discussion,

---

([25]) I hope to discuss this in a separate publication.

([26]) Cf. BOHLIN, op. cit., pp. 87-103.

([27]) JEROME, *Adversus Jovinianum*, II.3 (PL 23.286CD): "Liberi arbitrii nos condidit Deus, nec ad uirtutes nec ad uitia necessitate trahimur. Alioquin ubi necessitas, nec corona est". Augustine's affirmations of free will in his early writings were later appealed to by his Pelagian opponents.

([28]) Cf. RUFINUS, *Apologia ad Anastasium*, 6, ed. Simonetti, p. 27.

(^{29}) and he often speaks of the fail as if it were the fall of every soul in a previous existence (^{30}). In his earliest letter to Jerome, Epistle 28 written in 395, he welcomed Jerome's translations of Origen's biblical commentaries, but soon after this he became concerned about the attacks on Origen's errors and wrote to Jerome again asking for information (^{31}). By the time that he wrote his *De Diversis Quaestionibus ad Simplicianum* in 395-6 he no longer writes as if the fall were the individual fall of every soul. His own alternative view however presented a picture of divine justice, which, as I said previously, was found offensive and provoked a reaction. Both Origen and Augustine take a negative view of human life in the body under the conditions to which Adam was condemned in Genesis chapter 3, weighed down by the burden of the flesh and its lusts. Whereas however Origen is able to explain this by stating that it is as a result of each individual soul's own fall that God has sent it into this life for its own correction and education, Augustine finds himself having to draw the conclusion that God's justice is shown in his having taken Adam's sin alone as sufficient reason for condemning human beings not only to the penal conditions of life in the body but also to eternal damnation thereafter. The contrast between Origen and Augustine is increased by the fact that for Origen divine punishment is primarily corrective and purgative, for Augustine it is primarily retributive (^{32}). In addition Augustine's discussion of God's calling of Jacob and rejection of Esau seemed to leave very little role for human free will.

The earliest surviving writing to put forward characteristically Pelagian ideas such as were condemned at Carthage in 411 is the *De Fide* of a different Rufinus - Rufinus the Syrian. This work attacks the views of the fall to be found in both Augustine and Origen. With regard to the origin of the soul it denies traducianism (^{33}) and critici-

---

(^{29}) *De Libero Arbitrio*, I. 24 and III.57-59.

(^{30}) Cf. R. J. O'CONNELL, "The Plotinian Fall of the Soul in St Augustine", *Traditio* 19 (1963), pp. 1-35.

(^{31}) The enquiry and Jerome's reply to it are lost but they are referred to in Augustine's *Epistle* 40.

(^{32}) On Augustine's views on punishment cf. JOHN BURNABY, *Amor Dei* (London 1938), pp. 192ff.

(^{33}) 28, ed. Mary William Miller, *Rufini Presbyteri Liber de Fide* (Washington, D.C. 1964), p. 90.

ses Origen by name for his doctrine of pre-existence (³⁴). It rejects the idea that the conditions of human life are punitive as a result of Adam's fall and states that those who convict the whole world of iniquity and crime because of the one man Adam are mad and proclaim God to be unjust (³⁵). It denies that infants are baptised on account of Adam's sin (³⁶) or that children are punished for the sins of their parents (³⁷). The author of this work was no friend of Rufinus of Aquileia but on the contrary was probably one of the presbyters sent by Jerome from Jerusalem to Italy in 399 to campaign against Origenism. According to Caelestius' statement at the Council of Carthage he lived at Rome with Jerome's friend Pammachius (³⁸). It is likely that Caelestius was influenced by him in his own lost treatise entitled *Contra Traducem Peccati* (³⁹).

The other two surviving writings which put forward Pelagian ideas prior to 411 are the anonymous treatise *De Induratione Cordis Pharaonis* and Pelagius' own Commentary on the Pauline epistles. Both take issue with the views of Augustine and both were influenced by Rufinus' translations of Origen. The unnamed author of the *De Induratione Cordis Pharaonis* attacks Augustine indirectly without naming him, giving a positive view of the function of the law, emphasising the importance of free will, and refuting the idea that men are punished for the sins of their ancestors. In providing an alternative interpretation of Rom 9 to that given by Augustine he seems to have adopted certain ideas from Rufinus' translation of Origen on Romans (⁴⁰). It has been suggested that this work was written at the request of Rufinus' friend Paulinus of Nola, (⁴¹) whose

---

(³⁴) 27, ed. Miller, p. 88.
(³⁵) 39, ed. Miller, p. 112.
(³⁶) 40, ed. Miller, p. 114.
(³⁷) 38, ed. Miller, p. 110.
(³⁸) Cf. FLAVIO G. NUVOLONE, art. "Pélage et Pélagianisme", *Dictionnaire de Spiritualité* 12.2 (Paris 1986), col. 2890; C.P. Hammond, JThS, NS 28 (1977), pp. 425-6.
(³⁹) Cf. NUVOLONE, art. cit., col. 2891; TESELLE, art. cit., especially pp. 74-6.
(⁴⁰) Cf. TESELLE, art. cit., p. 84, note 86, and NUVOLONE, "Problèmes d'une nouvelle édition du *De Induratione Cordis Pharaonis* attribué a Pélage", *Revue des Études Augustiniennes*, 26 (1980), pp. 115-116.
(⁴¹) Cf. NUVOLONE, "Pélage et Pélagianisme", col. 2919; TESELLE, art. cit., p. 83.

interest in its subject matter is known from the fact that he had written a letter to Jerome enquiring about the same questions ([42]).

That Pelagius himself made use of Rufinus' translation of Origen's Commentary on Romans in his own Commentary on the Pauline Epistles is well known. He follows Origen particularly in his strong assertion of human free will ([43]). Rufinus will have been aware of the contemporary interest in this question and deliberately have provided a contribution to it. He was in Rome or its environs between about 404 and 408 and in contact with Paulinus of Nola and no doubt also with Pelagius ([44]). The first sentence of his translation of Origen's preface to the Commentary states that one of the chief difficulties of the epistle to the Romans is the basis it provides for the deterministic theories of heretics who use texts from it to attempt to overthrow the biblical doctrine of free will ([45]). Earlier he had undertaken the translation of Origen's *De Principiis* in order to help a friend called Macarius who was writing a book against fate ([46]). On the other hand it is interesting to note that although Pelagius shows awarenes of the debates about the transmission of sin he does not yet in his Commentary on the Pauline Epistles state his own view on the matter but only quotes arguments that have been used by others ([47]). It would seem that his opposition to Augustine at this period, about which we know from Augustine himself as well as from the internal evidence of his commentary ([48]), centered on his fear that Augustine was discouraging moral effort by denying human free will and responsibility.

([42]) The letter is lost but Jerome's reply is his *Epistle* 85 of 399 or soon after. Paulinus' interest in Adam's fall during these years is also shown in his *Epistles* 23.44 and 30 to Severus (ed. Hartel, C.S.E.L. 28, pp. 199 and 262ff.).

([43]) See above note 3.

([44]) Cf. C.P. Hammond, JThS, NS 28, pp. 372-429.

([45]) Ed. Lommatzsch, p.l.

([46]) Rufinus, *Apol. contra Hieronymum* I.11, ed. Simonetti, pp. 44-45. It is striking that Jerome when questioned by Paulinus of Nola about the texts in Romans 9 which appear to remove free will had referred him to Origen's *De Principiis* for an answer (*Epistle* 85; cf. note 42 above).

([47]) He does this in his commentary on Rom 5,15, ed. Alexander Souter (Cambridge 1926), pp. 46-7.

([48]) Cf. TeSelle, art. cit., p. 82; Giovanni Martinetto, "Les premières réactions antiaugustiniennes de Pélage", *Revue des Études Augustiniennes* 17 (1971), pp. 83-117. It is likely that it was Paulinus of Nola who made available Augustine's writings to Pelagius and others during this period.

It has only been possible in this paper to look briefly at two or three of the issues debated in the years leading up to the outbreak of the Pelagian controversy. Rufinus of Aquileia, Augustine, Jerome, Pelagius, Caelestius, Rufinus the Syrian and Paulinus of Nola no doubt each had their own individual viewpoints on these matters. During the lifetime of Rufinus the later protagonists of the controversy had not yet formed themselves into two opposing parties and the many and various ideas under discussion were not yet linked to form two opposing complexes of thought. The period was one of intellectual turmoil ([49]). The controversy over the ascetic movement had fueled debate and disagreement and the theological readjustments necessitated by the condemnation of Origenism had produced a variety of diverging views. Augustine's new ideas were provoking concern but not open attacks. Rufinus' own chief contribution was to make available a great wealth of relevant material in his translations of Origen. In these translations he may have played down Origen's characteristic ideas on the pre-existence and fall of the soul and on the purgative nature and limited duration of hell-fire, but he did not cut them out. It is likely that during his life-time he and his followers continued to regard Origen's own views as a viable alternative to the views being developed by Augustine and Caelestius. For those who did not, his translations provided not only expert biblical exegesis but also a storehouse of arguments and ideas and the challenge of finding a way of retaining the good in Origen's viewpoint while rejecting what were regarded as his characteristic "errors".

([49]) On the intellectual background to the Pelagian controversy cf. the excellent brief account by Vittorino Grossi in ed. Angelo di Berardino, *Patrology* IV (Westminster, Maryland 1988), pp. 463ff.

INDEX

Acacius of Caesarea [Acacius von Cäsarea]:
XIV 158
Acts of John: II 74; VI 7
Acts of Martyrdom [of Ignatius]: II 65
Acts of Paul: VI 7
Acts of Paul and Thecla: I 629
Acts of Peter: VI 7
Adimantus: XVI 2 ff.
Alexander, the 'ancient heretic' [der 'alte Häretiker']: XV 189 f.
Alcibiades [Alkibiades]: XIV 159
Alypius: XVI 11; XVII 342 f.
Ambrose [Ambrosius]: VI 6; VII 292;
VIII 100; X 135; XII 69, 84, 90, 93;
XV 188; XVI 12, 24; XVII 343, 347 f.,
358
Ambrosiaster: XIV 157, 167 f.; XV 189;
XVII 353, 355, 361
Anastasius of Rome: XVII 343
Andrew: I 630; II 95
Apocalypse of Peter: I 626
Apollinarius of Hierapolis [Apollinaris von Hierapolis]: III 61; VII 284, 287;
IX 201 f.
Apollinarius of Laodicea [Apollinaris von Laodicea]: V 195; IX 195, 200, 202,
204 f., 206; X 145; XIV 157 f.;
XV 189 f., 196 f.
Apollonius: II 73; XIV 159
Apostolic Constitutions: II 71, 77, 91; IX 204;
XI 475
Aquila: X 129 ff.,135 f., 138, 143 f., 146;
XII 72
Aristeas: X 129
Aristides: II 85, III 59, 67
Athanasius: VIII 99 f.; XII 62
Athenagoras: III 59 ff., 67; VI 1, 5; XIV 159
Augustine [Augustin]: III 66; VII 291 f.;
VIII 100; IX 195, 204 f., 207; X 137,
146 ff.; XI 476; XII 62, 84; XV 188,
193 f., 196; XVI *passim;* XVII *passim;*
XVIII 132 f., 135 ff., 138 ff., 141 f.

Bardesanes: VI 9
Barnabas: II 84, 92
Basilides: II 76; III 67

Basil of Cäsarea [Basilius von Caesarea]:
VIII 100 f.; X 135; XII 65, 69 f.;
XVII 343
Caelestius: XII 62; XVII 356 ff., 361, 363;
XVIII 131 ff., 140, 142
Callistus: V 195, 197
Celsus: I 622; III 55, 66; VI 1 f., 4 f., 7;
VIII 102 f.; IX 198; XI 464, 469,
472 ff.; XII 64, 66, 72, 79 f., 85 f.,
88 ff., 91 ff.; XIII 145; XIV 160; XVI 9 f.
Cerdo: VI 7
Cerinthus: II 86, 88, 90, 95 f.; V 197
Chrysostom, John [Johannes Chrysostomus]:
VII 290; VIII 100; IX 195, 203, 204 ff.;
XI 475; XIV 157, 160, 163 ff., 166 ff.;
XV 194; XVII 351
1 Clement [*1 Klemensbrief*]: II 89 f.; III 67
2 Clement: II 71, 74
Clementine Homilies: XI 465
Clementine Recognitions: II 77; XI 467; *see
also Pseudo-Clementines*
Clement of Alexandria [Klemens von
Alexandrien / Clemens Alexandrinus]:
I 630; II 75, 85, 90 f., 96 f.; III 65;
IV 1 f.; VI 5 ff., 13; VII 284, 287, 291;
VIII 101; IX 197, 200 ff.; X 129;
XI 466; XIV 159; XV 195
Contra Noetum: V *passim*
Cyprian: V 195; VI 11, 13; VII 286 f., 291 f.;
VIII 98
Cyril of Alexandria [Cyrill von Alexandrien]:
IX 195, 205, 207; XI 475; XIV 157, 166

De Induratione Cordis Pharaonis: XVIII 140
Dialogus Montanisti et Orthodoxi: XIV 161 f.
*Dialogue of Timothy and Aquila [Dialog von
Timotheus und Aquila]*: X 129, 131, 136
Didache: II 92; XI 466
Didascalia: I 622; II 67, 84, 93; VI 5;
VII 292; IX 203; XI 465, 468
Didymus the Blind [Didymus der Blinde]:
IX 195, 206; XII 63, 69 f., 74 ff., 86, 88,
90 f., 93; XIV 157 f., 162 f.; XV 188 ff.,
196 f.
Dio Chrysostomus: III 54

4 INDEX

Theodore of Mopsuestia [Theodor von
Mopsuestia]: IX 195, 200 f., 205 f., 146;
XIV 157, 161, 163, 167 f.
Theodoret: V 195, 197, 199; IX 203; XII 69,
88 f.; XIV 157, 165
Theodotion: X 130, 136, 138, 141, 143 f.,
147; XII 74
Timothy [Timotheus]: II 91; VI 4; VII 283;
XII 74, 79; XIII 148; XIV 161; XVI 3,
5, 7 f., 20 f.

Titus: XIV 161; XV 188, 191
Tyconius: XVII 351 f., 356

Valentinus [Valentin]: I 624; II 75; III 67;
IV 1 f.; V 197; VI 7; VII 283
Venerius: XVII 358
Victor of Capua: XII 89
Victor of Rome [Viktor von Rom]: II 76;
VI 9 f.; VII 284, 287 ff.; IX 202
Victorinus of Pettau: IX 203

DATE DUE

APR 1 9 2002			
			Printed in USA